Philosophy and Human Flourishing

THE HUMANITIES AND HUMAN FLOURISHING

Series editor: James O. Pawelski, *University of Pennsylvania*

Other volumes in the series

Philosophy and Human Flourishing
Edited by John J. Stuhr

History and Human Flourishing
Edited by Darrin M. McMahon

Literary Studies and Human Flourishing
Edited by James F. English and Heather Love

Religious Studies, Theology, and Human Flourishing
Edited by Justin Thomas McDaniel and Hector Kilgoe

Theater and Human Flourishing
Edited by Harvey Young

Cinema, Media, and Human Flourishing
Edited by Timothy Corrigan

Music and Human Flourishing
Edited by Anna Harwell Celenza

Visual Arts and Human Flourishing
Edited by Selma Holo

The Humanities and Human Flourishing
Edited by James O. Pawelski

Philosophy and Human Flourishing

Edited by

JOHN J. STUHR

OXFORD
UNIVERSITY PRESS

OXFORD
UNIVERSITY PRESS

Oxford University Press is a department of the University of Oxford. It furthers
the University's objective of excellence in research, scholarship, and education
by publishing worldwide. Oxford is a registered trade mark of Oxford University
Press in the UK and certain other countries.

Published in the United States of America by Oxford University Press
198 Madison Avenue, New York, NY 10016, United States of America.

Library of Congress Cataloging-in-Publication Data
Names: Stuhr, John J., editor.
Title: Philosophy and human flourishing / John J. Stuhr, editor.
Description: New York, NY, United States of America : Oxford University Press, [2023] |
Series: The humanities and human flourishing |
Includes bibliographical references and index.
Identifiers: LCCN 2022018928 (print) | LCCN 2022018929 (ebook) |
ISBN 9780197622179 (paperback) | ISBN 9780197622162 (hardback) |
ISBN 9780197622193 (epub)
Subjects: LCSH: Success. | Conduct of life. | Well-being. | Philosophy.
Classification: LCC BJ1611.2 .P46 2023 (print) | LCC BJ1611.2 (ebook) |
DDC 158.1—dc23/eng/20220615
LC record available at https://lccn.loc.gov/2022018928
LC ebook record available at https://lccn.loc.gov/2022018929

DOI: 10.1093/oso/9780197622162.001.0001

1 3 5 7 9 8 6 4 2

Paperback printed by Marquis, Canada
Hardback printed by Bridgeport National Bindery, Inc., United States of America

Contents

PART II: HUMAN FLOURISHING IN PRACTICE

Series Editor's Foreword

Imagine being invited to a weekend meeting to discuss connections between the humanities and human flourishing. You talk about ways in which the humanities can help us understand what human flourishing is—and is not. You explore how the humanities can help increase human flourishing. And you consider whether human flourishing is an absolute good, or whether it comes with certain limits and even potential dangers. How do you imagine the conversation playing out? What contributions might you make to the discussion?

The volumes in this series were borne out of just such a meeting. Or rather a series of such meetings, each gathering including some dozen scholars in a particular discipline in the humanities (understood to be inclusive of the arts). These disciplines include philosophy, history, literary studies, religious studies and theology, theater, cinema and media, music, and the visual arts. Participants were asked to consider how their work in their discipline intersects with well-being (taken to be roughly synonymous with human flourishing), along with a series of specific questions:

- How does your discipline conceptualize, understand, and define well-being?
- What does your discipline say about the cultivation of well-being? How does it encourage the implementation of well-being?
- In what ways does your discipline support flourishing? Do some approaches within your discipline advance human flourishing more effectively than others? Are there ways in which certain aspects of your discipline could more effectively promote well-being?
- Does your discipline contribute to well-being in any unique ways in which other endeavors do not?
- Are there ways in which your discipline can obstruct human flourishing?

As might be expected, the conversations in these meetings were rich and wide-ranging. Some of them headed in expected directions; others were more surprising. Each of them yielded opportunities to question assumptions and deepen perspectives. The conversations were rooted in disciplinary contexts and questions but yielded many generalizable insights on how to conceptualize human flourishing more clearly, how to cultivate it more effectively, and how to avoid negative consequences of understanding it in incomplete or overblown ways. I cannot properly describe or even summarize the richness of the discussions here, but I would like to point out a few of the highlights included in each of the resulting volumes.

Philosophy and Human Flourishing, edited by John J. Stuhr, addresses a number of fundamental questions. What is the value of discussing human flourishing in a world that in so many ways is decidedly not flourishing? In what ways is flourishing similar to and different from happiness? What is the role of morality in human flourishing? How does it relate to systemic privilege and oppression? To what degree is flourishing properly the concern of individuals, and to what degree is it a function of communities and societies? What are key factors in the fostering of flourishing? In addressing these questions, philosophers explore concepts such as mattering, homeostasis, pluralism, responsibility, and values, and consider the roles of individuals, educational institutions, and governments.

History and Human Flourishing, edited by Darrin M. McMahon, centers on the question, What is the value of history for life? This core question leads to a number of further inquiries. Is history only about the past, or does it have important implications for the present and the future? If the latter, then how can historical inquiry most effectively contribute to well-being? Does such inquiry currently focus in an imbalanced way on ill-being—on prejudices, class struggles, and wars? Such work is doubtless of great importance, not least by investigating how claims about happiness can serve as propaganda for continued oppression. But would hope for the future be more effectively kindled and concrete steps toward its realization more adeptly guided by increased attention to what has actually gone well in the past and what we can learn from it, or by more focus on how human beings have responded positively to adversity?

Literary Studies and Human Flourishing, edited by James F. English and Heather Love, focuses on the transformative power of literature. Scholars examine a range of topics, including the reparative possibilities of a literary encounter, the value of bibliotherapy and of therapeutic redescription, the genre of "uplit," and evolving methods for studying the activities and experiences of actual readers. A central question of this volume concerns the limits on transformations effected through literature. Several contributors worry that harnessing literary studies to the enterprise of human flourishing might lead readers merely to conform rather than to transform. To what extent might human flourishing serve as a palliative, enabling and encouraging readers to adapt to individual lives that lack moral depth and to social conditions that are rife with injustice, and thus obstruct the difficult and unsettling work of disruptive transformation needed for lasting individual and collective betterment?

Religious Studies, Theology, and Human Flourishing, edited by Justin Thomas McDaniel and Hector Kilgoe, explores ways in which individual and collective well-being can be increased through various religious perspectives and practices, including the Hindu concept of *sanmati* ("goodwill, wisdom, and noble-mindedness"), Buddhist meditation, and the cultivation of spiritual joy even while facing adversity. Scholars consider challenging questions concerning the proper contexts for learning *about* religion and for learning *from* religion, the right balance between the acknowledgment of suffering and the fostering of well-being, and the relationship between human flourishing and nonhuman worlds (including both natural and supernatural domains). A concern of some of these scholars is whether human flourishing entails a false universalism, one that seeks to reduce cultural diversities to one particular notion of what is desirable or even acceptable, and whether such a notion could be used to rate the value of different religions, or even ban religious practices (e.g., fasting, celibacy, or other ascetic austerities) that might be deemed misaligned with well-being.

Theater and Human Flourishing, edited by Harvey Young, considers the unique resources of theater and performance for imagining and enhancing well-being. Because theater involves both performers and audience members, it is inherently communal in ways many humanities disciplines and art forms are not. Theater allows groups of people—often strangers—to come together and experience the world in new ways. More than just an escape from ordinary life or a simple mirroring of reality, theater can provide opportunities for communal reimagining of the world, exploring new ways of thinking, feeling, and relating that can be experienced and then enacted to bring about a more flourishing future. Scholars examine connections between theater and human flourishing in more and less traditional spheres, looking at ways performance practices can be used to critique inadequate notions of human flourishing and to increase well-being in a wide variety of contexts, ranging from community theater to organizations serving soldiers with post-traumatic stress disorder (PTSD), and from oppressed groups to politically divided societies.

Cinema, Media, and Human Flourishing, edited by Timothy Corrigan, looks to film and a whole range of contemporary forms of digital media for what they can teach us about the nature of human flourishing and how it can be cultivated. These forms of communication have vast audiences and thus great power to support or subvert well-being. Contributors to this volume observe that human flourishing often seems to come piecemeal and as a hard-won result of conflict and struggle, and they explore ways in which well-being can be supported by collaborative practices for creating content, by the particular ways narratives are crafted, by certain genres, and by the various values that are embraced and transmitted. Contributors also consider how these popular forms can support individuals and groups on the margins of society by making more visible and sympathetic their struggles toward flourishing.

Music and Human Flourishing, edited by Anna Harwell Celenza, complements the commonly accepted and scientifically supported view that participating in music—as a listener, performer, or composer—can increase individual well-being. Instead of focusing on music as a performing art, this volume examines music as a humanities discipline, emphasizing the importance and value of music scholarship for fostering individual and collective human flourishing. How can music scholars (musicologists, ethnomusicologists, and music theorists) strengthen the effects of music on flourishing through a consideration of broader cultural, social, and political contexts? Contributors explore how processes of contemplation, critique, and communication within music scholarship can deepen the experience of music, resulting not just in the enhancement of individual well-being but in the more effective cultivation of wisdom and the greater realization of social justice.

Visual Arts and Human Flourishing, edited by Selma Holo, begins with the experience of artists themselves and the function of art in our society. If well-being is thought of as the happiness of self-satisfied complacency, then it would seem to be the antithesis of art, which is often disruptive, unnerving, and unsettling, asking viewers to question their assumptions and inviting them to see the world in new ways. But if well-being is understood more deeply as the flourishing that can arise from the full range of human experience, including the discomfort of contending forms of meaning and contested visions of reality, then it is difficult to think of it without art. Contributors to this volume consider the overwhelming personal necessity artists have to create, the role of well-being in art history, the increasing emphasis on human flourishing in architecture and public art, and salient questions of ethics, accessibility, and social justice in the context of art museums.

The Humanities and Human Flourishing, for which I serve as editor, is an interdisciplinary, capstone volume that contains contributions from the editors of the eight disciplinary volumes. After the disciplinary meetings were concluded, we gathered together to discuss what we had learned through the process. We considered both similarities and differences across the disciplinary discussions on human flourishing, identifying social justice and pedagogy as two common themes that emerged in the meetings. Like the other volumes in the series, this volume does not pretend to provide simple solutions or even unified answers to questions of how the humanities are or should be connected to the conceptualization and cultivation of human flourishing. Rather, it provides thoughtful questions and perspectives, distilled as it is from a deliberate process of extended engagement from diverse groups of scholars across eight different arts and humanities disciplines.

I would like to welcome you, the reader, to this book series. I hope you find it stimulating and even inspiring in its explorations into the complexities of the relationship between the humanities and human flourishing. And I hope you read across the volumes, as they are written in an accessible style that will yield valuable insights whether or not you have particular expertise in the discipline of the author whose work you are reading. To whatever degree you immerse yourself in this book series, though, I am sure of one thing: You will find it incomplete. As deep and as broad ranging as we tried to be in our explorations, none of the participants are under the illusion that the discussions and volumes brought it to a conclusion. We are keenly aware that a group of a dozen scholars, no matter how diverse, cannot speak for an entire discipline, and we realize that a focus on eight disciplines does not cover the entire domain of the humanities. Furthermore, our discussions and most of the writing were completed before the COVID-19 pandemic, which has made the nature and importance of flourishing all the more salient and has raised a host of new questions about well-being. Instead, we think of our work as an important beginning, and we would like to invite you to join the conversation. We hope a greater number and diversity of scholars, researchers, creators, practitioners, students, leaders in cultural organizations and creative industries, office holders in government, philanthropists, and members of the general public will bring their interests and expertise to the conversation, perhaps leading to new volumes in this series in the future. Investigations into human flourishing contribute to our knowledge and understanding of the human condition, and they have practical implications for the well-being of scholars, students, and societies. We hope our ongoing work together will enable the humanities to play a greater role in these investigations, effecting changes in scholarship, research, pedagogy, policy, and practice that will make them more supportive of human flourishing in academia and in the world at large.

Background and Rationale

For readers interested in more information on the background and rationale of this book series, I am happy to share further details on the perspectives, aims, and hopes that motivated it. A key catalyst for the development of this series was the dual observation that a growing number of individuals and organizations are focusing on human flourishing and that most of the headlines in this domain seem to be coming from the social sciences. Yale psychology professor Laurie Santos, for example, made the news when she developed a course on "Psychology and the Good Life"—and some 1200 students (nearly a quarter of Yale's undergraduate population) signed up for it.[1] As of this writing, her subsequent podcast, "The Happiness Lab," has reached 65 million downloads.[2] On an international scale, dozens of countries around the world have adopted psychological measures of subjective well-being as a complement to economic indicators, and a growing number of nations have embraced well-being, happiness, or flourishing as an explicit governmental goal.[3] The Organization for Economic Co-operation and Development (OECD), founded in 1961 to stimulate economic progress and world trade, has acknowledged the insufficiency of economic indicators

---

[1] David Shimer, "Yale's Most Popular Class Ever: Happiness." *The New York Times*, January 26, 2018. https://www.nytimes.com/2018/01/26/nyregion/at-yale-class-on-happiness-draws-huge-crowd-laurie-santos.html

[2] Lucy Hodgman, and Evan Gorelick, "Silliman Head of College Laurie Santos to Take One-Year Leave to Address Burnout." *Yale News*, February 8, 2022. https://yaledailynews.com/blog/2022/02/08/silliman-head-of-college-laurie-santos-to-take-one-year-leave-to-address-burnout/

[3] https://weall.org/; https://www.ons.gov.uk/peoplepopulationandcommunity/wellbeing/articles/measuresofnationalwellbeingdashboard/2018-04-25; https://www.gnhcentrebhutan.org/history-of-gnh/; https://www.worldbank.org/en/news/feature/2013/10/24/Bolivia-quiere-replicar-el-indice-de-felicidad-de-Butan; https://u.ae/en/about-the-uae/the-uae-government/government-of-future/happiness/;

alone for tracking progress. It launched its Better Life Initiative in 2011 to measure what drives the well-being of individuals and nations and to determine how countries can best support greater progress for all.[4] The United Nations publishes the World Happiness Report every year, releasing it on March 20, the UN International Day of Happiness.[5]

These are examples in the social sciences of what I have elsewhere called a "eudaimonic turn," an explicit commitment to human flourishing as a core theoretical and research interest and a desired practical outcome.[6] Over the last several decades, there has been a growing interest in human flourishing in economics, political science, psychology, and sociology, and in fields influenced by them, such as education, organizational studies, medicine, and public health. Perhaps the most well-known example of this eudaimonic turn in the social sciences occurred in psychology with the advent of positive psychology. Reflecting perspectives developed in humanistic psychology in the mid-twentieth century and building on increasing empirical work in self-efficacy, self-determination theory, subjective and psychological well-being, optimism, flow, passion, hope theory, positive emotions, and related areas, Martin Seligman and his colleagues launched the field of positive psychology. During a 1998 presidential address to the American Psychological Association, Seligman pointed out that mainstream psychology had become fixated on understanding and treating psychopathology. He argued that, although extremely important, healing mental illness is only part of psychology's mission. More broadly, he claimed, psychology should be about making the lives of all people better. He noted that this requires the careful empirical study of what makes life most worth living, including a deep understanding of flourishing individuals and thriving communities. Such study, he believed, would both increase well-being and decrease ill-being, since human strengths are both important in their own right and effective as buffers against mental illness. Known as "the scientific study of what enables individuals and societies to thrive,"[7] positive psychology has had a

[4] https://www.oecd.org/sdd/OECD-Better-Life-Initiative.pdf
[5] https://worldhappiness.report/
[6] James O. Pawelski, "What Is the Eudaimonic Turn?," in *The Eudaimonic Turn: Well-Being in Literary Studies*, ed. James O. Pawelski and D. J. Moores (Madison, NJ: Fairleigh Dickinson University Press, 2013), 3; and James O. Pawelski, "The Positive Humanities: Culture and Human Flourishing," in *The Oxford Handbook of the Positive Humanities*, ed. Louis Tay and James O. Pawelski (New York: Oxford University Press, 2022), 26.
[7] Constitution of the International Positive Psychology Association, Article 1, Section 2.

transformative effect on psychology and has deeply influenced many other fields of research and practice.

What role do the humanities play in all of this? What role could and should they play? How can the humanities help us conceptualize human flourishing more deeply, cultivate it more effectively, and critique it more insightfully? As a philosopher working in the field of positive psychology for more than twenty years, I have been concerned that there are not more voices from the humanities centrally involved in contemporary work in human flourishing. One of the core aims of this project and book series is to make a way for humanities scholars to play a larger role in this domain by inviting them to consider explicitly what contributions their work and their disciplines can make to the theory, research, and practice of human flourishing.

Historically, of course, human flourishing is at the root of the humanities.[8] The humanities were first defined and developed as a program of study by Renaissance scholars dissatisfied with scholasticism, which they perceived as leading to an overly technical university curriculum removed from the concerns of everyday life and unable to guide students toward human flourishing. They advocated, instead, a return to the Greek and Roman classics, reading them for insights and perspectives on how to live life well. Indeed, the Greeks and Romans had developed comprehensive programs of study (*paideia* and *artes liberales*, respectively) designed to teach students how to flourish individually and how to contribute to collective flourishing by participating effectively and wisely in civic life.

This emphasis on the understanding and cultivation of human flourishing that was so important to the Greeks and Romans was also of central concern to other philosophical and religious traditions that developed in the ancient world during what Karl Jaspers called the Axial Age.[9] Hinduism, Buddhism, Confucianism, Daoism, and Judaism, for example, along with the later Christianity and Islam, addressed the problem of human suffering and offered ways of promoting individual and collective flourishing. Although different in their cultural context and specific details, each of these traditions counseled against lives exclusively devoted to pleasure, wealth, power, or fame. They held that such lives only magnify suffering and that flourishing is actually fostered through a cultivation of virtue that allows

---

[8] Pawelski, "The Positive Humanities," 20–21; and Darrin M. McMahon, "The History of the Humanities and Human Flourishing," in *The Oxford Handbook of the Positive Humanities*, ed. Louis Tay and James O. Pawelski (New York: Oxford University Press, 2022), 45–50.

[9] Karl Jaspers, *The Origin and Goal of History* (Abingdon, UK: Routledge, 2011), 2.

for the transcendence of narrow, individual concerns in favor of a connection with the larger social world, the broader universe, or even the divine. Cultural forms such as literature, music, visual art, architecture, theater, history, and philosophical reflection were employed in the cultivation of virtue and the establishment of the broader and deeper connections valued for human flourishing.

Today, the humanities tend to be thought of less as a comprehensive program of study or means to cultivate virtue and more as a collection of academic disciplines. These disciplines are located largely within colleges and universities and are thus shaped by the values of these institutions. Much of higher education is driven more by the aim of creating knowledge than the goal of applying wisdom. To succeed in such an environment, scholars are required to become highly specialized professionals, spending most of their time publishing books and articles for other highly specialized professionals in their discipline. The courses they teach often focus more on the flourishing of their discipline than on the flourishing of their students, requiring students to learn *about* course content but not necessarily to learn *from* it. When human flourishing is addressed in the classroom, it is all too often done in a way that makes it difficult for students to apply it to their lives, and in many cases, it focuses more on obstacles to flourishing than on the nature and cultivation of well-being. It is important, of course, to understand and resist alienation, injustice, and malfeasance in the world and to expose corrosive ideologies that can permeate texts and other forms of culture. But it is also important to understand that flourishing is more than just the absence of languishing. And the argument has been made that "suspicious" approaches in the humanities need to be balanced by reparative approaches[10] and that critique needs to be complemented by a "positive aesthetics"[11] and a "hermeneutics of affirmation."[12] Meanwhile, students in the United States, at least, are reporting astonishingly high levels of anxiety, depression, and suicidality,[13] while at the same time coming under increasing economic

[10] Eve K. Sedgwick, "Paranoid Reading and Reparative Reading: Or, You're So Paranoid, You Probably Think This Introduction Is About You," in *Novel Gazing: Queer Readings in Fiction*, ed. Eve K. Sedgwick (Durham, NC: Duke University Press, 1997), 1–37.

[11] Rita Felski, *Uses of Literature* (Malden, MA: Blackwell, 2008), 22.

[12] D. J. Moores, "The Eudaimonic Turn in Literary Studies," in *The Eudaimonic Turn: Well-Being in Literary Studies*, ed. James O. Pawelski and D. J. Moores (Madison, NJ: Fairleigh Dickinson University Press, 2013), 27.

[13] Publications and Reports, National College Health Assessment, American College Health Association, accessed December 11, 2021, https://www.acha.org/NCHA/ACHA-NCHA_Data/Publications_and_Reports/NCHA/Data/Publications_and_Reports.aspx?hkey=d5fb767c-d15d-4efc-8c41-3546d92032c5

pressure to select courses of study that will directly help them find employment. Students who in the past might have followed their interests in the humanities are now more likely to major in STEM fields or to enroll in pre-professional tracks. Consequently, the number of students earning bachelor's degrees in the humanities is decreasing significantly.[14]

Would a eudaimonic turn in the humanities be helpful in addressing these obstacles of narrow professionalism, imbalanced focus, and student pressure? Would it help with what Louis Menand has called a "crisis of rationale" in the humanities, with scholars unable to agree on the fundamental nature and purpose of the humanities and thus unable to communicate their value clearly to students, parents, philanthropists, policymakers, and the general public?[15]Could the eudaimonic turn provide a unifying rationale in the humanities? Of course, there is a sense in which such a turn would actually be a eudaimonic *return*. This return would not be a nostalgic attempt to recover some imagined glorious past. The human flourishing historically supported by the humanities was significant, as mentioned above, but it was also very far from perfect, often embracing perspectives that supported unjust power structures that excluded many people—including laborers, women, and enslaved persons—from participating in flourishing and that enabled the exploitation of these individuals to the advantage of those in power. Tragically, our society suffers from some of these same injustices today. Instead of a glorification of a problematic past, which could well reinforce these injustices, a eudaimonic re/turn would invite us to focus our attention on perennial questions about human flourishing, building on wisdom from the past, but committing ourselves to a search for more inclusive answers that are fitting for our contemporary world.[16]

Not surprisingly, there is disagreement among scholars in these volumes, with some contributors endorsing the eudaimonic turn in the humanities and working to advance it and others putting forward a variety of concerns about the limitations and potential dangers of such an approach—and some even doing both. Scholars supporting a eudaimonic turn believe it could

[14] Jill Barshay, "PROOF POINTS: The Number of College Graduates in the Humanities Drops for the Eighth Consecutive Year," *The Hechinger Report*, November 22, 2021, https://hechingerreport.org/proof-points-the-number-of-college-graduates-in-the-humanities-drops-for-the-eighth-cons ecutive-year.

[15] Louis Menand, "The Marketplace of Ideas," American Council of Learned Societies Occasional Paper No. 49 (2001) http://archives.acls.org/op/49_Marketplace_of_Ideas.htm.

[16] Pawelski, "What Is the Eudaimonic Turn?" 17; Pawelski, "The Positive Humanities," 26; and McMahon, "The History of the Humanities and Human Flourishing," 45, 54.

revitalize the humanities by encouraging deeper investigations into the eudaimonic hopes that initially gave rise to their disciplines and the various ways in which contemporary work can support and develop these hopes. They believe these investigations could bring together scholars across the various humanities disciplines to create a common understanding and language for an examination of questions of human flourishing appropriate for our times. To be successful, such a project would not require complete agreement among scholars on the answers to these questions. On the contrary, diverse perspectives would enrich the inquiry, opening up new possibilities for human flourishing that are more equitable and widespread and that support the flourishing of the nonhuman world as well. Some contributors see significant potential in collaborating with the social sciences in their eudaimonic turn, a process that can be facilitated through the Positive Humanities, a new, interdisciplinary field of inquiry and practice focused on the relationship between culture and human flourishing.[17]

Scholars endorsing a eudaimonic turn in the humanities believe it could also inform, inspire, and support the work of museums, libraries, performing arts centers, and even creative industries (in music, movies, publishing, and other domains) to advance human flourishing more broadly in our society. They see a eudaimonic turn as also being of potential value to the millions of students who study the humanities each year. Without expecting humanities teachers and professors to take on therapeutic roles, they see considerable possible benefits in a pedagogical focus on how human flourishing can be understood and cultivated, with resulting courses intentionally designed to promote and preserve students' well-being and mitigate and prevent their ill-being.[18] Indeed, these scholars believe the volumes in this series might serve as useful texts for some of these courses.

Scholars with misgivings about a eudaimonic turn, on the other hand, raise a number of important concerns. Some contributors wonder whether human flourishing is a proper ideal in a world with so much suffering. Would such an ideal raise false hopes that would actually contribute to that suffering? Furthermore, are there more valuable things than human flourishing

---

[17] For more information on the Positive Humanities, see Louis Tay and James O. Pawelski, eds., *The Oxford Handbook of the Positive Humanities* (New York: Oxford University Press, 2022), especially the first three foundational chapters. Also, visit www.humanitiesandhumanflourishing.org.

[18] Furthermore, would students who perceive real life value in humanities courses be more likely to make room for them in their schedules, as suggested by the students who enrolled in Laurie Santos's course on "Psychology and the Good Life" in such large numbers? If so, could a side benefit of the eudaimonic turn be greater numbers of students signing up for courses in the humanities?

(e.g., ethics, the environment), and should flourishing be limited in favor of these greater goods? Is human flourishing inextricably linked to problematic ideological perspectives, perhaps ones that place too much emphasis on the individual and downplay or ignore issues of systemic injustice, or perhaps ones that serve the interests of a small number of persons in power and encourage everyone else to conform to the status quo? Is human flourishing a false universalism that might result in a failure to see and acknowledge deep cultural differences—or worse, that might see these differences as deviances that need to be suppressed and punished? Could an emphasis on well-being be employed to exploit individuals or groups of people, as notions of happiness have sometimes been used in the past? Are there other unexpected harms that might arise from a eudaimonic turn?

The unresolved tensions among the various chapters are part of what makes these volumes compelling reading. Are there ways to overcome concerns about the eudaimonic turn by clarifying its nature and aims, avoiding the dangers raised? Or will these concerns always persist alongside efforts to achieve individual and communal betterment through a theoretical and practical emphasis on flourishing? I welcome you, the reader, to join this discussion. What are your views on the perspectives expressed in these volumes? What points might you contribute to the ongoing conversation?

Process and People

I would like to conclude with a fuller account of the process by which the various volumes were created and an acknowledgment of the individuals and institutions who have made this book series possible. With the desire to give contributors ample time to reflect on how their work and their discipline relate to human flourishing, as well as to create opportunities to discuss these ideas with colleagues, we put into place an extended process for the creation of these volumes. After deciding on the eight disciplines in the arts and humanities we would be able to include in the project, we invited a leading scholar to chair the work in each of these disciplines and asked them to bring together a diverse group of some dozen noted scholars in their discipline.[19] For each group, we provided participants with some background

---

[19] For a full list of project participants, visit www.humanitiesandhumanflourishing.org.

reading[20] and asked them to prepare a draft essay on how their scholarly work informs the conceptualization and cultivation of human flourishing. Many participants chose to address the background reading—appreciatively, critically, or both—in their papers, although none were required to address it at all. We then circulated these drafts to the entire group in preparation for a three-day, face-to-face meeting, during which the disciplinary chair led a discussion and workshopping of the drafts. These disciplinary consultations, held in 2018 and 2019, were also joined by a junior scholar (usually a graduate student) in the field, one or two social scientists with work on relevant topics, and the Core Team.

Following these meetings, participants were asked to revise their drafts in light of our discussion, with the chairs serving as editors for the resulting disciplinary volumes. Given the nature of the project, I also read each of the contributions, providing comments along the way. From beginning to end, the process for creating and editing each of the volume manuscripts took well over a year and allowed for deep engagement with the subject matter and with other scholars. The disciplinary chairs and I were careful to emphasize that these discussions were intended to be robust and the writing authentic, with no foregone conclusions about the nature of human flourishing or the value of exploring it, and we were pleased by the range and depth of thinking undertaken by each group.

As mentioned above, after we held the eight disciplinary consultations, we held a ninth meeting where we invited the chairs of each of the disciplinary groups to present and discuss drafts of essays for a ninth, interdisciplinary volume sharing what they and their colleagues had learned through the process. We also invited a few humanities policy leaders, including past National Endowment for the Humanities Chairman William Adams, to join us and help think about the broader implications of this work.

---

[20] Martin E. P. Seligman and Mihaly Csikszentmihalyi, "Positive Psychology: An Introduction," *American Psychologist* 55 (1) (2000): 5–14; Darrin M. McMahon, "From the Paleolithic to the Present: Three Revolutions in the Global History of Happiness," in *e-Handbook of Subjective Well-being*, ed. Ed Diener, Shigehiro Oishi, and Louis Tay (Champaign, IL: DEF Publishers, 2018); James O. Pawelski, "Defining the 'Positive' in Positive Psychology: Part I. A Descriptive Analysis," *The Journal of Positive Psychology* 11 (4) (2016): 339–356; James O. Pawelski, "Defining the 'Positive' in Positive Psychology: Part II. A Normative Analysis," *The Journal of Positive Psychology* 11 (4) (2016): 357–365; James O. Pawelski, "Bringing Together the Humanities and the Science of Well-Being to Advance Human Flourishing," in *Well-Being and Higher Education: A Strategy for Change and the Realization of Education's Greater Purposes*, ed. Donald W. Harward (Washington, D.C.: Bringing Theory to Practice, 207–216); and Louis Tay, James O. Pawelski, and Melissa G. Keith, "The Role of the Arts and Humanities in Human Flourishing: A Conceptual Model," *The Journal of Positive Psychology* 13 (3) (2018): 215–225.

The compiling of the volumes was organized and overseen by the Humanities and Human Flourishing (HHF) Project at the University of Pennsylvania. HHF was founded in 2014 to support the interdisciplinary investigation and advancement of the relationship between the humanities and human flourishing. As the founding director of HHF, I am pleased that it has developed into a growing international and multidisciplinary network of more than 150 humanities scholars, scientific researchers, creative practitioners, college and university educators, wellness officers, policy experts, members of government, and leaders of cultural organizations. In addition to the disciplinary consultations described above and the resulting book series, we have published a number of conceptual papers and systematic reviews, developed conceptual models to guide empirical research, and created and validated a toolkit of measures. Designated a National Endowment for the Arts Research Lab, HHF has developed ongoing programs of research (including on art museums and human flourishing and on narrative technologies and well-being) to understand, assess, and advance the effects of engagement in the arts and humanities on human flourishing. We have published *The Oxford Handbook of the Positive Humanities* to help establish the Positive Humanities as a robust field of inquiry and practice at the intersection of culture, science, and human flourishing. For more information on HHF, including each of these endeavors as well as its current undertakings, please visit www.humanitiesandhumanflourishing.org.

I am deeply grateful to all the individuals and institutions whose collaboration has made this book series possible. I would like to begin by thanking Chris Stewart and Templeton Religion Trust for the generous grants that have underwritten this work. Thanks also go to the University of Pennsylvania for their robust institutional and financial support. (Of course, the views expressed in these volumes are those of the authors and do not necessarily reflect the views of Templeton Religion Trust or of the University of Pennsylvania.) I am grateful to the more than 80 contributors to these volumes for accepting our invitation to be a part of this work and bringing more depth and richness to it than I could have imagined. I am especially grateful to the chairs of each of the disciplinary groups for their belief in the importance of this work and their long-term dedication to making it a success. I also wish to express my appreciation for the hard work of the entire HHF Core Team, including Research Director Louis Tay, postdoctoral fellows Yerin Shim and Hoda Vaziri, Research Manager Michaela Ward, and especially Assistant Director Sarah Sidoti, who meticulously planned and oversaw each of the disciplinary consultations and used her expertise in academic publishing to help shape this book series in countless crucial ways. Most of the disciplinary consultations took place on the beautiful grounds of the Shawnee Inn & Golf Resort along the banks of the Delaware River. I am grateful to Charlie and Ginny Kirkwood, John Kirkwood, and all the folks at Shawnee for their gracious support and hospitality. Additionally, I am grateful to Jonathan Coopersmith and the Curtis Institute for donating space for the music group to meet, and to Bill Perthes and the Barnes Foundation for similarly donating space for the visual arts group. Thanks to the Penn Museum for a beautiful setting for the first day of our Chairs consultation and to Marty Seligman and Peter Schulman for donating further space at the Positive Psychology Center. Finally, I am grateful to Peter Ohlin and all the staff and reviewers at Oxford University Press for their partnership in publishing the volumes in this book series. I hope these volumes inspire further conversation, welcoming more people from a larger number of disciplines and a greater range of nationalities and cultural and ethnic backgrounds to inquire into what human flourishing is, how its potential harms can be avoided, and how its benefits can be more deeply experienced and more broadly extended.

James O. Pawelski
February 19, 2022

List of Contributors

Lori Gallegos is an associate professor of philosophy at Texas State University. Her recent work is on intergenerational autonomy-building in Latinx families, linguistic oppression, and cultural assimilation. Her articles have appeared in *Journal of Intercultural Studies, Inter-American Journal of Philosophy, Critical Philosophy of Race, Journal of Speculative Philosophy*, and *Topoi: An International Journal on Philosophy*. She has also contributed to the volumes *Latin American Immigration Ethics*, edited by Amy Reed-Sandoval and Luis Rubén Díaz, and *Latin American and Latinx Philosophy: A Collaborative Introduction*, edited by Robert Eli Sanchez, Jr. Gallegos is the editor of the *American Philosophical Association Newsletter on Hispanic/Latinx Issues in Philosophy*. She is a recipient of the Ford Foundation Pre-Doctoral Fellowship and the Ford Foundation Dissertation Fellowship. She is a winner of the American Philosophical Association Essay Prize in Latin American Thought. She has also been awarded the Texas State University College of Liberal Arts College Achievement Award for Excellence in Teaching.

Rebecca Newberger Goldstein is a philosopher and novelist. The recipient of numerous prizes for her scholarship and fiction, including a 1996 MacArthur prize, in 2012 she was named Humanist of the Year by the American Humanist Association, and in 2015 she received the National Humanities Medal from President Obama in a ceremony at the White House. Her fellowships include those from the Guggenheim Foundation, the American Council of Learned Societies, Radcliffe Institute, the Santa Fe Institute, and the Whitney Center for the Humanities, Yale University, where in 2014 she delivered the Tanner Lectures in Human Values. In 2005, she was elected into the American Academy of Arts and Sciences. She is the author of ten books, the most recent of which is *Plato at the Googleplex: Why Philosophy Won't Go Away*.

Jennifer L. Hansen is a professor of philosophy at St. Lawrence University. Her research focuses on the normative and gendering aspects of the definition of depression as a mental disorder. She has also written on the epistemological and ethical questions that emerge in the neuroscientific turn in psychiatry, specifically psychopharmacological treatment of depression. In addition to working in the area of philosophy of psychiatry, Hansen contributes to the fields of feminist phenomenology and American pragmatism, specifically William James and John Dewey. Her recent publications include, "The Hopeful Hashtag: Digital Feminist Publics in the Trump Era," in *Dewey Studies*, "Truth and Discursive Activism: The Promise and Perils of Hashtag Feminism," in the *Journal of Speculative Philosophy*, a chapter entitled "Cosmopolitan Hope," in *Cosmopolitanism and Place*, eds. Wahman, Medina and

Stuhr, and a co-authored article entitled "Prozac or Prosaic Diaries? The Gendering of Psychiatric Disability in Depression Memoirs," in *Philosophy, Psychiatry, and Psychology* with Ginger Hoffman.

Daniel M. Haybron is the Theodore R. Vitali C.P. Professor of Philosophy at Saint Louis University. He received his PhD in philosophy at Rutgers University. His research focuses on ethics, psychology and political philosophy, particularly issues of well-being. He has published numerous articles in these areas. In 2015 he was awarded a $5.1 million grant for a three-year project, *Happiness and Well-Being: Integrating Research Across the Disciplines*, funded by the John Templeton Foundation and Saint Louis University. He is the author of *The Pursuit of Unhappiness: The Elusive Psychology of Well-Being* (Oxford University Press, 2008), and *Happiness: A Very Short Introduction* (Oxford University Press, 2013).

Mark Johnson is the Philip H. Knight Professor of Liberal Arts and Sciences, emeritus, in the Department of Philosophy at the University of Oregon. His research focuses on the philosophical implications of the role of human embodiment in meaning, conceptualization, reasoning, and values, especially from the perspective of the interaction of embodied cognitive science and pragmatist philosophy. In *Moral Imagination* (1993) and *Morality for Humans* (2014), he develops a naturalistic account of human morality that emphasizes the role of moral imagination. His work in embodied cognition theory includes *The Body in the Mind* (1987), *Philosophy in the Flesh* (with George Lakoff, 1999), *The Meaning of the Body* (2007), *Embodied Mind, Meaning, and Reason* (2017), and *Out of the Cave: Toward a Natural Philosophy of Mind and Knowing* (2021).

John Lachs is Centennial Professor of Philosophy at Vanderbilt University. Two of his recent books are *Stoic Pragmatism* and *The Cost of Comfort*. He has taught about 10,000 undergraduates over 59 years and directed over 70 dissertations. John Lachs's *Practical Philosophy: Critical Essays on His Thought with Replies and Bibliography* includes discussion by a broad range of international scholars of Lachs's writings on art, education, epistemology, ethics and the good life, freedom, justice, pluralism, pragmatism, relativism, and the history of philosophy. His current project is a book on the philosophy of education.

José Medina is Walter Dill Scott Professor of Philosophy at Northwestern University, with affiliations in the Departments of African American Studies, Gender and Sexuality Studies, and Spanish and Portuguese. His work focuses on the intersections of race, gender, and sexuality and his primary fields of expertise are critical race theory, gender/queer theory, Black and Latinx feminisms, communication theory, applied philosophy of language, social epistemology, and political philosophy. His books include *The Epistemology of Resistance: Gender and Racial Oppression, Epistemic Injustice, and Resistant Imaginations* (Oxford University Press; recipient of the 2013 North-American Society for Social Philosophy Book Award), and *Speaking from Elsewhere* (2006). His most recent co-edited volume is *Theories of the Flesh: Latinx and Latin-American Feminisms, Transformation, and Resistance* (2020).

His forthcoming book, *The Epistemology of Protest*, discusses protest movements and kinds of activism (including what he terms "epistemic activism") that can be mobilized to resist oppression.

Michele Moody-Adams is Joseph Straus Professor of Political Philosophy and Legal Theory at Columbia University, where she served as Dean of Columbia College and Vice President for Undergraduate Education from 2009–2011. Before Columbia, she taught at Cornell University, where she was Vice Provost for Undergraduate Education. She has also taught at Wellesley College, the University of Rochester, and Indiana University. She is the author of *Fieldwork in Familiar Places: Morality, Culture, and Philosophy (1997)* and *Making Space for Justice: Social Movements, Collective Imagination and Political Hope* (2022). She also writes on democracy, academic freedom, justice, and moral psychology. Moody-Adams has a B.A. from Wellesley College, a second B.A. from Oxford University, and earned the M.A. and Ph.D. in Philosophy from Harvard University. She is a lifetime Honorary Fellow of Somerville College, Oxford and a Fellow of the American Academy of Arts and Sciences.

James O. Pawelski, is professor of practice and director of education in the Positive Psychology Center at the University of Pennsylvania, where he also serves as adjunct professor of Religious Studies. Having won a Fulbright Scholarship and earned a Ph.D. in philosophy, he is the founding director of the Humanities and Human Flourishing Project, which has been designated a National Endowment for the Arts Research Lab. He has published five books, including *The Oxford Handbook of the Positive Humanities*, and is the editor of the Humanities and Human Flourishing book series with Oxford University Press. He is an award-winning teacher, the founding director of Penn's Master of Applied Positive Psychology Program, the founding executive director of the International Positive Psychology Association, and a member of the executive committee of the International Council for Philosophy and Humanistic Studies, and he has served as a member of the steering committee of the International Positive Education Network, and as president of the William James Society.

John Z. Sadler, M.D. is currently a professor of psychiatry and data and population sciences and the Daniel W. Foster, M.D. Professor of Medical Ethics at the University of Texas Southwestern Medical Center. Dr. Sadler directs the Division of Ethics in the Department of Psychiatry and is the institution-wide director of the Program in Ethics in Science & Medicine at UT Southwestern. He is editor-in-chief of the Johns Hopkins University Press journal, *Philosophy, Psychiatry, and Psychology* and co-editor of the Oxford University Press book series, "International Perspectives on Philosophy and Psychiatry," the latter currently spanning over 50 volumes. Dr. Sadler has published dozens of articles, edited or co-edited six books, several special issues of professional journals, and authored a comprehensive monograph, *Values and Psychiatric Diagnosis*, published in 2005. In collaboration with philosopher Jennifer Radden, he coauthored *The Virtuous Psychiatrist: Character Ethics in Psychiatric Practice* (2009).

John J. Stuhr is Arts and Sciences Distinguished Professor of Philosophy and American Studies at Emory University. He received a B.A. from Carleton College and M.A. and Ph.D. from Vanderbilt University, has held visiting appointments in Australia, France, Germany, and Russia, and previously worked at Vanderbilt University, Penn State University, the University of Oregon, and Whitman College. Focused on ethics, social/political philosophy, 19th and 20th century American and European thought, and contemporary cultural issues, he is the author of scores of articles and book chapters and the author or editor of more than a dozen books including *Genealogical Pragmatism: Philosophy, Experience, and Community*; *Pragmatism, Postmodernism, and the Future of Philosophy*; and *Pragmatic Fashions: Pluralism, Democracy, Relativism, and the Absurd*. He is the Editor of *The Journal of Speculative Philosophy*, the *American Philosophy* series general editor, and the founding Director of the American Philosophies Forum.

Valerie Tiberius is the Paul W. Frenzel Chair in Liberal Arts and Professor of Philosophy at the University of Minnesota. Her work explores the ways in which philosophy and psychology can both contribute to the study of well-being and virtue. She is the author of *The Reflective Life: Living Wisely With Our Limits* (Oxford 2008), *Moral Psychology: A Contemporary Introduction* (2015), and *Well-Being as Value Fulfillment: How We Can Help Others to Live Well* (Oxford, 2018). She has published numerous articles on the topics of practical reasoning, prudential virtues, well-being, and the relationship between positive psychology and ethics, and has received grants from the Templeton Foundation and the National Endowment for the Humanities. She served as President of the Central Division of the American Philosophical Association from 2016–17.

Jessica Wahman is the author of *Narrative Naturalism: An Alternative Framework for Philosophy of Mind* and co-editor of *Cosmopolitanism and Place*. She researches and publishes on topics in American philosophy, particularly the work of George Santayana, and philosophical psychology (including the philosophy of mind). She is Director of Undergraduate Studies and Senior Lecturer in Philosophy at Emory University.

Editor's Introduction

Philosophy and Human Flourishing: Good Lives and How to Lead Them

John J. Stuhr

Deep and lasting happiness. Thriving. Self-actualization, self-fulfillment, and the fullest development of opportunities, interests, aims, and talents. Lives that grow, bloom, and flower. Prosperous, lush, and exuberant lives. Lives in top form and on a roll. Lives marked by peak experiences and lots of joy. Good lives. Well-being. Days and years and decades that are meaningful, purposeful, and difference-making. Lives that matter and feel like they matter. Flourishing. Characteristic and continuous flourishing.

Genuinely flourishing lives and genuinely flourishing societies.

Flourishing: What a concept!

It is a concept that now can seem so *distant* as to be downright out of touch with human experience. It can appear so far from present realities as to be fundamentally fiction, simply the stuff of pleasant bedtime stories for adults who have moved on—but only a little—from the Tooth Fairy, Easter Bunny, and bejeweled unicorns of some childhoods. Anyone who thinks about human flourishing must begin by acknowledging that there is something justified in critical reactions to the very notion of flourishing, that at least some suspicion about a focus on human flourishing is warranted initially. Simply put: Ours is most surely not a world of human flourishing. Experiences and cultures differ but they all seem shot through with sufferings and emptiness and some mix of hope for something different and better and despair about the possibility of realizing such hopes. Even scholars who claim that there has never been a better time to be alive recognize that vast numbers of people simply are not leading flourishing lives[1] and that many other people who do

---

[1] See, for example, Pinker, *Enlightenment Now*. In a similar vein, in his book, *Happiness: A Very Short Introduction*, Daniel Haybron, a contributor to this volume, notes both that "In all of human

John J. Stuhr, *Editor's Introduction* In: *Philosophy and Human Flourishing*. Edited by: John J. Stuhr, Oxford University Press. © Oxford University Press 2023. DOI: 10.1093/oso/9780197622162.003.0001

report themselves as thriving live in ways that are not sustainable, cannot be made available to all, and, in fact, often depend on the immiseration of others.

As I write these words, our world is one of worsening, rapidly worsening human-caused climate change and environmental destruction that now impact the quality, sustainability, and the continued existence of human life and much of the rest of life on our planet. It is a world of habitat loss and species loss, hotter temperatures and rising oceans, violent weather, lethal toxins, and climate refugees. Our world is a pandemic world, a world in which a novel coronavirus has infected millions, killed hundreds of thousands, and effected sweeping restrictions, loss, isolation, suffering, and despair across all countries, cultures, groups—some far more than others, of course. It is a pandemic that still rages on, still thousands dying day after day, still scarring the living with revelations of the precarity of our lives and the insecurity of our societies—direct and indirect scars that will remain even after treatment or prevention for this particular virus is discovered and distributed. Our world is one of violence and hate—war, terrorism, genocide, ethnic cleansing and racism, murder, torture, imprisonment, human trafficking, rape, domestic abuse, coercion, intimidation, greed, exclusion, school shootings, and social media attacks. Individual acts of violence often command attention, but much of the violence in our world is structural violence—no less real for being less noticed and built into and reinforced by associations, practices, and institutions that are national, legal, political, technological, economic, familial, and educational. And our world is one of massive inequalities: Resources and powers and positions and opportunities and securities and support and recognition and dignity are anything but shared or equitable. From the standpoint of flourishing, our world seems to be an oligarchy: the cultural preconditions for well-being are mostly the private possessions of the very few, the lucky few.

In the face of climate change and environmental destruction; a pandemic and global health crisis; incalculable and numbing individual, group, and structural hatred and violence; and indefensible inequalities across all aspects of life—these examples could be multiplied almost without end—the concept of flourishing can appear not only distant to the point of fiction but

history there may never have been a better time to be alive" and also "It cannot be stated too emphatically that many poor people are by no means flourishing," pp. 1, 7.

also badly out of touch. In the face of the extreme suffering, sickness, and despair experienced by so many, attention to flourishing can seem *obscene, even cruel*. No matter how well intentioned, any tour of a palatial estate serves as a reminder that you do not actually live there. We actually live in the world of environmental crisis, viral pandemic, chronic violence, and constraining and unfair inequality. Concern with flourishing can appear to be a luxury available and affordable only to a gated fortunate few. It can appear a misplaced priority when it comes to the lives of everyone else.

At the very least, a focus on flourishing can seem to be *premature* given the way the world really is. Flourishing? A would-be pragmatist or practical problem solver is tempted to respond that maybe we can make some time to think about all that later—if and when we make a lot of progress on our many pressing problems. When you are drowning—drowning in rising oceans, drowning in fluid building in your own lungs, drowning in violence, or drowning in debt, deprivation, and the hardness of everyday life—you don't need a treatise on the nature of what life might be like in heaven, what it is to flourish. You need a helping hand. You need a hand that helps you get to a better place, not one distributing brochures about the good place or the best place or some perfect place. When you can't breathe, you don't need an account of the full and fine points of the art of breathing. You need air. First and foremost you need air.

There is something to this suspicion that concern with human flourishing is something distant, obscene, and, perhaps at best, premature. Yet, attention to our world's most pressing problems is in no way at odds with reflection on human well-being. Moreover, the important point here is not simply that we can do two things at once—address real difficulties and also articulate worthy ideals. The point is not simply that these things are not mutually exclusive. Rather, the crucial point is that any long-term effective response to personal and social ills presupposes and requires ideals that frame and guide our striving. The concept of human flourishing is just such an ideal. It is a never fixed, never final articulation of desirable human lives and an account of the means to realize them—to realize them more and more fully if not ever completely. As an ideal, the concept of flourishing is a wager on the future, a melioristic belief in possibilities not yet realized. Philosopher John Dewey put it this way more than a century ago: "Faith in the power of intelligence to imagine a future which is the projection of the desirable in the present, and to invent the instrumentalities of its realization, is our salvation. And it is a faith which must be nurtured and made articulate: surely a sufficiently large task for our philosophy."[2] And as an ideal, the concept of human flourishing has immense critical power. It is the basis for judgments that climate change, pandemic illness, systemic violence, and cultural inequalities and disenfranchisement are not features of the lives we aspire to lead or of the way the world and human life just are. It is impossible to identify the shortcomings of the present without some reference, explicit or implicit, to some ideal of a more flourishing future. The notion of human flourishing is not a utopian daydream. It is an activist ideal.

Accordingly, this volume addresses the two most important clusters of issues about human flourishing:

- What does it mean for a human being to lead a flourishing life—a good life, a life of significance and value, a life of genuine fulfillment? And how can the presence or absence of flourishing be identified, determined, or measured?
- How can individuals and societies create flourishing lives—what are the conditions of flourishing and how can they be achieved, nurtured, and sustained? For particular times and places, what activities, associations, policies, and institutions lead to—or block—human well-being?

These questions are personal and they confront each individual: What should I do? How should I act? What sort of life should I live? What sort of person should I strive to be? They are also interpersonal and social: What should we together do? How should we live with others—including both those like us and those unlike us? What resources and opportunities must a society create and utilize so that its members live well? Finally, these questions are educational in the broadest sense: What habits, feelings, skills, and knowledge are required for flourishing lives? How can they be taught and learned—what kind of education provides these things? What argument, evidence, and facts—as distinct from assertion, speculation, and opinion—can be brought to bear to answer these questions?

These questions are not brand new. Indeed, they long have been at the heart of philosophy and humanistic inquiry more generally. At his death, Socrates reminded his friends that the goal of life is living well—good days—and not just mere existence—more days. Plato told his readers that the unexamined life is not worth living. And Aristotle stressed that we must study the good

[2] Dewey, "The Need for a Recovery of Philosophy," p. 48.

life—something quite different from instrumentally successful actions—not simply to know the good but to live well—to flourish. Understood as love of wisdom, philosophy for more than two thousand years has been the pursuit and practice of human flourishing.

The opportunity at present for philosophers to rethink these questions, however, is new. Just as positive psychology revolutionized psychology and other social science disciplines, the time is ripe for a critically positive, explicitly flourishing-centered, eudaemonic philosophy to reorient our understanding of the meaning of lives of flourishing and the practical means to flourishing lives. This is possible in part because philosophers today (unlike Socrates, Plato, and Aristotle) now can draw on the accomplishments of positive psychology and also a wide range of other fields that include psychiatry, cognitive science, evolutionary biology, and behavioral economics. And it is possible also because of new work in philosophy itself in areas that include philosophical psychology, neuro-ethics, feminist theory, critical race studies, pragmatism, and epistemologies of ignorance. As a result, this volume charts new directions for philosophy and it aims to function as a leading wave of humanistic scholarship focused on human flourishing.

To seize this opportunity, the volume draws on the insights of a carefully selected, diverse, pluralistic group of highly accomplished philosophical thinkers whose interests and writings range across several fields concerned with the meaning and conditions of human flourishing. Their expertise spans philosophy of science and evolutionary theory, cognitive science and philosophy of mind, psychiatry and neuroscience, moral psychology and moral philosophy, social epistemology and education, social and political philosophy, philosophies of race and gender, and both clinical practice and the arts. Though informed throughout by current scholarship in these areas, this volume aims to avoid technical jargon and soporific academic prose. The essays are crisp and clear. They do not assume background familiarity or knowledge of other texts or authors. Because the subject matter—flourishing lives—is engaging, the volume's style aims to be engaging too. Beginners will find the chapters accessible and informative; more advanced scholars will find the volume an original and intellectually sophisticated set of claims and challenges.

It is important to stress in this introduction that this volume is not simply a collection—a kind of volume, unfortunately now commonplace, that puts under one title a bunch of separately conceived and separately written chapters. Instead, *Philosophy and Human Flourishing* is a coherent, carefully integrated endeavor—a pluralistic and inter-stitched whole that is much more than the sum of its parts. This volume is also not simply a collection in a second sense. It does not seek to provide simply a neat and tidy catalogue of different, supposedly opposed or mutually exclusive theories of human flourishing and then trot out supposedly compelling and non-question-begging arguments for just one of them—presumably a given author's favorite theory—and counter-examples to all the other theories—presumably not the author's favorites. Instead of labeling flourishing as simply pleasure or happiness or desire-fulfillment or capacity-fulfillment or optimism and positive attitude or virtue or freedom or achievement or a sense of purpose or self-knowledge and the examined life or close friendships and love or security, stability, and sustainability or . . . , the chapters in this volume strive to set forth more nuanced and complex accounts of flourishing lives—accounts that recognize the multiple and interwoven strands—sometimes conflicting and contested strands—of such lives.[3] These accounts also recognize that it is not formal arguments in philosophy books that establish what human flourishing must or must not be; an account of human flourishing is established only in and by everyday experiences and the extent to which someone's experience is illuminated and enlarged by that account and, in turn, the extent to which that account is verified and confirmed in that experience.

In light of the two central questions—what is a flourishing life for human beings?; and, by what means are flourishing lives possible?—this volume consists of two parts. Part I, "The Meaning of Human Flourishing," takes up the philosophical tasks of conceptual clarification and critical analysis—tasks that Martin Seligman, positive psychology's founder, has stated succinctly must be developed by philosophers and then provided to psychologists and social scientists.

The six chapters in Part I take up several complex, interwoven questions, including the following:

---

[3] Valerie Tiberius, one of this volume's contributors, points in this direction in the "Introduction" to her *The Reflective Life: Living Wisely with Our Limits*, p. 3: "We might think that the way to answer these questions [about how one should live] is to argue for a theory of the human good . . . The problem with this approach is that it is difficult to get consensus on the target, especially if it is described in enough detail to be helpful to all of us. Philosophers, and more recently, psychologists have presented us with a diverse array of options, none of which is the obvious answer to everyone. A different approach is to ask how to live our lives given that we don't know just what the target is, and without assuming that we would agree about the matter."

1. What is the relation of human flourishing to *happiness*? Are they the same—so that a flourishing life just is a happy life? Or is happiness merely one part of flourishing? If so, what part? Is happiness simply subjective well-being? Is happiness a necessary part of flourishing— or can one flourish even if one feels unhappy from time to time (or maybe even more frequently)? Or is a flourishing life always accompanied by happiness? And if there is more to flourishing than happiness, what more?[4]

2. Is it possible to construct any useful *general* account of flourishing at all, or does the huge diversity of human lives make this an impossible or merely abstract and empty project? Is flourishing in some ways the same across all peoples and cultures, all times and places? Is it, for example, the fulfillment of values rooted in our natures or in our particular selves and senses of self? Is it a self-chosen life? Is it a self-enjoyed life? If not, and if all these things differ from person to person, what is a sufficiently *pluralistic*, difference-sensitive way of understanding human flourishing?

3. Is flourishing something ultimately *subjective*, such that whether or not individuals are flourishing wholly depends on whether or not they feel or find or report that they are flourishing? Are you happy if you think you are happy?[5] Is it possible to feel that one is flourishing and be self-deceived or wrong in other ways?[6] Or is flourishing *objective*— something that depends on the presence or absence of particular conditions and independent of how one feels or whether or not one correctly perceives the conditions and nature of one's own life? Can other people be the best judges of whether an individual is or is not

---

[4] I note that in *Happiness: A Very Short Introduction*, Daniel Haybron claims that "well being seems to require more than just happiness," but this is largely due to the fact that he defines happiness as a certain psychological condition or state of mind. Aristotle's very different account of happiness as an activity in accordance with human virtue draws together happiness and flourishing. Haybron suggests that some will find Aristotle's view overly objectivist—though experience often shows that what is good for someone is not what that person thinks is good—and overly externalist—though, again, experience often shows that who we are is not entirely a matter of our own creation or choice pp. 10, 77–85). A feature of many of the chapters that follow is a focus on understanding flourishing in a manner that does not assume or accept subjective/objective or internal/external dualisms.

[5] Rubin, *The Happiness Project*, p. 234.

[6] In a related context, Valerie Tiberius (*Well-Being as Value Fulfillment*, p. 8) has noted that "we know there has been a lot of attention paid recently to how little we really know about ourselves and what makes us happy and it is sometimes implied that we know others *much better* than we know ourselves. I agree that we lack self-knowledge, but I think we shouldn't infer from that we know our friends a whole lot better."

flourishing?[7] Or is flourishing best understood not as subjective or objective but, instead, as something *relational*—as spanning both individuals and their environments, spanning what philosopher William James called the *how* of experience and also the *what* of experience?[8]

4. What is the relation of human flourishing to moral goodness and *morality* more generally? Can a morally bad person nonetheless lead a flourishing life? Can a morally good person, perhaps as the result of the bad deeds of others or just bad fortune, fail to flourish yet succeed at being moral? And if a flourishing life and a moral life are not the same, does flourishing have any moral worth at all? Or, to frame this the other way around, does morality have any role or worth for flourishing? Is a morally good person simply a person who lives a flourishing life, a person whose character and habits facilitate a full, satisfying, meaningful life?[9] Or, is the very idea that virtue might have any role in flourishing or happiness deeply unlikely, a judgment Julia Annas attributes to philosophers of the past two hundred years?[10]

5. What is the temporality of flourishing? That is, can there be brief moments of flourishing in lives that otherwise do not flourish? Is flourishing a kind of peak experience, a quickly passing high point that exists only in relation to lots of other moments that are relatively flat or low? Or is flourishing something that applies only to longer, larger stretches of time—for example, a flourishing childhood in the apartment on Amsterdam Avenue, a flourishing liberal arts college experience, a flourishing career, a flourishing journey abroad, or a flourishing experience of parenting children? Or is it really only whole lives that

[7] Badhwar, *Well-Being: Happiness in a Worthwhile Life*, p. 3, divides account of well-being into those that are subjective (and sharply distinguish prudential value for an individual from moral value and a person's goodness) and those that are objective (and hold that prudential goods for an individual entail the moral goodness of the individual). In this sort of conceptual scheme, there is no space for a relational account of flourishing.

[8] This radically empirical, pragmatic view of human experience has affinities with Jonathan Haidt's final formulation of his "happiness hypothesis," in which happiness is presented not as something internal or as something external but as something "that comes from between." Haidt, however, does not draw upon pragmatism or note the similarities between his view and the century-earlier writings of leading pragmatists(The *Happiness Hypothesis*, p. 223). See also Annas, who, in discussing subjective and objective accounts of flourishing, writes, "It soon emerges, then, that we can find convincing counterexamples to both the subjective and objective accounts of happiness. This very fact, though, is an indication that we have a false choice here, and that it would be unpromising to follow up either alternative. . . . This strongly suggests that this whole approach to thinking of happiness is systematically unpromising" (Intelligent Virtue, pp. 142–43).

[9] See Lear, *Happiness, Death, and the Remainder of Life* p. 2 and the first chapter, "Happiness" more generally.

[10] Annas, *Intelligent Virtue*, p. 119; see chapter 8, "Living Happily," more generally.

either are or not flourishing affairs? Is flourishing something momentary or something longer-lasting, something more enduring?[11]

6. Are some people just by nature more able to more fully flourish than some other people? Just as some theorists have claimed that individuals have different base "set points" for happiness, do different people have different flourishing set points—different levels of flourishing that are their default states? Or is human flourishing something broadly available to all human beings? Is it possible to educate for flourishing—to develop knowledges and skills that are the means to or constitutive parts of flourishing lives? Is it possible to practice flourishing, to acquire high levels of skill in the art of flourishing? Is it possible to acquire a character of flourishing, to characteristically engage in flourishing? If so, how?

7. What is the relation between a flourishing life and a life of purpose and meaning? If a flourishing life has meaning, what is that meaning? Is it a life that just feels like it matters and is important to the individual living it? Or is it a life that other people recognize and communicate as making a difference to them? If so, which people? (This is a question with practical urgency, given the multiple and contested nature is of almost all judgments—what matters to some people either matters differently or does not even matter at all to others). Or is a flourishing life one that matters both to the individual and to others? And if all lives end in death, does even a flourishing life really matter in the end?[12] What could it mean to be finite and flourish?

In response to these questions, the chapters in Part I develop understandings of human flourishing as follows:

- Lives of meaning and self-awareness, lives that matter to others and to one's self;

---

[11] See Fletcher's analysis of well-being and the shape of a lifetime or whole-life; *The Philosophy of Well-Being*, 2016, pp. 132–44. A very different view is present by Lebar in his *The Value of Living Well*, pp. 38–55. In part he argues against what he terms "telic pluralism" because he conceives of "Ultimate Ends" as having logical and normative status rather than temporal status such that all ends, in the phrase of John Dewey, are simply ends-in-view. This notion of "ultimate end" is examined critically from the very different standpoint of psychoanalysis by Lear in *Happiness, Death, and the Remainder of Life*.

[12] See, for just one example, chapter 8 in Fletcher's *The Philosophy of Well-Being*, pp. 145–58.

- The achievement of homeostasis at multiple levels—biological, inter-personal, communal, and the quest for meaning;
- Lives of empowerment, self-narratives of empowerment, and genuine agency rather than passive mechanism;
- The fulfillment of the values a person holds and the development and nourishment of the very capacity to hold values;
- The capacity to formulate, identify, pursue, and reach goals, the goodness of which depends on individual attitudes, emotions, and experiences;
- Attunement to differences among individuals and cultures, and thus a recognition of the fact and value of pluralism both in a human life and across human lives.

In light of the overlapping account of human flourishing set forth in Part I, the seven chapters in Part II are directed to questions that emerge from a focus on the means to human flourishing. These questions include the following:

1. Can the concept of flourishing be applied effectively to social groups, peoples and cultures, regions and nations, or the whole of humanity? Or is flourishing significant only at the level of individuals? Is a flourishing society simply a collection of flourishing individuals? Or is it something more? And if the notion of flourishing societies is an irreducibly normative notion, who is or should be empowered to determine what counts as flourishing across varied times and places? Instead of asking which concept of flourishing is correct, should we ask how a particular concept of flourishing either advances of fails to advance well-being in particular contexts?

2. Are there pre-requisites for human flourishing? Is human flourishing possible only if particular conditions and resources are present? Or is it simply more likely to occur if particular conditions and resources are present? If so, what are the conditions? Do they include environmental sustainability?[13] Public health measures and personal well-being regimes? Economic and material conditions? Particular political forms or social ways of life? Support and security programs for the most

---

[13] Curren and Metzger discuss the "normative heart" of sustainability in their *Living Well Now and in the Future,* MIT Press, 2017).

vulnerable members of social groups? Warranted expectations for future flourishing? Educational practices? Loves, friendships, and close
personal relationships?[14] Other?

3. What policies, practices, institutions, and governments create and sustain these conditions? What counts as evidence of this?

4. What is the relation of flourishing to social justice? Can individuals
or groups of individuals flourish in unjust societies? For example, can
some individuals flourish even if (or maybe because) they live in societies that are racist or sexist or characterized by huge economic inequalities? Can some individuals flourish even if (or maybe because) they live
in societies that are colonial, fascist, or dictatorial and authoritarian?
Can an age flourish even as it lives in ways that damage future generations? Can a few people flourish—genuinely flourish—on the backs of
many others? Conversely, can everyone flourish? Or do inequalities in
flourishing harm everyone? Must everyone flourish for any individual
to flourish? Is virtue primary for flourishing?[15]

5. What responsibilities do individuals have for the flourishing—or the
relative absence of flourishing—in the lives of other persons? Is trust or
confidence that other persons and institutions will meet these responsibilities itself a major component of flourishing?

6. Is it possible to measure flourishing in a given society or to measure
flourishing across different societies? Of course, the math for such
measurement is easy after specified components of flourishing have
been operationalized and quantified, but what should be the basis
of this operationalization? Should the presence of a particular per
capita number of parks be a measure of a given city's flourishing? Or
the absence of corruption or perceptions of the generosity of others?
Should experienced freedom be a larger or smaller measure than per
capita hospital beds or average levels of formal education or relative
extent of ethnic diversity? Who should determine the answer to these
questions—what counts as freedom or generosity or corruption and
the relative importance of each of these? On what basis is this sort of
measurement made?

[14] In *The Happiness Project*, Rubin observes that "One conclusion was blatantly clear from my happiness research: everyone from contemporary scientists to ancient philosophers agrees that having
strong social bonds is probably the most meaningful contributor to happiness," p. 141.

[15] For example, in *Well-Being*, Badhwar argues that virtue is necessary—villains don't fully
flourish— but insufficient by itself—Stoic self-control is not enough because some external resources
are needed—for human flourishing. See especially Chapter 7, pp. 183–221.

7. Is it possible to educate—not just school, but most broadly and fully educate—people for virtuous, rewarding, and flourishing lives? What would such a civic education include, how would it work, who would it include, and how would it be supported? What is the role of the arts in such an education? What is the role of the humanities generally and philosophy specifically in such an education?

In response to these questions, the chapters in Part II squarely situate flourishing lives in social contexts: Human beings are biological and social organisms and so human flourishing is an environmental and social affair—a point recognized and stressed for the first time in the 2020 *World Happiness Report*.[16] Individuals are irreducibly and inseparably constituted by, and bound up in, social relations and social conditions, real and imagined.[17] Any account of human flourishing that overlooks this fact is an abstraction. In this context, these chapters analyze enabling conditions and limiting moral and political realities of flourishing. They include the following:

- The recognition that flourishing is a multivalent affair with multiple dimensions that must be explicitly specified in light of our many and different purposes, frequently fixed habits, and changing life conditions;.
- The nature of often seemingly irreconcilable conflicts between individual flourishing and communal well-being and justice, produced in part by individuals over-claiming on their own behalf as the result of egocentric bias and self-deception;[18]
- Our epistemic responsibility to attend to these linkages of one's own flourishing and the withering of the lives of others;
- The role of values literacy and the skill of values analysis in the public life of a society committed to the flourishing of all;

---

[16] *World Happiness Report 2020* . See also Lebar's dual focus on the fact that social relations are an important component of living well and that living well for a social being is always living well in community. *The Value of Living Well*, pp. 89–104.

[17] In *The Happiness Hypothesis*, Haidt terms this "ultrasociality," p. 47.

[18] See chapter 5 of Tiberius *Well-Being as Value Fulfillment*. Tiberius concludes: "I've argued that cultivating habits that make us less self-centered and more aware of our limitations is a good way to try to overcome some of the biggest barriers we face as friends who want to help. This is good for us insofar as we value friendship as part of what it is to live a good life for ourselves. Of course, becoming better at helping is also better for those we aim to help," p. 173. See also Lear's discussion of the unconscious and the possible inclusion of the unconscious in character formation in *Happiness, Death, and the Remainder of Life*, pp. 3–17.

- Ways in which the teaching of philosophy can contribute not only to theories of flourishing but also to practices of flourishing—individual and social well-being;
- Some opportunities for broadly educational institutions in democratic societies to nurture thought and action that enable creative lives rather than mere technological expertise and efficient professionalism;[19] and
- The central role of artistic dimensions of everyday experiences and the need to developed skills of imagination, creativity, and expression.

* * *

In the first chapter of Part I, "The Conatus Project: Mattering and Morality," Rebecca Newberger Goldstein draws from the philosophy of Spinoza to explain that the essence of each individual thing is *conatus*: the drive to persist in its own being and to flourish. Using evolution—especially as it has been updated to focus on genes rather than organisms—one can explain, she argues, both why *conatus* is so fundamental to biological systems and why, in humans, it is converted into the drive to matter, which can be thought of as the drive to justify the seriousness with which we have to regard our life just in order to pursue it. Properly analyzed, the drive to matter—not necessarily to matter more than others (which is obnoxious) nor to matter cosmically to the universe at large (which is the religious impulse)[20]—can offer a more precise way at getting at the fuzzy concept of the meaning of life and the concept of a flourishing life as a meaningful life. For Goldstein, we are creatures of matter who long to matter.

Also focused on evolution, biology, and embodiment, in chapter 2, "Flourishing in the Flesh," Mark Johnson explains that the conditions of human flourishing transcend those of mere survival and fitness, but nonetheless are built upon and engage those conditions of our biological well-being. In this sense, flourishing is rooted deeply in our embodiment. Here Johnson notes the importance of arguments by Antonio Damasio that the fundamental value for organic life is homeostasis—the maintenance of a suitable dynamic equilibrium within the boundaries of the organism as it

---

[19] For example, Curren and Metzger set forth "an education for sustainability" to enable communication, understanding, shared norms, trust, and leadership in action. The policies and curriculum they set forth suggests the possibility for an education for flourishing. *Living Well Now and in the Future*, pp. 153–79.

[20] Compare this with the distinction that Haidt makes in *The Happiness Hypothesis* between the purpose of life and purpose within life, pp. 217–18.

interacts with its physical, interpersonal, and cultural environments. This perspective echoes Jonathan Haidt's account of human beings as multilevel systems (bodies, minds, cultures) that require "cross-level coherence" to flourish.[21] From this perspective, Johnson investigates the issue of how far the notion of homeostasis can be taken as the supreme value underlying human flourishing at four levels of organization and complexity. Homeostasis goes a long way, he contends, toward explaining what flourishing consists in at the levels of our biological functioning, our interpersonal relations, and our communal practices and institutions, and it can even help us understand what constitutes our well-being and well-doing at the level of our quest for lives that are meaningful and significant.

An essential element of meaningful lives is our sense of empowerment—our ability to direct our own paths and to make some positive difference in the world on our own terms. Jessica Wahman develops this view in chapter 3: "Pragmatic Stories of Selves and Their Flourishing." This sense of empowerment is both advanced by and in part constituted by the narratives we tell about our individual trajectories and the general stories we tell ourselves about human nature and human life. These narratives, Wahman shows, can shape our sense of agency. Mechanistic models of human behavior, particularly when treated as foundational, can promote a narrative that alienates the conscious subject from her own empowerment and her agency in nature and society. This makes human beings passive observers in their own life stories—a result that runs counter to flourishing. As a means of reconstructing the narrative and providing an alternative, Wahman turns to pragmatic psychology in which the self is conceived as a system of habits. She shows that identifying the self with the entire organism—one which is not merely a mechanism and of which consciousness is an integral part—allows for a different and fuller kind of agency, one that better recognizes both our limitations and our choices. This sort of narrative, she concludes, identifies concrete possibilities for increasing the self's freedom and well-being.

This connection is affirmed and developed in chapter 4 by Daniel M. Haybron: Because an understanding of human flourishing depends upon an account of the human self, flourishing is constituted at least partially by self-fulfillment. Distinguishing a person's self—the fragile existence of consciousness—from that person's identity, Haybron develops two

---

[21] Haidt, *The Happiness Hypothesis*, pp. 226–29. Interestingly in this context, Lear claims that Aristotle's ethics of flourishing amounts to "recommending a different level of homeostasis for the best human life. *Happiness, Death, and the Remainder of Life*, p. 47.

new arguments for his self-based account of flourishing as self-fulfillment. These arguments embody a different strategy from two prior arguments that claim that both happiness and authenticity are best explained in terms of self-fulfillment. The "convergence argument" seeks to establish that currently popular alternatives to self-fulfillment accounts of flourishing—accounts of flourishing as pleasure or desire-satisfaction or nature-fulfillment, for example—are plausible only when understood as self-fulfillment. Supposed alternatives, that is, converge or collapse into self-fulfillment theories of human flourishing. The "piggybacking argument" aims to show that any substantive conception of the self requires an account of a flourishing self that rationally coheres with that view of the self—that a conception of the prudential value of flourishing as self-fulfillment "piggybacks" on any (and every) conception of the self—whatever that conception of the self may be, however one may "wade into the dark waters of the self."

If flourishing is understood as the flourishing of a self, does that mean that it is something subjective and relative to that individual self? Or is a self's flourishing something objective, something that depends upon the realization of certain conditions or standards even if an individual is not aware of them or does not care about them? Surveying the battles between subjectivists and objectivists, Valerie Tiberius argues for an account of flourishing that "sits on the line" right between subjectivism and objectivism. In chapter 5, "Well-Being, Value Fulfillment, and Valuing Capacities: Toward a More Subjective Hybrid," she sets forth this line-straddling view under the banner of "value-fulfillment theory," a subjectivist theory (because it holds that persons must have a positive attitude toward something for that thing to be a good for that person) that has objectivist elements as well—and thus is a hybrid theory. Understanding flourishing as the fulfillment of values appropriate to or psychologically fitting to a particular self, Tiberius moves beyond consideration of the criticism that a self's values or desires may be defective, that they may be desires for things that turn out not to be good for us, to the criticism that depressed persons may have no desires at all, may suffer complete conative breakdown. It seems that subjectivist accounts of flourishing flounder here: The depressed self may have no desires and so desire-fulfillment is an impossibility. Tiberius responds, however, that mental health and the capacity to formulate and pursue goals need not be understood as objective goods but, rather, as a self's pre-requisites for the pursuit and fulfillment of any goals at all. This view retains what is most important and insightful about subjectivism: its internalism about practical reasons, its rejection of evaluative realism, and its requirement that goods have some "internal resonance" with the individual for whom they are goods. And it adds what is best about objectivism: the requirement that the capacity (or restoration of capacity) for internal resonance is a good for a person even if that person does not desire that good (as a result of depression, poor mental health, etc.). This may be a departure from or rejection of subjectivism as it was originally conceived or is strictly practiced, but it maintains subjectivism about human flourishing (as value fulfillment) except when faced with the question of why having any values at all is a good thing.

When we try to think about flourishing from the perspectives of different individuals in this way, no matter how much we struggle to include the amazingly rich array of fulfilling human lives and the important differences among them, still the "allure of the all" is difficult to resist. No matter how we restrain ourselves from generalizing, sooner or later we almost always think we have discovered some essential feature of all reality or all human beings that is universally present—or should be universally present. In chapter 6 "The Allure of the 'All,'" John Lachs shows that this is how, with the best of intentions, we arrive at accounts of human flourishing that are not descriptive inventories of the many ways many different people successfully make sense of life, but instead selective cheerleading for single characteristics whose presence supposedly guarantees happiness and well-being for all. Even Aristotle, a master of human diversity, succumbed to this temptation, Lachs shows. He wisely wrote that happiness is an activity in accordance with virtue, but then associated virtue only with his narrow view of the golden mean. Lachs provides an account of human flourishing that does justice to the pluralities of human beings and the variety of ways they gain satisfaction and meaning. Human flourishing is simply a class name for multiple, diverse, plural human flourishings.

Taking seriously this pluralism focuses attention on the ways in which habits of flourishing require supportive social conditions if they are to be developed and sustained. Part II examines social aspects of human flourishing and conditions that limit or prevent it. In chapter 7, "Flourishing: Toward Clearer Ideas and Habits of Genius," John J. Stuhr identifies ten pitfalls that must be avoided on the way to any concept of human flourishing that has both practical or operational meaning and critical, normative use. They are (1) viewing flourishing in a wholly third-person or "objective" way; (2) conceiving flourishing only in a first-person or "subjective" way; (3) ignoring or under-recognizing the limits of individual or aggregate preference claims;

(4) taking homeostasis or similar conditions as a sufficient basis or full model for human well-being; (5) underestimating (or worse) human differences and the resulting need for an account of plural flourishings rather than any singular, one-size-fits-all account; (6) failing to recognize this pluralism (and selves as multiplicities) at intra-personal as well as inter-personal levels; (7) paying too little attention to the role of loss and tragedy in every realization of ideals, goals, and goods; (8) embracing only a plant-based notion of flourishing as a brief flowering season rather than a complete life; (9) conflating a life of meaning or purpose with a life of value (and some but not any and all meanings and purposes); and (10) considering flourishing in overly individualistic terms abstracted from its constitutive social relations and cultural conditions. In this light, he then sets forth a multivalent, five-dimensional, pluralistic account of flourishing—plural concepts of flourishing, each of which explicitly addresses flourishing across the following five axes: (1) the what of flourishing (e.g., health, happiness, purpose, creativity, etc.); (2) the when and where of flourishing (e.g., at a given moment, during a short span, across a longer period of time, over a whole life, in particular place, at many similar or different places, in the presence of what customs and habits, etc.); (3) the who of flourishing (e.g., an individual, a family, a neighborhood, a country or diaspora, a socio-economic group, etc.); (4) the how of flourishing (e.g., by whom—an individual, a third-party group of experts, some other social group, a liberal or conservative think tank, etc.—and how—by an appeal to authority, long-standing doctrine, experimental method, etc.); and (5) the why of flourishing (for what purpose, on the basis of what beliefs, in the service of what purpose or whose interests, etc.). To insist on this, Stuhr claims, is to endorse a form of pragmatism: We should stop asking which concept of flourishing is really the correct one and instead ask how and why it is illuminating and useful to take up any particular one. Finally, drawing on this multivalent account of flourishing, he takes seriously the claim that human beings are creatures of habit and the consequence that because our world is dynamic rather than static, these habits must change and evolve if they are to be successful. A flourishing life in this context is a life of creative habits, habits of flexibility, and habits attuned to possibilities.[22] This involves imagining, perceiving, thinking, and acting on the

---

[22] This focus resonates with Tiberius's account of "wisdom and flexibility" in chapter 3 of her *The Reflective Life*. She characterizes her approach as "in the tradition of Hume"—looking at "our experience as the only source of answers to our normative questions" and viewing the norms that govern

unhabitual—an undertaking James termed "genius" or the capacity to recognize, invent, and engage the unhabitual. This sort of life—one for which philosophy provides many skills and insights—is marked by fluidity and ease but also by self-interruption and discomfort and its hopes.

In chapter 8: "Navigating Irreconcilable Conflicts: Philosophical Thinking for Better Lives," Lori Gallegos asks about the role of philosophy with regard to efforts to live a good life. She notes that the answer to this question depends on how the good life is understood. If we view the good life as Aristotle did, for example—as a life in which pleasurable emotion, well-being, and virtue are largely integrated—then philosophy definitely can help us live better lives to the extent that it can guide us to live more virtuous lives. However, we may find that life is all-too-often full of irreconcilable conflicts and unintegrated elements. In this case, pursuing one central commitment comes at the cost of another. And so in this case, she suggests, philosophy's role may be to help us navigate our limitations and responsibilities in a more authentic way. Here Gallegos charts an alternative third course between these two approaches by bringing into focus key aspects of the social and political contexts within which we live our lives. She argues that life's irreconcilable conflicts are exacerbated by conditions of well-being inequality,[23] particularly for those who are oppressed. Gallegos shows that those who are disadvantaged may consistently find themselves in a position in which they must choose between their empowered, autonomous preferences and their own physical and psychological well-being; between cultivating and exercising certain virtues and their own well-being; and between pursuing their most meaningful commitments and their well-being. Although she finds it important to recognize the goodness of lives that involve great sacrifice, she also appreciates that imposed sacrifices involve real and lamentable loss for those who make them. Focusing on the way that unjust social conditions exacerbate these irreconcilable conflicts, Gallegos asks: What can philosophical thinking contribute in our efforts to understand what it means to live a good life and to pursue this vision? She concludes by proposing that philosophical thinking affords us both conceptual and practical resources. First, it allows us to make

how we ought to live as contingent on our commitments" (pp. 6, 20). This, in turn, suggests James's characterization of his pragmatism as "a new name for an old way of thinking."

[23] See the section on "Inequality and Happiness" in chapter 2, "Social Environments for World Happiness," *World Happiness Report 2020*. The extensive data here confirms this point.

helpful conceptual distinctions, such as distinctions among kinds of good lives, and between those limitations on our choices which are socially produced and those which are not. Second, philosophical thinking permits us to gain reflective distance from our lives, values, and choices so that we may more effectively pursue--and help others pursue--good lives.

While the goodness of some lives involves great sacrifices, so too the flourishing of lives of some persons often involves and depends upon the lives of other persons who are not flourishing. In chapter 9, "Relational Insensitivity and the Interdependence of Flourishing and Withering," José Medina begins with the fact of pluralism: Human beings seek flourishing in many ways, sometimes in conflicting ways. These lives and their pursuits are interconnected and interdependent in multiple, complex ways. And the flourishing of some, he observes, is very often pursued at the cost of the withering of others. Medina argues that in individualistic societies, agents, groups, and institutions typically have a blind spot for how the flourishing they pursue in their own paths of development may be entangled with the differential flourishing possibilities and even the withering of others. Recognizing this fact, he argues that this blind spot is a cultivated insensitivity or active ignorance— a *relational insensitivity*. He argues that this relational insensitivity reflects failed epistemic responsibility: the epistemic responsibility of being attuned to the interdependence of ways of flourishing and withering entangled with our own flourishing and withering. Drawing from feminist theory and critical race theory and critically engaging with William James, Medina argues that there is a Will-Not-to-Know that is at the core of American individualism and has been at the service of white privilege and neo-colonial attitudes and policies. There are practices in American culture that have produced social death, but there are also what he calls practices of *social deadening*: practices that desensitize people about the lives of others (especially those others who are very different from ourselves) and make them blind to aspects of their own lives and well-being and their connections (or lack thereof) to others. Practices of social deadening include practices of epistemic deadening that numb our sensibilities and make us inattentive to the interrelations between ways of flourishing and ways of withering. In response, Medina argues that we need *epistemic activism* in order to unmask and uproot our relational insensitivity and resist practices of social deadening. Here he uses contemporary political art to illustrate how epistemic activism can wake people up from their epistemic slumbers and promote more relational sensitivity to the flourishing of others—and ultimately to their own flourishing.

Activism on behalf of flourishing in the public sphere encounters an inter-related set of social problems that interfere with and block it. In chapter 10, "Values Literacy and Citizenship," John Z. Sadler addresses in practical terms some of these problems. He begins by describing the contemporary break-down of public civil discourse in the realms of political discourse, social media use, and education for civic engagement. He then introduces skills and attitudes for recognizing, analyzing, and interpreting values—including the value of flourishing. In light of these skills and attitudes, he develops a method of values recognition and analysis and defines values operationally as attitudes or dispositions that are action-guiding and subject to praise or blame. With this understanding, texts or human discourses can be "searched" for value terms (words with specified evaluative meanings), value semantics (sentences in which evaluations are semantically or pragmatically implied), and value entailments (practices which involve one or more evaluations). These philosophical concepts, Sadler shows, then can be applied in a con-crete way to cultural artifacts—texts, talk—to identify the values explicitly or implicitly present. This method of values analysis, Sadler contends, is in-tuitive and teachable, and he provides concrete illustrations of how to do this. The problem of "values blindness" refers to our tendency to not recog-nize values we and other hold, and this values blindness can be addressed by the method Sadler develops and outlines. Through a hierarchical order of value types, often implicit but commonly encountered and structured by Western liberal democratic societies, Sadler argues that educating the polity in values-analysis can deepen and expand civil discourse—and thus deepen and expand public flourishing. The primary importance of this education is the empathy it builds among stakeholders and the abilities it cultivates for conscientious consumption of communications, independent of ideological commitments, contents, and prejudices. Instead of taking values for granted, or simply accepting a claim to values (e.g., "family values," "progressivism"), Sadler concludes that the sincere seeker of human flourishing can use values analysis to explode simplistic accounts into complex sets of value trade-offs and compromises, exposing the insincere while revealing potentials for common ground and shared flourishing.

The development of this potential for shared, public flourishing is the focus of chapter 11. In "Teaching Philosophy: The Love of Wisdom and the Cultivation of Human Flourishing," James Pawelski examines how the teaching of philosophy can be more than mere theory about flourishing lives but, instead, can be a crucial component of practices of human flourishing.

Of course, philosophy and its teaching frequently have failed to make good on this goal, as Pawelski explains by examining its history from the ancient Greeks and Romans to the present and by identifying current obstacles to the cultivation of flourishing in actual practice. These obstacles include understanding schooling in narrow vocational terms and success in school in narrow GPA terms. And they include practicing philosophy itself in equally narrow academic specialization terms. Of course, the need for habits of well-being does not vanish just because theorists turn away from it. Accordingly, Pawelski calls for a "eudaimonic turn" and explains in terms of his own experience as a teacher some of its key components that he refers to as "applied" and genuinely "experimental pragmatism."

Pawelski's focus on the ways in which practical applications of philosophy can be philosophy points directly to Jennifer Hansen's focus in chapter 12, "A Reconsideration of the Role of Philosophy in the Reconstruction and Promotion of Leisure." Hansen argues that human flourishing has an autotelic character—that activities of flourishing "flow" and are experienced as intrinsically valuable. (To this point, she notes, that philosophical activity itself often has been thought—at least by many philosophers!—to be a prime instance of this sort of activity, such that a fully flourishing life has been taken to have a *philosophical* character or dimension.) To understand flourishing in terms of autotelic activities is a value paradigm very different from, and in many ways opposed to, the now more dominant values of technological rationality that pervade much of social life. Autotelic activities do not simply happen naturally or on their own. Hansen argues instead that they must be cultivated and that attention must be paid to the conditions on which they depend. In a democratic culture, this must be a matter of conditions open and widely available to all. Accordingly, she argues for educational policies and reforms necessary for cultivating habitual capacities for autotelic activities and experiences.

The cultivation of the capacity for flourishing is an art, Michele Moody-Adams explains in chapter 13: "Philosophy and the Art of Human Flourishing." Philosophy best supports and advances human flourishing, she shows, when it acknowledges, and deepens understanding of, the contributions that art can make to a satisfying and well-lived life. Philosophers who promote what Arthur Danto has called the "disenfranchisement of art" thus divert us all from a critical source of human flourishing. Moody-Adams contends that art can promote constructive transformations in individual lives, encourage and sustain social and political reconciliation, and provide unmatched consolation in response to suffering and adversity. Yet, as John Dewey urged, if we are to fully realize the contributions that art can make to human flourishing, we must find ways to restore continuity between art and everyday experience. This means acknowledging that art is the exercise and application of imagination, creativity, and skill in many domains of interest and concern that are not limited to the preoccupations of the "fine arts." Further, it means recognizing that living well is itself an art that draws on ways of knowing, and sometimes creatively reimagining, the world that are not accessible except by means of art. If we hope to promote human flourishing, we must therefore restore continuity between art and "everyday" experience in our individual lives, as well as in the social, political, and economic institutions within which we share our lives.

* * *

Genuinely flourishing lives and genuinely flourishing societies.

Flourishing: What a concept!

Flourishing does not happen automatically, naturally, by default. It requires reflection—reflection on its nature and reflection on the conditions needed for it. Without acting as a cheerleader in advance for any particular result of this reflection, philosophy can take up this reflection: imagining new possibilities, clarifying concepts, analyzing lines of thought, describing carefully, enlarging and enriching meanings, expanding awareness of oneself and others, integrating theory and practice, and cultivating skills and habits of practical wisdom. And in taking up this reflection, philosophy may confirm hope in its efficacy and sustain action based in the hope of human flourishing—surely a sufficiently large and sufficiently crucial task for philosophy.

Works Cited

Annas, Julia. Intelligent Virtue. Oxford University Press, 2011.

Badhwar, Neerea K. Well-Being: Happiness in a Worthwhile Life. Oxford University Press, 2014.

Curren, Randall, and Ellen Metzger. Living Well Now and in the Future: Why Sustainability Matters. MIT Press, 2017.

Dewey, John. "The Need for a Recovery of Philosophy," 1917. John Dewey: The Middle Works, 1899–1924, vol. 10. Southern Illinois University Press, 1980, p. 48.

Fletcher, Guy. The Philosophy of Well-Being: An Introduction. Routledge, 2016.

Haidt, Jonathan. The Happiness Hypothesis: Finding Modern Truth in Ancient Wisdom. *Basic Books*, 2006.

Haybron, Daniel. Happiness: A Very Short Introduction. Oxford University Press, 2013.

Lear, Jonathan. Happiness, Death, and the Remainder of Life. Harvard University Press, 2000.

Lebar, Mark. The Value of Living Well. Oxford University Press, 2013.

Pinker, Steven. Enlightenment Now: The Case for Reason, Science, Humanism, and Progress. Viking Press, 2018.

Rubin, Gretchen. The Happiness Project. Harper Books, 2009.

Tiberius, Valerie. "Introduction." The Reflective Life: Living Wisely with Our Limits. Oxford University Press, 2008.

Tiberius, Valerie. Well-Being as Value Fulfillment: How We Can Help Each Other to Live Well. *Oxford University Press, 2018.*

World Happiness Report 2020, Sustainable Development Solutions Network, a Global Initiative for the United Nations, 2020. https://worldhappiness.report/ed/2020/

PART I
MEANINGS OF HUMAN FLOURISHING

1

The Conatus Project

Mattering and Morality

Rebecca Newberger Goldstein

For the ancient Greek moral philosophers, the questions of morality were intimately conjoined with the questions of human flourishing. Socrates, Plato, and Aristotle concurred that living well was a central aim of philosophy and that virtue is crucial to the well-lived life. From Socrates' refusal in the "Apology" and "Crito" to compromise his virtue even were it to prolong his life, to Plato's claim in the "Gorgias" that the self-indulgent tyrant inflicts greater harm on himself than on his victims, to Aristotle's systematic investigations in the *Nicomachean Ethics* of the virtues whose habitual practice results in *eudaimonia*, there is the shared conviction both that human flourishing is an unquestionable good in itself, and that living as one morally ought does not detract from one's flourishing but rather conduces to it, even if, as was the case with Socrates, it shortens one's life.

With the eventual triumph of Christianity over Europe's normativity, the notion of virtue as tied up with flourishing no longer enjoyed its unquestionable moral status. "For to you it has been granted for Christ's sake, not only to believe in him, but to suffer for His sake," writes Paul in his Epistle to the Philippians (1:29), a valorization of suffering that is not only repeated throughout the New Testament but is vividly represented in the most central iconography of the faith.[1,2]

The moral philosophers of early modernism aligned themselves with the ancient Greeks in again focusing on human flourishing, denying suffering

---

[1] For example, Philippians, 3:10; Acts 5:14, Acts 9:16; Romans 8:17, Romans 8:36; Corinthians 1:7, Corinthians 11:23, Corinthians 4:11; Timothy 2:12; Hebrews 11:25; James 5:10.

[2] See Jensen 130: "Medieval and Renaissance sculpture and painting was saturated with scenes of the Lord's passion, a theme probably second only to the depiction of the Virgin and child. In general, Christ on the cross is probably the most recognizable Christian image, one that traverses both geographical and chronological boundaries" (Jensen 130).

Rebecca Newberger Goldstein, *The Conatus Project* In: *Philosophy and Human Flourishing*. Edited by: John J. Stuhr, Oxford University Press. © Oxford University Press 2023. DOI: 10.1093/oso/9780197622162.003.0002

its redemptive quality. To live ethically is, if not constitutive of flourishing, at least essential to it, which is an experience deeply positive.[3] With modernity, it becomes, once again, an essential question of ethics to determine what flourishing truly consists in.

No modern philosopher had more to do with restoring the moral salience of human flourishing than Baruch Spinoza, a singularly important figure in seeding the intellectual and political movement that would, roughly a hundred years after his death, effloresce in the European Enlightenment.[4] Spinoza is the first of the moderns to try to establish ethics on purely naturalist foundations, and his ethics, deduced in the work he titles, simply, *Ethica,* is an attempt to determine what are the attitudes and beliefs, emotions and goals that truly conduce to our flourishing.

Like the ancients, Spinoza recognizes the positive experiential aspect of well-being—it *feels* good—while not allowing the positive feeling to itself determine what well-being is. In other words, we take pleasure in things in which we shouldn't. But he assures us, by way of his systematically progressing proofs álà Euclid, that the positivity associated with flourishing, being a pleasure or joy or delight (*laetitia*) that draws forth the full expansive potentials of human nature, surpasses all other positive experiences. It is intense and deep, as well it should be, given all the work that Spinoza tells us is required in order to experience it, which is nothing less than coming to understand reality, in order that we might come to know our relation to it. We must be realists in order to flourish, not living in our self-aggrandizing ontological fantasies, no matter how shallowly pleasurable those fantasies might be.

And since "the eyes of the mind, whereby it sees things and understands, are none other than proofs," such realism requires nothing less than the emendation of the intellect, a notion that furnishes the title of another of Spinoza's works, *Tractatus de Intellectus Emendatione,* which he never completed, choosing instead to present his radical epistemology within the larger philosophical context, which he first attempts in his next work, *Short Treatise on God, Man, and His Well-Being,* also unfinished, and ultimately succeeds in doing in *The Ethics* (Proposition XXIII, Note).

---

[3] There was disagreement among the ancients as to whether virtue was sufficient for flourishing (Socrates, Plato, and the Stoics) or whether other circumstances—such as economic security, physical health, the well-being of the polis—were also necessary (Aristotle). This disagreement continues into the modern age.

[4] See Goldstein *Betraying Spinoza: The Renegade Jew Who Gave Us Modernity.*

But the *Tractatus de Intellectus Emendatione* is nevertheless uniquely important for one reason. It is in this work, which is uncharacteristically personal, that Spinoza confides the desire that prompted his formidable project, one which would cause him not only to be excommunicated from his own Jewish community, at the tender age of 23, but to be excoriated throughout greater Christian Europe, often denounced as Satan's emissary on earth, well into the Age of the Enlightenment. The driving desire was none other than to flourish:

> After experience had taught me the hollowness and futility of everything that is ordinarily encountered in daily life, and I realized that all the things which were the source and object of my anxiety held nothing of good or evil in themselves save insofar as the mind was influenced by them, I resolved at length to enquire whether there existed a true good, one which was capable of communicating itself and could alone affect the mind to the exclusion of all else, whether, in fact, there was something whose discovery and acquisition would afford me a continuous and supreme joy to all eternity. (*Treatise of the Emendation of the Intellect* 3)

Spinoza assumed that human flourishing rested on discovering and acquiring "a true good," the same for all of us, no matter our individually variable histories, dispositions, interests, resources. And to indulge in a bit of autobiography myself, I confess that for many years I was convinced that Spinoza, by promoting reason above all, had laid out a common path to human flourishing, wide enough to carry us all to a well-lived life.

But what has become increasingly obvious to me is that there can be no one path. And in trying to understand exactly why, the concept of mattering has emerged as central to human flourishing, to the extent that I would assert that *an essential aspect of a person's flourishing is the sense of their own personal mattering, to which everybody has a right.* The more that I've approached the question of human flourishing by way of the concept of mattering, observing the diverse ways in which people seek it, the less adequate Spinoza's univocal solution to the problem of human flourishing has seemed.

Each person, just as soon as the basic requirements for living a recognizably human life are secured (for to lack these requirements is to be made desperate), needs to feel that her life has not been wasted, that it has not come to nothing, that it is not the case that she might as well never have been born for all the difference she has made. Such a feeling is not consistent with flourishing.[5, 6] It is the very opposite of flourishing. There is a reason why the name of the website for the U.S. National Suicide Prevention Lifeline is "You Matter."

And though Spinoza's notion of the well-lived life can answer to the requisite sense of mattering for some people, yielding them the sense of flourishing it certainly yielded him, it will do nothing or even worse at the deeply personal level at which each person confronts her own existential need to matter.

Self-Mattering and Self-Identity

Such a great deal of energy and attention and passion goes into pursuing a human life—any human life. A condition for such single-minded pursuance—and who *else's* life is one going to pursue, if not one's own?—is that one's own life matters, at least to oneself. Such first-person mattering is baked into one's very identity.

Conatus, a concept which is foundational in Spinoza's system, serves very well to capture the idea of first-person mattering. "The conatus with which each thing endeavors to persist in its own being is nothing but the actual essence of the thing itself" (*The Ethics,* Part III, Proposition 7).

This is an extraordinarily prescient insight on the part of a seventeenth-century philosopher, speculating at the very dawn of science. It is almost as if he had *a priori* intuited a law of nature so fundamental that many scientists argue it yields the unidirectionality of time.[7] This is the Second Law of Thermodynamics, and what it states is that in a closed system, with no input of energy, entropy will, over time, increase. Entropy is the measure of disorder within a system; it is the notion of disintegration made quantitatively precise. Since order demands a relatively small subset of all the possible configurations the elements within a system can assume—and the more complex the system, the more numerous the possible configurations—the laws of probability dictate that entropy increases over time.[8]

---

[5] I mean by these basic requirements for living a recognizably human life, such necessities as are catalogued by Martha Nussbaum under her capabilities approach to the evaluation of human welfare (2000, 72).

[6] John J. Stuhr, this volume, contrasts a notion of a meaningful life with a notion of a valuable life, and identifies flourishing with the latter.

[7] See, for example, Carroll *From Eternity to Here.*

[8] This makes it sound as if The Second Law of Thermodynamics is entirely *a priori,* which it isn't. One needs to have a particle theory of matter in order for this law of probability to become a law of thermodynamics.

The Second Law of Thermodynamics tells us that a thing, simply to preserve the order wherein its existence consists, must resist entropy. In the face of this law, Spinoza's insistence on each thing's essential *striving* as a condition of its very identity seems prescient. Self-preservation is a prerequisite to an entity persisting rather than entropically falling apart, and, in living organisms, the genes' best strategy—for modern Darwinism displaces the mechanics of natural selection from the level of the organism to the level of the gene—is to keep an organism intact for as long as the genes need it in order to get themselves replicated into the future. And so it is that each organism is endowed with an unthinking ceaseless drive to survive and to flourish: to seek sustenance, flee the predator, avail itself of opportunities to successfully mate, be devoted 24/7 to seeing another dawn. The genes have programmed the organism in the ways of resisting entropy, which will of course get it in the end. But until then no organism has to think about whether it has the right to put its survival and flourishing first and foremost. The genes don't have time to waste with tortuous and fallible justifications, not even in us, the creatures who specialize in tortuous and fallible justifications. The advances in the sciences—in both physics and biology—have lent empirical content to Spinoza's *a priori* intuition.

Spinoza is, of course, most interested in drawing out the implications of conatus for one particular kind of thing—the kind of thing that is capable of not only behaving as if its own flourishing mattered but of reflecting on the question of whether it really does matter, in the larger scheme of things—the kind of thing that requires a treatise on ethics. The gist of making conatus foundational in a work of ethics is to accept, first of all, that one's own life can't help mattering to one in a quite distinctive way. This distinctive first-person mattering is why we never have difficulty, short of agonizing mental illness, identifying ourselves.[9, 10] Not even the swami, devoting himself to the disciplined rituals that allow him the experience of transcending the

[9] "Current psychopathological phenomenology has gained ground, emphasizing that the roots of mental illness are to be found in the patient's pre-reflexive or pre-thematic experience. From this viewpoint, it is argued that schizophrenia involves a particular disturbance of basic self-awareness, more specifically a disorder of "ipseity," normally occurring tacitly or pre-reflexively. Ipseity (ipse is Latin for *self* or *itself*) refers to the fundamental configuration of self-awareness, corresponding to the first-person perspective tacitly given in experience. This perspective is oriented intentionally "from within" toward the world, and presupposes an immediate sense of "mineness" of the experience, as "being mine" or as "my own doing," that is, a quality of "personally belonging" or of "personalization." The diminishment of this perspective mode of self-experience would lead to characteristic anomalies or basic disorders of the schizophrenic spectrum" (Irarrázava).

[10] See Jessica Wahman's account of the role of our narratives of ourselves in creating agency, this volume.

limitations of his own ego, bypasses first-person mattering. After all, it's *his* ego he devotedly seeks to transcend. He won't be satisfied by knowing that someone or other's ego—maybe the swami meditating on the next mountaintop over—has successfully transcended his ego. Being a human demands engagement in one's own life. It demands mattering to oneself.

First-person mattering—my mattering to me, as a very condition of my pursuing my life—is how conatus plays out in the mental life of humans. But, as a rule, our feelings of mattering don't confine themselves merely to the first-personal. True, it's quite possible to step outside one's life, so to speak, to view its web of contingencies *sub specie aeternitatis* and to pronounce life absurd.[11] Such episodes seem to come more frequently to some people than to others, and I wouldn't be surprised if one's susceptibility to the occasional sense of the absurd was highly correlated with a philosophical bent. Be that as it may, even the most philosophical among us doesn't pursue her life with any less focus than others. And in the course of pursuing one's life, with the whole structure of the emotions, both positive and negative, giving one feedback regarding how well that life of ours is going, one smoothly slides beyond mere first-person mattering to something less hedged, more categorical.[12] The transition carries with it, however obscurely, the human need to justify the seriousness with which we can't help taking our lives simply in order to pursue them, the need to ground that seriousness in something outside the arbitrary fact that one just happens to be who one happens to be. It's as if we want some external justification for mattering so inescapably to ourselves. It's as if we demand it.

In fact, one of the deepest manifestations of the insistence on categorical mattering is the denial that we are indeed nothing but matter—impressively organized matter, but matter nevertheless. The reasoning behind the denial seems to be: If we are truly to matter, we can't possibly be mere matter; ergo we are not mere matter. The insistence on mattering plays a definitive role in the history of metaphysics.

But it's not just in metaphysics that the transition beyond mere first-personal mattering makes itself felt. Human history has churned up a great diversity of claims regarding what is required in order for a person to matter: that we be made in the image of God; that we instantiate a particular

---

[11] See Nagel 716–727.
[12] This is yet another key insight of Spinoza's, that our emotions all follow from the conatus—that first-person mattering—which is one with our identity.

race, or sex, or class, or religion, or nationality, or ideology, or I.Q. range, or specific talent; that we be *Übermenschen*, distinguishing ourselves from the common herd by way of an originality capable of carrying our species to its next stage in development. Some of these criteria demand that we exert ourselves in order to achieve our mattering, accomplish something or other; others of the criteria assert that we—or at least some among us—inherit a special share of mattering as our birthright.

In the complex things that humans are, the conative striving to resist entropy is transformed into a striving to matter, which is why nothing can provoke more intensely negative emotions, whether passions of anger or despair, than a challenge undermining an individual's striving to matter. A person, in order to flourish, must have a sense that, in the ways that matter to her—and she must be able herself to determine what are the ways that matter to her—she herself matters, which means that she must also have the means of appropriately validating her mattering.

Normativity and Mattering

What exactly does it mean to say that something—or someone—matters? The notion of mattering is intimately linked with the notion of attention. To say that something matters is to assert that attention is due it, the kind of attention that both recognizes and reveals its reality. Something that matters has a nature that demands to be known, and the knowledge may yield other attitudes and behavior due it. If I say that something doesn't matter, I'm saying that it's not worth paying attention to.

And the notion of mattering is also normative, meaning that it implies an *ought*, an obligation—namely the obligation to pay appropriate attention to the thing that matters. The normative implications of the term come through loud and clear in the slogan that was adopted for the social protest movement prompted in the United States after several unarmed African-American young men, including Trayvon Martin and Michael Brown, were killed by police officers or others representing the law: Black Lives Matter.

I think it is a demonstrable moral truth that, to the extent that any of us insist on our mattering—and I hope I've gone some distance in explaining why we do all tend to insist-—it follows that we should extend that same degree of mattering to all humans (which isn't, of course, to assert that only humans matter).

And yet, merely acknowledging that the concept of mattering applies as much to oneself as to others—the starving serf knowing that yes, he matters, in virtue of his very humanity, just as much as the crapulous landowner exploiting the bloody hell out of him—isn't going to result in a life of flourishing. We require not only to experience our own mattering, as close and present to us as our very own identities, but also to be treated as if we matter. For if we indeed matter then certain attention on the part of others is due us. When it is denied to us, most especially when it is systematically denied to us, or denied to us in the specific areas in which we strive most strenuously to matter (more about those specific areas later), then we might very likely feel defeated in our striving to matter, a feeling so inconsistent with our flourishing that it might be called a sickness in the soul.

The striving to matter plunges us into the world of others, able to offer or withhold the attention that signals to us our mattering.

We are a gregarious species, generally needing and so acutely attuned to the attention of others. Here, too, specifics of human evolution seem relevant, in particular the "gaze detection" system, which is exquisitely sensitive to whether another person is looking directly at you. Studies that record the activity of single brain cells find that particular cells fire when someone is staring right at you, but not when the observer's gaze is averted just a few degrees to the left or right of you, when different cells will fire. Aiding us in detecting so subtly where another's gaze is directed is the fact that human eyes possess the greatest amount of visible white sclera. This contrast between the white sclera and the dark center makes it much easier to determine precisely where someone is looking. We have evolved in such a way as to highlight how important the attention of others is to us.

Nobody has better expressed what the attention of others means to us than William James:

> We are not only gregarious animals, liking to be in sight of our fellows, but we have an innate propensity to get ourselves noticed, and noticed favorably, by our kind. No more fiendish punishment could be devised, were such a thing physically possible, than that one should be turned loose in society and remain absolutely unnoticed by all the members thereof. If no one turned round when we entered, answered when we spoke, or minded what we did, but if every person we met 'cut us dead,' and acted as if we were non-existing things, a kind of rage and impotent despair would ere long

well up in us, from which the cruelest bodily tortures would be a relief; for these would make us feel that, however bad might be our plight, we had not sunk to such a depth as to be unworthy of attention at all. (James, "The Consciousness of Self," 293–94)

Bishop Berkeley had a motto that summed up his metaphysical idealism: *Esse est percipi.* To be is to be perceived. Some among us are systematically subjected to a withholding of the kind of attention due to all persons. Such situations point to the deepest injustices of our social, political, and economic structures. Ongoing moral progress depends on our recognizing and correcting these injustices that can't help but vitiate the general flourishing we want to promote, for "those who are governed by reason desire nothing for themselves which they do not also desire for the rest of humankind" (*The Ethics,* Part IV, Proposition XXXVII).

The Mattering Map

But beyond these intolerable societal injustices, there are still other variations in how well people fare in securing the sense of mattering requisite for their flourishing. Beyond the attention due us simply in virtue of our humanity is the attention we seek in more differentiated channels. For if our striving to matter is universal, the ways in which we go about trying to realize our mattering are more specialized. It's from this diversity that human culture emerged, the complexities of our public and private lives, and the creativity of both our collective achievements and collective atrocities.

To capture this multiplicity, I want to introduce the notion of a conatus project, using it roughly as Bernard Williams had written of ground projects.

Here we need only the idea of a man's ground projects providing the motive force which propels him into the future and gives him (in a sense) a reason for living. For a project to play this ground role, it does not have to be true that if it were frustrated, or in any of various ways he lost it, he would have to commit suicide, nor does he have to think that. Other things, or the mere hope of other things, may keep him going. But he may feel in those circumstances that he might as well have died. ("Persons, Character, and Morality")

These long-term projects, providing the motive force to project us into our futures, become the bearers of our striving to matter and thus the loci of some of our deepest emotions. We evaluate how well our lives are going by how well our conatus projects are going. Our conatus projects assign us to specific domains of what can be called "the mattering map."[13] The criteria for evaluating the progress of one's conatus project, upon which our sense of flourishing depends, are domain-specific.

Fracturing the universal striving to matter into a multitude of mattering-domains shifts many of the questions of human flourishing onto the sphere of the specific domains, where they can be usefully compared and a host of significant differences between them explored in the hope of isolating variables significantly correlated with measures of human flourishing, both individual and collective. Not only conceptual, but also empirical work is required.

Although these conatus projects are intimately personal, suffused with our profoundest emotions regarding what our lives are all about and how well they are going, it does not follow that these projects must be narrowly self-centered. Yes, of course, one is always going to give one's own life more attention than any other life, because such attention is a condition for pursuing one's own life. But that doesn't mean that our conatus projects must be shaped around selfishly constricted aims. They can be outwardly directed toward truth (science, mathematics, philosophy, history, journalism, etc.), beauty (the arts, craftsmanship, architecture, gardening, fashion, biophilia, etc.), and goodness (acts of mercy, spiritual purity, service to others, social justice, philanthropy, etc.).

Nor is there any contradiction in acknowledging that sometimes a person's conatus project—the very thing that gives him a reason for living—will demand his martyrdom. "It is a far, far better thing that I do, than I have ever done; it is a far, far better rest that I go to than I have ever known," was the dying sentiment not only of a fictional character—Sydney Carton, in Charles Dickens' A Tale of Two Cities—but of real-life counterparts, including

---

[13] The mattering map was a concept I'd first introduced in The Mind-Body Problem (1983). "People occupy the mattering map. . . . The map in fact is a projection of its inhabitants' perceptions. A person's location on it is determined by what matters to him, matters overwhelmingly, the kind of mattering that produces his perceptions of people, of himself and others: of who are the nobodies and who the somebodies, who the deprived and who the gifted, who the better-never-to-have-been-born and who the heroes. One and the same person can appear differently when viewed from different positions" The term and the concept have since been taken up by various researchers. See, for example, "How Mattering Maps Affect Behavior," by the behavioral economists Loewenstein and Moene, in which the concept is used to challenge the rational agent model of economics. See also "The Mattering Map" by Kaschak.

Socrates, whose conatus projects entail that, under certain circumstances, death is a requirement of the very project that has kept one going through one's life.[14] It's such conatus projects that fit the so-called heroic ideal, which some have mistakenly considered the sine qua non of all conatus projects.[15]

It should also be clear that the striving to matter need not be the striving to matter *cosmically*, to establish that one will matter for all time, or that one matters to the universe at large. Those who speak about the meaning of life generally have in mind some universal purpose to human life, some sort of role that we're asked to play in the unfolding of cosmic history. This seems to be the background assumption behind the question regarding life's meaning, and religious conatus projects, of course, satisfy this assumption. But a person might well reject that the cosmos has anything in mind for any one of us, believing that it is utterly indifferent to the sapiens who, perhaps as a consequence of evolving their big brains, seek to justify the seriousness with which they can't help taking their lives. She might then say that life is meaningless. But even if she does, her statement isn't going to undermine her commitment to her own life, to pursuing it with all the attention and energy and emotional reactions that it demands, as funneled, most especially, into her conatus projects. Perhaps she'll devote herself to publishing books on life's meaninglessness.

It should also be clear that conatus projects need not be intrinsically competitive, although many of them are. A saying, often attributed to La Rochefoucauld, captures the spirit of competitive conatus projects: "It is not enough that I succeed; others must fail."

In fact, it seems that although some mattering-domains are intrinsically zero-sum—such as projects devoted to the pursuit of power—almost any conatus project can be "competitivized," so that the sense of mattering, yielded by way of engagement in, say, science or mathematics or philosophy or poetry or motherhood or stylishness (I knew a woman whose conatus project, she confessed to me, was to be the best-dressed person in any room

---

[14] Carton's extended soliloquy, that of the fictional character awaiting his turn at the guillotine, is a meditation on how his voluntary death, in place of another, will allow him to achieve the mattering that has agonizingly eluded him. And the mattering that he seeks is delivered by the attention he imagines for himself from those he loves after his death: "I see that I hold a sanctuary in their hearts, and in the hearts of their descendants, generations hence. I see her as an old woman, weeping for me on the anniversary of this day. I see her and her husband, their course done, lying side by side in their earthly bed, and I know that each was not more honoured and held sacred in each other's soul, than I was in the soul of each."

[15] See, for example, *The Denial of Death*, by Becker: "What I have tried to do . . . is to suggest that the problem of heroics is the central one of human life" (7).

she entered) or even piety and philanthropy, is secured only by beating out others and so feeling that one matters more than they.[16] It was once said to me, about a certain Nobel Laureate in biology, that he was only happy for all of fifteen minutes in his life, initiated when he received the call from Stockholm and terminated when it dawned on him that other people had been awarded the prize as well. It would be interesting to test whether the difference between competitivizing and not competitivizing conatus projects correlates with measures of well-being.

There are other variables among conatus projects that might be correlated with differences in well-being. So, for example, consider "mattering-adjudicators." It's no surprise, given the close attention between mattering and attention, that, in the great majority of mattering-domains, the criteria for evaluating the progress of one's conatus project demands the right kind of attention from the right kind of others—the domain-specific "mattering adjudicators."[17]

So, for example, if a conatus project locates a person in the mattering-domain of professional philosophy, then it's the community of professional philosophers who will constitute her mattering-adjudicators—or perhaps some subset of these whom she most respects. There is a story about the young Ludwig Wittgenstein and his encounter with Bertrand Russell. Wittgenstein had been studying aeronautical engineering at the University of Manchester but, becoming interested in some mathematical problems, arrived at Cambridge University to audit some classes with Bertrand Russell. One day Wittgenstein demanded of Russell, "Will you please tell me whether I am a complete idiot or not? If I am a complete idiot, I shall become an aeronaut; but, if not, I shall become a philosopher." Russell assigned him a paper and, after he had read it, told Wittgenstein not to become an aeronaut.

---

[16] One of my favorite explorations on the theme of competitivizing philanthropy comes from the television series *Curb Your Enthusiasm,* created by and starring Larry David, in an episode called "Anonymous." David donates a new wing to a hospital, his name up on the wall, but then is outdone by Ted Danson, who, David learns from his wife, anonymously donated a wing. Larry is furious that now everybody, including his wife, is praising Danson over David. "Nobody told me that I could be anonymous and not tell people. I would have taken that option, okay? You can't have it halfway. You're either anonymous or you're not . . . It's fake philanthropy and it's faux anonymity."

[17] Not all the domains have mattering-adjudicators who are human, as opposed to divine. Great theological disputes—such as that between Martin Luther and the Church of Rome, which resulted in the Reformation and Counter-Reformation—have revolved around the question of how one can ascertain that one is getting the right kind of attention from the only mattering-adjudicator who, in the religious mattering-domain, matters. Some people find the validation of their mattering neither in the attention of other people nor from the believed-in attention of their god(s), but from the attention of animals. Again, it would require empirical testing to see how much well-being they experience (and if the well-being of dog-lovers exceeds the well-being of cat-lovers).

Even so independent a thinker as Wittgenstein had recognized at least one mattering-adjudicator. Interestingly, Wittgenstein soon became Russell's mattering-adjudicator, whose perceived attitude caused Russell to conclude that he could no longer do foundational work in philosophy. "The conviction produced in him an almost suicidal depression" (Monk 82). Switching roles as mattering-adjudicator had a devastating effect on Russell's conatus project.

The various fine arts, including literary fiction, are highly dependent on mattering-adjudicators *of the right kind*—with the approbation of the wrong kind capable of adversely affecting the assessment of one's conatus project.[18] Consider the case of Jonathan Franzen. In 1996, Franzen published an essay in *Harper's* bemoaning the situation of literary artists in a culture ruled by "the banal ascendency of television."[19] But then, a few years later, his novel *The Corrections* was chosen for her book club by the queen of daytime television, Oprah Winfrey. Franzen was horrified and initially refused Winfrey's invitation to appear on her program, explaining that attention from her was out of keeping with his place in "the high-art literary tradition" (Kirkpatrick).

For some domains the mattering-adjudicators are people with whom there is a special personal relationship, with the quality of the personal relationship providing the content of the conatus project.[20] So consider someone whose conatus project is fostering a happy family life, or someone whose conatus project is bound up with (a) romantic partner(s) or in a relationship with a charismatic figure, as in various cults. The wife of Ron Hubbard, the man who invented Scientology, explained the special power he had over his followers: "He would hold hands with them and try to talk them into these phony memories," she recalled. "He would concentrate on them and they loved it. They were so excited about someone who would just pay this much attention to them" (Wright 81).

---

[18] In her chapter in this volume, Michele Moody-Adams discusses the role of the arts in the cultivation of well-being.

[19] The essay was published in Harper's under the title "Perchance to Dream." It was republished under the more attitudinally expressive title "Why Bother?" in Franzen's book of essays, *How to Be Alone.*

[20] *The Psychology of Mattering,* considers only conatus projects of this kind. "Mattering is unique because it captures the powerful impact that other people have on us and it reflects our need to be valued by the people in our lives. People are strongly influenced by their beliefs about how they are seen and regarded by other people, and feelings of mattering or not mattering to other people reflect these perceived evaluations. Mattering also reflects core questions that people ask themselves, such as "Who really cares about me?" and "Who would miss me if I was not around?" and "Do people realize how much they matter to me?" (Flett 5).

In contrast, there are domains that, though highly dependent on mattering-adjudicators, don't depend on any kind of personal relationships with them. So, for example, consider the pursuit of fame as a project in and of itself. Kanye West perhaps epitomizes, in our day, the pursuit of fame, not just because he is extremely famous, but because he himself is so fascinated by fame, a man as star-struck by the phenomenon as his own fans.[21] West doesn't know the identities of the millions who know of him, and he doesn't need to know them. He just needs to have those millions, whoever they are, paying him attention.

And then there are domains that are quite independent of mattering-adjudicators. So, for example, suppose one's conatus project is a moral or spiritual one, where the progress to be made is, say, the deepening of one's own compassion, or of one's inner purity, or the performance of acts of do-goodism.[22] Such projects are—at least if performed not to attract any kind of attention, whether divine or human—independent of mattering-adjudicators. But then so, too, is the conatus project devoted to the accumulation of wealth for wealth's sake.

Or suppose one's conatus project is to deepen the richness and variety of one's observations of others, striving to be, as Henry James put is, someone on whom nothing is lost. Or one devotes oneself to refining one's aesthetic sensibility, which is the course that Schopenhauer recommends as effective in dulling the otherwise persistent pain of existence, reading the best that has been written and attending concerts, theater, and museums.[23] Or perhaps the project lies in bird-watching, success measured by the number of specimens recorded in one's "life-list." These projects, too, are independent of mattering-adjudicators.

Or maybe one's conatus project involves participating in physically risky challenges that wonderfully concentrate the attention and force one to

---

[21] In the video that accompanies West's 2016 song, "Famous," there are life-size, uncannily realistic wax figures of Kanye West, Taylor Swift, Kim Kardashian, George W. Bush, Donald Trump, Anna Wintour, Rihanna, Chris Brown, Ray J, Amber Rose, Caitlin Jenner, and Bill Cosby, all sleeping nude in a shared bed. And at the 2016 MTV awards, West gave a free-associating speech that contained this interesting fragment: "But for people to understand just how blessed we are, it was an expression of our now, our fame right now, us on the inside of the TV. You know, just the audacity to put Anna Wintour right next to Donald Trump. I mean, like, I put Ray J in it, bro. This is fame, bro."

[22] For accounts of the conatus projects of some extraordinary do-gooders see MacFarquhar's, *Strangers Drowning*.

[23] Schopenhauer describes aesthetic experience, which lifts us out of the stream of time and all other relations, in singularly rapturous terms. "It is then all one whether we see the sun set from the prison or from the palace" (255).

experience the moment with great intensity, obliterating both past and future. Here, too, it's the qualities of the experience that constitute the conatus project, making the project independent of mattering-adjudicators.

On Cape Cod, where I have a home, there is a community of surfers whose conatus projects are independent of mattering-adjudicators. Many of them travel the world, not to compete, but just to catch the big waves. Among them is Kai Potter, who occasionally writes about the surfer's life in luminously philosophical prose: "If you ask yourself why you surf, part of the answer should be, quite simply, to have fun. Achieving joy in one's life is the most worthy pursuit—in whatever form it takes. I love that through surfing you get little glimpses into absolute presence, moments where you are fully and completely present. When you're standing in the most momentary, intense, dynamic place a person can be, a spinning tube of water, or pushing through a big, deep bottom turn, it demands that you be completely in that crystalline moment with a clarity difficult to reach elsewhere. It allows for a chance to fully exist" ("The Young Man and the Sea"). I'm grateful that Potter writes so vividly about what it's like to surf, so that I don't have to venture onto a board and experience it myself.

Among academics, mathematicians come closest to being able to dispense with mattering-adjudicators, there being (1) objective criteria for determining which, among the outstanding problems, are the hardest and most consequential to solve and (2) objective standards for when a problem is solved. When the Russian Grigori Perelman solved a problem that had long been considered of the first importance, the Poincaré Conjecture, and was, in recognition of his achievement, awarded the Fields Medal, which is mathematics' answer to the Nobel, he refused it, the first time in the history of the medal that it was refused. "It was completely irrelevant for me," he explained to a reporter who had sought out the reclusive Perelmen in St. Petersburg, where he lived with his mother. "Everybody understood that if the proof is correct then no other recognition is needed" (Nasser and Gruber, "Manifold Destiny"). Perelman clearly wants to contribute to the advance of mathematics, a subject that gave him joy, but beyond that goal all attention was undesirable. "I'm not interested in money or fame," he was quoted to have said at the time that he was being urged to accept the award. "I don't want to be on display like an animal in a zoo. I'm not a hero of mathematics. I'm not even that successful; that is why I don't want to have everybody looking at me" ("Maths Genius Urged to Take Prize").

I am only scratching the surface in presenting here the range of concerns out of which people fashion their individual conatus projects, and in suggesting a few of the of variables—zero-sum versus non-zero-sum, degree of dependence on mattering adjudicators—that might be utilized in investigating how features of conatus projects correlate with differences in the quality of well-being. There are empirical hypotheses to be tested here, and the results can go some way—though not all the way—toward answering the most basic questions we ask when confronting the vast variety of conatus projects: Are any of them superior to others? Is any one of them *the right one*, the one to which we all ought to commit ourselves to achieve a life of maximum flourishing?

Faulty Projects

Spinoza's ambitious conatus project—which was, by emending the intellect, to attain a transformative grasp of reality that would reconfigure one's sense of oneself and purge the negative emotions—certainly yielded him, as it can so many others, the requisite sense of mattering demanded for flourishing.[24] Despite the hardships of his short life, he closes *The Ethics* on a note of triumphant transcendence, leaving the reader with little doubt that he had found that continuous and supreme joy that had been his stated goal. "If the road that I have pointed out as leading to this goal seems very difficult, yet it can be found. Indeed, what is so rarely discovered is bound to be hard. For if salvation were ready to hand and could be discovered without great toil, how could it be that it is almost universally neglected? All things excellent are as difficult as they are rare."

Spinoza was recommending his conatus project to us all. One could argue, on his behalf, that a conatus project ought to be devoted to something that objectively matters, and one could argue even further that the more the something matters, the better the conatus project. And what could matter more than coming to understand the nature of reality and adjusting oneself, and all of humankind, accordingly? Still, must we censure the bird-watchers and surfers, the culture-vultures and pure mathematicians? Couldn't we argue that if devotion to something provides a person with the motive force

---

[24] Spinoza's view was that, reality being subject to the strictest determinism, it is irrational to feel anger or hatred or fear or any of the negative emotions. The best way to proceed, in a deterministic universe, is to understand, which in itself engenders a host of positive emotions.

that propels him into the future, then, just because each person matters, that something ipso facto matters?[25]

Still, broadening the range of acceptable conatus projects so as to accommodate the great variety in individual temperaments and talents and interests and passions, there still does emerge the possibility that some conatus projects are failures, either psychologically or morally, or both.

A conatus project might conduce more to a sense that life isn't worth living than that it is worth living, which is a serious defect for a conatus project. The defect may just stem from a misfit between a particular person's talents and temperament and the conatus project to which she's given herself. She may need therapy to pry herself away from her particular mattering-domain.

Or it may be that some conatus projects are generally defective: they tend not to yield a sustained sense of mattering. So, for example, our culture promotes, as a conatus project, the pursuit of fame, a tendency intensified by social media. And given how the concept of mattering is so intimately connected with attention, it's not surprising that people would try to derive their sense of mattering by acquiring a great deal of attention, even from perfect strangers—which is what fame is. But perhaps the pursuit of fame, as a goal in itself, doesn't yield a sustained sense of mattering. Maybe such a culturally encouraged conatus project is doing damage to people.

And then there are conatus projects that go even more seriously amiss, because in pursuing them one has to deny the mattering of things that really do matter. A conatus project that consists in the pursuit of power can lead one not only to dismiss truth as mattering but also any people who happen to get in one's way. Any project requiring that for the requisite sense of mattering to be achieved other people's sense of mattering must be subverted, their conatus projects thwarted, is, to say the least, morally defective.[26] It's on these grounds that all racist, sexist, classist, and all other forms of bias—many of which we haven't gotten around to yet naming—are morally abhorrent.[27]

[25] Jeremy Bentham famously wrote, in *The Rationale of Reward*, "Prejudice apart, the game of push-pin is of equal value with the arts and sciences and music and poetry." John Stuart Mill, his fellow utilitarian, disagreed, holding that the quality of the pleasure, and not just the quantity, must be taken into account.

[26] In their essays in this volume, Lori Gallegos, José Medina, and John J. Stuhr each explores ways in which the flourishing of some people—or what those people take to be their flourishing—is possible only because of ways in which some other persons are not provided with resources and opportunities to flourish.

[27] But perhaps, it can be objected, these biases aren't sufficient in themselves to become a conatus project; no racist or sexist, no matter how incorrigible, is going to feel that his being a "European" or a male, in itself provides "the motive force which propels him into the future, and gives him (in a sense) a reason for living"—that is unless he feels the need to impress the fact of superior mattering on those

I want to end by addressing another way in which we can go wrong in our conatus projects, and this is to commit the fallacy of false universalizing. Galen Strawson writes, in another context, of "that special fabulously misplaced confidence that people feel when, considering elements of their own experience that are existentially fundamental for them, they take it that they must also be fundamental for everyone".[28] This is what so often happens when it is presumed that the domain-specific conatus project, which answers to one's own need to provide a reason for living, must of necessity be the reason for anyone's living and is thus exalted into the very meaning of human life.

There are certain domains in which the tendency to universalize is all but entailed. These are domains associated with ideologies, whether religious or secular.[29] And although the denizens of these domains may individually flourish, having a single-minded sense of purpose, value, and efficacy, the non-negotiable universalizing of the conatus projects that such domains demand often wreak havoc on our collective flourishing.

But the tendency to falsely universalize—John Lachs in his essay in this volume calls it "the allure of the 'all'"—lurks in just about every mattering-domain and contributes to our human capacity to amaze, baffle, and horrify one another. I close by giving some examples from across the mattering map.

> For the sommeliers, sensory scholars, wine makers, connoisseurs, and collectors I met, to taste better is to live better, and to know ourselves more deeply. And I saw that tasting better had to begin with the most complex edible of all: wine.
>
> Bianca Bosker, author of *Cork Dorks*

---

who aren't convinced of it. And then—especially if the skepticism he faces is perceived by him to be stiff, if he feels that the whole of society is getting it wrong—the attitude, which before had functioned as a kind of background assumption, can become transformed into a conatus project, as in the recent phenomenon of the alt-right. As one of my colleagues remarked to me, "I suspect that, as is often the case, and as Joni Mitchell wrote, 'you don't know what you've got till it's gone.'" A biased sense of mattering becomes a project when its automatic character is threatened.

[28] Galen Strawson, "Against Narrativity." First printed in *Ratio: An International Journal of Analytic Philosophy*, November, 2004. Reprinted in *Things That Bother Me: Death, Freedom, the Self, Etc.* (*New York Review of Books*, 2018). Strawson is addressing those who presume that a narrative sense of one's life is essential for deriving a sense of personal identity.

[29] This might well be a tautological statement; an ideology might very well be defined as restricting all who matter to one specific domain of the mattering map.

We as human beings are unique in that we can ask questions about our grander environment. It's what makes us great. And societies that don't do that die.

—Margaret Geller, astrophysicist

You gotta have style. It helps you get down the stairs. It helps you get up in the morning. It's a way of life. Without it, you're nobody.

—Diana Vreeland, editor-in-chief, *Vogue*

"Music is the heart of life. Without it, there is no possible good and with it everything is beautiful.

—Franz Lizst

"I teach you the superman, because humanity can only pursue one goal; the creation of a superior man of superior culture.

—Friedrich Nietzsche

But if you really want to send yourself into a tragic spiral of depression, call down for a room service hamburger when you're alone in your room. You will inevitably be disappointed and more than likely sent into a manic-depressive state for days.

—Anthony Bourdain, celebrity chef

According to the Christian world view, God does exist, and man's life does not end at the grave. In the resurrection body, man may enjoy eternal life and fellowship with God. Biblical Christianity therefore provides the two conditions necessary for a meaningful, valuable, and purposeful life for man: God and immortality. Because of this, we can live consistently and happily. Thus biblical Christianity succeeds precisely where atheism breaks down.

—William Lane Craig, Christian apologist

It's a perfectly fine choice to never become a parent, but there is absolutely *no* chance that your life will be as full or meaningful, or that you will learn as many essential truths about existence, as you would if you had kids. Because when it comes down to it, there are certain truths about life that you literally *cannot* know until you've become a parent. The list of those truths could go on forever (no, it really could), but the core truth behind all of it is about what human life is about."

—Sarah Larson, mommy blogger

It is not the goal of grand alpinism to face peril, but it is one of the tests one must undergo to deserve the joy of rising for an instant above the state of crawling grubs.

—Lionel Terray, mountaineer, author of *Conquistadors of the Useless*

The satisfactions of manifesting oneself concretely in the world through manual competence have been known to make a man quiet and easy. They seem to relieve him of the felt need to offer chattering *interpretations* of himself to vindicate his worth. He can simply point: the building stands, the car now runs, the lights are on. Boasting is what a boy does, because he has no real effect in the world. But the tradesman must reckon with the infallible judgment of reality.

—Mathew Crawford, motorcycle mechanic,
author of *Shop Class for Soulcraft*

I firmly believe that any man's finest hour, the greatest fulfillment of all that he holds dear, is that moment when he has worked his heart out in a good cause and lies exhausted on the field of battle—victorious.

—Vince Lombardi

The unexamined life is not worth living.

—Socrates

The more we live by intellect, the less we understand the meaning of life.

—Leo Tolstoy

[O]ne doesn't want to read badly any more than live badly, since time will not relent. I don't know that we owe God or nature a death, but nature will collect anyway, and we certainly owe mediocrity nothing, whatever collectivity it purports to advance or at least represent.

—Harold Bloom, literary critic

Works Cited

"Anonymous" (Season 6, Episode 2). *Curb Your Enthusiasm*, written by Larry David, HBO Enterprises, 2007.

Becker, Ernest. *The Denial of Death*. The Free Press, 1973.

Bentham, Jeremy. *The Rationale of Reward*. Wentworth Press, 2019 (1825).

Carroll, Sean. *From Eternity to Here: The Quest for the Ultimate Theory of Time*. Dutton, 2010.

Flett, Gordon. *Psychology of Mattering*. Academic Press, 2018.

Franzen, Jonathan. "Why Bother?" *How to Be Alone*. (Re-print of "Perchance to Dream." *Harper's Magazine*.). Farrar, Straus and Giroux, 2007.

Goldstein, Rebecca Newberger. *Betraying Spinoza: The Renegade Jew Who Gave Us Modernity*. Pantheon Press, 2006.

Goldstein, Rebecca Newberger. *The Mind-Body Problem*. Random House, 1983.

Irarrázava, Leonor. "The Lived Body in Schizophrenia: Transition from Basic Self-Disorders to Full-Blown Psychosis." *Frontiers in Psychiatry*, vol. 6, no. 9, 2015. https://www.frontiersin.org/articles/10.3389/fpsyt.2015.00009/full.

James, William. "The Consciousness of Self." *The Principles of Psychology*. Henry Holt and Company, 1890, pp. 293–94.

Jensen, Robin Margaret. *Understanding Early Christian Art*. Routledge, 2000.

Kaschak, Ellyn. "The Mattering Map: Integrating the Complexities of Knowledge, Experience, and Meaning." *Psychology of Women* Quarterly, Vol. 37, No. 4, 2013, pp. 436–43.

Kirkpatrick, David D. "'Oprah'Gaffe by Franzen Draws Ire and Sales." *The New York Times*, October 29, 2001.

Loewenstein, George, and Moene, Karl. "How Mattering Maps Affect Behavior." *Harvard Business Review* Case Study, September 1, 2009, pp. 22–27.

MacFarquhar, Larissa. *Strangers Drowning: Grappling with Impossible Idealism, Drastic Choices, and the Overpowering Urge to Help*. Penguin, 2015.

"Maths Genius Urged to Take Prize," BBC News. March 24, 2010.

Monk, Ray. *Ludwig Wittgenstein: The Duty of Genius*. Penguin, 1990.

Nagel, Thomas. "The Absurd." *The Journal of Philosophy*, Vol. 68, No. 20, Sixty-Eighth Annual Meeting of the American Philosophical Association Eastern Division, Oct. 21, 1971, pp. 716–27.

Nasser, Sylvia and Gruber, David. "Manifold Destiny." *The New Yorker*, August 28, 2006.

Nussbaum, Martha. *Women and Human Development: The Capabilities Approach*. Cambridge University Press, 2000.

Rorty, Amélie, ed. "Persons, Character, and Morality." *The Identities of Persons*. University of California Press, 1976, pp. 197–216.

Schopenhauer, Arthur. *The World as Will and Representation*, vol. 1. 3 vols. Translated by R. B. Haldane and J. Kemp, Routledge & Kegan Paul, 1883–1886.

Spinoza, Baruch. *The Ethics*. Translated by Edwin Curley, Princeton University Press, 1994.

Spinoza, Baruch. *Treatise of the Emendation of the Intellect and on the Way by which It Is Best Directed to the True Knowledge of Things*. Translated by Samuel Shirley, Hackett Publishing Company, 2002, p. 3.

Strawson, Galen. "Against Narrativity." First printed in *Ratio: An International Journal of Analytic Philosophy*, Nov., 2004. Reprinted in *Things that Bother Me: Death, Freedom, the Self, Etc.*, New York Review of Books, 2018.

"The Young Man and the Sea," EasternSurf.com August 29, 2017. https://www.easterns urf.com/news/kai-potter/.

West, Kanye. 2016 MTV Awards. Speech.

Williams, Bernard. *Moral Luck: Philosophical Papers 1973–1980*. Cambridge University Press, 1981.

Wright, Lawrence. *Going Clear: Scientology, Hollywood, and the Prison of Belief*. Knopf Doubleday Publishing, 2013.

2

Flourishing in the Flesh

Mark Johnson

Owen Flanagan (2007) correctly observes that in the human drama of survival and well-being, fitness has to come first, then flourishing. Our first order of business is to ensure the bodily conditions necessary for survival. However, as we will see, these same life-regulation processes so crucial for survival also play a major role in our well-being, growth, and flourishing. I want to explore the hypothesis that fitness and flourishing are different, but nevertheless intimately related and interdependent processes, so that understanding the conditions for our survival takes us a long way toward explaining what constitutes our well-being, even at the most complex levels of our existence. I want to examine the idea that the very conditions that make the continuation of life possible are also important for the unfolding of our many potentialities, allowing us to transcend our current formations and habits and to develop capacities for growth in meaning, values, and interpersonal relations.

We need to begin, then, by investigating what conditions are required for life in an organism (here, mostly human organisms) to see whether they might also supply a profound insight into the basic requirements of the organism's well-being and well-doing. This approach assumes that human flourishing develops "from the bottom up," so to speak, by recruiting the structures and processes necessary for our animal survival, but then expanding and enriching them to suit the new levels of interaction and meaning-making that emerge as we develop. As the human organism and its corresponding situation get increasingly complex, new dimensions and even new forms of flourishing arise. This multi-dimensional, pluralistic notion of human flourishing is an emergent functional matrix of values and activities of embodied social creatures with particular capacities, needs, values, and systems of meaning. I will argue that the homeostasis or dynamic equilibrium that keeps a human alive also plays a key role in our realization of our highest capacities and possibilities. In short, there is continuity between

Mark Johnson, *Flourishing in the Flesh* In: *Philosophy and Human Flourishing*. Edited by: John J. Stuhr, Oxford University Press. © Oxford University Press 2023. DOI: 10.1093/oso/9780197622162.003.0003

the processes of life maintenance and our most grand attempts to live meaningful and moral lives.

Homeostasis and Allostasis as Fundamental Values

Before we can crawl, before we can speak, before we can fall in love, before we can construct communities of meaning and value, and before we can solve quadratic equations, we first have to master the ongoing maintenance of the critical life processes within our organic bodies. Neuroscientist Antonio Damasio stresses the need of every organism to sustain the conditions of life within the boundary of its physical body:

> Life is carried out inside a boundary that defines a body. Life and the life urge exist inside a boundary, the selectively permeable wall that separates the internal environment from the existence of that boundary . . . If there is no boundary, there is no body, and if there is no body, there is no organism. Life needs a boundary. I believe that minds and consciousness, when they eventually appeared in evolution, were first and foremost about life and the life urge within a boundary. (*The Feeling of What Happens*, 137)

With regard to the functioning necessary for survival, the key is to maintain a certain homeostatic balance of conditions within the boundary of the organism. In *The Wisdom of the Body*, Walter B. Cannon defined homeostasis as "the coordinated physiological reactions which maintain most of the steady states of the body" (1932). Over the course of evolutionary history, animals have established automated processes for correcting imbalances that arise in their internal bodily state that occur as the animal responds to changing conditions in its environment. These processes evolved to preserve, and when disrupted to recover, the dynamic equilibrium within the organism that is necessary for life-maintenance. At the biological level, this includes such things as maintaining in the blood the right levels of oxygen, carbon dioxide, glucose, sodium, pH, and an internal temperature within the quite narrow margins requisite for the continuation of life. Too hot, you die. Too cold, you die. Too little oxygen, you die. Not enough glucose, you become dysfunctional. Life maintenance is a marvelous dance requiring constant monitoring of our internal states, leading to mostly unconscious changes to the brain and body in order to tune the dynamic balance necessary for life.

It is important to understand that homeostasis is not just the preservation or recovery of a pre-established set-point level of oxygen, sugars, temperature, or salts. Such fixed points are, indeed, necessary for life-regulation, but it is not enough merely to reproduce a fixed, pre-given set-state; in addition, we need to adapt to changing conditions by creating *new* states of dynamic equilibrium that take into account the new conditions we have encountered. Those who want to limit the notion of homeostasis to a set-point equilibrium tend to use a different term—*allostasis*—to capture cases where a new dynamic equilibrium is generated. Neuroscientists Don Tucker and Phan Luu define allostasis as "an extension of homeostasis wherein an organism actively anticipates challenges to internal parameters that can vary by a wider range (e.g., blood pressure) than those regulated by homeostatic processes. Allostasis emphasizes that an animal anticipates challenges to the system and adjusts both physiological and behavioral systems to meet the challenges" (*Cognition and Neural Development*, 70). To capture this future-directed change aspect of homeostasis, Damasio suggests in his latest book (2018) the term *homeodynamics*, in which "*life is regulated within a range that is not just compatible with survival but also conducive to flourishing, to a projection of life into the future of an organism or a species*" (*The Strange Order of Things*, 25 [italics in original]). In spite of having introduced "homeodynamics" as an apt term to cover both homeostatic and allostatic processes, Damasio reverts to using the more mellifluous term "homeostasis" for both processes. In what follows, I will use "homeodynamics" to capture the full range of monitoring and transformative processes included under the notions of both homeostasis and allostasis.

What, one may wonder, does homeodynamics have to do with human flourishing? As Dewey (*Art as Experience*) observed, the history of a living creature is an adventurous journey of falling in and out of harmony with its environment. Most of the time organisms operate on autopilot, according to reinforced habits, physiological set-points, and conditioned and non-conditioned responses operating beneath the level of conscious awareness. However, in the normal course of life, there will be instances when an organism falls out of harmony with its changing surroundings—cases in which its normal habits are inadequate to deal with the complexities of some newly encountered situation. When this happens, its brain and body automatically initiate processes directed toward finding a new dynamic equilibrium in response to the emerging conditions that have upset or are in conflict with prior habits of living and doing. This homeodynamic process occurs first at the organic, biological level, but, as we will see, it is operative at other levels, such as our interpersonal relations and our activities within larger communities.

In other words, we might consider homeodynamics to be the *Ur-Value* upon which, and out of which, everything else pertaining to our functioning is built. This does not mean that everything we do is directly in the service of homeodynamics, but it does regard that process as providing the most adequate framework for explaining our responses and actions. Damasio summarizes this hypothesis: "I see value as indelibly tied to need, and need as tied to life. The valuations we establish in everyday and cultural activities have a direct or indirect connection with homeostasis. [. . .] Value relates directly or indirectly to survival. In the case of humans in particular, value also relates to the *quality* of the survival in the form of *well-being*" (*Self Comes to Mind*, 47–48).

You will have noticed that Damasio has moved in this passage almost imperceptibly from survival (fitness) to well-being (flourishing). How is that possible? How does flourishing all of a sudden emerge from an account of survival and fitness? To assert that homeostasis (i.e., homeodynamics) is the "primitive" of value is to regard it as the fundamental value operating, in one form or another, at all levels—not just at the level of biological functioning, but also at the levels of intimate interpersonal relations, larger communities, and cultural institutions and practices that give our lives meaning and direction. Damasio summarizes this somewhat radical thesis as follows:

> My hypothesis is that objects and processes we confront in our daily lives acquire their assigned value by reference to this primitive of naturally selected organism value. The values that humans attribute to objects and activities would bear some relation, no matter how indirect or remote, to the two following conditions: first, the general maintenance of living tissue within the homeostatic range suitable to its current context; second, the particular regulation required for the process to operate within the sector of the homeostatic range associated with well-being relative to the current context. (*Self Comes to Mind*, 49)

The monumental challenge here is to explain how our "higher" values thought to be critical to our flourishing, and thus beyond mere survival, might be forms of homeodynamics. Can flourishing really be just an appropriation of values and processes that first evolved to regulate our basic life processes?

How Much Can Homeodynamics Explain?

The hypothesis I am exploring here is based on what one might call a continuity thesis—the idea that our so-called higher values, meaningful activities, and forms of social engagement that contribute to our flourishing are emergent from our biological capacities and operations, rather than coming on the scene from some transcendent normative source of values.[1] This assumes an evolutionary perspective, in which higher functions are exaptations from earlier evolved functions for bodily perception, movement, body-state monitoring, and feeling. Our supreme values, upon which we typically assume that our sense of flourishing is based, are manifestations of the basic homeodynamic processes and capacities we have developed over the course of our evolutionary history. If this is correct, then there is not as great a gap between survival and flourishing as one might think. On the contrary, human flourishing recruits capacities and processes that evolved for the biological survival and well-being of the human organism, even though these activities acquire new significance and value when they operate at higher levels than was possible at lower levels of interaction.

In *Morality for Humans: Ethical Understanding from the Perspective of Cognitive Science*, I described four levels of organism-environment interaction from which our most basic and important values emerge. I now want to suggest that each of these four levels gives rise to its correlative notions of flourishing. Homeodynamics is operative at every level, but it becomes more complex, less hard-wired, and more pluralistic as we move up the levels. Consequently, there is no overarching, homogenous conception of flourishing appropriate for all four levels. Instead, human flourishing is a many-splendored state, complex and multi-dimensional, requiring the weaving together of values and activities at all four of these levels.

Here are the four levels, with a brief account of the corresponding notion of well-being and flourishing relative to each level and an account of what homeodynamics might mean at each level:

---

[1] In "Flourishing: Toward Clearer Ideas and Habits of Genius," this volume, John J. Stuhr sets forth a more critical account of human well-being as homeostasis or allostasis in his fourth point about the nature of flourishing, its normative dimensions, and the multivalent character of this concept.

1. **Organic Functioning and Well-being**

Since the very notion of homeostasis was first formulated to explain the biological functioning of organisms, it should come as no surprise that it operates most evidently at the particular level of organization. As we have already noted, the first and most fundamental requirement for any living human creature is the maintenance of the homeodynamic balance necessary for sustaining life within the boundaries of the organism. In order to survive, we humans need at least the following conditions and capacities:

- Bodily systems (e.g., digestive, circulatory, immune) to preserve life and to deal with pathogens, bodily injury, and psychological dysfunction
- Systems capable of monitoring our internal body states
- The ability to modify our internal milieu in response to changing conditions in the environment
- At least some capacity for minimal movement of body parts and our whole body
- Energy (through food) adequate to sustain life processes
- Shelter from the elements (sun, rain, snow, etc.)
- A moderate climate that avoids extreme heat or cold that would kill the organism
- Sufficiently clean air and water
- Protection from predators or others who might do us harm
- Care and nurturance necessary for a child to traverse their typical developmental trajectory for forming up their physical, cognitive, and emotional capacities that serve their life functions

This is a partial yet extensive list of all that goes into our biological survival. Flourishing at this level of organic functioning therefore requires the joint satisfaction of these, and perhaps other, conditions necessary for the preservation of life. Furthermore, it is a good thing that we have evolved systems for managing these needs for the most part by automated, nonconscious processes shaped by our evolutionary development.

At this level of organic biological functioning, survival and flourishing are so intimately interwoven that flourishing reduces to exemplary fitness. In other words, we don't usually regard someone who is merely surviving, barely hanging on, as flourishing. Flourishing here requires a more robust expression of our life processes and capacities for getting on in the world. There is thus a continuous gradient from merely meeting the minimal conditions for staying alive all the way up to the most robust and exemplary realization of our animal capacities for perception, bodily movement, physical exertion, and growth. Within such a framework, the accomplished athlete, dancer, and singer become exemplars of superlative human physical achievement that most of us can only admire and dream of. We see in such performances the fulfillment or even perfection of our bodily activities—the very activities by which we manage to survive, interact with others, and achieve a broad range of goals. In such cases of extraordinary physical skill and performance, we see the living creature in all its physical glory, fully alive and fully realized.

To sum up: In the biological realm, flourishing is fitness on steroids—our most basic capacities for life maintenance and regulation activated to their fullest. Homeodynamics at this level is the harmonizing and balancing out of all the various conditions for our physical functioning.

2. Intimate Interpersonal Relations

In John Donne's much celebrated words, "No man is an island/ Entire of itself/ Every man is a piece of the continent/ A part of the main." Masculine nouns aside, the point is that we humans are not atomic, autonomous individuals who come into the world fully formed up with our bodily identities, and who then choose our social and cultural attachments. Instead, we are social creatures from the get go. We exist at the level of what has been called "primary intersubjectivity"—living in and through others in a reciprocal process of shared experience and intentionality. We are inescapably dependent on others both before and after birth for the care, nurturance, and social interaction without which we would either die or fail to develop normally. Our identity is formed up through our ongoing intimate relationships, first with our caregivers, and then with our siblings and close social others. Such nurturance and caregiving supports more than mere survival. It is a major component of our intersubjective flourishing.

Developmental child psychologists Daniel Stern (*The Interpersonal World of the Infant*) and Colwyn Trevarthen ("Communication and Cooperation in Early Infancy") describe the many ways that infants and their caregivers attune themselves to each other in a finely choreographed dance of mutual intentionality that binds them together into a unified intersubjective process of co-self-formation. Early on, babies learn their charming and seductive eye contact with their caregivers. They eventually participate in shared gaze toward objects and locations, and they reproduce (imitate) facial gestures and vocal contours, creating a marvelous back-and-forth mimetic dance with their caregivers, in which self and other are co-constituted. Humans are intrinsically social creatures whose physical, emotional, psychological, and cultural development depends on the nature and quality of their engagement with others, so much so that we exist only in, with, and through others.

The implications of our intrinsic ultrasociality for our well-being are profound. Our full development into caring beings capable of forming healthy and constructive bonds with others requires a basic capacity to imitate others and to experience empathy by projecting ourselves imaginatively into the perceptions, feelings, and perspectives of other people. At this level we do not flourish as autonomous, independent agents; rather, our well-being is socially constituted and maintained with and through others. The early stages of this intersubjective self-formation rely on innate and mostly nonconscious capacities and processes for engaging caregivers, but once infants begin to have conscious feelings, they can even have some modest measure of control over their transactions with others.

The emergence of the ability to experience feelings was a huge step forward in human evolution. Feelings enabled us to become aware of our own current body states and of how we are being affected by our surroundings (both material things and other people). In our individual development, from womb to adulthood, we come to appreciate how others are feeling, which enables appropriate social and ethical relations. Creatures without feelings can have systems for maintaining homeostasis via automated, unconscious, and unthinking responses to environmental encounters, but feelings, by allowing us to become conscious of how we are being changed by our interactions with our environment, liberate possibilities for more conscious control of our well-being and flourishing. Damasio articulates the general relation of feelings, homeodynamics, and well-being as follows:

We have discussed feelings as mental expressions of homeostasis and as instrumental in governing life. [. . .] Feelings are *for* life regulation, providers of information concerning basic homeostasis or the social conditions of our lives. Feelings tell us about risks, dangers, and ongoing crises that need to be averted. On the nice side of the coin, they can inform us about opportunities. They can guide us toward behaviors that will improve our overall homeostasis and, in the process, make us better human beings, more responsible for our own future and the future of others. (*The Strange Order of Things*, 139)

This last sentence is a decent reminder of the nature of flourishing with respect to our intimate interpersonal relations. We have to learn that the well-being of *others* with whom we interact is a crucial condition for, and a part of, our *own* well-being. We have to learn to live, not just directed toward our own perceived happiness, but instead also toward taking into consideration and fostering the well-being of others.

Our well-being and flourishing thus ideally require the fullest exercise of our capacity for empathetic imagination, as the basis for our ability to dwell cooperatively and meaningfully with and through others. The highly problematic notion of radical autonomy and independence from others is not a basic ontological fact, and even less is it an ideal to be pursued. Instead, it is actually a symptom of developmental failure to attach ourselves to others and to establish the kind of intensive sociality that makes us who we are and that gives us a sense of connectedness, cooperation, and moral responsibility toward others—all of which are conducive to our flourishing. Our living with and through others requires a delicate balance between our own needs, desires, and dreams for fulfillment and those of others. The homeodynamics no longer operates only within individual subjects, but instead operates in and through others in what might be viewed as a larger social organism of sorts.

3. **Communal Interactions, Institutions, and Practices**

Our sociality that begins in intimate interpersonal relations eventually develops into participation in larger groups that emerge first at the level of the family and later at the level of various communities and institutions (neighborhoods, clubs, schools, religious groups, and city, state, and federal governmental institutions). At this high level of social organization, certain problems about how to secure homeodynamics emerge that, at the level of intimate interpersonal social relations, were either not present or were easier to solve. Even at the interpersonal level, we already encounter the possibility of conflicting needs, desires, projects, temperaments, and feelings separating two or more people. When we then expand the community to tens, hundreds, or thousands of members, the occasion for conflict increases exponentially and the homeostatic processes that worked well at the biological level seem inadequate for the larger communal level. Damasio explains the problem:

> The physiological rationale and primary concern of basic homeostasis is the life of an individual organism within its borders. [. . .] It can be extended with more or less effort to the family and to the small group. It can be extended further out, to large groups, on the basis of circumstances and negotiations in which the prospects of general benefits and power are well balanced. But homeostasis, as found in each of our individual organisms, is not *spontaneously* concerned with very large groups, especially heterogeneous groups, let alone with cultures or civilizations as a whole. (*The Strange Order of Things*, 219)

The potential within large groups for conflicts about resources, goods, services, power, and social status makes it unlikely that the automated and nonconscious processes that maintain homeostasis within individual organisms are automatically going to be able to do the same for large groups.[2] In spite of this difficulty, Damasio argues that it is still possible to identify homeodynamic processes operating in large group relations. He seems to suggest that homeostasis can indeed explain our higher values that we regard as constituting our most important social and ethical accomplishments. Referring to cultural practices and institutions, such as communal story-telling, group cooperation (e.g., hunting, building shelter, farming), social units (family, clan, city, state, nation), and legal systems, Damasio suggests that

> the engine behind these cultural developments is the *homeostatic impulse*. [. . .]. In one form or another, the cultural developments manifest the same goal as the form of automated homeostasis to

---

[2] In their chapters in this volume, both Lori Gallegos and José Medina argue that these conflicts are not only possible but that they are actual and thus constitute real limits on the extent to which a homeostatic or homeodynamic account of flourishing can succeed.

which I have alluded [...]. They respond to a detection of imbalance in the life process, and they seek to correct it within the constraints of human biology and of the physical and social environment. (*Self Comes to Mind*, 292)

Damasio gives the name "sociocultural homeostasis" (292) to processes within these higher-order practices, systems, and institutions that are created by creatures capable of reflective thought and engaged in forms of cooperative social activity, such as language use, other forms of symbolic interaction, and cooperative participation in cultural institutions and practices. In *Looking for Spinoza: Joy, Sorrow, and the Feeling Brain* (2003), Damasio suggests that "social conventions and ethical rules may be seen in part as extensions of the basic homeostatic arrangements at the level of society and culture. The outcome of applying the rules is the same as the outcome of basic homeostatic devices such as metabolic regulation or appetites: a balance of life to ensure survival and well-being" (168–69).

Obviously, groups can have competing goals, conflicting values, and incompatible practices, and the result is that homeostasis can seem illusive at best and impossible at worst. The problem is that, at this high level of social and political engagements, homeostasis ceases to function as a more or less automated process within an individual person, and, instead, it requires intense work, reflection, and imagination to discern how a dynamic equilibrium might be achieved among people and groups that have diverse cultural backgrounds and interests.

Consequently, at this third level (and even partly, as we just saw, at the second level, i.e., of intimate interpersonal relations), homeodynamics becomes, not an automated nonconscious systemic response process, nor even a consciously entertained problem-solving process (though it *is* that, too), but rather an *ideal* to be imagined, pursued, and held up to give us hope that human intelligence is not without resources to improve our human condition. For example, values and virtues that were necessary for healthy interpersonal relationships must be scaled up to the complexities of large communities. Therefore, at every level, from our ties to our parents and siblings, all the way up to our national, and even global, allegiances, we must develop the virtues and dispositions of character that further social cohesion, harmony, cooperation, and creativity, if we ever hope to flourish in our communal environments. A representative, though highly selective and partial, list of these crucial virtues would include at least truthfulness; personal integrity; courage (physical and intellectual); acknowledgment of legitimate authority; loyalty; responsibility; civic-mindedness; altruism; perseverance; and many more. MacIntyre (*After Virtue*) and Flanagan (*The Really Hard Problem*) have provided multiple catalogues of the similar kinds of virtues that have been recognized historically within different social practices and across sometimes very different cultural institutions.

The significant upshot of this view is that certain social and cultural virtues will be considered critical for our fullest flourishing. Just as Aristotle observed, whatever catalogue of virtues is sanctioned by a particular social and cultural community will determine what flourishing amounts to at that level of human intercourse and transaction. The realization of such values and virtues is an expansion and enrichment of the self that becomes possible at higher (social and cultural) levels of complexity in organism-environment interactions. We humans thus have more ways (and degrees) of flourishing (and, correspondingly, of failing) than are available to our primate ancestors.

4. **Our Search for Meaning, Growth, and Self-cultivation**

It is an important fact, often observed, that as we age and enter into "retirement," we have to guard against retiring from the activities, connections, and commitments that have given our lives meaning and value. Our well-being requires that we stay connected to others, to our communities, and to our physical and cultural environment, practicing the relevant virtues, if we hope to experience growth of meaning and value. In short, at the level of interaction that we humans tend to consider the most important for our flourishing (at least once our survival is relatively secured), it is our sense of being engaged in meaningful relationships and activities that strikes us as most important for our flourishing.

Ontologically, as we move up the scale of increasing complexity of organism-environment interactions—from single-celled creatures, to animals capable of perception and feeling, and on up to animals capable of imagination, thought, and language—we encounter increasingly expansive and rich notions of flourishing. However much we might share with our animal ancestors, we humans have possibilities for flourishing that they cannot even imagine. For instance, the emergence of language and other forms of symbolic interaction in humans affords many new opportunities for enhanced kinds of well-being and well-doing. To cite just one obvious example, our human ability to engage in social intercourse through communicative symbol systems opens up an entire universe of possibilities for meaning-making (in language, art, music, dance, theater, and ritual practice) that other primates either lack or share only to a very limited degree.

Our humanity is inextricably tied up with our capacity for *meaning-making*, through bodily gesture, language, the arts, and multiple forms of symbolic interaction. We have evolved memory capacities that make it possible for us to connect past experiences to present occurrences, and then to imagine their implications for future events. We can thus situate our own lives, and the lives of others, within narrative arcs of developing meaning and significance played out in imagination and lived as history. The good news is that we can anticipate the fulfillment that may come if we can realize projected possibilities for meaningful action, but the bad news is that we can also, by virtue of the same capacities, suffer the agony of broken relationships, failed projects, and lost opportunities.

Positive psychology has gone a long way in exploring some of these levels of flourishing that have been overlooked or under-valued in most traditional psychology and philosophy concerned with value, goodness, and well-being (Seligman and Csikszentmihalyi, *The Really Hard Problem*; Gable and Haidt "What (and Why) Is Positive Psychology?"; Paweleski Defining the 'Positive' in Positive Psychology"). One area that may merit even further development in this literature is the importance of the making and experience of meaning that looms so large in human life and generates such distinctive and marvelous achievements. The capacity to make and experience meaning is a high and very recent development in the human species, and it is a game-changer in respect to what humans need in order to flourish. In *Authentic Happiness*, the first book published in the field of positive psychology, Martin Seligman includes meaning as one of the key components of human well-being. In his later and current model of well-being and happiness, meaning is one of the five core elements—along with positive emotions, engagement, relationships, and achievement.[3] Similarly, researcher Michal Steger has focused extensively on the role of meaning in the quality of life.[4]

Philosopher and cognitive scientist Paul Thagard has observed that a *meaningful life* is not necessarily or always co-extensive with a *happy life*: "A meaningful life isn't just one where happiness is achieved through accomplishment of goals, but one where there are worthwhile goals to pursue. Many of the goals that people value most—for example, raising children and working at challenging tasks—are not always sources of happiness. [...] Hence a meaningful life is not just one in which all your goals are satisfied, but one that provides reasons for doing things. Because meaning requires pursuing goals that are not yet satisfied, it cannot be identified simply with the satisfaction of goals as measured by happiness or well-being" (*The Brain and the Meaning of Life*, 148–49).

I want to suggest that certain virtues are conducive to the pursuit of meaning in our lives, so that the correlative virtues are a central component of any suitably broad notion of human flourishing. Faced with his imminent execution, Socrates famously summed up his supreme values when he said, "the most important thing is not life, but the good life . . . and . . . the good life, the beautiful life, and the just life are the same" (*Crito* 48b). Owen Flanagan offers a de-transcendentalized, more naturalistic interpretation of this passage, suggesting that Plato's notions of " 'the good,' 'the true,' and 'the beautiful' are ways of gesturing at, or describing, the three fundamental and universal ways humans orient themselves in and toward the world in order to live well and meaningfully" (*The Really Hard Problem*, 40). The idea here is that we experience meaning, purpose, and fulfillment in our lives primarily by exercising our capacities for intelligent inquiry (the true), moral behavior (the good), and aesthetic sensitivity (the beautiful).

This list of virtues and activities that arise in relation to our pursuit of meaning will include many of the other virtues mentioned earlier as pertinent to our well-being at other levels of complexity of interaction with our physical, interpersonal, and cultural environments. To the extent that human beings have a somewhat distinctive capacity to

---

[3] See, for example, Seligman, 333–35.
[4] See Martela and Steger, 531–45. See also Steger, "Meaning and the Quality of Life," http://www.michaelfsteger.com/

grasp and explore the meaning of their experience, they need to culti-vate virtues of inquiry, communication, and intellectual cooperation. I have in mind capacities and virtues of the following sort. *Intelligence* is our ability to engage in inquiry that reveals the meaning of what we are experiencing and makes it possible to transform our experience for the better. *Aesthetic sensitivity* is our bodily, affective, and imaginative ca-pacity to grasp the meaning of a situation through perception, feeling, and emotion. *Open-mindedness* permits us to take up the perspective of others and to submit our own point of view to critical assessment of its shortcomings and partiality. *Flexibility of thought* means that we are not entirely enslaved by our prior habits of experiencing, thinking, and val-uing, but instead can imagine and enact new modes of thought.[5] Such flexibility in our thinking is closely tied to our capacity to imagine pos-sibilities previously unrecognized. This capacity for *creative imagina-tion* is crucial for intelligent moral deliberation (Dewey, *Human Nature and Conduct*; Fesmire, *John Dewey and Moral Imagination*; Alexander, *The Human Eros*; Johnson, *Morality for Humans*), insofar as it allows us to empathically understand others and also to imagine how a mor-ally problematic situation might develop under the guidance of certain habits and values.

My claim is that at this fourth (meaning-enacting) level of com-plexity of human-environment interaction, flourishing in its fullest (and most distinctively human) sense requires cultivation of these, and other, virtues of perception, thought, feeling, and action. The opposite of these virtues—such vices as close-mindedness, fundamentalism, aesthetic insensitivity, and lack of moral perceptiveness—impoverish our experience and understanding by drastically narrowing and lim-iting them, thereby diminishing our capacity for intelligent engage-ment with our world and our fellow human and non-human others. Intelligent action requires an ability to grasp the full (most comprehen-sive) meaning of our present situation, which is a fundamental prereq-uisite for our flourishing.

---

[5] Several other authors of chapters in this volume develop this point in significant detail and in the context of pluralism. See, for example: Jessica Wahman's analysis of flexible habits in her "Pragmatic Stories of Selves and Their Flourishing"; John Stuhr's Jamesian account of genius as the habitual ability to perceive and act in unhabitual ways; Jennifer Hansen's discussion of the cultural conditions prerequisite for autotelic activities; and Rebecca Newberger Goldstein's discussion of the dynamic character of mattering.

John Lachs (this volume) has suggested that some people can be quite satisfied without exercising any of these reflective and critical capacities of mind. That is certainly true, and it is not to be sniffed at by eggheads with their noses in the air. Once you have a job that pays the bills, keeps you busy most of the day, and pays your beer tab on the way home every evening, what more could be needed or even wanted? For some folks, nothing more is required. My response is to acknowledge this mode of being as legitimate, and to take at face value the satisfied individual's self-assessment. To the extent that this person's world remains relatively fixed and does not confront him or her with conflicting values and demands, that person may be happy. However, the ability to sustain such a happy state depends precisely on remaining relatively encapsulated in one's small world, rather than realizing our shared fate with larger communities, from our local institutions all the way up to a global perspective. Consequently, there are many people (I would venture to say, *most* people) who want and need more, and they are at least moderately self-reflective about that reality. They want their lives to *matter*, and they construe mattering (in the brief instances that they do think about it) to involve engagement with people and activities that they believe contribute to more lasting values—often values connected to the well-being of others and to the betterment of the world in which they live. Some believe that for their lives to matter, those values must be transcendent and eternal, while others are satisfied with believing that they are part of an ongoing, creative transformation of the natural world, without any need for a transcendent supernatural ground of meaning and value. Either way, it is an essential part of their sense of meaning that they are able to pursue certain tasks that are valuable relative to the development of the human and more-than-human world.

Homeodynamics at this highest level of complexity and pluralism of values is using our aesthetic capacities for feeling and imagination to explore the meaning of our current situation in the most comprehensive and clear-sighted way. We need an imaginative grasp of the possibilities within a conflicted and problematic situation, in service of using our intelligence and capacity for nurturance to help reduce conflict, harmonize competing ends, and engender cooperative engagement. The "balance" or "dynamic equilibrium" we are seeking here is both among our own values and interests and those of others (including the more-than-human world) and also among the multiple things we value and find meaningful in our individual lives, such as the various goods, relationships, and states that seem to matter to us individually. In this way, we move into the ideal of artfully composing situations, with respect to both our own lives and well-being, and also that of others. This sort of homeodynamic transformation of experience is something that has to be intentionally and imaginatively wrought, and it is based on our ability to take the measure of the difficult situations in which we find ourselves.

Is Homeodynamics the Basis for Our Flourishing?

I have been describing four of the more important levels that, via their increasing complexity, give rise to ever richer and more expansive notions of human well-being and flourishing. We pursued Damasio's suggestion that homeodynamics is the supreme value that ultimately underlies our flourishing at all of these levels of complexity and emergent functions just described. The case for this is most compelling on the biological plane, since the securing of the conditions for life processes within the bodily boundary of the organism is clearly based on maintaining the proper dynamic equilibrium that is necessary: first, for survival, and second, for growth.

Damasio also suggests that what we might call *interpersonal/social homeostasis* is equally important in creating positive, cooperative, and nurturing relations with other people (e.g., parents, siblings, close friends, lovers) with whom we are intimately connected. The "balance" or "equilibrium" at this interpersonal level of interaction consists of our ability to harmonize potentially competing values, needs, and ends that can create disharmony, conflict, and social disintegration. This process, in turn, depends on our ability to appreciate empathically the experience and perspective of others, and to imagine ways to resolve conflict at the intimate interpersonal level.

Moving to the level of what I have called larger communities, the idea of homeostasis can be recruited from the level of intimate interpersonal relations. Moral action toward others requires a balancing of sometimes conflicting or incompatible perspectives, goals, and values. The ideal is to establish practices, institutions, and social arrangements that allow for the reduction of conflict and that support cooperative behavior that is experienced by members of the larger community as fair, in spite of the inherent tensions that arise within human communities and the inevitability of cases where no agreement seems possible.

When we move, at last, to the "highest" level—that of our human quest for meaningful and ethically responsible action that matters to us—it may seem as though we are doing more here than trying to maintain a homeostatic balance. Yet even at this level, finding meaning, purpose, and significance in our lives remains a matter of harmonizing a number of fundamental values and finding life activities that allow them to be realized in a manner that creates an ever-expanding dynamic equilibrium. The ideal of living a balanced, harmonious, and ever-expanding (in its inclusiveness) life is a genuine and enduring good. It is a highly developed art to accomplish such a state of being and doing. It is a matter of artfully composing a life that expansively realizes one's many potentialities, cares for and cooperates with others, and finds ever more possibilities for growth of meaning.

Homeodynamics has to be a pluralistic notion, because the different levels at which it can be realized may have different ontologies, different layers of complexity, different functional processes, and different values. Moreover, as we saw, what happens mostly automatically and nonconsciously at the biological level has to be transformed, at other levels (the intimate interpersonal, large group, and meaning-making levels), into a far more consciously controlled imaginative process of aesthetic creation. In short, we moved from homeodynamics as a built-in, automated value to homeodynamics as a consciously entertained imaginative ideal to be pursued and realized in our lives in an artful fashion.

Eudaemonistic Pluralism

The analysis I have developed highlights the pluralistic character of human flourishing. Flourishing is not one homogenous thing, but rather many activities blended in a fluid equilibrium. There are at least four levels at which different modes of flourishing emerge, and, however one might count and carve up various levels, there is no single univocal concept of well-being and well-doing that is adequate to the complexity of the relevant constituents of our flourishing. Even the notion of homeodynamics (i.e., homeostasis and allostasis) does not have the same meaning or application at each of the four levels. Consequently, we need to learn how to balance out our many needs, values, and interests, both within each level of functional organization and then across all four levels. The depth and scope of meaning that arises as we attempt to negotiate all of these dimensions of our being is crucial for developing our more distinctively human ways of flourishing. The art of living requires a continuous re-making of experience (and, concomitantly, of oneself) while staying "present" to the meaning of what is happening and to the possibilities for growth of meaning and value.

Works Cited

Alexander, Thomas. *The Human Eros: Eco-ontology and the Aesthetics of Existence.* Fordham University Press, 2013.

Cannon, Walter. *The Wisdom of the Body.* Norton, 1932.

Damasio, Antonio. *The Feeling of What Happens: Body and Emotion in the Making of Consciousness.* Harcourt Brace and Company, 1999.

Damasio, Antonio. *Looking for Spinoza: Joy, Sorrow, and the Feeling Brain.* Harcourt Inc., 2003.

Damasio, Antonio. *Self Comes to Mind: Constructing the Conscious Brain.* Pantheon, 2010.

Damasio, Antonio. *The Strange Order of Things: Life, Feeling, and the Making of Cultures.* Pantheon, 2018.

Dewey, John. *Human Nature and Conduct,* 1922, vol. 14 of *The Later Works, 1925–1953,* edited by Jo Ann Boydston, Southern Illinois University Press, 1988.

Dewey, John. *Art as Experience,* 1934, vol. 10 of *The Middle Works, 1899–1924,* edited by Jo Ann Boydston. Southern Illinois University Press, 1987.

Edelman, Gerald. *Neural Darwinism: The Theory of Neuronal Group Selection.* Basic Books, 1987.

Fesmire, Steven. *John Dewey and Moral Imagination: Pragmatism in Ethics.* Indiana University Press, 2003.

Flanagan, Owen. *The Really Hard Problem: Meaning in a Material World.* MIT Press, 2007.

Gable, Shelly, and John Haidt. "What (and Why) Is Positive Psychology?" *Review of General Psychology,* vol. 9, no. 2, 2005, 103–10.

Johnson, Mark. *Morality for Humans: Ethical Understanding from the Perspective of Cognitive Science.* University of Chicago Press, 2014.

MacIntyre, Alasdair. *After Virtue.* University of Notre Dame Press, 1981.

Martela, Frank, and Michael Steger. "The Three Meanings of Meaning in Life: Distinguishing Coherence, Purpose, and Significance." *Journal of Positive Psychology,* vol. 11, no. 5, 2016, 531–45.

Pawelski, James. "Defining the 'Positive' in Positive Psychology: Part I. A Descriptive Analysis." *Journal of Positive Psychology,* vol. 11, no. 4, 2016, 339–56.

Plato. *Crito, Complete Works.* Hackett, 1997.

Seligman, Martin. *Authentic Happiness: Using the New Positive Psychology to Realize Your Potential for Lasting Fulfillment.* Atria Books, 2004.

Seligman, Martin. "PERMA and the Building Blocks of Well-being." *Journal of Positive Psychology,* vol. 13, no. 4, 2018, 333–35.

Seligman, Martin, and Mihaly Csikszentmihalyi. *The Really Hard Problem American Psychologist,* vol. 55, no. 1, 2000, 5–14.

Steger, Michael, "Meaning and the Quality of Life," http://www.michaelfsteger.com/, 2013.

Stern, Daniel. *The Interpersonal World of the Infant: A View from Psychoanalysis and Developmental Psychology*. Basic Books, 1985.

Thagard, Paul. *The Brain and the Meaning of Life*. Princeton University Press, 2010.

Trevarthen, Colwyn. "Communication and Cooperation in Early Infancy: A Description of Primary Intersubjectivity." *Before Speech*, edited by M. Bullowa. Cambridge University Press, 1979, pp. 321–47.

Tucker, Don, and Phan Luu. *Cognition and Neural Development*. Oxford University Press, 2010.

3

Pragmatic Stories of Selves and Their Flourishing

Jessica Wahman

Organisms flourish—machines do not. Your car may perform optimally or poorly, but it would be odd to say that it thrives. "Machine-talk" about human functioning can therefore make for an unhelpful framework for thinking about our well-being. A psychology that concerns itself with human flourishing should instead conceive of human beings as organisms: living beings who sustain themselves, develop, reproduce and—most important for my purposes here—function as purposive self-directing agents.

Computational and mechanistic models of the mind-brain currently dominate cognitive science and psychology, and, through the popularization of neuroscientific information and the ubiquity of psychopharmacology, have given rise to a story that, I argue, promotes a sense of helplessness and passivity that is at odds with our flourishing. This is to say, when we conceive of our brains and bodies as computers or machines, we start to think of ourselves as without agency. Deterministic models like these invite us to view ourselves as objects and our behavior as the inevitable result of a chain of efficient causes. Or, more accurately, we find ourselves powerless witnesses to the behavior of our own mechanical bodies. To call the popular attitudes inspired by these models "interpretations," moreover, would be somewhat misleading. Rather, they function as intuitions or assumptions, serving as bases for conclusions about who we are and how we affect one another. This sort of mechanistic outlook promotes a narrative that can alienate the conscious subject from her own material organism, making us passive observers in our own life stories.

As a means of reconstructing the narrative from a mechanistic to an organismic one, I turn to pragmatic psychology, where the self is conceived, not as a conscious yet inactive witness to machine behavior, but as a dynamic

Jessica Wahman, *Pragmatic Stories of Selves and Their Flourishing* In: *Philosophy and Human Flourishing*. Edited by: John J. Stuhr, Oxford University Press. © Oxford University Press 2023.
DOI: 10.1093/oso/9780197622162.003.0004

system of material habits. I will show that identifying the self with the entire organism—one which is not merely a mechanism and of which consciousness is an integral part—allows for a different kind of agency, one that better recognizes both our limitations and our choices and that identifies concrete possibilities for increasing our freedom and happiness.

Narrative Explanation and Self-Understanding

An important aspect of human flourishing is our empowerment—our ability to direct our own paths and to make some positive difference in the world. The narratives we tell about our individual trajectories can shape this sense of agency. Whether we understand ourselves as significant and influential or unimportant and ineffectual can influence both our sense of well-being and our capacity to improve our situations. Broad cultural narratives—about who we are in our social roles, about human nature in general, and even our place in the cosmos—can influence individual self-perceptions and thus the stories we tell about ourselves. Our individual self-understanding, in other words, is affected by the cultural narratives that pervade our environment, which can influence our sense of agency and thus our ability to flourish.

In order to see how mechanistic models have shaped psychological narratives, it is important to clarify what I mean by narrative explanation in general and, more specifically, by its role in individual self-conception. As I have argued extensively elsewhere, we explain the world we experience through the construction of narratives (*Narrative Naturalism*). These can range from flights of fancy to meticulously crafted theories, depending on the aims and purposes of the storytellers. I use *narrative* here in the broad and not uncommon sense of a description or account of phenomena involving subjects engaged in some form of activity and usually described in both diachronic and causal terms, such as those involving events. Furthermore, as Cheryl Misak explains, "[n]arratives are not simply chronological accounts of events. They are accounts that give coherence or shape to events and are thus freighted with interpretation, motivation, and other dents to what we think of as objectivity" (616). That is to say, when we narrativize some phenomenon, we orient it within a broader explanatory and interpretive context, much of which may be implicit but is nonetheless crucial for making sense of the phenomenon in question. This act of giving coherence to an occurrence by placing it within a relational and meaningful web fits well with

Paul Ricoeur's notion of narrative "emplotment." This activity, as Kim Atkins describes it in her account of his work,

> brings the diverse elements of a situation into an imaginative order, in just the same way as does the plot of a story. Emplotment here has a mediating function. It configures events, agents and objects and renders those individual elements meaningful as part of a larger whole in which each takes a place in the network that constitutes the narrative's response to why, how, who, where, when, etc. By bringing together heterogeneous factors into its syntactical order emplotment creates a "concordant discordance," a tensive unity which functions as a redescription of a situation in which the internal coherence of the constitutive elements endows them with an explanatory role. ("Paul Ricoeur")

To "emplot" various phenomena, then, is to tell a cohesive story about them. This is not limited to literary activities but serves as the very act of explanation. In the most basic sense, when we explain the behavior of objects, whether animate or no, we provide a narrative about who or what acted, the location and time in which the action took place, the manner in which the action occurred, and—in order to serve as an explanation—some reason for or cause of the event in question. So, while this sense of narrativization would certainly include the literary meaning we frequently associate with the term—where *narrative* may also imply such criteria as plot development, a singular protagonist, conflict and resolution, etc.—I use the term more broadly to indicate our general acts of explanation.

Explanatory systems of physical, physiological, and psychological behavior (everything from cultural and religious origin myths to scientific theories), furthermore, influence the storylines of individual histories. Though the latter are more likely to include literary elements that make a story dramatic, funny, suspenseful, tragic, etc., these specific narrative arcs nonetheless take place in the context of an overarching explanatory background. Based on a person's broader belief system, she may explain a dramatic element of her life story—a grave social transgression, perhaps—as the result of her fallen and sinful nature, her childhood upbringing, a chemical imbalance, or her self-determined creative choice (or some combination of the above). Furthermore, her subsequent decision to either repent, reflect and process, seek medication, or stand alone against the herd similarly depends on a web of background assumptions about the nature of the world and her role in it.

Explanatory structures, then, not only give meaning to past actions but, in turn, contribute to the choices an individual makes as she continues to craft her story. Nietzsche was perhaps one of the earlier noteworthy philosophers to suggest that we (or at least some of us) are artists composing our own life stories, but this idea has subsequently been taken up by many others. Philosophers as otherwise distinct as Albert Camus,[1] Daniel Dennett,[2] and Charles Taylor[3]; and psychologists like Jerome Bruner[4] and Otto Rank[5] have argued that we give coherence and meaning to our lives through creative acts of self-understanding and that these symbolic constructions in turn shape our future choices. In chapter 13 of this volume, "Philosophy and the Art of Human Flourishing," Michele Moody-Adams claims that "living well is itself an art," suggesting that creative and interpretive, not only logical, acts shape our life choices. Some (e.g., Dennett) have gone so far as to identify the self with this sort of narrative, suggesting that a self is nothing other than the story each person tells about the choices and behaviors of her or his individual spatiotemporal being. (For reasons that I will soon explain, I take issue with Dennett's identification of the self with its narrative, though I would readily agree that this sort of story can certainly contribute to one's own self-concept.) Anthropologist Ernest Becker explicitly ties this sort of storytelling to human flourishing, arguing that an important aspect of our functional denials of death, our self-esteem, is closely tied to whether we view ourselves as a heroic protagonist in our own story. These individual stories, he claims, are constructed within the symbolic context of a culture with whom a person identifies. Meanings derived from our cultural worldviews, Becker claims, serve as death-denying forces by giving our lives significance. They enable us to suppress the terror associated with our own mortality so that we may focus instead on building a meaningful and (hopefully) satisfying life.[6] A worldview, therefore, that reduces individuals to physical objects—as

---

[1] In "The Myth of Sisyphus," Camus suggests an authentic life involves a refusal of absurdity through self-aware constructions of meaning and value. Sisyphus, he thinks, must be found to be happy because he knows and embraces the fact that his task has no meaning other than what he gives it.

[2] See Dennett, 103–115.

[3] See Taylor, *Sources of the Self.*

[4] Bruner uses *narrative* in the more restrictive sense of a literary construction involving people as the subject matter, reserving *paradigm* for scientific explanation (41–54). My use of *narrative* accommodates both senses. It is, in fact, part of the point of this paper that scientific paradigms give form to stories about events in nature, including the sorts of stories people tell about themselves.

[5] See Rank, *Art and Artist: Creative Urge and Personality Development*

[6] Becker, of course, also argues that this death-denying function causes problems of its own, such as attachment to one's own cultural meanings and hostility and even violence toward anything or anyone that threatens the veracity of one's belief system. Dealing with the problem of human flourishing

some versions of physicalism do—could undermine a person's ability to for-mulate a tale in which s/he can be seen as a self-determining agent playing a heroic role in her or his given cultural context.

This notion of narrative self-understanding has become so common, even "fashionable," as Galen Strawson puts it, that it might hardly seem worth defending except for the fact that Strawson devotes an entire article to refuting the idea in both its descriptive and normative senses. That is, Strawson argues that it is not the case that all people experience themselves in narrative terms, nor should this be an expectation for a well-lived life ("Against Narrativity" 428–52).[7] While many of the details of Strawson's ar-gument are not directly relevant to my thesis, two specific criteria are worth considering here, precisely because addressing them will help me to clarify my own position. First, the object of Strawson's refutation is a strong sense of *narrative*, where the term denotes a literary account of one's entire subjec-tive life treated as a unity. He, in fact, stresses this strong sense by assigning the term a capital letter to distinguish a Narratively lived life from just any sort of story about oneself as a human being ("Against Narrativity" 429, 440). Second, Strawson identifies the self (the object of the self-reflective account) as "an inner mental entity" or "self-experience," and explicitly distinguishes the self from the human being taken as a whole ("Against Narrativity" 429). This distinction is reminiscent of John Locke's famous discrimination be-tween personal identity, or self-consciousness, and being one and the same man, or living organized being.[8] Strawson rejects the Narrativity hypothesis because he does not believe all people experience their subjective selves in a diachronic manner and even fewer find it beneficial to turn that chron-ological experience into an overarching life story. He asserts that his own conscious experience would be better characterized as *episodic* and that an episodic self can make prudent and ethical decisions without formulating an overarching Narrative about a string of subjective experiences with which he may no longer identify.

The two assumptions behind Strawson's argument against Narrativity—that Narrativity implies an integrated and self-conscious history possessing

on a social level, then, becomes a complicated issue of balancing individual needs for self-esteem with social requirements for tolerance of conflicting worldviews (*The Birth and Death of Meaning*).

[7] My thanks to Rebecca Newberger Goldstein for bringing this article to my attention.
[8] This distinction is reminiscent of John Locke's famous discrimination between personal identity, or self-consciousness, and being one and the same man, or living organized being.

a dramatic structure and that a self is an inner consciousness—are important to note because they depict Narrativity as a position meaningfully different from my own claims about narrative explanation. First of all, my own sense of narrative can easily accommodate Strawson's episodic experiences. He readily acknowledges that his string of episodic selves all pertain to one and the same human being named Galen Strawson ("Against Narrativity" 433). Insofar as any one of his episodic selves would make sense of his actions in the context of a remembered past and anticipated future belonging to Strawson the human being, that self would be providing a kind of narrative about what he is doing. Episodes can, after all, be stories, too; and, as aspects of something larger, they are only partially self-contained. An episode of a television sitcom, for example, might present a restricted tale with elements that never appear in any other installment of the program, but to be an episode of that sitcom, it will involve characters, situations, and themes that transcend the subject matter of any particular half-hour slot. Strawson may not be composing a Narrative about a singular diachronic self-consciousness, but to engage in any basic reasoning or planning in his day-to-day life—to give any action coherence or purposiveness—each of his episodic selves would draw (even if only implicitly) on both a particular history and a set of broader cultural narratives about social and natural realities.

The second factor that distinguishes Strawson's position from mine is his equation of selfhood with self-consciousness. Such an association has a long history in philosophy, and it is thus not at all surprising that Strawson would identify the self with a sort of Cartesian thinking subject, albeit one wholly physical in origin.[9] However, it is precisely this characterization of the self that my position calls into question. The traditional identification of the self with consciousness and the brain and body with a machine, when interpreted through a physicalist lens where only material things have causal power, contributes to a narrative of a self without agency. All activity, in this case, is taken up by the machine, which the conscious self merely witnesses. Pragmatic concepts of the self, by contrast and as I will show, have more in common with Strawson's notion of himself as the same human being than with his notion of a life-long self-consciousness. The object of self-narrative, in this sort of pragmatist account, becomes the entire organism, which includes its lived experience but is not limited to it. Identifying the self

---

[9] In *Consciousness and Its Place in Nature*, Strawson (2006) defends a physicalist panpsychism, explicitly distinguishing physicalism from "Physicsalism," which assumes that the only physical realities are those described by the scientific subject matter of physics.

with the organism as a whole—one with both active and adaptive powers—maintains a scientifically explicable account of human behavior while ascribing agential power to the human subject.

Mechanistic Stories in Humane Practices

Where scientific research is concerned, explanatory tales are expected to adhere closely to experimental data and to illuminate the regular and predictable features of experience. However, and as Misak has explained, this mode of operation sometimes disguises the fact that theories are deeply laden with creative elements that shape the construction of research projects and the interpretations of evidence. Scientific explanations do not just relate a chronology of facts. They construct frameworks for—they "emplot"—systematically chosen data in order to provide a coherent and meaningful explanation of what is observed. Such constructions lead us to imagine specific kinds of subject matter in particular sorts of relations, and the storylines they inspire will prove more effective for analyzing some features of experience over others. When we neglect the creative contributions of the scientific imagination and treat models and interpretive explanations as straightforward facts—even worse, as facts exhaustive of reality—we can blind ourselves to the limitations of a given model and fail to note its potential for misunderstanding a situation to which it ill applies.

Where the topic of human flourishing is concerned, reducing well-being to mechanical function, with its connotations of efficiency and instrumentality, can lead us to misunderstand what flourishing means and to prescribe solutions that may even inhibit it. Neurobiological explanations can, of course, play an important role in understanding the workings of the human organism, but physicalist inclinations—both within and beyond scientific communities—often tempt us to interpret our feelings and behavior too reductively, with counterproductive and possibly harmful effects for humane social practices, such as those involving mental health treatment. A relevant example of this involves a rubric called the Research Domain Criteria (RDoC) put forward by the National Institute of Mental Health (NIMH). Early language devoted to explaining RDoC evoked behavioristic and computational metaphors and celebrated the greater precision that mechanistically understood data can provide mental health research ("The Road to Precision Medicine Starts Here"). It makes sense that a field that increasingly views its subject matter in neuroscientific terms would want to diagnose psychological disorders as neurological ones and to propose solutions that address the mechanisms directly. However, too close a focus on mechanism invites researchers and practitioners to prioritize quantitative methods and to ignore the more "imprecise" methods of research and treatment that deal with human beings in their various aspects as biological, psychological, social, and even spiritual organisms. To be fair, the NIMH cautions that it is not promoting RDoC as a unitary solution to a complex problem. Rather, it celebrates the emergence of a new system of constructs as an addition to a wealth of existing models of studying and treating mental illness, and it no longer requires that researchers seeking funding include a neurobiological level of inquiry, though it does recommend computational approaches ("RDoC Frequently asked Questions"). Certainly, the inclusion of neurobiological information, where relevant to a given study, is a good idea. However, RDoC's continuing focus on neurobiology and computation reflects the current cultural predilections for that which can be mechanized and mathematized. The appeal of precise measurement can lead researchers to ignore non-mechanistic (e.g., teleological, qualitative) interpretations of organismic phenomena and psychological behavior and thus to impoverish approaches to our well-being. Even in cases where one thinks of the human body as an intricate machine—and this is a metaphor with limited efficacy even at the biological level—it turns out to be a machine whose functioning is influenced by qualitative conditions, purposiveness, and other conceptual factors, such as how an individual thinks about his own condition and to what extent his life choices are up to him. Experiences and their meanings irreducibly affect attitudes, behaviors, and self-images and should remain important subject matter for psychological research and treatment.[10]

A wealth of arguments in the philosophy of psychiatry show how mechanical models can influence the attitudes of both practitioners and clients and help to create a problematic presumption that wellness is equivalent to the smooth functioning of a machine. As Jennifer Hansen explains in chapter 12 of this volume, the technological features of psychiatry have come to dominate the discussion and crowd out the "purposes or ends for which humans . . . have invented technological devices" and, I would add, technological explanations (273). She references psychiatrist John Sadler's

---

[10] This was nicely articulated in a recent *New Yorker* article on the history of psychiatry: "Words can alter, for better or worse, the chemical transmitters and circuits of our brain, just as drugs or electroconvulsive therapy can" (Groopman, 69).

concept of *hyponarrativity*, the tendency for symptom-driven language in the *Diagnostic and Statistical Manual of Mental Disorders* (DSM) and pharmaceutical treatment in the psychiatric profession to prevent patients from cultivating richly narrative forms of self-understanding. As a result, "people are used and regarded primarily as instruments of larger social projects."[11] Sadler, *Values and Psychiatric Diagnosis*, 2004, cited in Hansen, this volume, 274). The disease model of psychiatry, Hansen notes, tends to focus on the patient as an inefficiently operating cog in some larger socio-economic apparatus and to characterize wellness as the restoration of its operationality. The doctor-patient dialogue that would enable a client to make sense of her situation in more humane terms becomes attenuated, as consultation focuses instead on a list of ameliorated (one hopes) symptoms in response to prescribed medication.

Ginger Hoffman similarly draws on Sadler's notion of hyponarrativity to criticize pharmaceutical treatment of mood disorders for its implicit mechanistic connotations and, in doing so, points to the role of self-understanding in wellness. As she puts it, "[o]ne task for philosophers of psychiatry is to understand how different aspects of psychiatric practice may influence patients' self-understandings, which is important because such self-understandings can have dramatic effects on their prospects for flourishing" (Hoffman 2015, 318.) In other words, and as expressed in the terms of my own argument, the more general explanatory tales relied on by the practitioner—whether explicitly relayed to the patient or implicitly communicated via therapeutic practices—shape the way the patient understands her nature, her individual story, and her role in her own healing. Hoffman notes, in a related article (2013), that treating depression with medication can lead both the psychiatrist and the patient to treat the suffering individual as an object, and that, as a result, the patient may begin to see herself as without agency. She "treats herself in some sense as a mere object or a mere machine—as a thing to be manipulated rather than reasoned with" (Hoffman 2013, 166). Hoffman explains that human beings are, of course, natural objects, but they are "non-mere objects" in that they possess mental features (2013, 167, 171).[12] This distinction between mere and non-mere objects is not unlike the existentialist distinction between an *in-itself* and a *for-itself*, the latter of which is

---

[11] Sadler, John. *Values and Psychiatric Diagnosis.* Oxford University Press, 2005.

[12] Mental states are understood here as features of wholly physical phenomena (her argument is not concerned with the metaphysical question of in what sense this is so), so the affirmation of mentality is not an attempt by Hoffman to introduce a supernatural aspect to the human condition.

aware of its condition, interested in its well-being, and capable of taking steps that promote (or hinder) its flourishing. Hoffman's point is that feelings, thoughts, and goal-oriented behavior render people importantly different from those natural objects whose behavior is well-explained in mechanistic terms. Treating a patient's suffering from a mood disorder—which would include emotional issues, thoughts about the meaning of such feelings, and their implications for future life choices—as essentially an issue of chemical imbalance is, Hoffman explains, treating the patient as a mere object—a malfunctioning machine—rather than an organism with a subjective life and purposive reasoning capacities. This form of treatment can then influence the patient to understand herself in a similar manner when she makes sense of what is happening to her (rather than what she is doing) in the therapeutic process.

Sadler's concept of hyponarrativity, which influences both Hansen's and Hoffman's positions, is significant in its attention to the role of self-understanding in human flourishing and the risks associated with narrowly instrumentalist interpretations of health and wellness. Given my focus on the influence of mechanistic narratives, however, I would qualify the prefix *hypo*-, which would suggest something weak or underdeveloped. While it is certainly the case that symptom-driven diagnoses and pharmaceutically oriented treatments limit therapeutic opportunities for the patient to participate in crafting her own narrative about her situation, her suffering, and her goals for wellness, it is not the case that there is an insufficiently robust (in the sense of influential) story taking place. On the one hand, neurological accounts of the role of the brain in psychological maladies can themselves be well-developed and compelling narratives about the organ pivotally responsible for thought, feeling, planning, and acting. On the other hand, when treated as the primary explanation of a given disorder, they become a powerful but possibly harmful influence on beliefs about who—or what—the patient is: Is the person who seeks psychological help an agent, however naturally, socially, and culturally embedded, or is she a mere object or social instrument? Can she be influenced by reasons and goal-oriented attitudes and behaviors, or do the machine workings merely require adjustment? Whether the patient understands herself as a mere object who has things done to her or an agent who participates in her own healing—and, hopefully, even flourishing—can affect that healing and flourishing by influencing the patient's sense of her own power and significance.

In chapter 1 of this volume, "The Conatus Project: Mattering and Morality," Rebecca Newberger Goldstein argues that a distinctively human requirement for flourishing is the belief that one matters. Her claim is that we are creatures who "strive to matter" in some way and that these mattering projects—which she terms "conatus projects," after Spinoza's concept of the drive to persist in being—are tied to the question of "what our lives are all about and how well they are going." Part of believing that one matters, then, is the ability to tell a story—if only to oneself—about how one is faring. This need not imply that one must construct an overarching life narrative in the strong sense objected to by Strawson, only that one view oneself as a human being engaged in a meaningful project, one that may be tied to one's own flourishing or that of others (or, in the best case scenario, both). The drive to matter, furthermore, seems reasonably connected to the issue of agency in that it is grounded in an internal striving to act in the world in ways that are significant. By contrast, if one sees oneself as a mere object—an *in-itself* rather than a *for-itself*—then this attitude would likely seriously undercut one's sense of mattering, for an object cannot have a sense of its own significance or impact. One who comes to see herself as an object to be "fixed" by mechanistic means so that she can return to playing her automatic part in the gearworks of technocratic society is, arguably, alienated from the possibility of discovering and developing her own conatus project.

I am in no way claiming that attention to symptoms of suffering and pharmaceutical treatments aimed at their amelioration are wrong or always misguided. To be sure, symptom language can provide a useful framework for identifying a patient's distress, and medication has helped many people to lead happier and more productive lives (though it has harmed others). The issue in question is how practitioner and patient interpret what is taking place when medication is prescribed and how exclusively symptoms and medication become the focus of illness and treatment. When stories of complex organisms with rich subjective lives and who are capable of acting in their own interests are reduced to stories of brain behavior and technical functionality, we omit important aspects of the human condition that are relevant to flourishing, including the role of the patient, or client, in her own healing.[13]

---

[13] It is not insignificant that psychologist Carl Rogers referred to his form of therapy as "client-centered." Not only does it focus on the subject's own understanding of herself and her goals, it transforms a term associated with disease and passivity—*patient*—into a term associated with one who actively chooses service.

The Organismic Self

Up to this point, it has been asserted that neurochemical explanations of mental function can cause us to view ourselves as objects, or as helpless witnesses to the mechanical behavior of our bodies. The reasons for this are no doubt complex, but one major factor at work here is the traditional identification of the self with self-consciousness. Because physicalism—which generally equates reality with the subject matter of the sciences—locates all agency in material existence, consciousness, under this rubric, cannot itself have causal power. According to reductive forms of physicalism, conscious experience is nothing other than brain activity and thus does not itself will or choose but merely witnesses the acts and choices of its brain, acts and choices that are, themselves, entirely physically determined. All bodily behaviors—including brain behaviors—are treated as material results of equally material efficient causes and are wholly determined by their antecedent conditions. If we are nothing but our consciousness, then it is our deterministic brains and bodies, not our conscious selves, that determine what we do.[14]

The physicalist view is popular, in part, because it suggests that one is being properly scientific and not introducing supernatural forces or substances. It is not the case, however, that physics is the only or best way to tell a scientific story, particularly where organisms are concerned. The biological sciences, though they draw deeply on mechanistic metaphors where appropriate, also incorporate teleological language into explanations of behavior, and so the efficient causal story of physics gets supplemented with the language of final causes, or, aims and purposes. Natural behavior, therefore, can be scientifically expressed in terms where wholly material beings are themselves centers of agency capable of goal-oriented behavior. Organismic behaviors are not just automatic effects of prior states of affairs but can also be acts that transform materials and redirect energies in accordance with particular ends.

The organism, furthermore, given its self-interested behavior—its drive to persist in being against entropic forces—is arguably a better candidate for being a self than is self-consciousness, despite longstanding philosophical tradition. There is indeed precedent in American philosophy—specifically

---

[14] As I argue in *Narrative Naturalism*, this is an ironic conclusion for a reductionist to make, for the reductionist asserts that consciousness really is just brain activity. It makes no sense, by this reasoning, for "us" to be essentially our self-consciousness *rather* than our brains and bodies, when consciousness and the brain are supposedly one and the same. Nonetheless, Cartesian dualist intuitions are powerful ones and work their way into positions to which they should be antithetical.

in the thought of George Santayana and John Dewey—for equating the self with the organism as a whole, not just with its conscious awareness. When we understand each self as an individual's entire organism instead of just its conscious aspects, we reintroduce to the self the possibility of, not only causal power, but self-directing and purposive activity. The self, in this context, is wholly material but not mechanical: it is a self-maintaining and self-replicating system of habits capable of adaptation, growth, and acting in its own personal, social, and altruistic interests.

The notion that we are our consciousness seems, on the one hand, intuitive. That which appears to be most intimately *us* is likely our experiences of our own thoughts, desires, and plans. Indeed, consciousness is not only the basis of our self-awareness, it is the condition for the possibility for us being aware, in a reflective sense, of anything at all. Furthermore, there is a long tradition in the history of Western philosophy of identifying the self with consciousness and treating the body as its possession. Present-day mechanistic formulations, such as those in RDoC and dominating the language of the pharmaceutical industry, are twenty-first century versions of longstanding beliefs about nature, the body, and consciousness, going back as least as far as Rene Descartes and his clockwork theory of material existence. This is to say, what scientism treats as straightforwardly objective fact is, in truth, an enduring metaphysical story that works very well in some contexts but poorly and confusedly in others. The assumptions that the body is a machine and the self is the conscious subject have combined to form a myth that we are helpless spectators of our own behavior—passive witnesses with little more than illusions of agency.

However, there is no reason for us to believe that our bodies are nothing but machines or that we are, essentially, our self-consciousness. An alternative conception—one tracing back to Aristotle and reconstructed in Classical American thought—is the equation of a self with an entire organism, or more accurately, with its overarching system of self-organization, the psyche, or soul. Aristotle's notion of the soul as the form of the body—that which gives its matter life, structure, organization, power, and purpose—finds new expression in the psychologies of both Santayana and Dewey. Not only do both characterize the self as a functioning system rather than an awareness of that system, they both interpret the living body as a fundamentally habitual and adaptive form of organization aimed at survival and growth.

In his ontological framework, Santayana distinguishes consciousness, or *spirit*, from the material psyche, identifying the latter as the organizing principle of life and the source of conscious awareness. The psyche, then, would be the overarching system that makes someone the same human being over time and through various material changes. "The psyche," Santayana claims, "is the self which a man is proud or ashamed of, or probably both at once . . . " (*Realms of Being*, 338). For Santayana, then, that conscious experience of our own thoughts, desires, and plans is, in truth, our awareness of the psyche's own interests. These thoughts and feelings are indeed our own, but *we* are not just awareness of these feelings, for ". . . mental discourse is not, and cannot be, a self nor a psyche. It is all surface . . ." (*Scepticism and Animal Faith*, 149). There is some similarity, here, with a physicalist position (though, for a host of reasons, not a reductive one), in that Santayana is denying causal power to spirit, rendering it instead a sort of surface awareness of the bodily inclinations and activities that are really driving things along. But Santayana's position is different from the physicalist one in two key respects that are immediately relevant to this discussion: (1) spirit may be a witness, but the self is not spirit, so the self is not a helpless spectator; and (2) the organismic self is not a mere machine but a naturally, socially, and culturally embedded system that is responsive to and transformative of its environment, so our selves may be understood as, while not radically and transcendentally free, nonetheless capable of genuine agency.

A key aspect of Aristotle's conception of the soul is the idea that the form of the body is not an inert structure but a coordination of integrated functions. Santayana and the pragmatists pick up on this notion when they characterize life as essentially habitual. Santayana frequently speaks of the psyche in these terms, calling it "that habit in matter which forms the human body and the human mind" ("The Psyche," 221). William James viewed life as "a bundle of habits," (173) as John J. Stuhr notes in Chapter 7 of this volume, "Flourishing: Toward Clearer Ideas and Habits of Genius." And John Dewey placed habits—their nature and range, from rigid and automatic to flexible and reflective—at the heart of his humanistic psychology. Living things, according to Dewey, are systems of habits, and it is these that comprise the self and its agency. A habit "is an immensely more intimate and fundamental part of ourselves than are vague, general, conscious choices. All habits are demands for certain kinds of activity; and *they constitute the self* [my italics]. In any intelligible sense of the word will, they *are* will" ("Human Nature," 21). Like Santayana, Dewey asserts that organic dispositions, not mental discourse, make up the self and that these habits are more reasonably the source of our will than some supernatural faculty possessed by a Cartesian subject.

This implies, of course, that a will does not arise *sui generis* but out of material conditions and within a context of multiple environmental influences. At the same time, the willing self can be understood as an active center of experience, capable of creative change of both itself and its environment. Natural impulses are not all reflexes or knee-jerk reactions but can be "agencies for transfer of existing social power into personal ability; they are means of reconstructive growth. Abandon an impossible individualistic psychology, and we arrive at the fact that native activities are organs of re-organization and re-adjustment" ("Human Nature," 68.) Understanding the self as an adaptive habitual system, as Dewey does, enables us to recognize willful activity as something both formed and *empowered* by its surroundings in that existing conditions and forces become raw material for an organism to reconstruct its environment according to its needs and interests.

The possession of agency by a self-directing system, therefore, does not imply a radically free will where we can desire, think, choose, or do anything under the sun. As Dewey notes, "[w]e cannot change habit directly: that notion is magic" ("Human Nature," 18.) Furthermore, objective conditions produce and sustain our habits and "can no more be dismissed by a direct effort of will than the conditions which create drought can be dispelled by whistling for wind" ("Human Nature," 24). Our organic conditions, then, shape what we think and want as much as they form and express our other bodily powers and limitations. For example, just as I can breathe air and run a few miles but cannot breathe underwater or sprout wings and fly, I am similarly able to think, dream, and reason but not able to find feces a delightful repast nor to do complex math at the speed of a digital computer. And while these limitations hold for most human beings and are unlikely to change (in some cases, this may be a good thing!), I am also not, at present, capable of enjoying organ meats or performing statistical analyses, though others do, and I could, conceivably, in the future develop these tastes and skills. A reasonable concept of agency does, then, imply that one is capable of retraining and redirecting one's energies over time and often rationally and in one's own interest. So, while we cannot immediately change our manner of mental or physical activity just by wanting to, "we can change [habits] indirectly by modifying conditions" both external and internal ("Human Nature," 18–19). In other words, we can *practice*. We can put ourselves in environments more conducive to the development of a desired habit, and we can rehearse new ways of moving, and even thinking, over time until the novel pattern itself becomes something habitual. The human organism is highly plastic—adaptive, flexible, and capable of self-transformation through acquired skills and associations—and so it is unknown to what extent I may improve my skills or alter my tastes and preferences.

The overarching point I wish to make in embracing the pragmatists' conception of an agential organismic self is that the traditional argument over whether we are free or unfree is a false dichotomy heavily influenced by Cartesian dualism and sustained by its legacy of mechanistic materialism. Agency is not an on/off switch, something organisms either do or do not possess, but is instead a relative concept. While it is senseless to imagine ourselves entirely untethered from environing conditions, it does not follow that we are helpless witness to the automatic behavior of a body that is ours but, paradoxically, not us. As Dewey notes, "[t]here are in truth forces in man as well as without him." Our thoughts and actions do not take place out of all causal context, but neither is human behavior limited to mechanical reactivity, for "all conduct is *interaction* between elements of human nature and the environment, natural and social." The human organism acts *on* her or his environment as much as (s)he acts within it. When we understand agency in this way, "we shall see that . . . freedom is found in that kind of interaction which maintains an environment in which human desire and choice count for something" ("Human Nature," 1983, 9). A meaningful notion of agency, then, is not freedom from causal conditions but a spectrum of possible responses to them. The relatively free individual has a wider range of responses under her reflective and deliberate control while the less free person may find herself buffeted and frustrated by forces both within and around her that she does not understand. The freer individual is thus more capable of wisely assessing conditions and actualizing goals, that is, of acting in the service of her own well-being as well as that of others. The pragmatic story of the organismic self, with its associations of embodied agency, provides a more constructive psychological framework for thinking about human empowerment and, as a result, a more useful means of assessing concrete possibilities for flourishing.

Flexible Habits and Flourishing

A realistic notion of agency is important to human flourishing because it helps us to conceive of our own empowerment and influence in meaningful ways and, at the same time, to more accurately assess genuine possibilities for empowered activity. As I have argued, a narrative in which we are effective protagonists is more conducive to positive self-understanding, which itself can promote well-being. This is because we can accurately view ourselves as persons whose actions matter and whose choices can and do make a difference in the world to varying degrees. In addition, a notion of organic and relative agency is empirically supportable. It helps to explain our actual experiences of success and frustration, and it enables us to investigate which forms of life possess greater agency and which concrete conditions support and promote that freedom. Whereas a putative "free will," a transcendental but scientifically inexplicable power, flies in the face of widespread observable facts about the influence of our natural, social, and cultural environments on the ways in which we think and act, a situated agency can be scientifically investigated to see which sorts of habits better enable us to creatively respond to and materially transform both ourselves and our surroundings.

Because organisms may be understood as habitual systems, an understanding of flourishing requires a conception of habitual function. In short, we need to know what our habits *do* in order to conceive of what it means for them to function *well*. "Habits," Dewey explains, "give control over the environment, power to utilize it for human purposes. Habits take the form both of habituation . . . and of active capacities to readjust activity to meet new conditions. The former furnishes the background of growth; the latter constitute growing" ("Education as Growth," 497). Habits, according to Dewey, enable us to adapt to our environments in two ways. First, through experience we develop patterns of response that become so automatic as to seem instinctive. With habituation, we do not need to parse each event anew to figure out how to respond to it. These background conditions, particularly when they involve habits that are themselves flexible, then empower us to respond to novel situations in more functional and beneficial ways, in other words, to grow.

Flourishing, for even the simplest organism in the most stable conditions, requires the capacity for growth. For a simpler system, such as vegetative life, growth from a seed to maturation is a relatively straightforward affair. Given a functioning internal structure and a supportive environment, a plant can develop to its capacity. At the other end of the spectrum, we find the human organism, with its greater organizational complexity, plasticity, and dependence on the environment for its development. Given this complexity and the inevitability of a changing world, human beings require flexible habits in order to flourish, ones that can not only adapt to a changing situation but purposively construct a more suitable environment. Human flourishing, then, depends on habits that are conducive to creativity, autonomy, and ingenuity.

Several arguments in this volume effectively explain the importance of flexible habits to human flourishing. In "Philosophy and the Art of Human Flourishing," Michele Moody-Adams discusses the importance of artistic activity to our fullest realization. In her argument, she discusses many projects that would be commonly recognized as artistic but, significantly, also stresses that "artistic activity involves the exercise and application of imagination, creativity and skill in many domains of human interest and concern. Art, on this stance, is not confined to those activities and projects often labelled 'fine arts'" ("Philosophy and the Art of Human Flourishing," p. 281). The cultivation of creative abilities is important to human flourishing, not only because artistic endeavors represent the actualization of our imaginative powers, but because those very powers are crucial to success in many aspects of life. Problem-solving, except in the most ordinary and familiar situations, requires the ability to take existing materials and imagine new and better forms of organization for them.

Jennifer Hansen, in Chapter 12 of this volume, "A Reconsideration of the Role of Philosophy in the Reconstruction and Promotion of Leisure," addresses what is perhaps the ultimate expression of flexible habits—*autotelic* activities—and explains their role in flourishing. Stressing both an Aristotelian and Deweyan influence on Mihalyi Cskikszentmihalyi's concept, Hansen characterizes autotelic activities as "transactions between organism and environments that open up the possibility for greater control and creativity over those environments" ("A Reconsideration of the Role of Philosophy in the Reconstruction and Promotion of Leisure," 266). Flourishing involves autotelic activities because these practices, which would include artistic ones, represent flexible habits at their most playful and joyful—self-directed and imaginative interactions with the environment for the sake of both themselves and the enjoyment the activities bring. While, of course, not all flexible habits are performed and utilized for their own sake— indeed, they are particularly significant to instrumental problem-solving— those very habits that enable us to thrive in our environments can, Hansen claims, produce great enjoyment through the very experience of excellence in one's own autonomous and creative activity.

In "Flourishing: Toward Clearer Ideas and Habits of Genius," chapter 7 of this volume, John J. Stuhr presents a most fully articulated explanation of flexible habits, characterizing them as a kind of genius that is itself tantamount to flourishing. Stuhr characterizes genius as "an openness and responsiveness to unhabitual ways" and effectively communicates what makes habits of genius flexible rather than rigid: "In a life of flourishing, openness and responsiveness must themselves become habitual—the cultivation of a habit of being open to the unhabitual in imagination, perception, conception, purpose, and action—in one's own life and in the lives of others" (174). Though one might be tempted think of habits as rather inflexible due to their almost instinctive nature, Stuhr shows that this need not be the case. First, as we have seen, not all habits are equivalent to what Dewey calls habituation, the rather automatic background conditions of activity. Some habits are themselves exercises in growth and thus involve expansion in new directions. Second, however, and as Stuhr explains, some forms of habituation are, in fact, flexible ones. While rigid habits might cause someone to ignore or unimaginatively respond to novel aspects of a situation, other forms of habituation are inherently suited to adaptation and change: sensitivity to nuance, openness to difference, variety in ready-to-hand responses to given conditions, and a willingness to experiment with different endeavors. These sorts of background patterns give shape to activities that provide an organism with the flexibility needed to be creative, autonomous, and ingenious and thus with the agency it needs in order to flourish.

Conclusion: The Value in Pragmatic Stories of Selves and Their Flourishing

There are at least two major reasons why we speak of organisms, but not machines, flourishing: the concepts of health and growth. While machines can function as intended and can be made larger, there is something more to health and growth than just operationality and size. The flourishing of an organism implies an internally generated drive toward, not just persistence, but development. A healthy organism maintains itself by drawing on its environment and—using internal principles of organization—grows, transforming itself and its surroundings to suit its well-being (and for highly social organisms like ourselves, this includes the well-being of others). Flourishing, then, is inextricable from a being's own interests and its ability to act on them. Human beings have such interests—machines do not. Psychological discussion of flourishing, then, needs to meaningfully distinguish organisms from machines, no matter how useful mechanistic metaphors may be in explaining aspects of our physiology.

Because the very concepts of health and growth entail the interests of an organism, concerns about a flourishing life are essentially about its quality and value. That is, flourishing is a normative concept regarding what forms of individual and social life are worth living and for whom, which experiences are worth having, and what sorts of life choices are worth aiming for. A mechanistic account of human nature, with its aim at "objectivity," can neglect the qualitative and teleological factors essential to telling meaningful stories of our health and development. After all, even our conceptions of "mere" machines entail qualitative and teleological aspects that go beyond mechanistic language, such as the distinction between a fine driving machine like a luxury sports car and a merely functional automobile. It is much more the case that a non-mere object, a life that matters to itself and aims to matter to others as well, should be conceived in terms of its ability to value wisely and to act in accordance with those values. Pragmatic versions of the self, with its environmentally embedded agency, are arguably a better—perfectly accurate and more useful—way of understanding our empowerment to act on what we value than are deterministic accounts of causation and volition that alienate the conscious subject from its organic origins and ignore the creative and transformative powers of the self. By instead examining the relative degrees of flexibility in our habits, we can analyze actual psychological and environmental conditions to see which sorts are conducive to thriving and which hinder it. If psychology is to concern itself with flourishing, where the very quality of life is in question, we need to tell stories that assess the meaning and purpose of our lives and that treat us as subjects capable of directing ourselves towards those ends.

Works Cited

Atkins, Kim. "Paul Ricoeur (1913—2005). *The Internet Encyclopedia of Philosophy*, ISSN 2161-0002, https://www.iep.utm.edu/ricoeur/. Accessed May 28, 2019.

Becker, Ernest. *The Birth and Death of Meaning: An Interdisciplinary Perspective on the Problem of Man*, 2nd edition. The Free Press, 1971.

Bruner, Jerome. "The Remembered Self." *The Remembering Self: Construction and Accuracy in the Self-Narrative*, edited by U. Neisser and R. Fivush. Cambridge University Press, 1994, pp. 41–54.

Camus, Albert. *The Myth of Sisyphus and Other Essays*. Vintage Books, 1955.

Dennett, Daniel. "The Self as the Center of Narrative Gravity." *Self and Consciousness: Multiple Perspectives*, edited by Frank S. Kessel, Pamela M. Cole, Dale L. Johnson, and Milton D. Hakel, Psychology Press, 1992, pp. 103–15.

Dewey, John. "Education as Growth." *Pragmatism and Classical American Philosophy*, edited by John J. Stuhr, Oxford University Press, 2000, p. 497.

Dewey, John. "Human Nature and Conduct." *The Middle Works of John Dewey 14*, edited by Jo Ann Boydston, Southern Illinois University Press, 1983, p. 21.

Goldstein, Rebecca Newberger. "The Conatus Project: Mattering and Morality." *Philosophy and Human Flourishing*, edited by John J. Stuhr, Oxford University Press, 2022, ch. 1.

Groopman, Jerome. "Medicine in Mind: Psychiatry's Fraught History." *The New Yorker*, May 27, 2019, p. 69.

Hansen, Jennifer. "A Reconsideration of the Role of Philosophy in the Reconstruction and Promotion of Leisure." *Philosophy and Human Flourishing*, edited by John J. Stuhr, Oxford University Press, 2022, ch. 12.

Hoffman, Ginger. "How Hyponarrativity May Hinder Antidepressants' 'Happy Ending,'" *Philosophy, Psychiatry, and Psychology*, vol. 22, no.4, 2015, p. 318.

Hoffman, Ginger. "Treating Yourself as an Object: Self-Objectification and the Ethical Dimensions of Antidepressant Use." *Neuroethics*, vol. 6, 2013, p. 166.

Misak, Cheryl. "Experience, Narrative, and Ethical Deliberation." *Ethics*, vol. 118, no. 4, 2008, pp. 614–32.

Moody-Adams, Michele. "Philosophy and the Art of Human Flourishing." *Philosophy and Human Flourishing*, edited by John J. Stuhr, Oxford University Press, ch. 13.

Rank, Otto. *Art and Artist: Creative Urge and Personality Development*. W.W. Norton and Co., 1989.

"RDoC Frequently Asked Questions (FAQ)," National Institute of Mental Health https://www.nimh.nih.gov/research/research-funded-by-nimh/rdoc/resources/rdoc-frequently-asked-questions-faq#2. Accessed May 28, 2022.

Research Domain Criteria Science Update. "The Road to Precision Medicine Starts Here." National Institute of Mental Health, May 1, 2015. https://www.nimh.nih.gov/news/science news/2015/the-nimh-research-domain-criteria.shtml. Accessed November 15, 2015—no longer live.

Sadler, John. *Values and Psychiatric Diagnosis*. Oxford University Press, 2005.

Santayana, George. "The Psyche." *Soliloquies in England and Later Soliloquies*. Charles Scribner's Sons, 1922, p. 221.

Santayana, George. *Realms of Being*. Charles Scribner's Sons, 1942, p. 338.

Santayana, George. *Scepticism and Animal Faith*. Dover Publications, Inc., 1955, p. 149.

Strawson, Galen. "Against Narrativity," *Ratio (new series)*, vol. 17, no. 4. 2004, 428–52.

Strawson, Galen, "Realistic Monism: Why Physicalism Entails Panpsychism." *Consciousness and Its Place in Nature: Does Physicalism Entail Panpsychism?* edited by Anthony Freeman. Imprint Academic, 2006

Stuhr, John. "Flourishing: Toward Clearer Ideas and Habits of Genius," *Philosophy and Human Flourishing*, edited by John J. Stuhr, Oxford University Press, chapter 7.

Taylor, Charles. *Sources of the Self*. Cambridge University Press, 1989.

Wahman, Jessica. *Narrative Naturalism: An Alternative Framework for Philosophy of Mind*. Lexington Books, 2015.

4

Well-Being

Taking Our Selves Seriously

Daniel M. Haybron

Introduction

Lizards, it seems, have a welfare: things can be good or bad for them, and they can do well or badly. Ideally, they thrive.[1] What exactly this amounts to admits of a few plausible answers: having pleasant rather than painful experiences, for instance; getting what they want, perhaps, or succeeding in their endeavors—feeding, mating, etc.; or just succeeding in the leading of characteristically lizard-y lives.

Human beings are a little more complicated. Most of them, at least, are persons. Not surprisingly, they have personalities. They have not just desires but heart's desires; they have values, and care about things; they have not just pleasures and pains but rich emotional lives that range from the heights of elation to the near-total-shutdown of the organism of severe depression; and they are rational, reflective creatures who not only reason through simple tasks as a lizard might but about all these matters, including about their own reasoning. Standardly, at least in the healthy case, these things are the inner determinants of a person's basic manner of living. And each person does them a little differently from the next, in ways that are more or less characteristic of that individual—indeed, that define her as the person she is . . . as *who* she is. We say that they define her character, her identity . . . and her *self*. And we ordinarily attach great importance to this self, to who a person is. If her behavior in no way reflects who she is, say because she was sleepwalking, we tend not to hold her morally responsible for it. If addiction or compulsive disorder dictates her activities against her values and best judgment, we

---

[1] A tip of the hat is due to John Doris, whose excellent book, *Talking to Our Selves* (2015), probably inspired this title.

Daniel M. Haybron, *Well-Being* In: *Philosophy and Human Flourishing*. Edited by: John J. Stuhr, Oxford University Press.
© Oxford University Press 2023. DOI: 10.1093/oso/9780197622162.003.0005

lament her unfreedom, her lack of autonomy or self-determination. If she suffers serious brain injury we are keen to know if it's still "really her" in there, or if she's no longer herself, and we grieve if we learn that the person we knew is gone. If a young man fails badly to understand who he really is, or is unable to come to terms with it, the identity crisis is at best a severe growing pain, at worst tragic. Likewise, if his occupation conflicts with who he is, leaving him empty and listless. Were a parent forced to betray her deepest commitments she may be shattered by a sense of loss to her integrity as a person, perhaps to the extent that she no longer wishes to live.

Lizards, so far as we know, don't have identity crises, or any of these problems. The fact of our personhood, the fact that we have (or are) selves, is pervasive in thinking about practical matters, across most if not all cultures, and if that is not already apparent it will become so in the pages to follow. And when thinking about well-being in the human case, the natural question is: "what is good for a person?" "What is good for Ishani?" Not "what is good for this creature?" We tend to think of human welfare as, in the first instance, a question about what benefits some*one*, not what benefits some organism. Given that the pedestrian concerns listed above hinge on the notion that each of us has a distinct self that is defined at least partly by certain characteristics, and that it is of first importance that this self be preserved, honored or accommodated, an obvious thought presents itself: *human well-being is at least centrally a matter of how things stand with respect to the self.* What's good for Ishani, for instance, depends on who Ishani is, what sort of person she is, or what defines her as the individual she is. This should seem fairly obvious on its face even without reflection on the above concerns, and the answers to it can vary enormously. Ishani's sister may have a very different personality and identity. If Ishani lives in Jaipur, then who she is may be less about her personal inclinations and more about her relationships and social roles than if she spent her life in San Diego. Selves can be regarded as collectivist entities, and indeed most selves reside in collectivist rather than individualistic cultures, so there is nothing especially parochial about these ideas. It seems unlikely that the members of any culture would generally welcome the prospect of Granny's personality being scrambled by a device so that she has a completely different personality, or having Granny replaced by a duplicate. Selves appear to be fundamental, universal concerns in human life.[2]

---

[2] There may well be exceptions, but these are likely marginal. I suspect the point holds even where official doctrine is skeptical about selves, such as among Buddhist populations in Bhutan or Tibet. These of course are empirical conjectures, so data might yield a different picture, but the appearances

To understand what is good for a person, then, we need to know what manner of self she has: who she is. If this is right, then to understand human well-being generally we need some account of the self. Well, perhaps we could get by without one: we might stumble accidentally on a theory of well-being that happens to accord with the nature of selves. But this would be a poor way to go about things, and in any event our understanding would have at least this much of a gap: we wouldn't grasp the connections between welfares and selves.

As it happens, there are rather sizable philosophical literatures on both well-being and the self, so we should be in pretty good shape on this count. The odd thing is, the intersection of these literatures appears to be remarkably small, and few philosophers, contemporary Western philosophers at least, explicitly ground their theories of well-being on some account of the self.[3] This is strange. What gives? One reason, no doubt, is that the topic of the self is a philosophical swamp, and it is not easy to tell what all the hubbub is even about, except that there appears to be a variety of hubbubs, each obscure, whose relation to each other is still more obscure.[4] Theorizing about well-being is hard enough already, and what I'm suggesting is that we first need to sort out a whole other and much more difficult sort of theory; despair would be an understandable reaction. It also may not help that there is outright skepticism in some quarters about the existence of selves, in Buddhism for example, which furnishes a convenient excuse simply to ignore the matter. Finally, it is unlikely that a self-based account of well-being

seem pretty robust. For some relevant research, see De Freitas et al., "Origins of the Belief in Good True Selves"; Strohminger et al., "The True Self: A Psychological Concept Distinct from the Self." For good, recent cross-cultural discussions of the self, see also Ivanhoe, *The Oneness Hypothesis: Beyond the Boundary of Self.*

[3] For some examples or near relations, see, e.g., Brink, "Prudence and Authenticity: Intrapersonal Conflicts of Value"; Clark, "Pleasure as Self-Discovery"; Clark, "Narrative, Self-Realization"; Haybron, "Happiness, the Self and Human Flourishing."; Haybron, *The Pursuit of Unhappiness: The Elusive Psychology of Well-Being*; Haybron, "Flourishing and the Value of Authenticity"; Russell, *Happiness for Humans*; Višak, "Sacrifices of Self," Yelle, "Alienation, Deprivation, and the Well-being of Persons." The words "self-fulfillment," "self-actualization," or "self-realization" figure in a wider range of theories, mostly historical—for instance among Marxist, Existentialist, Hegelian, or Hindu writings—but often do not include an explicit account of the self, and these terms sometimes refer more generally to nature-fulfillment ideals. A good general discussion of such ideals is Gewirth's *Self-Fulfillment*. In this volume, see John Lachs's account of human natures that provides the basis for his pluralistic account of flourishing in his "The Allure of the 'All'" and Valerie Tiberius's view of human nature as goal seeking that underlies her "Well-Being, Value Fulfillment, and Valuing Capacities: Toward a More Subjective Hybrid."

[4] *The Oxford Handbook of the Self* is an excellent reference, but the diversity of its chapters highlights the difficulties here.

would center on goods that don't tend to correlate pretty strongly with, if they aren't in fact identical to, the usual suspects in the philosophy of well-being: pleasure, desire-fulfillment, objective goods like knowledge, achievement, friendship, or Aristotelian goods like the life of excellent activity. All of these proposed constituents of well-being can without difficulty be linked to common understandings of the self. If you can get the goods while dodging the swamps of the self, why not do so?

One reason is that you'll be getting the goods for the wrong reason, or at least be unable to explain the connections between well-being and another major cluster of topics in ethics. And the fact that we have independent reasons to think about the self in certain ways in those domains is liable to place constraints on plausible theories of well-being; to the extent that it does, we need to take account of them in our reflections. At any rate, we may not in fact get the goods if our welfare theorizing isn't self-aware (as it were). I have argued, for example, that authenticity—a notion rooted in the idea of the self—is an important aspect of well-being, and if that's right then most extant theories are ruled out ("Flourishing and the Value of Authenticity").

In what follows I will assume a basic familiarity with philosophical theories of well-being, with typical candidates including hedonism, desire theories, (objective) list theories, and eudaimonistic or nature-fulfillment theories such as Aristotle's that see well-being as a matter fulfilling one's nature. In earlier work I argued that the intuitive value of happiness, understood along the lines of an emotional state theory, is best explained in terms of one form of nature-fulfillment, self-fulfillment: well-being consists at least partly in self-fulfillment, which in turn consists at least partly in (authentic) happiness—the fulfillment of one's emotional nature. The assumes a view of the self as partly defined by one's emotional nature, understood in terms of what sorts of lives make one (authentically) happy. We can group the points mobilized in favor of this conclusion together as the *argument from happiness* (Haybron 2008b, 2008a). A more recent argument, *the argument from authenticity*, defended the significance of ideals of authenticity for theories of well-being, and that this in turn supports a self-fulfillment approach ("Flourishing and the Value of Authenticity"). In what follows I will offer two further arguments focusing on a different strategy: namely that for many philosophers, other theoretical commitments exert considerable pressure to accept some ideal of self-fulfillment in the domain of well-being. In a manner of speaking, all roads lead to self-fulfillment. In total, the case rests on four arguments:

1. The argument from happiness
2. The argument from authenticity
3. The convergence argument
4. The piggybacking argument

My aim here is to make the case for self-based theorizing about well-being—thinking about well-being in terms of self-fulfillment. I will not offer a particular account of self-fulfillment.

Concepts of the Self

Thankfully, we can proceed largely without much explication of the various notions and theories of the self, as the arguments rest mainly on intuitive considerations. But a few distinctions will be helpful. One concept I will set aside is that of numerical identity—whether A is the same individual as B, who emerged from a teleportation device, or a different one. Of greater interest for our purposes is the question of qualitative or substantive identity, or self, or *who* one is, as opposed to *which* individual one is. Here it seems to me that the philosophically important issues center on two different notions, or clusters thereof: what is commonly called the *soul*, or the person or self strictly speaking; and what is most often denoted when we speak of a person's *identity*. One's identity is a representation having to do with who you are "seen" as, either by your self or by others. Identity is important in the first instance because it shapes how a person regards herself and reasons about what to do. Being a philosopher is one part of my identity, and being a father is another. These self-representations are very important to how my life goes; if I were no longer able to do philosophy, or if I seriously violated the basic norms of the profession, for instance through gross plagiarism, I would likely have cause to be shattered. One may have multiple identities as well, for instance a person's social identity, say as a Black woman, which might shape how others regard them and treat her, even if she does not internalize this as part of her own identity, though in the standard case we should expect these identities to be more or less intertwined. For purposes of thinking about well-being we can probably set aside notions of social identity, though there are interesting questions to explore about whether individuals are necessarily or always the right unit of analysis. (In bees they might not be, and perhaps something analogous obtains for humans.) I shall assume that they

are, however, and that our social natures are reflected in the ways we are constituted and think of ourselves, for instance as having a good that cannot be
defined apart from the good of our families or communities, as might historically be the case in most cultures.

It is helpful to regard the self proper, or the person or soul, as distinct from
a person's identity. Mention of the soul can raise eyebrows, but it is helpful
to draw on the historical term, especially as it figures in religions that chart
a person's destiny in terms of their passage through lives and/or afterlives.
Suppose you believe in an immaterial soul that is essentially "you," so that if
your soul passes into heaven or hell, it is *you* making that journey. The person
survives death. It is very natural to regard the self as an entity in something
like the way a soul is, something that persists through time and is the vehicle
for survival, at least the sort of survival we care about. Arguably, it is the object
of the varied self-concerns listed earlier, at least for those who trade in soul-
talk: the character of your soul just is your character. Of course, many of us
do not believe in immaterial souls, and may cast a suspicious eye on any kind
of "soul" talk. While I find the term helpfully evocative and well-entrenched
in ordinary thought quite apart from religious convictions, the word itself is
dispensable if we find it unhelpful, and those so inclined can simply speak of
the self or person to denote the relevant part of one's psychology.

Whether we call the self a soul or not, and whether it is immaterial or material, there remains a distinct question about a person's *identity*, in the collo-
quial sense: one's self-conception, for instance. Huck Finn is thought to be a
good person, to have a good soul, and his decision not to betray Jim to slavers
reflects his character, who he truly is. Yet that's not his identity: as he sees
himself, he is someone who believes in slavery, or at least in accepting the
property claims of slavers, and in his view he is not such a good person. He
is in fact a good person who doesn't accept slavery, but his identity is quite
different. Such mismatches are commonplace: a man who doesn't realize that
he is gay and identifies as heterosexual; a kind and generous person who has
read some Ayn Rand and identifies as a hard-nosed, selfish egoist; a man who
deems himself generous and fair but in fact is an overbearing bully toward
his wife and children; a young woman who leaves the banking industry and
declares herself an artist and acquires the trappings of an artist, but has not
yet acquired the skills, commitments, habits and personality of an artist, for
these will only come with time—for now her eye is untrained and her tastes
remain materialistic and unattuned to beauty. In later years she will realize
that she was not yet really an artist. In each case a person's identity does not

reflect her true self. In this ordinary sense your identity is not literally you, but only a representation of you.

This distinction is easily overlooked, first because many of us do not believe in the soul or anything like one, and second because our opinions on the two matters tend not to be distinct in practice. It would be odd if not incoherent to identify as X, but think your true self is really not-X. Perhaps our identities literally embody our views about our selves or souls. Moreover, our self-conceptions probably tend to be reasonable accurate. Finally, the self proper is often viewed in terms that are closely bound up with our identities. The self might be defined in terms of one's values, for instance; but so too is it likely that your identity will also be substantially a matter of your values. Huck Finn-type cases aside, living in a way that clashes with your identity is likely to be at odds with who you are, your true self, as well your self-conception.

If you believe in souls, you'll still need the notion of identity, and should not be tempted to equate the two. If you do not believe in souls, then you'll still need some notion in that ballpark because the notion of identity is no substitute: you need some way to talk about Huck Finns and similar cases, where a person's identity clashes with her . . . what? Her self. In plainer terms, it is problematic to think there is nothing more to a person, or to the self, than a representation.[5] Which brings us to skeptical doubts about the self, which seem to advocate just this sort of view. When it is claimed that there is no self, it need not be maintained that we do not have identities, and in fact identities offer a natural explanation for the presumed mistake: what do you mean I don't have a self? I'm a philosopher, a father, I care about these things, certain ways of living make me happy, etc.—all these together constitute my self, so how can it be illusory? Because, the thought goes, there is no stable underlying entity that answers to these descriptions. Just a bundle of impressions and mental states in constant flux, in synchrony with events

---

[5] How does the identity/soul distinction relate to the notion of narrative, which is often invoked in connection with the self? Briefly, it depends on what narrative concept is in play: *narratives* themselves are presumably representations and one way to understand identity (perhaps your sense of who you are is constituted by a narrative). Second, we might distinguish self as the narrative's *protagonist*, or "center of narrative gravity" as Dennett puts it—the character posited by or implicit in the narrative; this appears to be a different and perhaps more compelling notion of identity. Finally there is the *narrator*, the one spinning the story; this might correspond to the soul or self proper. The importance of these concepts of narrative is a question I'll leave aside here; clearly narrative is an important feature of human life, but I am skeptical that any particularly important notion of self can be reduced to narrative. I suspect that too much of life is just one damn thing after another, our tales too easily respun, for narrative to have that kind of significance.

in the environment around us, perhaps so interrelated that the person-environment distinction itself is dubious. There is no soul, no homunculus or person-object in our heads that answers to the notion of the self, and our identities are eminently changeable—think of our example of the newly-declared artist. To think otherwise is to become irrationally attached to our identities, believing these mere representations are fixed to some deeper reality. But they signify nothing save a fiction, and the sooner we accept that the better off we'll be.

From a Buddhist perspective doubts about the self make good sense because the reality of just about everything is placed in doubt—impermanence is a feature of things generally, not just selves; all is flux. I'm not sure that isn't a useful perspective to take up for some purposes, but there's another perspective one can also occupy: the point of view from which my many malfunctioning electronic devices, including the one that just landed on my foot, are all too real. They are impermanent all right, but questioning their existence will do nothing to still the howls of indignation from my children, themselves showing all the signs of existing, about the stuttering internet connection. Whimsical cosmic farts we may be, but until the wind carries us off there's work to be done.

What could it mean for a sentient being to lack a self? One possibility: a "film projector" mind that rapidly cycles through a succession of personalities, one moment a painter, the next a banker, then a torturer, then a saint, then a soldier, then a zookeeper . . . . No continuity at all, with no personality lasting long enough for us to say "this is who that is." There is no who, no person it seems. This science fiction scenario is more extreme than simply lacking continuity of memory, as the protagonist of *Memento* does; he may lack a fully formed identity or narrative, but it seems to be one person who persists through the story.

A different sort of individual could be like a lizard: no reflection, no depth of feeling, no sense of past and future, not seeing anything as worth caring about, if it cares in any way at all; wanting but not valuing or loving. No soul—reptilian, one might say. Just a flow of consciousness, reasoning perhaps but not reflecting, all reflex, instinct and drive. Maybe it is possible for an outwardly functional human adult to come very close to this, perhaps even achieving high public office. But it is doubtful whether such an individual would even *be* a person: behind the *papier mâché* exterior there is very little, perhaps nothing, that one could call a self. Be that as it may, such cases must be very rare at best.

In the ordinary case, human adults have a broad repertoire of strong and deep emotions and desires; they engage in complex chains of reasoning and reflect on their inner lives and their ways of living; they do not merely want but also value and care about things, seeing them as meriting desire, and these values tend to be more or less coherent; they have a sense of continuity with the past and anticipate the far future; and they have reasonably stable and lasting personalities and characters that typically evolve in gradual fashion, a far cry from "film projector" minds. If an individual has all these characteristics, then what more do we need before we can conclude that it— no longer comfortably deemed an "it"—is a person, has a self? Should a radical discontinuity arise in the individual's psychology, so that she wakes up one morning drastically altered in all these respects, we should suspect that it's no longer really her, the person we knew. It would rightly be deemed a massive transformation, or loss, of self. But you can't transform a self that isn't there to begin with.

Skeptical doubts about the existence of selves ask too much of the self. Selves do not require homunculi, ghosts in the machine, or "mind pearls" like those inserted in the heads of robots in *Westworld*. They certainly do not require anything permanent, as most selves seem to be all too aware. They need little more than what is already manifest from experience: that something is conscious—or if one wants to be really fussy, that there is consciousness, more or less distinguishable from other consciousnesses—and that it has something like the qualities just noted. In principle one's consciousness could be nothing more than a sequence of random emanations in the cosmos, not subserved by any remotely stable reality. But we have no reason to believe that or even to take the possibility seriously.

All of this is consistent with the ideas that selves are fragile and easily disrupted, and that they change a great deal over time, that they are fragmented rather than organized into global personality and character traits, and that they are highly permeable and elastic, constantly altering in response to situational factors. In fact I have argued for all these points save the first: human beings are highly adaptable if not chameleon-like (Haybron, 2008b, 2014). My personality, even the way I talk, is one way in a low-key island setting, and quite another in a typical mainland environment. If you migrated some time ago to the United States from China, you've likely undergone extensive changes in your psychology, and even strangers might be able to gauge the length of your tenure from little more than your facial expressions; if you maintain connections with China then you might find that you revert somewhat to your old self when visiting your old home town, changing back to the new one on your return. But an elastic self is a far cry from no-self, and there is still a perfectly familiar sense in which it is you in both environments. Part of who you are may in fact be defined by how you tend to respond to such changes—some people are more rigid, perhaps to a fault, while others are more prone to blend in, perhaps to a fault. Likewise, older you may be quite different in deep respects from younger you, yet it is still you. Saul was evidently a zealous jerk, and then he took the road to Damascus where, legend has it, the scales fell from his eyes and he underwent the most radical of transformations into Paul—who, also, might fairly be deemed a zealous jerk. There is not the slightest reason to doubt the existence of selves in these cases, any more than there is to doubt the existence of chameleons and caterpillars. The apparatus of the soul need not be exotic, and is easy enough to come by.

The more pertinent question, to which we now turn, is whether we should care very much about selves, as such, or whether the character of the self places meaningful constraints on theories of well-being.

The Convergence Argument

Preliminaries

Self-fulfillment theories of well-being do not enjoy a great deal of support these days, and indeed the very expression "self-fulfillment" often arouses some hostility—and not entirely unreasonably as its use in popular culture is associated with New Age self-indulgence if not narcissism. Let's see if we can't take the fight to the skeptic's own turf, then: suppose one favors a popular alternative, such as hedonism, desire theory, or nature-fulfillment theories along Aristotelian or other traditional lines. I will argue that the intuitive appeal of these views is best explained in terms of self-fulfillment. At bottom, each view is either founded on some notion of self-fulfillment or faces strong pressure to collapse into a self-fulfillment theory. All roads lead to the self.

Almost. One well-known family of views I will not discuss are objective list, or just list, theories, that identify well-being with some list of intrinsically beneficial goods like knowledge, achievement, friendship, pleasure and so forth. Unlike the other theories, list views generally aren't motivated by any particular insight. This is widely taken to be a deep problem for them: they can seem not to be motivated at all, except as a last-ditch effort to cope with the diversity of intuitively plausible goods. One might try to show that each list item bears some connection to the self, but lists are as diverse as list theorists and the task would never end, and for the most part list items aren't motivated even individually except by brute intuition: imagine a life without that good; don't "we" think such a life is worse than a life with it? (Often enough, for what it's worth, my response is "no," and it is telling that list theorists themselves rarely agree on the list of goods.) Without any animating principle to one's theory, it is hard to say that the theory could have any latent tendency, except perhaps to multiply brute posits without end. In any event, I think most of the more popular list contents could readily be explained either within a plausible self-fulfillment theory or through noninstrumental values other than well-being, such as excellence and beauty. If it turns out—as I believe to be the case—that those are non-welfare goods, then it should not be surprising if efforts to accommodate such values exert some pressure to abandon more coherent or unified approaches to well-being.[6]

Hedonism

Take pleasure, to begin with: when asked to describe what well-being looks like in practice, hedonists tend not to focus, explicitly at least, on people experiencing lots of physical pleasure. Rather, the examples typically involve "happy" people, who in turn are standardly characterized as being in good spirits, untroubled, and generally in a good mood. This is probably not just a marketing ploy, meant to defuse prejudices about libertinism. Rather, it seems to reflect the sensible observation that among the most important pleasures are emotional pleasures: being in a good emotional condition.[7] An obvious thought is that this is because one's emotional condition typically has a bigger impact on the quantity of pleasure one experiences: if one wants

[6] It bears remarking that my present view of well-being, a "Millian hybrid" approach, in fact amounts to a two-item list theory—the items being self-fulfillment and pleasure—so I am not well-positioned to cast many stones on this count. But that fact is a problem, and I believe it requires some metaethical footwork to show that such a list is not in fact unmotivated; it just isn't motivated in the usual way.

[7] I will not elaborate much on the distinction between hedonic state and emotional condition, or emotional well-being, here; see Haybron, 2001; 2005; 2008b; and 2016a). The term "emotional well-being" is meant to be purely descriptive, not entailing anything about well-being proper, like "subjective well-being."

to lead a pleasant life, emotional well-being seems likely to have a larger impact than, say, sensory pleasures.

But sheer quantity of pleasure seems not fully to explain the significance of our emotional conditions for well-being, and the reason seems to be that emotional states bear a more intimate relation to the self. Thus we naturally distinguish between things that merely hurt, or are painful or unpleasant or annoying, and things that "get to you," or "get you down." And, conversely, between things that are merely pleasant or amusing and things that "lift your spirits," "fulfill" you, or, to paraphrase a popular song, "satisfy your soul." The distinction in question concerns what I've called "central" versus "peripheral" affective states, where the former, but not the latter, implicate what we intuitively regard as our emotional conditions. Happiness, I've argued, has to do with central affective states—our emotional conditions, or alternatively, emotional well-being. Peripheral affective states either don't bear directly on happiness, or do so only to the extent that they exhibit the characteristics of central affective states (if the distinction proves to be merely one of degree). This distinction seems tacitly to be recognized in diverse moral psychologies, including Stoic and Buddhist thought among others—indeed, I suspect in all cultures—where it is deemed important to regulate the emotional, but not so much the merely hedonic, impact of events. As one Buddhist texts advises:

> Just as a person might be pierced by a dart, but might not be pierced by a second dart. In that case, one would feel only one feeling from the one dart. Thus, the learned noble disciple, when touched by an unpleasant feeling, does not grieve, is not wearied, does not lament, does not weep beating one's chest and does not become confused. Such a person feels only one feeling, a bodily one, but not a mental one. (*Samyutta Nikaya* 4.207–210, trans. John Holder)[8]

Similarly, Epictetus remarks:

> "I have a headache." Well, do not say "Alas!" "I have an earache." Do not say "Alas!" And I am not saying that it is not permissible to groan, only do not groan in the centre of your being. (Epictetus, 1925)

---

[8] I am grateful to John Holder for directing me to this passage.

Your emotional condition, and what impacts your emotional condition, seems to reflect who you are, including your character. That being stuck by a needle is painful and unpleasant may be inevitable, saying little about you; but that you let it get you down, or alternatively just "shake it off," does say something about you, and may be morally or ethically quite significant.[9]

The same distinction comes into play in ordinary thinking about how to treat different sorts of unpleasantness. The rise of antidepressants, anti-anxiety medications and other mood enhancing pharmaceuticals has brought attendant worries about whether they undermine—or perhaps enhance—the authenticity of the person's emotional responses. Perhaps you're happier now, but is it really *you*? (Or again, maybe the happier you is really more fully you, no longer squelched by a psychiatric disorder.) People tend not to have such concerns about taking analgesics for bodily pain, or anti-nausea medications. When concerns do arise, they have a different flavor: some people just don't like taking medicine of any sort, or worry about becoming dependent on the pills, or feel it would be better to accept the pain and develop better skills for coping with it emotionally—which again illustrates how we think differently about emotional states. I'm not sure if anyone ever thinks, "my wrist doesn't hurt anymore; this just isn't me."

Emotional states, then, seem to raise special concerns regarding well-being and authenticity; people care about whether their emotional responses to their lives are genuinely theirs, reflecting who they are—their true selves. And when not, then there seems to be a tension between hedonic value and authenticity: we benefit from the drugs, insofar as they make life more pleasant; but that benefit is diminished, possibly reversed, insofar as the resulting emotional responses seem phony, out of step with who we really are . . . inauthentic. Many of us are willing to accept some tradeoff of this sort, but only within limits, and would not take such drugs if they radically altered our personalities, or undermined the expression of our personalities, even if that would yield a more pleasant life.

---

[9] The reader might wonder if in fact pains are really unpleasant when we aren't troubled by them. There is indeed good evidence that people can experience pain without being bothered by it, and sometimes this is thought to support the idea that such pains aren't unpleasant after all. I am not aware, however, of research that takes care to distinguish between finding the pain unpleasant and being bothered by it, so such claims might conflate the two issues. I have asked a Buddhist monk, an expert meditator who has participating in neuroimaging studies along these lines and been found to experience pain without discernible emotional distress—not being bothered by it—and been told that the pain was indeed unpleasant. He still felt the one dart, as it were, just not the second.

Similarly, we might live in ways that don't suit our personalities, and this possibility again raises distinctive concerns that extend beyond the hedonic. If your work as a copyeditor gives you wrist pain, that is one sort of problem; but if it makes you depressed, or leaves you hollow, or stresses you out, or bores you, then that's a very different sort of problem. In the latter sorts of cases, your friends are apt to observe that your job doesn't suit you, or fit your personality; you're living in conflict with your nature. Those would be odd things to say in the former case. You might take a pill to deal with sore arms, and have no qualms about it; but if your job is unfulfilling or enervating, taking a pill that made you happy in it would at best be problematic: you've got a mismatch between life and self, and might be better advised to find a different line of work if you can. The basic point here is a wizened trope of countless novels and films: the creative type languishing in respectable work that ill suits him; the repressed Victorian daughter; the gay man pretending to be straight. These are conventionally regarded as sad cases, and sad in a different way from afflictions of physical discomfort: they are sad because it matters for well-being that we live in a manner that expresses and suits, and fulfills, our natures, our selves. To flourish is, at least in part, to achieve self-fulfillment.

It is revealing, I think, that such sentiments have received no finer expression than in the writings of a self-avowed hedonist, John Stuart Mill, in his discussion of individuality in *On Liberty*. Arguably, his distinction regarding quality of pleasures reflects, at least in part, a wish to reconcile his hedonism with his eudaimonism. It is a good question just what conception of self-fulfillment animated him—there may be no determinate answer to that—and I know of no evidence he understood that ideal in exactly, or even approximately, the way I do here. But considerations of the sort I've been discussing suggest that self-fulfillment is at least partly a matter of the fulfillment of our emotional natures—of happiness, understood along the lines of some sort of emotional state view (or, to put it in eudaimonistic terms, "psychic flourishing"). Specifically, it seems to involve *authentic happiness*, a notion introduced two decades ago by L.W. Sumner (*Welfare, Happiness, and Ethics*). For who we are, at least in part, is defined by what manner of living makes us (authentically) happy: the self is, at least partly, an emotional self. Were you such that very different things made you happy, you would be a different person.

I have argued for these claims at greater length in earlier work and will be brief here, but it bears remarking that the idea of self-fulfillment, and of having an emotional nature, does not commit us to thinking of the self as a fixed quantity, or that self-fulfillment demands that the individual pursue some very specific personal destiny (being a painter, for example). Presumably, a given person can find authentic happiness in any number of ways; even if being a painter makes you happy, you might also have found happiness as a stockbroker. And our emotional natures are dynamic, evolving over time so that, in later stages of life, we are somewhat different people from who we were in young times. Should a young woman choose to become a concert pianist, then she will change accordingly, and find happiness in different things from before (when, for instance, she could not be happy playing the piano, having not yet learned it). But some transformations, intuitively, seem to be authenticity-preserving (learning piano), while others do not (getting a lobotomy). And there are limits to what can make an individual happy; probably most people would be unable to find happiness in an asocial existence.

It is plausible, in light of these reflections, that hedonism gains some of its appeal from its association with self-fulfillment, specifically authentic happiness. It also seems relevant that one prominent form of hedonism, Epicurean hedonism, is arguably grounded in nature-fulfillment as well.[10] As the tensions between self-fulfillment and hedonic value noted above suggest, the allures of hedonism may not be wholly explicable in eudaimonistic terms. Convergence between hedonism and self-fulfillment may be incomplete, then. But it suffices for our purposes if ideals of self-fulfillment are needed to explain at least part of hedonism's plausibility.

Desire Theories

Now consider another sort of view, also standardly posed in opposition to eudaimonistic theories: desire theories of well-being. Roughly, what's good for you is getting what you want, or what you would want under idealized conditions. As noted above, and as with hedonism, one can readily see the appeal of this sort of account without reference to notions of nature-fulfillment: it seems to honor popular ideals of agent sovereignty, and also to forge a strong link between welfare and motivation. It likely profits as well from the idea that it is somehow more respectable naturalistically: nothing mysterious about desires, or their fulfillment. That, however, is arguably a

[10] Julia Annas, *The Morality of Happiness.*

confusion: the desire theory of well-being is a position in normative ethics, and can be founded on any metaethic you like, including Platonism. Perhaps, if you really grasped the Forms, you'd see that the Good consists in the fulfillment of desire. This might be a curious move, but it is open to those so inclined. This sort of confusion is unsurprising, since informed desire theories of well-being so closely resemble ideal observer theories in metaethics, and indeed one variant of that metaethic just is an informed desire theory—but not of well-being, but of the metaphysics of value. One could take an informed desire account to fill both the metaethical and normative-ethical roles, but that requires a different sort of argument.[11] Showing, using conventional arguments involving experience machines and the like, that getting what you would want under ideal conditions is what's good for you may rescue us from the clutches of hedonism and Aristotelianism, but it doesn't solve any metaphysical problems at all. Because, again, that claim could rest on any metaphysical foundation. Just as any theory of well-being could be founded on an informed desire theory about the metaphysics of value. (Maybe what we'd want if informed is Aristotelian flourishing.) Put another way, the metaphysical problem is: what makes it the case that a given theory of well-being, such as a desire theory, is true? Establishing a desire theory of well-being gets you zero mileage on that question.

The motivational argument—viz., that desire theories ensure a link between well-being and motivation—has more to recommend it. But it is not obviously compelling, as it is not clear why well-being *should* bear any essential connection with the individual's motives. Granting, as a Humean probably should, that values generally need to connect somehow with *somebody's* motivation, why does your well-being have to be something you care about? One reason would be if the concept of well-being necessarily served to structure your deliberations about how to live. But that sort of claim is more naturally found among the ancient eudaimonists, who notably were not given to desire theories, perhaps because desire seems too flimsy a foundation for the ethical life. But even if well-being isn't the target of all your deliberations, it might be thought necessarily to be one of your targets, and hence something you must care about. Perhaps, but again this isn't obvious, and I've no inclination to buy it.

---

[11] One difference is that informed desire theories of well-being are normally relativized to the individual, whereas response-dependent theories in metaethics are more plausible when relativized to some larger population, or to humans or rational beings generally. You probably don't want the right theory of well-being to depend on the individual, for instance.

In fact, it is at least arguable that the notion of well-being is mainly a *third-personal* notion: a notion we employ chiefly to regulate our dealings with others.[12] When and whom do we help? How do we best look after our children? It is easier to see a need for the notion of well-being here than in thinking about our own lives.[13] (And where it does seem to have specially first-personal significance, which seems mainly to involve cases where non-first-personal concerns are salient: have I sacrificed too much in helping others?) And in those contexts, it seems if anything as if well-being *shouldn't* be essentially connected to the individual's motivation: as every parent and pet-owner knows, what the individual wants and what's good for her are often rather different things.

Perhaps the motivational argument is just a variant of the concern for agent sovereignty: it's my life, and what's good for me is for me to judge. Given that, my well-being has to be grounded in my concerns, and can't be completely unmotivating for me. This argument has some force but not, in my view, a whole lot: once we recognize the moral demands for respecting agent sovereignty, and allow that this may call for a great deal of deference toward individuals' judgments about their lives—to the point, perhaps, that we should refrain even from privately judging them to be wrong—then it is not clear what more we could need. The basic argument here seems to concern paternalism, but it is difficult to see what could possibly be paternalistic about an objective theory of well-being, as has often been noted. If that's the way things are, then that's the way things are—no insult to anyone's sovereignty. (Note that more than a few Aristotelians are libertarians.) Paternalism can arise only, if at all, in the application.

Is there a better argument for the desire theory? Perhaps the strongest, and the one that explains the appeal of the motivational argument, has to do with *alienation*. The thought here is that if what's good for me could be utterly divorced from my concerns, then that's an intolerably alienating view of well-being. It makes well-being too loosely connected with me, so that what's good for me need not suit me, and that seems wrong. Non-alienation seems a plausible constraint on a theory of well-being, and I happily endorse it.[14] The question is whether that constraint really supports a desire theory.

---

[12] Here see John Stuhr's rejection of the adequacy of both first-person and third-person accounts of human flourishing, "Flourishing: Toward Clearer Ideas and Habits of Geninus," this volume.

[13] Scanlon makes similar observations but goes further, casting doubt on the need for any single notion of well-being. Tiberius emphasizes the case of helping friends in defending a value-fulfillment theory of well-being.

[14] Non-alienation is often framed as a "resonance constraint," a seminal source being Railton, *Facts and Values*.

It does seem, at least, to rule out strongly objectivist views like the Moorean private-ownership theory, which seems only to require the conjunction of an individual with something that is, quite independently from his personal characteristics, a good thing. It also appears incompatible with views that, like Aristotle's, ground a person's well-being at least somewhat independently of what that individual is like, for instance in species norms.

Actually, it might also rule out desire theories, at least in their more basic forms. Take the case of alien desires, which are, nonetheless, desires. Is it good for you, at least to some extent, to fulfill your weird urge to touch the hot stove? Perhaps *you* don't think so. Yet you desire it all the same, and perhaps would continue to desire it given full information, reflection, etc. It's just stuck in your head and there's no ridding yourself of it. Similarly, you might crave money, power, status, and a gold iWatch, just for their own sakes, as you've been conditioned to crave such things, yet see those desires as having no reason-giving force whatever, and their fulfillment as bringing no benefit.

Perhaps alien desires are less alien to us than are species norms that have zero grip on us as individuals, just as the norms of bull-hood have no grip on gentle Ferdinand, who would rather smell flowers than fight.[15] But they seem, as the name suggests, to be alien all the same. If we are concerned with either agent sovereignty or non-alienation, then we need some way to claim that alien desires don't count. Perhaps an "ideal advisor" account might serve, though it seems we could imagine that you and ideal advisor both are afflicted, not just with disagreeable cravings, but with the disagreeable urge to advise others to fulfill such cravings (Railton, *Facts and Values*). At any rate, the move leaves unanswered the question of why the adviser's advice is supposed to carry more authority. Is your adviser channeling the will of the gods? Clearly, the adviser is standing in for some part of you, or variant of you, that has the requisite authority, but that's just to restate the problem. A more rewarding response is suggested by the name of the problem itself: identify the desires that matter with the part of you that decidedly isn't alien—*you*; that is, your true self.

In what is probably not a coincidence, it happens that the most popular views of the self in the philosophical literature center on some subset of our desires, such as our higher order desires, or our values.[16] (At least,

---

[15] From the children's story, *Ferdinand the Bull*.

[16] E.g., Doris, *Talking to Our Selves*; Frankfurt, "*Freedom* of the Will and the Concept of a Person"; Frankfurt, "Identification and Wholeheartedness"; Shoemaker, "Ecumenical Attributability"; Sripada, "Self-Expression: A Deep Self Theory of Moral Responsibility"; Watson, "Free Agency"; Wolf, "Sanity and the Metaphysics of Responsibility."

when talking about thicker notions of the self than numerical identity.) Who you are, roughly, is defined by what you care about. So, for example, you act freely when you act of your own volition, motivated in accordance with your higher-order desires. Or, you are autonomous or self-directed when guided in your actions by your own values. Working with this conception of self, we might say that alien desires fail to benefit, when fulfilled, because they don't reflect the true self: they don't reflect our values. And what's good for us is not just getting the object of any old whim or want, but getting the things we care about—the things we regard as giving us reasons. (Or, alternatively, getting the things we would value under ideal conditions.) So we handle the problem of alien desires by shifting the account of well-being to focus on those desires that constitute the self.[17]

We seem to have arrived, again, at a self-fulfillment approach to well-being, again starting from one of the classically "subjectivist" approaches that have traditionally been posed in opposition to eudaimonistic views. Admittedly, one could defend a desire theory that focuses on values, and thus dispatches alien desires and the like, without going this route. Recently Tiberius[18] and Raibley[19] have defended "value-fulfillment" theories that do not rely explicitly on reasoning about the self. This is understandable—why drag in problematic machinery if you can get results without it? But we seem already to need an account of the self in other domains, such as autonomy and responsible agency, and self-fulfillment approaches—and nature-fulfillment views more generally—have substantial independent attractions. Arguably, the best explanation for the attractions of a value-fulfillment account is a tacit appeal to ideals of self-fulfillment. Consider, for example, the loss of a spouse or child: even if you manage eventually to adapt emotionally and be as happy as you were before, it may still seem as though there is a lasting deficiency in your life: you remain worse off. A natural explanation is that you strongly value that person, and your relationship, and so are worse off in part because your life is missing something you deeply care about. The death has left a major gap in your life. Indeed, you may feel as if a large part of your *self* is missing, and the bereaved often report that it seems as if they've lost a limb.

---

[17] I do not claim agents always have a firm grip on their values, and it is entirely possible to sincerely endorse views that stand in conflict with one's values (e.g., a generous but benighted person who claims to value selfishness). In that case, one's own express views might prove to be alien, clashing with who one really is. Shifting a desire theory to center on values may not, then, preserve the kind of agent sovereignty many subjectivists hope for. This seems to me a virtue of the approach.

[18] Tiberius, Valerie. *Well-Being as Value Fulfillment.*

[19] Raibley, "Well-Being and the Priority of Values"; "Values, Agency, and Welfare."

This is arguably because you are in fact defined partly by the values in question, and so a significant part of the self is going unfulfilled. A similar phenomenology attends other major disruptions in people's lives: the failure of a career, being uprooted from one's home, community or culture, having to perform abhorrent acts to prevent even worse outcomes, and so on.[20] These—call them "core commitment failures"—are in fact among the gravest harms human beings can suffer, and can permanently mar or even ruin lives. For the values that define, in part, who we are and the way we structure our lives, have effectively had the rug pulled out from under them, leaving lives organized around now-empty goals. You become, to a significant extent, a person without a point—with one less reason for living.[21]

Note also that value-fulfillment views face significant pressure to incorporate an authenticity requirement: it would be odd, at least, to take well-being to consist in success regarding the things you care about—not just things you feel some craving for, say—and then deem it a matter of indifference whether your values are genuinely *yours* and not merely the products of brainwashing, manipulation, or neural tinkering. Indeed such values would themselves seem to be alien; in any event, it is unclear what could be the rationale for excluding whims, cravings and the like, but not the products of brainwashing. It seems that what matters is not, strictly speaking, value-fulfillment, but *authentic* value-fulfillment. And the notion of authenticity is most at home in a eudaimonistic framework, where well-being is grounded in the character of the self.[22]

[20] See Doris's discussion of Ishi, the last of his tribe, in *Talking to Our Selves*. There are interesting questions about the differences between failing to fulfill the self and actually losing part of the self. While people often speak as if the latter is the case rather than the former, it isn't clear why this should be so in the sorts of examples we are considering: you still value your spouse, so in what sense is a part of you literally lost? Such thinking may be somewhat confused, though Doris suggests that, with great enough losses, you lose the ability to maintain your values, and hence literally lose your self.

[21] As this remark suggests, value-fulfillment appears closely linked to the idea of a meaningful life: our values mark out at least part of what gives our lives meaning. Perhaps this thought lends further support to the self-fulfillment view, but I will not pursue it here.

[22] I argue at greater length for this in Haybron, "Happiness and Pleasure"; Haybron, *The Pursuit of Unhappiness: The Elusive Psychology of Well-Being*; and Haybron, "Flourishing and the Value of Authenticity." Grounding value-fulfillment in the self may also help address difficulties regarding "conative collapse" in certain cases of depression, where a person might lose all desires; see Tiberius, this volume, and Tully, Depression and the Problem of Absent Desires." It does seem beneficial, as she suggests, to restore such a person's capacities for valuing, but the benefit depends on whether those capacities, and the resulting values, are consistent with who that individual is. Suppose Eeyore to be in conative collapse: he no longer has any goals. You could give him an operation to "fix" that, but in one case you restore him to something recognizably related to his old conative nature, while in the other you equip him for a totally new set of goals, so now he's like Tigger. I take it that something important is lost in the latter transformation—namely, Eeyore. Whatever value-fulfillment Neo-Eeyore achieves seems less worth having, because the values aren't really his; they aren't authentic.

Aristotelian Nature-Fulfillment

Suppose now that you are drawn to some nature-fulfillment or eudaimonistic account of well-being. For the most part, such theories have not been grounded explicitly in any conception of the self. Aristotelian views, for instance, focus on the fulfillment of our species natures—one's nature *qua* human being—specifically through the idea of capacity-fulfillment, for instance realizing one's human potential through a life of excellent, characteristically human activity. Both of these features of the Aristotelian approach are problematic: even if well-being isn't subjective, the concerns about alienation noted earlier suggest that it must depend wholly on your individual characteristics, not on the norms for whatever species you're classified under. While there do seem to be intuitions to the contrary, for instance that the inability to enjoy goods that are normally part of human life such as sight is a lamentable deprivation, these might be explained in terms of a moral concern for equity—that no one be left out in the enjoyment of important goods that are ordinarily possessed. And the mere fact that you have the potential or capacity for something seems orthogonal to the question of whether it will benefit you, unless somehow you desire it or would welcome it. Even if it is independently valuable, whatever reasons you might have to pursue it may fall entirely under the heading of self-sacrifice.

These are not unfamiliar points and I will not argue for them at length here.[23] It suffices to note that the appeal of nature-fulfillment ideals of well-being does not hinge on the ideas of species nature or capacity-fulfillment, and there are plausible grounds for rejecting such notions.

Nature-fulfillment might instead be understood in subject-dependent terms—as grounded in the individual's arbitrarily idiosyncratic nature—and in terms of goal-fulfillment, where goals are understood broadly to include tendencies to respond positively to things—with joy or pleasure, say.[24] A natural thought is that the relevant goals are given by the nature of the *self*: the aspect of your nature that matters for well-being is the part that defines you as a person, as who you are—the character of your soul. Indeed, if we take the language at face value then it seems that strictly speaking your nature must be the nature you have *qua* person: what makes you *you*. This is all the

[23] But see Haybron, "Well-Being and Virtue"; Haybron, *The Pursuit of Unhappiness: The Elusive Psychology of Well-Being*.

[24] See Tiberius, "Well-Being, Value Fulfillment, and Valuing Capacities: Toward a More Subjective Hybrid," this volume.

more credible given that, as we just saw, the self is plausibly conceived in terms of the individual's goals: her values, and what makes her happy. In this way the ideal of nature-fulfillment naturally takes the more specific form of self-fulfillment.

Whether or not the nature-fulfillment theorist is persuaded to reject a focus on species norms and capacity-fulfillment, this much seems hard to avoid: if what's good for you is fulfilling your nature—living in a way that suits your nature—then it would be exceedingly odd to deny at least this: that your nature is at least *partly* given by the nature of your self. Indeed, one would veer sharply toward incoherence to adopt a view of the self, for instance as defined by some subset of one's desires, and then to cash out well-being in terms of the fulfillment of some nature you have that is independent of the self, in this case of your desires or values. What's good for you is to fulfill your nature, and yet this has nothing to do with who you are: such a claim is at the very least bizarre, and perhaps nonsensical. If your nature isn't at least partly a function of what constitutes *you*, then in what sense is this *your* nature? Perhaps: it is a nature that you possess, signified by qualifying reference to it as for instance your nutritive (physiological) or animal nature. But unless one takes a very strange position on the self, these cannot be all there is to your nature, if they are any part of it at all: they leave *you*, or at least a large part of you, out of the picture—namely the part that we can refer to without any qualifier, as "your nature," period.

The nature-fulfillment theorist has two options. One is to take up a skeptical position on the self, denying that there is such a thing and thus liberating themselves from any need to consider its nature. This would seem to be an unnatural juxtaposition of views, however, particularly as nature-fulfillment theorists are not noted for a fondness for desert landscapes. Thomistic theorists for their part would be in hot water if they took an eliminativist stance on the soul, and nontheistic Aristotelians hang rather a lot on airy abstractions like species norms to adopt a hard-nosed empiricism—or whatever it would be—about more earthy notions like the self which, as we saw in Section 2, requires nothing more than that we are not trapped in a nightmare skeptical scenario. The other option is to take the self seriously, incorporating the notion of self-fulfillment as at least part of the theory of well-being. I see no reason why Aristotelians couldn't make such a move, and arguably some do, though again explicit discussion of the nature of the self as constraining the character of well-being in that literature remains thin on the ground.[25] For example, an Aristotelian might incorporate a conception of self-fulfillment as a matter of authentic happiness and/or value-fulfillment, but add further provisions such as that one's self-fulfillment must involve objectively worthwhile activities, realizing one's human capacities, and include the full suite of characteristically human goods. So your well-being depends partly on who you are, but not entirely: Hannibal Lecter-style self-fulfillment does not constitute flourishing.

It is arguable, then, that the most prominent approaches to well-being, with the exception perhaps of list theories, are founded on insights that naturally lead us to the conclusion that well-being hinges on the nature of the self and involves some notion of self-fulfillment.

The Piggybacking Argument

I just noted that nature-fulfillment theorists are in a funny position if they take a certain view of the self, for instance as constituted by certain desires, while ignoring that view in their accounts of well-being. While the result is especially awkward for them, the basic problem generalizes, and we can call it the "piggybacking" argument, in that the ideal of self-fulfillment in thinking about well-being naturally rides piggyback on our commitments about the self in other realms. *If you have committed to some substantive conception of the self, then your theory of well-being needs to cohere with it.* Suppose, to take an example, that you think free, or autonomous, or responsible agency cannot be driven wholly by uncontrollable urges, compulsions or other desires conventionally regarded as alien, and that this is because one's agency needs to be *self*-determined.[26] That is, presumably, you think some motives reflect the self, while others do not. More broadly, you think certain psychological features reflect, or define, the self. And yet, turning to questions of well-being, you leave that view completely behind. For example, suppose you take the self to be defined by one's values: who you are is defined by what you care about. To the extent someone acts from her values, she is autonomous, etc. With this view in hand, would it then make sense to endorse *hedonism* about well-being? This would be an unseemly pairing of ideas, having the consequence that what's good for us could be utterly at odds with who we are.

---

[25] There are exceptions, e.g. Russell, *Happiness for Humans*.
[26] See the earlier references to desire-based theories of the self for discussion.

Someone like Nietzsche, for example, might be firmly committed to nonhedonistic ideals, indeed believing flourishing to consist in a life of passionate, often unpleasant, struggle. On the present view, that's *who he is*: were he to convert to Benthamite hedonism, that would be a deep change in personality; he'd be a different person. As it is, hedonism counsels him to reject those ideals, and hence his very identity—indeed, his integrity—to lead a more pleasant existence. Perhaps he'll need a lot of really good pills, or a lobotomy, to make that happen, but it's the life hedonism would recommend for him. It is not an attractive position, it seems to me, to claim that the pleasant life is completely at odds with who a person is, and yet it is in leading precisely that sort of life that his flourishing consists.[27] Note that the claim here isn't just that, all things considered, prudence counsels living in conflict with who he is. That claim is not obviously problematic, since we might think some people just have conflicted selves, for instance having values that clash with other aspects of their personalities. In those cases, one might have no choice but to live in ways that don't entirely suit who one is. Rather, the case at hand involves a much stronger claim: that what's good for us has *nothing at all to do with who we are*. Because the self is defined wholly by one's values, while one's well-being involves nothing more than pleasure. There's nothing to regret, so far as prudential value goes, about lobotomized Nietzsche, except perhaps that one's surgical methods couldn't alter him even more radically, to experience still more pleasure. It is hard not to suspect that Nietzsche might have preferred that a friend take a cue from *One Flew Over the Cuckoo's Nest* and put him out of his bliss, as it were.

It is arguable, then, that one's account of well-being should accord with one's account of the self. Perhaps it is not obvious that this commits us to a self-fulfillment view, and strictly speaking it doesn't. But all the ideal of self-fulfillment requires is some notion of the self and the claim that prudential value depends on fulfilling ideals derived from the constitution of that self. It is very hard to see how that could fail to obtain if we require that our views of self and well-being accord with each other.

Suppose, for example, that you think the self is defined by an individual's desires, and that well-being consists in desire satisfaction.[28] Your theory of well-being, then, obviously coheres in some natural sense with your theory

---

[27] The point remains if we use more neutral terms like "well-being," but that term doesn't clearly denote a very high level of welfare.

[28] I'm switching to "desire satisfaction" terminology to avoid worries about equivocation over the meaning of "fulfillment."

of the self. It is admittedly conceivable that this is mere coincidence, or that the account of self derives from the account of well-being, rather than the other way around. But coincidence is rankly implausible, and the arguments of this chapter strongly suggest that our understanding of the self does not simply derive from some prior understanding of well-being. As our understanding of who a person is varies, so does our sense of what would benefit her. It is much rarer, if it happens at all, to encounter reasoning from what's good for a person to conclusions about who she is. Note as well that if this were the order of explanation then many accounts of autonomy, free will and responsible agency, being grounded in views of the self, would likewise derive from the theory of well-being, and theorizing about such matters would need to be far more attentive to the well-being literature than it has been. A final possibility is that self and well-being are mutually dependent, with neither being prior to the other. But that just is a form of the self-fulfillment approach, which requires only that well-being be dependent on the self. It does not rule out that the character of the self also depends on facts about well-being.

These reflections may not impress those uncommitted to any view of the self, but many philosophers are so committed. And it is quite possible that many of those without such commitments simply haven't had occasion to put much thought into it, having not worked on issues, like autonomy, where talk of the self is hard to avoid. In any event, theorists of well-being need to attend to questions of self, whether drawn to eudaimonistic theories or not.

Many philosophers are understandably wary of theorizing about the self, but I hope it is reasonably clear that it is something we cannot easily do without. Consider also how important questions of self, particularly identity, are in moral and political thought, where it is widely deemed crucial to take people's identities seriously. (Here I take it that identity is congruent with the self properly speaking, and is not merely a self-conception along the lines of Huck Finn.) To require that someone act contrary to commitments that define her identity, for instance, is ordinarily thought to do her a grave harm, undermining her integrity.[29] Similarly, policies that leave people unable to live in accordance with their identities, such as prohibitions on religious practice, are widely considered to be deeply problematic, at least partly because they frustrate, in very deep ways, people's ability to lead good lives.

---

[29] E.g. see Williams, "A Critique of Utilitarianism," 77–150.

It is understandable that philosophers should be reluctant to wade into the dark waters of the self. But I don't see that we really have any choice.

Conclusion

I have argued that a wide range of philosophical commitments lead us to the same conclusion: human well-being hinges centrally on the nature of the self, so that well-being at least partly consists in self-fulfillment. Theories of well-being must be constrained by our understanding of the self. In other work I've suggested that the self is defined partly by one's emotional nature— what makes one authentically happy—and partly by what I now think of as a person's values (Haybron, "Happiness, the Self and Human Flourishing"; Haybron, *The Pursuit of Unhappiness: The Elusive Psychology of Well-Being.*). Accordingly, I am inclined to think well-being consists at least partly in authentic happiness and value-fulfillment. You might conceive of the self differently.[30] No matter: if you also find plausible a different view of well-being—one that more closely fits with your understanding of the self—then that might be a good sign that we've nailed down a central feature of the structure of well-being.

References

Annas, Julia. *The Morality of Happiness*. Oxford University Press, 1993.

Brink, David O. "Prudence and Authenticity: Intrapersonal Conflicts of Value." *Philosophical Review*, vol. 112, no. 2, 2003, pp. 215–45. https://doi.org/10.1215/00318 108-112-2-215

Clark, Samuel. "Pleasure as Self-Discovery." *Ratio*, vol. 25, no. 3, 2012, pp. 260–76. https://doi.org/10.1111/j.1467-9329.2012.00541.x

Clark, Samuel. "Narrative, Self-Realization, and the Shape of a Life." *Ethical Theory and Moral Practice*, vol. 21, no. 2, 2018, pp. 371–85. https://doi.org/10.1007/s10 677-018-9885-7

De Freitas, Julian, Mina Cikara, Igor Grossmann, and Rebecca Schlegel. "Origins of the Belief in Good True Selves." *Trends in Cognitive Sciences*, vol. 21, no. 9, 2017, pp. 634–36. https://doi.org/10.1016/j.tics.2017.05.009

[30] Compare, for example, Mark Johnson's account of homeostasis, allostasis, and flourishing as dependent on the conditions of survival of an organism, "Flourishing in the Flesh," this volume.

Dennett, D. C. "The Self as a Center of Narrative Gravity." *Self and Consciousness: Multiple Perspectives*, edited by F. Kessel, P. Cole, and D. Johnson. Psychology Press, 1992, pp. 103–15. Retrieved from http://www.citebase.org/abstract?id=37012428

Doris, John M. *Talking to Our Selves*. Oxford University Press, 2015. https://doi.org/10.1093/acprof:oso/9780199570393.001.0001

Epictetus. *The Discourses as Reported by Arrian, The Manual, and Fragments*. Harvard University Press, 1925.

Frankfurt, Harry. "Freedom of the Will and the Concept of a Person." *Journal of Philosophy*, vol. 68, no. 1, 1971, pp. 5–20.

Frankfurt, Harry. "Identification and Wholeheartedness." Responsibility, Character, and the Emotions, edited by Ferdinand Schoeman. Cambridge University Press, 1987, pp. 27–45.

Gallagher, Shaun. *The Oxford Handbook of the Self*. Oxford University Press, 2013. Retrieved from http://books.google.com/books?id=ueDTmQEACAAJ&dq=intitle:THE+OXFORD+HANDBOOK+OF+the+self&hl=&cd=1&source=gbs_api

Gewirth, Alan. *Self-Fulfillment*. Princeton University Press, 2009. Retrieved from http://books.google.com/books?hl=en&lr=&id=bvzxaB5KDUsC&oi=fnd&pg=PP1&dq=SELF+FULFILLMENT&ots=5f2g4xvo56&sig=EAQvMbXOt-qPGC2ScjwZjXW2Sgo

Hawkins, Jennifer. "Well-Being, the Self, and Radical Change." *Oxford Studies in Normative Ethics Volume 9*, edited by Mark Timmons. Oxford University Press, 2019, pp. 251–70. https://doi.org/10.1093/oso/9780198846253.003.0012

Haybron, D. M. "Happiness and Pleasure." *Philosophy and Phenomenological Research*, vol. 62, no. 3, 2001, pp. 501–28.

Haybron, D. M. "On Being Happy or Unhappy." *Philosophy and Phenomenological Research*, vol. 71, no. 2, 2005, pp. 287–317.

Haybron, D. M. "Well-Being and Virtue." *Journal of Ethics and Social Philosophy*, vol. 2, no. 2, 2007, pp. 1–27. Retrieved from http://heinonlinebackup.com/hol-cgi-bin/get_pdf.cgi?handle=hein.journals/jetshy2§ion=9

Haybron, D. M. "Happiness, the Self and Human Flourishing." *Utilitas*, vol. 20, no. 1, 2008a, pp. 21–49. https://doi.org/10.1017/S0953820807002889

Haybron, D. M. *The Pursuit of Unhappiness: The Elusive Psychology of Well-Being*. Oxford University Press, 2008b. Retrieved from http://books.google.com.ezp.slu.edu/books?hl=en&lr=&id=jAEBzgqniMAC&oi=fnd&pg=PR7&dq=The+pursuit+of+unhappiness+The+elusive+psychology+of+well+being+Haybron&ots=q3WfzVdo4C&sig=v5Vn1JcVPClU4dfxe9qgWgC5NY4

Haybron, D. M. "Adventures in Assisted Living: Well-Being and Situationist Psychology." *The Philosophy and Psychology of Character and Happiness*, edited by Nancy Snow and Franco Trivigno. Routledge, 2014, pp. 1–25.

Haybron, D. M. "Mental State Approaches to Well-Being." *The Oxford Handbook of Well-Being and Public Policy*, edited by M. D. Adler and M. Fleurbaey. Oxford University Press, 2016, pp. 347–78. https://doi.org/10.1093/oxfordhb/9780199325818.013.11

Haybron, D. M. "Flourishing and the Value of Authenticity." *Human Flourishing in an Age of Gene Editing*, edited by Erik Parens and Josephine Johnston. Oxford Scholarship Online, 2019, pp. 29–45. Retrieved from https://www.oxfordscholarship.com/view/10.1093/oso/9780190940362.001.0001/oso-9780190940362-chapter-3

Ivanhoe, Philip J., editor. *The Oneness Hypothesis: Beyond the Boundary of Self*. Columbia University Press, 2018.

Raibley, Jason. "Well-Being and the Priority of Values." *Social Theory & Practice*, vol. 36, no. 4, Oct. 2010, pp. 593–620.

Raibley, Jason. "Values, Agency, and Welfare." *Philosophical Topics*, vol. 41, no. 1, 2013, pp. 187–214. https://doi.org/10.5840/philtopics20134119

Railton, Peter. "Facts and Values," *Philosophical Topics*, vol. 14, no. 2, Fall 1986, pp. 5–31.

Russell, Daniel. *Happiness for Humans*. Oxford University Press, 2013.

Scanlon, T. *What We Owe to Each Other*. Harvard: Belknap Press, 1999.

Shoemaker, David. "Ecumenical Attributability." *The Nature of Moral Responsibility: New Essays*, edited by Randolph Clarke, Michael McKenna, and Angela Smith. Oxford Scholarship Online, 2015, pp. 115–40.

Sripada, Chandra. "Self-Expression: A Deep Self Theory of Moral Responsibility." *Philosophical Studies*, vol. 173, no. 5, Aug. 2015, pp. 1203–32. https://doi.org/10.1007/s11098-015-0527-9

Strohminger, Nina, Joshua Knobe, and George Newman. "The True Self: A Psychological Concept Distinct from the Self." *Perspectives on Psychological Science*, vol. 1, no. 4, 2017, pp. 551–60.

Sumner, Wayne. *Welfare, Happiness, and Ethics*. Oxford University Press, 1996.

Syed, Moin, Colin Deyoung, and Valerie Tiberius. "Self, Motivation, and Virtue, or How We Learned to Stop Worrying and Love Deep Integration." *Self, Motivation, and Virtue: Innovative Interdisciplinary Research*, edited by Nancy Snow and Darcia Narvaez. Routledge, 2019, p. 10.

Tiberius, Valerie. *Well-Being as Value Fulfillment*. Oxford Scholarship Online, 2018. Retrieved from http://books.google.com/books?id=mrRwDwAAQBAJ&printsec=frontcover&dq=intitle:Well+Being+As+Value+Fulfillment&hl=&cd=1&source=gbs_api

Tully, I. "Depression and the Problem of Absent Desires." *Journal of Ethics and Social Philosophy*, vol. 11, no. 2, 2017, pp. 1–16. https://doi.org/10.26556/jesp.v11i2.110

Višak, Tatjana. "Sacrifices of Self Are Prudential Harms: A Reply to Carbonell." *Journal of Ethics*, vol. 19, no. 2, 2015, pp. 219–29. https://doi.org/10.1007/s10892-015-9196-3

Watson, Gary. "Free Agency." *Journal of Philosophy*, vol. 72, no. 8, 1975, pp. 205–20.

Williams, Bernard. "A Critique of Utilitarianism." *Utilitarianism: For and Against*, edited by J.J.C. Smart and Bernard Williams., Cambridge University Press, 1973, pp. 77–150.

Wolf, Susan. "Sanity and the Metaphysics of Responsibility." *Responsibility, Character, and the Emotions: New Essays in Moral Psychology*, edited by Ferdinand Schoeman. Cambridge University Press, 1987, pp. 46–62.

Yelle, Benjamin. "Alienation, Deprivation, and the Well-being of Persons." *Utilitas*, vol. 26, no. 04, Dec. 2014, pp. 367–84. https://doi.org/10.1017/S095382081400017X

5

Well-Being, Value Fulfillment, and Valuing Capacities

Toward a More Subjective Hybrid

Valerie Tiberius

Introduction

Is well-being entirely relative to an individual person so that someone could be flourishing despite the fact that no one else in their community sees their life as worthwhile? Or are there objective constraints on what it is to flourish? Could a person achieve well-being if they have devoted their life to counting blades of grass or to becoming the best assassin they can be? Can someone flourish whose life contains no meaningful relationships? Or are meaningful work, moral virtue, and relationships necessary for well-being, no matter what? If they are necessary, could something really make a person's life go better, if she has absolutely no interest in it and would never come to develop one? This debate about whether well-being is subjective or objective is one of the central debates about well-being in analytic philosophy.

It is an important and philosophically interesting debate, but I think that the trenches have been dug too deep. The battle has consisted largely in lobbing nasty counterexamples back and forth: subjective theories throw the happy under-achiever who doesn't want the objectively good knowledge or achievement allegedly required for their flourishing; objective theories throw the perfectly satisfied, immoral mobster who "surely" cannot be said to be flourishing. Each side has its standard responses and few defect from their side. Even the recent addition of hybrid theories respects the lines that have been drawn. These theories take a tenet from each side and put them together, by arguing that well-being consists in the subjective appreciation of the objective good. With the battle lines drawn so clearly, it's difficult to recognize that some theories might actually sit quite close to the line.

Valerie Tiberius, *Well-Being, Value Fulfillment, and Valuing Capacities* In: *Philosophy and Human Flourishing*. Edited by: John J. Stuhr, Oxford University Press. © Oxford University Press 2023.
DOI: 10.1093/oso/9780197622162.003.0006

In this essay, I want to argue that the best version of the subjective theory I favor—the value fulfillment theory—actually sits on this line between subjectivism and objectivism. To do that, I'll need to explain the distinction between subjective and objective theories, introduce the value fulfillment theory, and show why it has one foot in the objectivist camp. I'll conclude with a discussion of what's at stake in the debate, and whether the value fulfillment theory preserves what's important.

Preliminaries

Since L. W. Sumner's highly influential book, *Welfare Happiness and Ethics*, philosophers working on the topic of well-being have distinguished subjective theories from objective theories by appeal to subjective attitudes. Subjective theories hold that a person must have a positive attitude (hypothetical, on some views) toward something for that thing to count as good for a person. Desire satisfaction theories are a classic case of a subjective theory, because they make prudential good dependent on a person's desires. According to desire satisfaction theory, well-being is getting what you want, or (on some views) getting what you would want under certain idealized conditions (Heathwood "Desire Satisfactionism" 539–64; Railton "Moral Realism" 163–207; Railton "Facts and Values" 5–31).

Objective theories deny the subjectivist claim; instead, they hold that something could be good for a person even absent any actual or hypothetical positive attitude on her part. Objective list theories are the paradigm example here, because they hold that certain objective goods like knowledge, pleasure, and achievement, are good for a person whether or not she wants them or would want them under hypothetical conditions (Finnis 2011; Rice 196–211).

Perfectionist theories, according to which it is good for us to develop our essentially human capacities, are also in the objectivist camp. Perfectionism, the descendent of Aristotle's eudaimonist theory, does not take our positive attitudes toward the development of our social or rational nature to be necessary for this development to count as good for us (Bradford "Problems" 244–364). I find it helpful to think about the distinction between subjective and objective theories of well-being in terms of the explanations they offer for the goodness of prudential values. On the former, that explanation ultimately makes reference to human attitudes. According to Aristotelian perfectionism, the explanation bottoms out in the facts about human nature and does not make reference to our subjective attitudes.

Objective theories of both types—objective list and perfectionism—have a similar unintuitive implication, namely, that some objective good (such as knowledge or the development of a capacity) could be good for a person even if it doesn't resonate with that person in any way. This possibility invites us to think up examples of hermits being forced to socialize or chill surfer dudes being required to achieve something meaningful for their own good. These intuitions fuel what has come to be called the "resonance constraint," a widely accepted constraint on well-being theories that is often used as part of an argument for subjectivism (Railton "Moral Realism" 166–207; Dorsey, "Why Should Welfare 'Fit'?" 685–24). Notice that a theory that ensures that what is good for a person "resonates" with them is one that is well suited to account for individual differences, which is a theoretical constraint that concerns psychologists (DeYoung and Tiberius, unpublished manuscript).

In response to this problem, and the general attractiveness of the idea that a person should not be alienated from her own good, objective theories have introduced hybrid versions of their theories. Richard Kraut defends a version of perfectionism (which he calls "developmentalism") according to which human flourishing consists in the possession, development, and *enjoyment* of our physical, cognitive, affective, sensory, and social powers (*What Is Good and Why* 137). Guy Fletcher's version of objective list theory insists that the objective goods (his list includes achievement, friendship, happiness, pleasure, self-respect, and virtue) "all have pro-attitudes as *necessary* components," that is, possessing these goods essentially involves various endorsements, desires, and affections (216).

Both of these modified objective theories have pursued the same strategy. They retain the objectivist explanation for the prudential goodness of the list of goods or the development of our capacities, and they add subjective appreciation of these goods.[1] Fletcher's objective list theory does not take positive subjective attitudes to be part of the explanation of the good-for relation; they are a component of the good itself. Similarly, Kraut's perfectionism takes the explanation for the goodness of developing our capacities to have to do with our human nature; it is not to be explained by our enjoyment of it, though enjoyment is included in the development of our

---

[1] These theories are similar to Susan Wolf's theory of meaning in life as what arises when "subjective attraction meets objective attractiveness" (1997: 211).

human capacities. Nevertheless, both theories seem more plausible because of these modifications. They have taken the most compelling feature of subjectivism—its respect for the resonance constraint—and found a way to build it into their theories.

I think this is a good strategy. In the well-being battle, we may be better off negotiating and learning from the other side than continuing to fight in the counterexample filled trenches.[2] However, it seems to me that so far in the negotiations, the objectivist camp has had more of their demands met. Can the same strategy be used by subjectivists? Could a subjective theory of well-being learn from the attacks from the other camp and yet retain the best of subjectivism? That is the question I turn to next.

Value Fulfillment and Human Nature

In order to explore this path for subjectivism, I'll start with a description of the specific subjective theory I favor, the value fulfillment theory. Value fulfillment or value realization theories take well-being to consist in the fulfillment or realization of one's own values. It can be helpful to think of value fulfillment theory as a development out of desire satisfaction theories. According to desire satisfaction theories, what is good for a person is getting what she wants, that is, obtaining the objects of her desires (as opposed to the mere feeling of satisfaction). Similarly, according to value fulfillment theory, what is good for a person is actually succeeding in terms of what she values. Not everyone agrees about the nature of values, but two of the main proponents of the view (myself and Jason Raibley) agree that they are complex patterns of attitudes including emotional dispositions, motivations, and judgments about what one has reason to do or to plan for (Tiberius "Beyond the Experience Machine" 398–415; Tiberius Well-being as Value Fulfillment; Raibley "Well-Being and the Priority of Values"; see Dorsey "Subjectivism without Desire" for a contrasting view).[3] For example, to value a friendship is to be disposed to want to spend time with your friend, to feel joy when you

2 Many of the authors of other chapters in this volume pursue a different but related strategy by rejecting the sharp distinction between subjective and objective theories of the prudential good and the assumptions that give rise to this distinction. From the perspective of this strategy, what is most striking about both subjective and objective theories is their common assumptions rather than the different inferences they draw from these assumptions.

3 See also John Z. Sadler's analysis of values as attitudes or tendencies to do things which the agent likes or does not like, "Values Literacy and Citizenship," this volume.

spend time together, and to think that the friendship warrants attention in your plans for how to spend your time.

According to my version of the theory, well-being consists in fulfilling, actualizing, or realizing, your appropriate values over time, where "appropriate" values are psychologically fitting—suited to your desires, emotions, and judgments—and mutually sustainable (Tiberius *Well-being as Value Fulfillment*). It's worth noting that I do not think there are bright lines between mere attitudes, values, and appropriate values; these are matters of degree. Whether your attitudes toward something are integrated enough to count as your valuing it, or to count as your valuing it appropriately, is often the subject of reflection aimed at improving your life. A person who wants to spend time with her friend but finds it emotionally draining when she does, has conflicting attitudes. Depending on the strength of her attitudes and other factors, we may count her as valuing the friendship or as wanting something she doesn't value. In either case, on my view, she would be better off with the conflict resolved. We improve well-being by creating more value fulfillment and we do this, primarily, by reducing conflicts among values or between values and our environment.

Such conflicts can be reduced by changing our values entirely, but we do not often change basic values like friendship, family, and career. More often, conflicts are reduced by changing our interpretations of our values, which means changing what we take success in terms of the value to mean. For example, a person whose valued job is very demanding may learn to stop thinking that being a good parent requires baking cupcakes from scratch for the school bake sale, or a person who has three young children may decide that publishing a novel before he turns 40 is not a realistic way of thinking about how to value creativity.

Because values are subjective attitudes (beliefs, emotions, desires, or some combination, depending on the particular theory), value fulfillment theories have been classified as a type of subjective theory. According to value fulfillment theory, friendship is good for a person (if it is) because that person values friendship, not because friendship has attitude-independent or objective value.[4] Desire satisfaction theories offer the same type of explanation for the prudential value of things like friendship.

---

[4] Note that this does not mean that a person's *reasons* for valuing friendship must make reference to her own desires or values. The reasons you value a particular friendship likely have to do with features of the friend and your relationship, not with your own mental states. The point here is about the underlying philosophical explanation of the "good for" relation.

One of the main problems for all subjective theories is that our subjective attitudes can be defective in various ways. We can desire things that just don't seem intuitively to be good for anyone, such as Rawls' grass counter who wants nothing else but to count blades of grass. Subjective theories have attempted to solve this problem by appeal to idealizing constraints such as full information (Railton, "Moral Realism") or rationality (Brandt *A Theory of the Good*), a focus on ultimate rather than instrumental desires or values, and also by appeal to total subjective fulfillment over the course of a lifetime (Heathwood "The Problem"; Tiberius *Well-being as Value Fulfillment*). There are many solutions to the problems of defective desires in the literature, and when the subjectivist response runs out, so do strong intuitions about the cases. For example, if the man who wants to spend his life counting blades of grass wants this for its own sake, understands what he's doing, wants nothing else, and will never come to experience any frustration because of it, many people lose the sense that his life is not actually good *for him*. When people are so unusual that the standard subjectivist responses to the objection don't work, they are also so unusual that we don't always have clear intuitions about their well-being. Indeed, defenders of goal fulfillment theories may take it as an advantage of their theories that they respect individual differences in interests and abilities.

The problem of defective desires or values is serious, but there are adequate lines of response available for goal fulfillment theories. A different problem for subjectivist theories will be my focus, one that does not yet have a clear line of response. For obvious reasons, subjective theories have trouble accommodating the unmistakable value of mental health, physical health, and the other capacities that make valuing and value pursuit possible (Raibley "Health and Well-being"). It seems that according to goal fulfillment theories health is good if you want or value it, but not if you don't. Similarly, for the capacity to endorse, maintain, and pursue the values that you have, they are good for you if you care, but not if you don't. We might characterize this as "the problem of absent desires": goal fulfillment theories seem to give the wrong results about people who do not have desires for certain obvious goods.[5]

This might not seem like a terrible problem. (Note that as I turn to solutions, I will sometimes talk about "value fulfillment theories" in particular, when I invoke specific features of this approach, though I believe other

---

[5] See Mitchell 2020 for a related objection to my 2018.

theories in the goal fulfillment family could follow the same general strategy I describe). First, health and valuing capacities are robustly instrumentally valuable because they are necessary for pursuing other values. These are prudential goods that will increase overall value fulfillment and, so, they are goods one ought to value, insofar as one values anything that requires them. Second, given what values are, most people already value their health and their valuing capacities at least implicitly. We do tend to have positive emotional responses toward good health, and to judge that it is something we have reason to plan for and protect. Further, part of what it is to value something is to want to fulfill that value, to be concerned to succeed in its terms. So, in valuing anything we are thereby concerned about our ability to fulfill our values; caring about our capacities to fulfill our values is just part of what it is to value something.

We can go some way to addressing the problem of absent values, then, by appeal to the strong, instrumental value of these capacities and to the fact that most of us do implicitly value them already. But this only goes so far. The problem of absent desires becomes deadly when we introduce the possibility of people who have no desires at all, as may happen in severe depression. Ian Tully has recently argued, on the basis of Victor Frankl's discussion of his experiences in Nazi concentration camps, that depression can cause "complete conative collapse," a state of utter desirelessness (Tully 2016 1–15). Since goal fulfillment theories identify our good with the fulfillment of our goals, it seems that a person who has no goals (no desires or values) cannot be benefited or harmed. There is no way to make the person's life better, because they have no desires to satisfy, no values to fulfill. There is no way to make their lives worse because there are no goals to frustrate and, presumably, no aversions to be triggered. And if there are no goals, then there is nothing for the good of health (for example) to be instrumental *to*, or to ground the implicit value of our valuing capacities. As Tully points out, this implies that a guard would do no harm to a prisoner in complete conative collapse by kicking him and would bring him no benefit by treating him kindly. Goal fulfillment theories seem to imply that the person in complete conative collapse is not a welfare subject at all, and this is not a tolerable result.

I am skeptical that severe depression results in *complete* conative collapse. Such a person is not averse to pain, not averse to humiliation or torture, in any way at all, not even a little bit. This is a person who would not pull their hand away from the flame if they could, would not scratch an itch, or sit down when their legs ache, or do anything else at all. Such a person is closer to someone in a coma than to a conscious human being. And it makes sense to say about people in comas that we act toward them in order to benefit the person who persists through the coma and will eventually come out of it with desires and aversions in place.

That said, it's hard to rule out completely the possibility of a person who is conscious yet desireless. Moreover, very young children raise a similar problem for goal fulfillment theories, insofar as they do not have the kinds of capacities to set and pursue their own goals that adults have (Lin 354–77). A solution to the problem of conative collapse may also help goal fulfillment theories account for the well-being of children.

So, what can be said about this possibility of a person with no desires, goals, or values? The idea that we harm the comatose or the conatively collapsed by harming the agent who persists through time gives rise to a strategy of response sympathetic to Aristotelian nature fulfillment theories. Notice that goal fulfillment theories do have an implicit view about human nature: they think of human beings as goal pursuing creatures or, to put it in terms borrowed from personality psychology, cybernetic organisms (DeYoung 38–58). From the point of view of value fulfillment theory, our capacities to acquire, maintain, and pursue our values are special in the sense that without them nothing would be good for us. Value fulfillment theory, then, might take the having of values itself (or, more precisely, the capacities that allow us to have and pursue our values) to be a precondition of well-being in the sense that it harms a creature capable of having values to interfere with the process of acquiring, maintaining, and pursuing them. On this view, if you are the kind of creature who could have values, it is bad for you to be prevented from returning to (or reaching) this state, and good for you to receive what you need to put you on the trajectory of a person who can acquire, maintain, and pursue her values. Having values and being appropriately disposed with respect to them, on this view, is a precondition for well-being that is itself prudentially good for goal-seeking creatures. A value fulfillment theory like this would hold that actions that destroy, damage, or forestall the return of the agent's valuing capacities are significantly harmful.

It is worth saying a little bit more about the value that valuing capacities have, on the hybrid theory I am proposing. Such capacities have obvious instrumental value, but their instrumental value is not sufficient to explain why it is good for people without values to have them. Valuing capacities must have something more than instrumental value. Jason Raibley is the clearest example of someone who takes this strategy and the way he puts it is that being stably disposed to realize our values is "directly" good for human agents (Raibley "Health and Well-Being" 207).[6] According to Raibley, it is directly good for us to be disposed in such a way that we can realize our values:

> Whichever states serve as the causal basis for the disposition to realize one's values will also be components of welfare, itself, so that when these states are present, this counts as directly and not merely instrumentally beneficial. These same states can therefore legitimately be thought of as "basic goods." The diachronic emotional condition of happiness; physical and psychological health; rationality; functionally appropriate emotional states (feeling good when one achieves goals; experiencing negative emotions when one's values are threatened or destroyed); and other personal characteristics (e.g., optimism, good judgment) are directly (and not just instrumentally) welfare-constituting, because they underwrite and serve as the causal basis for one's disposition to realize one's values (Raibley 205).

I have put the point in terms of our capacities to acquire, maintain, and pursue our values, rather than in terms of dispositions, but I don't take this to be an important difference.

Importantly, adding the non-instrumental good of capacities or dispositions is not *ad hoc*. Goal fulfillment theories are animated by a conception of human nature: human beings are goal seekers, value pursuers, desire satisfiers. It is this conception of human nature that underlies the claim that our valuing capacities are good for us. A hybrid value fulfillment theory is unified by this picture of human nature. Equally importantly, although there is a view about human nature that underlies the theory, because the theory is still a goal fulfillment theory, "fulfilling our nature as human beings" is not what grounds the theory's claims about what has prudential value. Rather, it is fulfilling our values that is good for us; certain capacities are the *sine qua non* of value fulfillment and are, therefore, good for us in a special, non-instrumental way.

On this improved version of a goal fulfillment theory, it is good for a person to be able to form and pursue her values, even if that isn't her goal. This bold way of putting it raises questions about how far we have now moved from subjectivism.

---

[6] Connie Rosati makes a related but more general argument in her defense of the rational fit theory of welfare; she argues that "the welfarist good-for relation is a reason-giving relation of fit between a welfare object and a welfare subject, where a welfare subject is a valuable being" (2020, 241).

Preserving What's Important from Subjectivism

Returning to Sumner's definition of a subjective theory, such theories require that a person has a positive attitude (at least under certain conditions) toward something for that thing to count as good for a person. On this definition, my hybrid value fulfillment theory is not a subjective theory. It is, however, still an internalist theory or what Alicia Hall and I have called a "subject-dependent" theory (as opposed to an externalist or subject-transcendent theory; Hall and Tiberius 175–86). Subject-dependent theories take well-being to depend on features of the individual well-being subject as opposed to features that transcend the subject such as species membership or objective goods. Such theories need not insist that there is nothing that can be good for a person without her having a pro-attitude of some kind toward it, however, because a feature of an individual agent (in this case, their valuing capacities) may not be the object of that agent's pro-attitudes. This subject-dependent version of value fulfillment theory contains an objective element, namely, that value fulfillment itself is good for people. Nevertheless, it may preserve what is important about subjectivism.

What is important about subjectivism? First, its respect of the resonance constraint, which allows it to respect individual differences. Recall that the resonance constraint requires that what is good for a person has some "internal resonance" with that person. As Railton puts it, "It would be an intolerably alienated conception of someone's good to imagine that it might fail in any such way to engage him" (Railton "Moral Realism" 9). The hybrid value fulfillment theory I have put forward respects the resonance constraint in one important respect, which is that it doesn't place external constraints on what people may value as part of their own good. This is certainly a stark contrast to objective list theories. It also respects the resonance constraint in almost every actual case, since goal seeking capacities have instrumental value for, or are implicitly valued by, anyone with values. However, it does imply that there's something that is good for us even if we don't value it. What does this mean for the resonance constraint?

Worries about the resonance constraint only arise for the special good of value fulfilling functioning itself—the good of endorsing, maintaining, and pursuing values (what Raibley calls our agential capacities). This kind of functioning is good for people even if they do not value it, because it is a necessary condition for anything being good for us in the first place. The essential capacities of a goal seeking agent, on this view, are non-instrumentally good for a person, whether she will come to value them or not, and whether or not they will turn out to be instrumental to greater value fulfillment in the future.

This certainly does not respect the resonance constraint. But how much of a problem is it, really? The resonance constraint, after all, is supported by the intuition that a conception of the good that didn't resonate with a person would be an "intolerably alienated" one. Examples that fuel this intuition are examples of people who lack the capacity to appreciate certain goods, but who are perfectly capable of enjoying many other activities: the cognitively impaired person who has little interest in acquiring knowledge, but who loves to play and be with people; the neurologically atypical person who does not want to develop intimate relationships with others, but who enjoys solving puzzles and learning new things; or the happy couch potato who is completely unmoved by the idea of achieving anything, but who really enjoys the pleasures of food and trashy movies. These are people who are capable of being alienated from a conception of the good that leaves out their subjective perspective; they can find something alien. The severely depressed person in complete conative collapse, however, cannot find anything alien, because they (by definition) neither like nor dislike anything (if they did, then they would have at least something in the way of goals).[7]

The problem with conative collapse is that literally nothing resonates: not having an opportunity to eat, drink, or feel pleasure, not living another day, and not being spared pain. As mentioned above, this is certainly an extremely unusual and rare sort of case. It is hard to imagine that there is nothing aversive or painful about the condition, and aversions would allow a goal fulfillment theory to get a foothold into attributing goods that resonate with the person. If such a person is possible, however, the intuitions that support the resonance constraint don't obviously apply. In such cases it seems like common sense to say that what is good for this person is to be brought back to the capacities that would allow them to find some things attractive and other things alien. This is just to say that the addition of nature fulfillment to our subjective theory does put a limit on the resonance constraint, but it is an intuitive limit. Since the resonance constraint is itself supported by common sense intuitions, I see no reason not to accept such a limitation. It remains to

---

[7] If alienation is a condition rather than a feeling, another way to describe the case might be that the person in complete conative collapse is alienated from *everything*. Thanks to Dan Haybron for this suggestion. I think what I say below is compatible with this alternative description.

be seen whether this restriction on the resonance constraint causes us to sacrifice other attractive features of subjectivism.

Before we turn to these other attractive features, it is worth emphasizing the point that what is good for a person is the capacities that are a necessary condition for their well-being as a goal seeking creature.[8] Notice that this gives goal fulfillment theories a good basis for discussing child well-being, because it allows for the idea that the development of capacities for deliberation, choice, and planning are good for children independently of their current goals.[9] This development is good for them because they are creatures whose good is defined relative to their goal seeking nature. The hybrid value fulfillment theory does not entail that it would be good for creatures who have never had, or would not normally develop, the capacities to deliberate about, choose, plan for, and act toward their goals (artificial intelligences, for instance) to gain them.[10]

A second and related feature of subjectivism that is found attractive by some philosophers is its compatibility with internalism about practical reasons. According to reasons internalism, normative reasons for action always bear a close relationship to motivation, so that a person couldn't have a reason to do something she has no motivation whatsoever to do.[11] Though one might have qualms about reasons internalism when it comes to moral reasons, it is a plausible thesis about prudential reasons (the reasons generated by well-being) (Railton "Moral Realism" 163–207). Examples that pump the internalist intuition here are similar to the examples used to add force to the resonance constraint (and, indeed, some authors take these to be two descriptions of the same phenomenon). For our purposes, what's important here is the fact that a person in complete conative collapse would have no reason to promote her own valuing capacities if internalism is true. So, the hybridized value fulfillment theory has two options: it can stick with

---

[8] It may be that the right understanding of what's happening here is that blocked or suppressed capacities and goals are being reanimated or "woken up." On this understanding, the physical basis for these capacities and goals is there to be restored, and if it weren't, the case would have to be treated similarly to cases of human beings in permanent comas or persistent vegetative states.

[9] On child well-being in general see Raghavan and Alexandrova. On the problems raised by children for subjective theories see Lin.

[10] Though this does raise some interesting questions about the ethics of designing goal directed artificial intelligence. At what point would we say that a robot has the capacity to set and fulfill its own goals, and at what point would we be harming it by withholding enhancements that would develop these capacities? I don't think the answers are obvious.

[11] Different versions of internalism will spell out this relationship to motivation in different ways. See Finlay and Schroeder for discussion.

internalism and accept that the collapsed person has no such reason, or it can hold that internalism is not true of all prudential reasons and hold that the collapsed person does have a reason to promote their valuing capacities.[12] I prefer the first route here, because of the oddness of saying that a person who has absolutely no preferences about the state of the world with respect to anything at all has reasons for action. This very oddness should make us less concerned about a theory of well-being that implies that people in complete conative collapse do not have reasons to act. Our concern should be about, as Tully's was, the reasons others have to help or harm them, and those reasons are preserved by weakening the resonance constraint as discussed above.

The third feature of subjectivism that one might take to be an advantage is that it does not rely on an evaluative realism that makes evaluative properties mind-independent.[13] It may be that objective list theories are a better fit with realist theories of value, while desire fulfillment theories pair more naturally with a Humean metaethical picture, but these are not necessary connections; we should be careful to distinguish between metaethics and normative ethics (Haybron 27–53). If goal fulfillment theories of well-being are taken to be explanatory, it's easy to see how they might be mistaken for theories of the metaphysics of value, but they should not be taken in that way. Metaphysical theories of value aim to explain what value is and why there is such a thing. Theories of well-being, on the other hand, aim to characterize a particular kind of value. The particular criteria of success for a normative theory of well-being are descriptive adequacy, normative adequacy, and empirical adequacy (Sumner 1996; Tiberius "Beyond the Experience Machine" 398–415).[14] In other words, we are looking for a theory that makes sense of our considered judgments about well-being, plays an appropriate role in our normative practices, and is compatible with what we know about human psychology and the world. A goal fulfillment theory of well-being, then, explains why x is good for y; it does not explain why there is value in the world in the first place. What this means for our purposes is that a goal fulfillment theory

---

[12] A third possibility would be to argue that the hybrid goal fulfillment theory does respect Rosati's two tier internalism, according to which (roughly) a version of you in "ordinary optimal conditions" would care about what your idealized self would want for you ("Internalism and the Good for a Person" 297–326). Two tier internalism is difficult to interpret to the case of someone in conative collapse, so I won't pursue this option here.

[13] Connie Rosati calls this the argument from the metaphysics of value for internalism ("Internalism and the Good for a Person" 297–326).

[14] Of course, we may also look for general theoretical virtues such as simplicity. For instance, as discussed above, it is a virtue of the current theory that the addition of goal fulfillment capacities as a non-instrumental good is not ad hoc.

that takes valuing capacities to be intrinsically good for people independently of their attitudes towards them need not be making any metaethical assumptions.[15]

Finally, some will surely wonder why we don't just opt for a full-blooded Aristotelian theory, if we're going to abandon thoroughgoing subjectivism anyway. After all, the Aristotelian theory comes with the added alleged bonus that vicious people cannot achieve well-being! Why prefer the subject-dependent (but not quite subjectivist) value fulfillment approach to the more substantive Aristotelean approach with its robust conception of human nature?[16] There are two reasons (Dorsey "Three Arguments for Perfectionism" 59–79). First, goal fulfillment theories in general do better accommodate the resonance constraint. To my mind, a robust conception of human nature in terms of normal human capacities or substantive goals has the wrong results for people who do not fit neatly into those norms. We are better off tolerating the unhappy result that the immoral can flourish than we are consigning people who are different to the category of those whose lives are defective. Second, it is difficult to articulate and defend a highly substantive conception of human nature that is plausibly normative. A descriptive, biological account of human nature provides substance, but it isn't clear why our biology should determine our good. A normative account of human nature avoids this problem but does not have an obvious advantage over other theories, given the controversy about what counts as human nature worth expressing. Goal fulfillment theories' thin conception of human nature lightens this philosophical burden by insisting that what's good for people is intimately tied to what they value, or what they would value if they could.

Conclusion

I said earlier that the hybrid value fulfillment theory holds that it is good for a person to be able to form and pursue their values, even if that isn't what they value. Now that we see what this means, we can see that the bold statement is a little overstated. The first point, after all, is that if we have values or goals, then

[15] For example, the hybrid goal fulfillment theory is compatible with a constructivist (Lenman 2010) or desire based (Schroeder 2007) metaethics. According to these naturalist, Humean positions, there is no need to resort to metaphysical extravagance to explain how something can be valuable even if a particular person doesn't value it.

[16] For discussions of the capacities central to the Aristotelian conception of human nature see Kraut 2007 and Nussbaum, 2001.

we do care about our ability to fulfill them. But in the rare case in which one has literally no goals, or in which valuing one's own goal seeking capacities is entirely absent or not yet developed, goal fulfillment theorists could accept that a person can be benefited and harmed by aiding or impeding their goal seeking capacities. This subject-dependent theory is a hybrid in terms of its list of prudential goods. First and foremost, the realization of what you value is good for you. If you value friendship and meaningful work, what's good for you is your friendships and you career, and valuing them in a way that you can succeed in their terms over the course of your life. But possessing the capacities necessary to set and pursue values is also good for you, whether you value these capacities or not. The ultimate explanation for this is that we are creatures whose well-being is defined in terms of our values, which re-quire valuing capacities as a necessary condition.[17] This is a departure from subjectivism as originally conceived, but it is a subjective-dependent posi-tion that preserves what's important about subjectivism.

My discussion leaves many unanswered questions, but I hope to have persuaded you that a hybrid option that starts with the insight of subjec-tivism –its commitment to the resonance constraint and the significance of individual differences—is worth developing. I hope it is also clear that the future development of this option creates a lot of work for philosophers who do not typically write about well-being. Questions about well-being are im-portantly related to questions about practical reasons, evaluative realism, and moral obligation. Research on well-being will be improved if we all join forces.

Acknowledgments

I would like to thank Dan Haybron and John Stuhr for helpful comments on previous draft of this paper.

---

[17] Compare in this volume both John Stuhr's claim that "any wholly third-person account or ex-ternal perspective on flourishing is inadequate and can provide only part of the story about flour-ishing" and John Lachs's claim that good empiricists who focus on facts "find a bewildering array of pursuits, every one of which renders some people happy and others miserable."

Works Cited

Bradford, Gwen. "Problems for Perfectionism." *Utilitas*, vol. 29, no. 3, 2017, pp. 344–64.

Brandt, Richard. *A Theory of the Good and the Right*. Clarendon Press, 1984.

DeYoung, Colin G. "Cybernetic Big Five Theory." *Journal of Research in Personality*, vol. 56, 2015, pp. 33–58.

DeYoung, Colin G., and Tiberius, Valerie. "Value Fulfillment from a Cybernetic Perspective: A New Psychological Theory of Well-Being." *Personality and Social Psychology Review,* 2022, https://doi.org/10.1177/10888683221083777.

Dorsey, Dale. "Why Should Welfare 'Fit'?" *The Philosophical Quarterly*, vol. 67, no. 269, 2017, pp. 685–724.

Dorsey, Dale. "Subjectivism without Desire." *Philosophical Review*, vol. 121, no. 3, 2012, pp. 407–42.

Dorsey, Dale. "Three Arguments for Perfectionism." *Noûs*, vol. 44, no. 1, 2010, pp. 59–79.

Finlay, Stephen, and Schroeder, Mark, "Reasons for Action: Internal vs. External." *The Stanford Encyclopedia of Philosophy*, edited by Edward Zalta. Fall 2017. https://plato.stanford.edu/archives/fall2017/entries/reasons-internal-external/.

Finnis, John. *Natural Law and Natural Rights*. Oxford University Press, 2011.

Fletcher, Guy. "A Fresh Start for the Objective-List Theory of Well-Being." *Utilitas*, vol. 25, no. 2, 2013, pp. 206–20.

Hall, Alicia, and Tiberius, Valerie. "Well-Being and Subject Dependence." *The Routledge Handbook of Philosophy of Well-Being*. Taylor and Francis Inc., 2015, pp. 175–86.

Haybron, D. M. "The Philosophical Basis of Eudaimonic Psychology." *Handbook of Eudaimonic Well-being*. Springer, pp. 27–53.

Heathwood, Chris. "Desire Satisfactionism and Hedonism." *Philosophical Studies*, vol. 128, no. 3, 2006, pp. 539–63.

Heathwood, Chris. "The Problem of Defective Desires." *Australasian Journal of Philosophy*, vol. 83, no. 4, 2005, pp. 487–504.

Kraut, Richard. *What Is Good and Why: The Ethics of Well-Being*. Harvard University Press, 2007.

Lenman, J. "Humean Constructivism in Moral Theory." *Oxford Studies in Metaethics,* edited by Ross Shafer-Landau. Oxford University Press, vol. 5, 2010, pp. 175–93.

Lin, Eden. "Against Welfare Subjectivism." *Noûs*, vol. 51, no. 2, 2017, pp. 354–77.

Mitchell, Polly. "Review of Well-Being as Value Fulfillment: How We Can Help Each Other to Live Well By Valerie Tiberius." *Analysis*, vol. 80, no. 1, January 2020, pp. 196–98, https://doi.org/10.1093/analys/anz090

Nussbaum, Martha. *Women and Human Development: The Capabilities Approach* (Vol. 3). Cambridge University Press, 2001.

Raibley, Jason. "Health and Well-being." *Philosophical Studies*, vol. 165, no. 2, 2013, pp. 469–89.

Raibley, Jason. "Well-Being and the Priority of Values." *Social Theory and Practice*, vol. 36, no. 4, 2010, pp. 593–620.

Raghavan, Ramesh, and Alexandrova, Anna. "Toward a Theory of Child Well-Being." *Social Indicators Research*, vol. 121, no. 3, 2015, pp. 887–902.

Railton, P. "Moral Realism." *The Philosophical Review*, vol. 95, no. 2, 1986, pp. 163–207.

Railton, P. "Facts and Values." *Philosophical Topics*, vol. 14, no. 2, 1985, pp. 5–31.

Rawls, John. *A Theory of Justice*. Harvard University Press, 1971.

Rice, Christopher. "Defending the Objective List Theory of Well-Being." *Ratio*, vol. 26, no. 2, 2013, pp. 196–211.

Rosati, Connie. "Welfare and Rational Fit." *Oxford Studies in Metaethics*, vol. 15, 2020, pp. 241–62.

Rosati, Connie. "Internalism and the Good for a Person." *Ethics*, vol. 106, no. 2, 1996, pp. 297–326.

Schroeder, Mark. *Slaves of the Passions*. Oxford University Press, 2007.

Sumner, L. W. *Welfare, Happiness, and Ethics*. Clarendon Press, 1996.

Tiberius, Valerie. *Well-being as Value Fulfillment: How We Can Help Each Other to Live Well*. Oxford University Press, 2018.

Tiberius, Valerie. "Beyond the Experience Machine: Philosophical Methodology and Theories of Well-Being." *Philosophical Methods: The Armchair or the Laboratory?* Edited by Matthew Haug. Routledge Publishing, 2014, pp. 398–415.

Tiberius, Valerie. *The Reflective Life: Living Wisely with Our Limits*. Oxford University Press on Demand, 2008.

Tully, Ian. "Depression and the Problem of Absent Desires." *Journal of Ethics and Social Philosophy*, vol. 11, no. 1, 2016, pp. 1–15.

Wolf, Susan. "Happiness and Meaning: Two Aspects of the Good Life." *Social Philosophy and Policy*, vol. 14, no. 1, 1997, pp. 207–25.

6

The Allure of the "All"

John Lachs

No matter how much we struggle to include the different, the allure of the "all" is difficult to resist. No matter how we restrain ourselves from generalizing, sooner or later we think we discover some choice feature of reality or of human nature that is universally present. This is how, with the best of intentions, we arrive at accounts of human flourishing that are not inventories of the many ways we make sense of life, but single characteristics whose presence guarantees happiness.

Even Aristotle, a master of human diversity, succumbs to this temptation. He wisely says that happiness is activity in accordance with virtue, but then associates virtue with his narrow view of the golden mean. I will attempt to sketch an account of human flourishing that does justice to the variety of ways humans gain satisfaction.

It is best to begin with facts. Some people swim in the milk of human kindness; others would like to boil them in it. There are persons whose dreams would come true if they were offered a deanship; others cannot stay far enough away from administration. We see individuals devoted to creating varied levels of what we call good and evil, while others gain satisfaction from accepting what comes their way. The only plan for flourishing I have not come across is to profit from performing exclusively evil deeds, and that is because of the extraordinary efforts required for thorough wickedness.

In light of such diversity, it is impossible to frame universal theories about the nature and conditions of happiness.[1] Anyone who speaks of a single "human nature" overlooks its varieties and embraces, without knowing it, a momentous fiction. Many fictions have value and among those that do, the

---

[1] In distinguishing plural meanings and dimensions of human well-being, John Stuhr affirms this point in "Flourishing: Toward Clearer Ideas and Habits of Genius": "Any practically relevant and critically applicable notion of flourishing must confront, acknowledge, and embrace the great diversity of human lives and the big fact of pluralism." A similar stress on, and explicit commitment to, pluralism and diversity is set forth by Rebecca Newberger Goldstein, Mark Johnson, Michele Moody-Adams, and Jessica Wahman in their chapters in this volume.

John Lachs, *The Allure of the "All"* In: *Philosophy and Human Flourishing*. Edited by: John J. Stuhr, Oxford University Press. © Oxford University Press 2023. DOI: 10.1093/oso/9780197622162.003.0007

idea of a single human race is preeminent. It demands special treatment for everyone who falls under its canopy and justifies extreme measures in its protection. In theory at least, humans enjoy rights not accorded to any other animals and they enjoy them in equal measure irrespective of accidents of birth or social position.

The idea of a single human nature has a troubled history, and even today it tends to serve as an ideal honored in the breach. But its role in protecting underprivileged minorities assures it a place among expressions of our most humane tendencies. In calling it a fiction I don't mean to impugn its value. Instead, I want to stress its usefulness, without losing sight of the vast differences it encompasses. And there is no better place to find these divergences than in the way people seek to flourish.

The list of ideas, things, and processes that promise happiness is nearly as long as the list of things in the world. Some want to win the lottery; others, as a child once told me, want to grow up to be able to earn ten dollars an hour. Some want a trusted partner for life; others desire to attract as many partners as possible. Some seek battles and want victories; others withdraw from contests and want to be lost in silent thought. Many of these people will experience disappointment during their lives, partly because their hopes will be dashed and partly because their hopes will come true and turn out to be unsatisfying. Others will change midstream and no longer pursue a dream or else switch their dream for something more attainable.

Designating one particular pursuit and satisfaction as *the* nature of happiness is arbitrary and flies in the face of facts. The diversity of strivings and enjoyments is overwhelming. Whose life is to set the standard? Am I to be declared unhappy for neither having nor wanting something that delights someone else? To make sure the arbiters of happiness do not acquire the right to tell us when our lives are worthwhile, it is best to embrace a radical pluralism, letting people pursue their fulfilments in their own ways.

This sounds relativistic, which is supposed to be bad. That impression can, however, be improved by calling it "relational" in the sense that it involves some relations. There is, of course, hardly a theory that fails to include relations, so it is easy to disinfect the view by explaining that the relations it introduces are not to momentary feelings or passing opinions, but to established natures. Because he thought there was just one human nature, Aristotle related human perfection to it. But he could not resist noticing that individual natures modify the human essence: what is appropriate for the monstrous wrestler Milo, he had to admit, is beyond the range of the rest of us.

The most plausible candidate for a general theory of happiness is probably Aristotle's. Its usual interpretation is that the good life consists of "activity in accordance with virtue," that is, in contemporary language, doing things and doing them well. But the question "Which activities?" arises immediately and receives no satisfactory answer. "The characteristically human ones" offers no help: those are precisely the ones we want to identify.

If we resolve to be good empiricists and turn to the facts, we find a bewildering array of pursuits, every one of which renders some people happy and others miserable. To deal with this profusion, we tend to permit our natural tendency to prevail and elevate the values of our society or our age to universal validity. Instead of respecting irreducible multiplicity, the "all" once again achieves an easy victory.

Even more damagingly, we can ask Aristotle why happiness should be a matter of doings rather than receivings. When we think of the blessed souls of the departed, we surely do not suppose that they do much, let alone labor mightily, for their privileged condition. Blessedness is an effortless delight, possibly like Mozart's music floating in elevators. Moreover, how are we to decide what counts as performing an activity well? Much depends on what we take the activity to be. But what surgeons and demented criminals do to human bodies may be physically identical, yet we set different standards for them, because we wish one of them to succeed and the other to fail.

The trouble with Aristotle's theory is the "all" that is supposedly essential for theories. My view, inspired by Aristotle, does justice to the diversity of human flourishings. The details of this theory are worked out in my "Human Natures."[2]

The starting point is that no universal trait defines the human. Instead, we categorize people on the basis of features broadly though not universally present. Scientists may be right that there are no purposes in the physical universe, but the human world is replete with them. With purposes go desires to recraft a portion of that world. The desires tend to lead to action and, under favorable circumstances, to satisfaction. Much but not all of our lives revolve around this trinity of activities.

It would be difficult to find three notions that can reveal more about individuals than what they want, what they are willing to work for, and what stills their drives. Of course, categorizing people on this basis can lead also to frightful triviality, but that is easily controlled by changing the defining

[2] See Lachs, "Human Natures," 22–39.

desires. For example, individuals who like to travel, often do, and find fulfil-ment in it can be seen as constituting one group of persons; those who find it delightful to eat lots of Italian food make up another. Matters turn more serious, however, if we select on the basis of willingness to surrender life for country or of lifelong commitment to a single person in marriage.

The number of groups we can identify in this way is indefinitely large. To the good: there are many conceptual jobs to do and we are free to choose whatever tools best advance our purposes. Because sorting and resorting occur on the basis of open criteria, there is less chance of hidden agendas or ill will prevailing. Moreover, the approach offers an additional benefit. If we learn to see people as transparently and non-threateningly different from us, we increase the likelihood of accepting their peculiarities. Obviously, there are no guarantees, but we are familiar with the sting of desire, the pain of hard work and the pleasure of achievement, and it is difficult not to see them in the struggles of others.

Sympathy tends to grow with selective identification, so a smaller group near us is more likely to mobilize the moral sentiments than is humanity at large. Something like this happened in the United States in relation to same-sex couples: in focusing on particular cases of intolerance, the entire machinery of feeling was engaged. This, incidentally, is why those, such as Fichte, Royce, Levinas, and Peter Singer, who would impose stringent uni-versal obligations on us, tend to remain dissatisfied: their moral psychology is flawed.

In the light of this preliminary description of human natures, it may be worth asking what constitutes flourishing. As usual, J. S. Mill offers the most obvious and commonsensical answer: it is a matter of feeling good. Subjective as this sounds, it captures the attention and imagination of people. Referring to it as a life of pleasure makes it sound risqué, but calling it enjoyment takes the overtone of sensuality out of it. Mill goes so far as to distinguish higher, intellectual and artistic, delights from the common, garden variety ones.

The pleasure calculus promises to eliminate the distinction between pri-vate delight and public good. The conviction that pretty much everybody likes to feel good erases concerns over a possible conflict between egoists and altruists and points in the direction of a world in which rationality at last prevails. The motto "Each is to count for one and no one for more than one" assures everyone equal standing; guided by such humane Enlightenment ideals, our lives acquire their proper value and flourishing becomes inevitable.

The trouble with pleasure has remained the same over centuries: work attains it with difficulty, drugs with ease. Marijuana, the latest generation of relaxants, or alcoholic haze does an excellent job of making life appear a pleasant diversion. The urgency of problems recedes and near-term pleasure crowds out concern over the future. What is left can hardly be called flourishing. It has only feeling and lacks plan, action, and victory.

Recognition that flourishing involves much more than feelings leads to the idea that it is simply getting whatever we like. The range of desired objects is broader than Mill suspected: it includes physical possessions, social standing, and remarkable achievements. We value these miscellaneous items for their own sake and not for the sake of the pleasure they create. Whoever doubts this has never seen a person drive a new Bentley.

The benefit of this view is that it focuses flourishing at the point of desire rather than at the far end of satisfaction. The modern industrialized world is designed to create desires and satisfy them: it is a huge engine of productivity. The view that flourishing is getting what we like appears invincible: we can reasonably ask how it is possible for people to remain unhappy if they get everything they want. This surely is what heaven must be like, although there we have to be more modest in our desires.

Some humans approximate this fashion of flourishing, but for most it is unreachable. Desires proliferate faster than satisfactions and the more quickly success follows craving, the less interesting it all becomes. The more assured and rapid the outcome, the more certain that it will be greeted by boredom. Further, so long as there are desires for the unique, all of them cannot be honored: you and I cannot both take possession of the same house by the sea.

If getting what we like does not make us happy, perhaps liking what we get does. Nature sooner or later defeats us: we are born with deficits, grow up to learn our limits and face inevitable death. On the last analysis much, some think everything, is beyond our power. The only way to fight back is to cease caring and embrace a profound indifference to whatever befalls us. In the grand scheme of things, what happens to us is of no significance; nothing matters but our readiness to accept the course of nature.

This stoic view of flourishing comes in a variety of versions. Those holding it tend to agree that the right attitude to the vicissitudes of life is quiet acquiescence. But some stress the importance of intellectual grasp: they want to understand what is happening to them. Others lay special emphasis on self-control, enduring terrible indignities with supernatural calm. But whoever endorses the view is likely to believe that emotions constitute the primary source of our unhappiness and should, accordingly, be extinguished.

These are sound strategies in times of tragedy. But life offers joy no less than disappointment. The exercise of our powers is intrinsically delightful. Making plans and carrying them out bolster self-confidence. Normally, a feeling of satisfaction accompanies the processes of life. Although it is true that fate can wipe us out at any moment, it is equally true that it does not over long stretches of time. Flourishing is a kind of flowering that involves the entire organism; it cannot be identical with the limited defensive posture of the stoic.

There is another view of flourishing focused on purposes and activities that is worth canvasing. The process begins with an idea of some plan or challenge worth taking on. The application of skill and hard work yield victory over the initial problem, but create new ones. Each challenge overcome adds to the agent's skill, energy, and confidence. The challenges must not be beyond the capacity of the individual to meet and their number must not be overwhelming. Flourishing is mastery of such problem-chains. Take the decision to become a physician as an example. It involves a series of challenges that can be overcome. Each course taken and each specialty rotation requires skill and hard work; each one mastered counts as a minor victory. Flourishing is the entire process when successfully performed.

There are such heady times in life and they feel wonderful. But once again we must careful not to capitulate to the "all." Many people perform their jobs with competence and yet gain little satisfaction. Physicians specialized to treat single organs, for example, tend to complain of burnout, no matter how successful their practice. Other individuals avoid challenges altogether and still lead happy lives. The exertions needed for a continued series of victories wear people out; many satisfy themselves with memories of better days.

Clearly, no single notion of flourishing can do justice to the variety of human satisfactions. Might we do better looking for universality among the conditions that make flourishing possible? Once again, Aristotle comes to the fore as the philosopher who has reflected on the details of these matters. He provides a list of conditions necessary for happiness. Being born into a good family and raised properly constitute just the beginning. Enjoying the benefits of friends, health, and money is important. It is difficult to thrive without peace and social stability. Even good looks and luck, he thinks, are essential to living well.

Of all these miscellaneous conditions none seems indispensable. People overcome their childhood deficits and learn to flourish without friends and family. Some report that times of turbulence make them come alive. Others glory in victory over disease. Individuals report that winning the lottery did not make them happy. It might appear difficult to compensate for the disadvantage of being plain or ugly, but the entire beauty industry is devoted to proving that assumption wrong.

That leaves luck. On one way of seeing it, everything is a matter of luck: it is sheer good fortune that a truck did not run over me at age ten. If it did not, it was because, luckily, I had been taught to be careful at intersections. That itself was, of course, the consequence of a fortuitous collocation of circumstances. At some point soon, it becomes clear that "luck" in this sense refers to the contingencies of nature when they favor our endeavors. In this sense, however, luck is not an independent agency whose activity serves as a condition of flourishing, but a way in which we praise compliant nature. This is an empty universality, not one that reveals the inner structure of flourishing. We have no better proof of this than the wide variety of what people consider lucky.

In reflecting on the capacity of people to render themselves happy, we must not overlook two talents that move them in the opposite direction. In the case of the first, the difference between humans and other animals is striking. When offered neither food nor chase, cats curl up and sleep. By contrast, humans are inclined to complain of being bored. Tedium is an awful by-product of successful societies: along with laziness, it is a luxury that eats away at the foundations of happiness.

If possible, the second talent is even more devastating. It is the uncanny ability to destroy happiness through a series of questions. Sometimes the queries come disguised as attempts at maximization. I have heard a rich and famous musician ask, "Is this all there is to life?" It was not clear what he was missing, but he wanted more. Insatiable appetite gobbles up innocent enjoyment and leaves us permanently dissatisfied. The result is a search for the magic bullet, the possession or activity that would at last yield peace.

Yet peace is never reached that way. Other people have better friends and seem happier or more fortunate. Their houses are larger, their mates finer looking, and their cars fancier. Instead of rejoicing with our neighbors, their possessions constitute invitations for us to outdo them. Comparisons feed competition and falling behind is to taste defeat. The contest is so all-encompassing that even the victors quiver: they fear losing their advantage.

In the process, everyone loses the sweetness of the moment. The ultimate way to render oneself miserable is to ask for the point of it all. This nihilistic move can begin with modest reflections on the shortness of life and the losses we suffer. It can spread from there, an awful cancer, questioning the value of human endeavors and achievements. From a cosmic perspective, what we do is, indeed, of no significance. Soon we will die and future generations will not remember our names. The dusty planet we inhabit in a small solar system may outlive our species, but in five million years the sun will be extinguished and permanent darkness will descend. How can we flourish when our prospects are so dim?

The wrongheadedness of this argument against happiness must be exposed. First, prognostications about events five million years in the future are, at best, ignorant guesses. Further, what may happen then has no relevance to us today. We can take reasonable steps to secure our next few years and the lives of our children and grandchildren. That may total a hundred years. Precautionary concerns, such as not allowing living conditions on the planet to deteriorate, are appropriate for another few hundred years, even though their exact nature is unclear. But for worries about what might happen millions of years from now to nullify the joy of a good conversation is absurd. Conversations offer intrinsic value even if they are terminated by the death of their participants. Plato made a related point about the death of Socrates.

So far, my argument has shown that there is no single, universally valid conception of human flourishing. What we have, instead, is a collection of ideas embraced and enacted by groups of individuals. Some of the notions resemble one another to varying degrees; others are so different that what would count as thriving for some human beings is sheer misery for others. We need to keep this in mind as we examine the relation of the humanities to human flourishing.

The study is particularly difficult because it requires tracing causation among embodied abstractions. The humanities are constituted by a collection of ideas and happiness is a subjectively reported condition of individuals. How can we determine their causal influence on one another? One way might be to start with existing claims and see if they are borne out.

Practitioners of the humanities frequently claim that the education they receive and the activities in which they engage provide them with unique sources of happiness. The humanities are supposed to open avenues of enjoyment and self-development that are not accessible from anywhere else.

And, indeed, those who enjoy philosophy, literature, and history testify to the benefits of these fields. Studying foreign languages is the nearest we can come to opening the secrets of other minds, reading novels is unmatched in expanding the imagination, and critical thinking remains our best hope for avoiding the contagion of ideologies.

It is important to add that although the humanities can achieve remarkable results, often they fail to do so. There are lamentable instances of scholars lending their names and their efforts to the promotion of noxious causes. In some cases, people who study the soaring achievements of the human mind remain untouched by them and treat students and younger colleagues with disdain. Many display a mean and vindictive streak and delight in driving whomever they consider lesser humans into the ground.

This combination of high intelligence and moral nastiness is not unusual. One can reasonably ask if the failure is of temperament or humanities materials. In either case, it demonstrates the limits of what words and ideas can do. In spite of rhetoric to the contrary, even works that address the imagination often fail to create empathy, in good part because of the dryness of their medium. This may sound like an attack upon words, but it is only a way of celebrating their surprising efficacy, along with notice of where they fail.

Humanities scholars tacitly admit the limitations of their art when they introduce service learning into their courses. The point is not so much to help others, valid as that is, but to add immediate experience to the mediation of words. Whole-body absorption in real-world events tends to generate enhanced understanding and appropriate sentiments. The ideal is to combine the grasp uniquely brought by words with direct sensory exposure. Without ideas, raw experience remains unintelligible; without a tie to the real world, concepts lose relevance.

Something like this loss of reality, and with it its loss of ancient mission, is what beset philosophy in the middle decades of the twentieth century. The striking success of science and the equally striking failure of philosophy to produce confirmed theories or even a few new facts, generated waves of self-hatred in the academy. A. J. Ayer's book, *Language, Truth and Logic*, decreed that what had hitherto been thought philosophy was literally nonsense. Unmindful of the contradiction, philosophers happily taught this new philosophy.

At roughly the same time, socio-political events in the academy made the situation of philosophy more dire. The power structure of the profession fell under the control of a few graduate schools in the East. The American

Philosophical Association, the premier society in the field, was taken over by graduates of a few schools, who kept handing positions of responsibility to their allies and friends. At one meeting of the largest (Eastern) Division of the society, seventeen members associated with a single school were represented on the program, with none from several major graduate schools.

Professional meetings were sites of bloodletting with displays of newly invented fallacies, of which unsuspecting philosophers were easily convicted. It was all an inside job played and appreciated by professionals alone. Undergraduate enrollments shriveled and the educated public ceased reading the work of academic philosophers. The American pragmatist tradition of tackling social problems was abandoned; in its place, American thinkers looked to Oxford for linguistic analysis and to Paris for something called post-structuralism.

Philosophy came near to losing its place in the academy. When philosophers spoke, colleagues from other fields rolled their eyes. Whenever possible, they were left off committees; when that could not be done, it was generally agreed that they conversed as if they were from another planet. In a way they were, demanding extreme precision when there was neither need nor possibility of it and showing no practical concerns. In the years I went through graduate school, we had interminable debates concerning what is a fact. The consensus was that we could argue about these matters without actually knowing any facts.

Sanity returned to philosophy after a revolt against the APA in 1978 and the realization that there was room for critical thinking in the hospital. The opening phase of medical ethics came as a surprise to philosophers: it seemed astonishing that their skills could be put to practical use. Little by little, philosophy regained its interest in reality and expanded its activities to business ethics, environmental ethics and journalistic ethics, along with other areas. The hardliners continue to hold that "applied" philosophy is a bastard field lacking legitimacy, but the bulk of the profession is happy with the new jobs and new respect that have been created.

Since the Centennial celebrations of the APA in 2000, the organization acknowledges that philosophy is of immense "personal value and social usefulness" to people. New journals have been started, some of them dealing with the problems of life in ordinary English. Books are being published that enhance the public appreciation of philosophy. Undergraduates make certain they enroll in bioethics courses before applying to medical school. Most important perhaps, the great American tradition of pragmatism has been revived. Graduate schools turn out new PhDs who meet rigorous professional standards, but also take a vital interest in the problems of ordinary people. Philosophy is beginning to reclaim its ancient task of serving as a guide to life.

This brief historical overview points to how much philosophy, and the humanities, can lose when it detaches itself from its natural functions in society. It also opens the door to a discussion of the unique contributions philosophy can make to good lives. Among the latter I count the vast enrichment of my life as a result of learning to attend to my immediate experience. Philosophy, especially the philosophy of Santayana, taught me the areligious spirituality of not looking past appearances for the meaning of things.

I and others have derived immense benefit from reading the Stoics. Sometimes naive about the power of emotions and occasionally offensive in their recommendations, they nevertheless capture the demands of good sense. People whose taste runs to religion have a rich choice between St. Thomas and Kierkegaard, and persons interested in the problems of civil society can reflect on works by a list of authors from Hobbes to Hegel.

These, however, are only fortuitous intersections between philosophical materials and individual interests. At its strongest, the connection is so tight that philosophy takes over the person's life and we find Stoics, libertarians and practicing Christians surrounding us. More frequently, a ragtag band of ideas is invoked to justify what one is inclined to do or to believe. In the latter case, professionals shudder at seeing what has become of their carefully formulated ideas.

Between thoughtful philosophy and garbled justification lie the swamps of ideology. To convert virtually any idea into an element of ideology we simply remove its limits and enhance its promise. This identifies it as a classic case of the "all." It promises to solve all problems on condition that all of its enemies are eliminated. The enemies are varied, ranging from infidels to capitalists and united only by their nefarious wickedness. This is no way to contribute to human flourishing: philosophers can do little more than point to the way in which edifices of prejudice shatter into shards.

There are two vital general contributions only philosophy can make to human flourishing. One relates to skepticism, the other to the future. A frequent response to a simple request is "Absolutely." This is said to indicate assurance and belongs with such locutions as "I feel certain" and "For sure." We throw around such sentences as though certainty were an attainable ideal. As an indication of promise or intention, the invocation of assurance might seem harmless, but even there it is misleading. Matters of greater urgency or changed relations might well nullify the commitment.

In spite of declarations to the contrary, there is no certainty in the realms of knowledge and emotion. Religious truths used to be considered inerrant; today, few take them to be truths at all. It is shocking to realize how much the content of common sense has changed. Science is more method than results; in the search for precision and scope, it undermines its own conclusions. If we could be certain of the affection of our mates, there would be far fewer divorces.

The plain fact is that humans have to make do without certainty. What stability we enjoy we carve out of often recalcitrant nature and the equilibrium does not last. A large hurricane or a small virus can lay waste to our finest creations. There is no assurance in defensive action: we are victorious until we are defeated and the human race loses its dominance. For many people this is difficult to imagine, but all it takes is a change or two in the germ plasm of the next wave of viruses.

No one knows human vulnerability and cognitive disappointment better than philosophers; the history of their field is, among other things, a history of skepticism. They are uniquely capable of deploying the questioning attitude largely missing in human interactions. It is missing because we desperately want stability and are willing to believe the first credible-sounding witness. Politicians profit by this naiveté, as do advertisers and lying lovers. This is an area in which obligation and the promotion of flourishing coincide: being skeptical is often a short-term pain but a long-term safeguard against disappointment.

Does this not hand the ever-present "all" a victory? The obligation to demand evidence for belief appears universal, as does its reward in flourishing. It is easy, therefore, to suppose that the connection runs deep and assures that the appearance of one brings with it the appearance of the other. The search for such conjunctions is one of the tasks of science, and it is not unreasonable to expect some success in physics. Human natures, however, are varied and the "wet blanket" role of questioning everything does not agree with them. Some persons reject the idea that this is a legitimate role for philosophy, others accept the task but feel miserable in carrying it out. In any case, important as it is, it is not the road to universal flourishing.

A second general service philosophers can render that promises an increase in happiness is their educational role. In looking over the curricula of universities it is striking how much time we spend on the past and how little on the future. Students are required to master a body of knowledge established some time ago. This is natural in history where the past explores the distant past, but extends to literature in our search for classical novels. The statistics of sociology and the charts of economics tend to be built on past experience, as are the rules of foreign languages. The picture of the world developed by physics and astronomy has been with us a long time and, although we rarely acknowledge it, whenever we ask for evidence we address the past.

The emphasis on the past comes at a cost to the future. What is yet to come lives in the womb of possibility and invites energetic people to bring it into existence. This interplay of the existent and the potential is the source of personal and social improvement. It operates by means of the imagination, sometimes warning of trouble, at others envisaging overlooked benefits. The emergence of the Corona19 virus is a classic case of the disaster that can befall people who try to deal with the world without imagination.

What a university curriculum focused on the imagination and the future would look like is a topic for another day. Philosophers would likely play a central role in it, though it is less clear whether that role would contribute to their flourishing. As with other occupations, some philosophers would happily throw themselves into the fray while others would busy themselves searching for reasons to complain. The "all" once again would not prevail.

There can be no doubt that philosophy of certain kinds has a beneficial influence on some areas of life. Careful theory construction, critical examination of claims, synthetic vision, and the search for relationships are finding their place in the toolbox of researchers. At the same time, personal philosophies such as stoicism offer themselves for serious consideration. Philosophers are team members in the treatment of difficult cases in hospitals. They give advice on business decisions and participate in developing environmental impact statements. Not every philosopher is involved in these activities, but the crucial change is that doing such things has become a valued regular part of the work of the profession.

Nevertheless, we must be sure not to succumb to the lure of the "all." There are some philosophers who prefer abstraction and believe that seeking relevance is to lose sight of what philosophy is to accomplish. In the university, these people are carried by their colleagues on their backs; their courses are poorly attended, and administrators think of them as burdens. Good teaching begins with interesting materials and requires connections to daily life. Abstraction has its value only in the production of new theories and the discovery of novel facts, and philosophy has not exceled at these tasks.

Does this mean that the humanities, in the form of philosophical thinking, are of use for everyone?[3] And is it as intrinsically delightful for people as it is for philosophers arguing into the night? The answer to both questions is in the negative. Drawing distinctions, making critical points, and creating room for the soaring imagination constitute exhilarating exercises for the mind. But only for the minds of a relatively small number of people. Some individuals simply cannot think that way. Perhaps that weakness is offset by other skills, and those who lack it never miss it. I have attempted to interest students over the last sixty years in thinking philosophically. Some of them have come alive with the discovery of their native powers, but many found thought difficult and disquieting.

Even if we deduct the personal and social harms created by harnessing the humanities to political ends, their contributions to some lives are overwhelming. The reference, once again, to "some" lives is intentional because many people of my acquaintance, some of them students, have no use for the humanities. Willie, my erstwhile plumber, confessed to two developmental goals in life: he wanted to solve the problems of pipes and faucets and he wanted to drink beer. His reading was limited to road signs and his thinking was focused on what excuse he could offer his wife for having stayed at the bar till late.

Willie was clearly flourishing; his life had challenge and satisfaction.[4] To say that he could have profited from some poetry is the empty blabbering of the overeducated elite. He didn't need much, he had what he needed and he was happy. Willie and his friends surround us, reminding us not to make a searing problem out of what has a simple solution. The downside of too much learning is the problematization of the everyday, providing depth of reflection but denying immediate enjoyment of the processes of life.

His desires, actions, and satisfactions identify Willie as a certain sort of human being. There are many sorts, and a proportion of them do not need to have their lives improved. This may sound like treason from an educator, but it is only a plea to leave well enough alone.

---

[3] Compare Jennifer L. Hansen's discussion of philosophy as an autotelic activity in "A Reconsideration of the Role of Philosophy in the Reconstruction of Leisure," her chapter in this volume. Hansen also stresses the fact that the humanities frequently fail to contribute to human flourishing—which she analyzes more in terms of technological rationality and economic market forces rather than matters of personal character or the structure and history of the professional discipline of philosophy.

[4] Here see Valerie Tiberius's goal fulfillment account of flourishing and her claim that in almost all cases "what's good for people is intimately tied to what they value," "Well-Being, Value Fulfillment, and Valuing Capacities: Toward a More Subjective Hybrid," this volume.

Works Cited

Ayer, A. J. *Language, Truth and Logic*, Dover, 1952.

Goldstein, Rebecca Newberger. "The Conatus Project: Mattering and Morality." *Philosophy and Human Flourishing*. Ed. John J. Suhr, Oxford University Press, 2022.

Johnson, Mark. "Flourishing in the Flesh." *Philosophy and Human Flourishing*. Ed. John J. Suhr, Oxford University Press, 2022.

Moody-Adams, Michele. "Philosophy and the Art of Human Flourishing." *Philosophy and Human Flourishing*. Ed. John J. Suhr, Oxford University Press, 2022.

Lachs, John. "Human Natures," *Proceedings and Addresses of the American Philosophical Association*, vol. 63, June 1990, pp. 22–39.

Stuhr, John. "Flourishing: Toward Clearer Ideas and Habits of Genius." *Philosophy and Human Flourishing*. Ed. John J. Suhr, Oxford University Press, 2022.

Wahman, Jessica. "Pragmatic Stories of Selves and Their Flourishing." *Philosophy and Human Flourishing*. Ed. John J. Suhr, Oxford University Press, 2022.

PART II
HUMAN FLOURISHING
IN PRACTICE

7

Flourishing

Toward Clearer Ideas and Habits of Genius

John J. Stuhr[*]

> My mission in life is not merely to survive, but to thrive; and to do so
> with some passion, some compassion, some humor, and some style.
>
> —Maya Angelou

> Poetry fettered, fetters the human race. Nations are destroyed or
> flourish in proportion as their painting, poetry, and music are
> destroyed or flourish.
>
> —William Blake

The Practical Question: How Does One Lead a Flourishing Life?

There is only one immediately and wholly *practical* question about flourishing. It is this: *How* does one lead a flourishing life? Put differently: *How*
does one genuinely thrive rather than merely survive?

Now, I recognize—and this is a point I want to stress as strongly as possible
at the outset and to make reverberate throughout this chapter—that it may
well seem that even to ask this question is to engage in an appalling activity—
an exercise of overlooking or looking past or just failing to attend to poverty,
prejudice, pain and illness, injustice, ignorance, abuse, violence, and the personal and structural harms that mark the lives of so many people today. It

[*] James Pawelski read and commented critically and constructively in great detail on drafts of this
chapter. I thank him for his insightful and generous thoughts—both those I have adopted and also
those I have not.

John J. Stuhr, *Flourishing* In: *Philosophy and Human Flourishing*. Edited by: John J. Stuhr, Oxford University Press.
© Oxford University Press 2023. DOI: 10.1093/oso/9780197622162.003.0008

may well *seem* that this is the case because, quite simply, in fact it often *is* the case. We live in a world in which vastly unequal and unfair differences in psychological, social, cultural, and environmental resources and opportunities afford a tiny minority of people, if they are so inclined, the relatively, even obscenely, large luxury of concern about their own flourishing. Meanwhile, others have no such leisure and struggle simply to keep threats to their survival at bay for yet another day. They are not actively engaged in flourishing activities—activities that require resources, many of which they simply do not have. They are focused on survival: getting through another day without health insurance; providing food and shelter for their children; holding on to a job, even one that pays too little or is mind-numbing; finding safe spaces or asylum from hate, violence, aggression, war; outlasting corruption, authoritarianism, and new technologies of control; being with loved ones. All this does not mean that the goal of flourishing should be abandoned or considered merely a matter of unalterable fortune.[1] Just the opposite: Flourishing needs to be extended—and not just in theory but in practice. What all this does mean, however, is that any acceptable theory of flourishing must not ignore or unwittingly reinforce the very conditions that now render a flourishing life genuinely out of reach for so many. These social conditions, moreover, in turn often sustain (and so are complicit in) a view of flourishing that presupposes and leaves intact these very conditions—rather than critically questioning and aiming to reconstruct them.[2] An acceptable account of flourishing cannot be simply a set of guidelines for how a few folks emerge as the winners of a stacked-deck bad game. It must be in part an imaginative, pluralistic vision of a more meaningful, more fulfilling and actualizing, more engaging life for all its diverse participants.

How to flourish? Because it is difficult to move toward *any* goal in life unless one understands to a significant degree what that goal is, so it is difficult (at least without continuous, and thus highly unlikely, good fortune) actually to lead a life of flourishing if one doesn't even know what flourishing is. Before we begin *any* journey toward flourishing, we'd better know its location and in what direction it lies. (This point can be generalized: Practice is not

---

[1] See McMahon, "From the Paleolithic to the Present: Three Revolutions in the Global Revolution of Happiness," p. 11.

[2] José Medina articulates related concerns in in his "Relational Insensitivity and the Interdependence of Flourishing and Withering," this volume (especially the third section: Epistemic Activism: Fighting against Relational Insenstivity).

likely to be very successful if it is not informed by intelligence. It is this fact that renders thinking pragmatic.)

Now, despite the fact that there are many popular and scholarly articles, essays, manifestos, books, and videos about flourishing, this idea remain to a significant degree both practically unclear and critically inapplicable. This is my first thesis. This means that the first task of any account of how to lead a flourishing life is the project of making this idea of flourishing clearer—much, much clearer.

In claiming that the idea of flourishing is *practically unclear*, I mean that this idea is not defined in terms of any practical effects or consequences that make it possible to determine effectively and consistently whether any given action, any cluster of habits, any set of practices or relations or modes of interaction, or any given life does or does not constitute an instance of flourishing.

In claiming that the idea of flourishing is *critically inapplicable*, I mean that the apparently central normative dimension of this idea—flourishing is a matter of prescription and value, not just description and fact—renders its application for any critical purpose to any particular and concrete situations in part a question-begging evaluation rather than any sort of (merely) empirically (or scientifically) warranted description.

It is easy to call names and to idly criticize. In claiming that the notion of flourishing is practically unclear and critically inapplicable, in contrast, my aim is constructive. I want to show that the notion of flourishing is *essentially and irreducibly multivalent*. In other words, the idea of flourishing has plural, often confused or contested, and at times incommensurable meanings, interpretations, values, and applications. I address these multiple dimensions of flourishing in the next section: Multiple and Partial Dimensions of Flourishing These differences must be identified, clarified, and made explicit if the idea of flourishing is to be rendered clear and have critical force in practice. I explain how to do this in a way that brings together insights from both a critical, pragmatic philosophy and an experimental, positive psychology in the third section: From Multiplicity to Clarity and Empirical Method. In the fourth section, Habits, Genius, and the Humanities, finally, I attempt to provide an example or case study of one clear and practical way to think about one important dimension of flourishing—the habit of ongoing growth or ability to reconstruct in fulfilling ways one's habits as one's environment changes and renders old habits less and less means to, and expressions of, well-being.

Multiple and Partial Dimensions of Flourishing

At present, the lack of practical clarity and the critical inapplicability of the notion of flourishing are manifest across several different dimensions or aspects of flourishing. Here are ten of them—different dimensions of flourishing each of which is merely partial and each of which becomes problematic when it is presented as more than partial and when the interests that have led to a focus on just this part or dimension of flourishing are not acknowledged and assessed.

1. Any wholly third-person account or external perspective on flourishing is inadequate and can provide only part of the story about flourishing. To assert that someone else is or partly is or is not much at all flourishing is to hold that the criteria of flourishing do not include how individuals actually experience themselves and their own lives. This would mean, for example, that a third party reasonably could hold that someone was thriving even if that person reported depression or indifference, disengagement and lack of affect, only superficial relationships and commitments, little meaning or value, and almost no sense of achievement or self-worth. The perspective and judgments of other persons are important and frequently crucial, and surely our own views about almost everything are shaped in important ways by the outlooks of others. Nonetheless, an experience of one's self as flourishing appears to be a necessary condition of a flourishing life. If after discussion and reflection with other persons, individuals just do not experience themselves as thriving, then the judgments of others seem at best incomplete and at worst wide of the mark. Third party judgments or assessments are not sufficient; flourishing is not merely an objectivist notion.[3]

2. At the same time and in a parallel fashion, first-person accounts, self-reports, or internal perspectives are also partial, incomplete, and insufficient as marks of flourishing or as bases for judgments about flourishing. If this were not the case, judgments about flourishing

---

[3] While I here undercut and, so, sidestep the subjectivist/objectivist dualism and the shared assumption made in common both by those who view values as subjective and those who take them to be objective, Valerie Tiberius in her "hybrid subjectivism" stresses this same point about the inadequacy of purely third-person accounts of flourishing: "The ultimate explanation for why something is good for a person must refer to that person's attitudes (in some way) . . . " ("Well-Being, Value Fulfillment, and Valuing Capacities: toward a More Subjective Hybrid," this volume).

would amount to the simple identification of flourishing with people's own judgment of their flourishing or lack of flourishing. This would be reasonable only on the assumption that everyone has zero self-deception and complete self-transparency, a self-understanding immune to manipulation and control, and, instead, complete self-knowledge. On this assumption, any belief I hold about myself is true and any ways in which I matter to myself is evidence that I do matter just because I am the one who believes or experiences it.[4] This assumption, of course, is contrary to the facts of life. Sadly, just because I believe that my current activities or my life constitute flourishing to the extreme, it does not follow that this is so. And just as sadly, ideals of flourishing held by individuals in societies in which anti-flourishing conditions are pervasive are apt themselves to be marked by these conditions. (Is it even possible to say what flourishing is under conditions of extreme anti-flourishing for so many—or all?) The experience of one's self as flourishing appears to be a partial, incomplete, insufficient measure of a flourishing life. First party judgments or assessments are not sufficient; flourishing is not merely a subjectivist notion. And to flourish is not simply to feel happy (something that, as Kant pointed out, reason is not especially suited to produce).

3. There is an important corollary to this second point—one with important substantive and methodological implications. Given that self-reports and personal statements about one's subjective preferences are merely partial, insufficient measures of a flourishing life—valuable but partial—it follows that any and all first-person surveys or questionnaires about these preferences are highly insufficient, limited, and flawed when treated as complete measures or sufficient evidence or a thorough mapping of flourishing (or "the positive" more generally).[5] That some one person or even a large collection of individual

[4] See Rebecca Newberger Goldstein's account of "first-person mattering" in her "The Contaus Project: Mattering and Morality," this volume.

[5] To the extent that any mapping of preferences and dispreferences takes those preferences and dispreferences to be matters of fact, it provides no space for a critical examination of them, the conditions of their formation, or the interests and persons that these conditions either serve or do not serve. So, if the positive is understood as that which is preferred, it leaves unexamined the issue of whether any particular preference is or is not preferable to any other particular preference. It leaves unexamined, that is, whether what is valued is also valuable. This point and its implications are developed in great detail by John Dewey in his *Theory of Valuation*. Historical examples can help illustrate this point. That many white American plantation owners had a simple preference for chattel slavery, for example, and the fact that this may have been a strong preference or a preference sustained over generations is insufficient evidence that the preference is positive or part of a positive, flourishing life. Indeed, if one looks at human history (including the present), slavery and domination appear to

persons prefers X to not-X or prefers X to some other Y does not by itself establish that X is any part of a flourishing life or that an increase in the preferred X is an increase in the "positive" aspects of life. It simply is evidence that someone prefers X to not-X and/or to some Y. The fact of this preference would count as a measure of flourishing only if we conceived of flourishing in terms of met or unmet self-aware and reported preferences. However, because persons who are surveyed or in other ways report on their preferences may lack self-knowledge or be deceived—human beings are not wholly transparent to themselves—and because these preferences may be products of intentional manipulation or merely the limits of any given historical/cultural perspective, flourishing is not simply a matter of individually perceived individual preference satisfaction. To fail to take seriously this point is to run the risk of reducing flourishing to a life of maximum preference satisfaction—even the satisfaction of preferences that (from the standpoint of other criteria of a flourishing life) may have no place at all in a flourishing life. This is not simply a theoretical possibility: It is a practical reality that people frequently desire the undesirable and that, sadly, the satisfaction of some preferences shows them not to be what they had seemed as we pursued them. Moreover, it is—with both rational choice theorists and more recently (but just as much) with behavioral economists—to treat reported preferences as explanations of why persons chose what they chose and it is to treat preference fulfillment and maximization (whether rational or misformed) as a method by which to aggregate human behavior. To do this is to engage in the social pathology of the social sciences—to mistake or uncritically equate the aggregate results of social science surveys of individuals for wisdom and the art of leading a flourishing life. The notion of flourishing in very large part does not admit of rational choice, economistic, social-scientific reductionism in substance or in methodology.

4. Fourth, in a related manner the notion of flourishing does not admit fully of biological, life-scientific reductionism either. Now, obviously

be thoroughly and strongly sustained preferences—preferences so great that they often include dismissal of the preferences of those who are enslaved and dominated and even refusal to view and treat those persons as full persons. For a helpful discussion of the concept of preference within positive psychology, see Pawelski, "Defining the 'Positive' in Positive Psychology" Part I, pp. 339–56 and Part II, pp. 357–65.

the notion of a flourishing life presupposes the notion of life itself. Flourishing requires life, and no organism can achieve in any continuous way a flourishing life unless it manages to be alive and stay alive. But this is a merely partial, if necessary, condition (or pre-condition) and not a sufficient condition of flourishing or a very full story of a flourishing life. Mere life itself and its physiological (or inner) and environmental (or outer) conditions provide no sufficient and justified criteria for what makes a life flourishing or thriving. As Mark Johnson explains in his chapter in this volume, no doubt a sufficient level of homeostatic internal stability and response to environment, for example, is a necessary component or condition (or pre-condition) of flourishing—because it is a necessary condition for life.[6] Nonetheless, this idea provides no practical implications for an account of flourishing—infants stunted by lead in their drinking water, children growing up in abject poverty or war-torn strife with little opportunity for escape, young adults in mind-numbingly repetitive wage labor, anxiety- or anger-filled retirees, and serial rapists and solitary confinement prisoners all may exhibit relatively high level of homeostasis and, simultaneously, relatively low levels of flourishing. Now, in an effort to address this problem and to avoid mistaking a part of flourishing for the whole, some theorists have defined homeostasis not simply in terms of *maintenance* of internal conditions of an organism but in terms of the *optimal* functioning of the organism (which seems to be more accurately a matter of growth than a matter of literal maintenance). Other theorists have set aside the notion of homeostasis and embraced the idea of "allostasis"—not really any sort of *stasis* at all but rather a constantly changing adaptation and challenge-meeting in the face of new conditions.[7] These shifts are very much at odds with the strictly biological meaning of homeostasis as Claude Bernard and Walter Cannon first used the term, but beyond that and more important they are shifts that convert the idea of homeostasis from a biological notion of survival to a normative one of flourishing. Given this shift, though, the question of what is to count as an organism's "optimal" or "flourishing" or "higher" function is begged—or, at least, unanswered. As philosophers since the days of Plato have known,

---

[6] Mark Johnson, "Flourishing in the Flesh," this volume. Johnson uses the term "homeodynamics."
[7] See, for example, Tucker and Luu, *Cognition and Neural Development*).

certainly the mere maintenance of life—the quantity of life—is not an adequate measure of flourishing—the optimization of life. When Socrates drank the hemlock, he was not renouncing living well, although he was abandoning biological homeostasis.

5. Any practically relevant and critically applicable notion of flourishing must confront, acknowledge, and embrace the great diversity of human lives and the big fact of pluralism. It is a fact: We are different—not absolutely or entirely different, but different. What counts as flourishing for me may not constitute flourishing for you. Succinctly put, flourishing is a relative or relational term: To assert that a life of some X constitutes flourishing is a shorthand or abbreviation for asserting that a life of X constitutes flourishing for person P at time T or situation S. Recognition of the real plurality of lives of different persons and different times and different situations constitutes a cautionary tale for any final, closed, monistic, narrow account of human flourishing. It is an antidote to what John Lachs in this volume has termed "the allure of the 'all.'"[8]

Here are two ways to understand and respond to this tale. The first way is to conclude that any successful account of human flourishing must escape all these differences, must rise above them, and so must be tremendously abstract and untethered to the particulars of any concrete situation (any concrete P, T, and S). This sort of project exhibits a Miss America Contestant Speech syndrome: It earnestly announces, for example, that a flourishing life involves Happiness, Meaning, Purpose, Achievement, and Social Engagements of recognition, respect, care, and love. Like most Miss America candidates, we almost all want, for example, World Peace. But this project is practically empty and has no critical application unless and until supposed commonalities are translated into and operationalized as specific differences in particular lives: Without this, such an account does not provide any actual, concrete person with any direction at all about how or with whom to lead one's life. These abstractions—to flourish you must live with happiness, meaning, purpose, achievement, and engagement—could be embraced equally by terrorists and teachers, cult followers and concerned parents, mean girls and nice girls, by wolves of Wall Street and altruistic philanthropists, and by

---

[8] John Lachs, "The Allure of the 'All,'" this volume.

liberal and illiberal democrats. A very different way to understand the implications of pluralism for an account of flourishing would be to avoid all context-free pronouncements, moral absolutes,[9] and false universalizations, to be very careful about speaking for others (especially others whose lives are more different than similar to one's own), and to strive to create conditions in which plural and different voices can articulate plural and different accounts of flourishing and motivate action to address its absence in their lives. As Jessica Wahman argues persuasively,[10] this would result in *narrative* understandings of flourishing—something much more like the stories provided by nuanced novels, plays, paintings, poems, photographs, music, dance, and science-informed humanities than merely a biology or cognitive science of homeostasis.

6. There is a brief but important corollary here: This pluralism is not simply inter-personal pluralism, not simply recognition that a flourishing life for person P may be quite different from a flourishing life for person Q. It is also *intra*-personal pluralism, recognition that what constitutes a flourishing life for person P at T1 (for example, as a sixteen-year-old) is likely not to be fully a flourishing life for that same person P at T2 or T3 (for example, as a thirty-six-year-old or as a seventy-six-year-old). This is an easy point to recognize in reflection, but because of the force of habit, it is a much harder point to take up in action. Habits that are part of a relatively flourishing life easily can remain habits long after the conditions in which they worked so well have vanished. When this happens, habits that worked so well over a particular time and place bad habits—habits that remain long after the conditions in which they were established have changed. And so, it is not simply that a full account of flourishing must recognize the plurality of persons and their lives—a plurality that includes both felt continuities and felt discontinuities, self-familiarity and self-distance.[11] It also must recognize that each self, each one of us, is a

---

[9] John Z. Sadler discusses the importance of reducing moral certainty in his "Values Literacy and Citizenship," this volume.

[10] Jessica Wahman, "Pragmatic Stories of Selves and Their Flourishing," this volume. See especially the section "Narrative Explanation and Self-Understanding," in which Wahman pinpoints two faulty assumptions in arguments against narrativity.

[11] See the related account of critical self-estrangement provided by José Medina, this volume. Medina finds in the writings of William James insufficient attention to this critical, self-critical dimension of experience. I think that James's constant attention to the irreducibly selective and partial character of any self-awareness (or of attention to anything at all) includes centrally this critical dimension—and so find that what Medina terms *guerrilla* pragmatism and its epistemic activism is

multiplicity. And so no partial, single, fixed, frozen-in-time account of any self's flourishing can be adequate.

7. Many accounts of flourishing are framed in terms of their answer to this question: Is the positive simply the absence of the negative, or is the positive something more than the absence of the negative?[12] Many traditional psychologists in effect have answered that the positive, to the extent they have theorized it at all, simply is the absence of the negative—that persons rid of depression, for example, have positive feelings and moods. By contrast, the work of many positive psychologists in effect generally illustrates the view that the positive is something more than the absence of the negative—that flourishing is something more than simply not suffering or not ailing or merely mitigating life problems. Now, if we think of the positive (flourishing, self-realizing) and the negative (suffering, self-diminishing) as poles of a continuum, then the positive psychologists surely are correct: Simply because one (whether as a result of treatment or not) is not at or near the negative pole of an arc or continuum, it does not follow that one is at or near the positive pole (as opposed, say, to being mired somewhere in the middle between the two poles). Just because someone is not deeply depressed, it does not follow that this person's life is happy. Surely it is possible not to be depressed and at the same time not to be very fully happy and in the flow of peak experience. However, if we employ a very different picture or image of the positive and the negative, then things look—surprise!—different. If we think of flourishing (the positive) as an Aristotelian golden mean in the middle of a continuum, with excess (a negative) at one pole and deficiency (also a negative) at another pole, then it is the traditional psychologists who

in practice a *melioristic* pragmatism. See also Sadler's philosophical psychiatry-informed account of value-blindness, this volume (especially the section on "Becoming Values Literate").

[12] See James O. Pawelski's contrast between philosophies that focus on understanding the world and those that focus on changing it and his contrast between human energies devoted to mitigating negatives and problems and other energies focused on promoting positives and goods. In pragmatic spirit, Pawelski concludes that we need to balance these concerns—and so to confront opportunities as much as problems. "Teaching Philosophy: The Love of Wisdom and the Cultivation of Human Flourishing," this volume. This stress on balance is also evident in his "Bringing Together the Humanities and the Science of Well-Being to Advance Human Flourishing" *Well-Being and Higher Education*, pp. 207–16. See also Seligman and Csikszentmihalyi, "Positive Psychology: An Introduction," pp. 5–14. Seligman and Csikszentmihalyi explain that traditionally, since World War II, psychology's "empirical focus shifted to assessing and curing individual suffering," (p. 14) and they argue that it must become also the study of "strength and virtue" (p. 7) and that it is not enough for psychology only "to help those who suffer" (p. 10).

appear largely correct: The positive (flourishing) is just the (positive) absence of the negative in any and all of its forms (both excess and deficiency). If someone is without both cowardice and foolhardiness, then that person is courageous; if someone is neither miserly nor extravagant, then that person is generous; persons who are not shy or arrogant are thus relatively modest. It is impossible to be neither cowardly nor foolhardy without thus being courageous. I suspect it is quite easy for one or the other of these images to grip our mind—to think of flourishing either as one end of a positive/negative continuum or as the midpoint of an excess/deficiency continuum. Or we may prefer yet some other image—for example, instead of opposites, or a linear continuum, we might prefer a two-dimensional graph in which flourishing is a point in the upper right (e.g., high positive affect over a sustained long period of time) or lower left (e.g., high positive affect and low negative affect). Or we may prefer a three-dimensional or four-dimensional model or a model with even more variables.[13] Rather than argue (in ways I think are fated to be inconclusive but stereotypically academically partisan) about which of these images is the *right* one or the *true* one, I suspect we would do better to ask in a pragmatic spirit *what purpose is served* by employing one or the other— and by demanding that anyone who uses one of these images make this purpose explicit. At present I am not concerned to lobby for the usefulness of either of these images in any specific context. My point here concerns the nature of the positive presupposed by these various images. Accordingly, I want to call attention to what I take to be a shared flaw and incompleteness in all of these images of flourishing. They typically assume that a constitutive condition of the presence of the positive (even when at the same time there may be present *other* negatives) is the absence of the negative always intrinsically and irreducibly within the positive itself; both assume that the presence of the positive *ipso facto* is not at once also the presence of the negative. The traditional psychologist often appears to believe that the positive—as a particular positive—simply is the absence of the negative (though of course other negatives may be present at the same time), while the positive psychologist appears often to believe that the positive is the

---

[13] See, for example, the following: Peterson, "The Values in Action (VIA) Classification of Strengths," pp. 29–48; and Pawelski, "Happiness and Its Opposites," pp. 326–37.

absence of the particular negative (though again other negatives may be present at the same time) plus the absence of the more or less neutral that lies between that specific positive and the negative of that same specific. But both agree that for the positive to be present, that specific negative must be absent or largely absent. However, in actual human experience, often this is not the case. Much of the time, our lives are messier, more complex, and less pure; our good are less comprehensive and complete.[14] Put in dramatic terms, life always is irreducibly more tragic (or more negative) than either the positive/negative image or the excess/mean/deficiency picture allow. It is not simply that sometimes one fails to attain a good (the positive, the golden mean) or that sometimes the good attained turns out not to be really quite as good as expected. Rather, it is that *even when one attains a good*, even when one is in the flow, even when one is flourishing, this comes necessarily at the cost of the real and permanent loss of many other possible goods. For example, to become a world-class pianist is to renounce forever the joys one might have had if all that time spent practicing had been put to other use developing other talents or pursuing other pastimes. To spend one's life with many people, as another example, is to sacrifice forever a kind of relationship possible only with significantly more time spent with just one or a few other persons. And vice versa. And to journey to an academic meeting to receive a book prize is forever to lose that very same time with your aging parents, young children, or good friends. As William James forcefully put it, the attainment of any positive good requires that the ideal—the fully, flowing positive or the glittering golden mean—be "butchered." The realization of any and every possibility comes only with the destruction of many other possibilities—sometimes only the destruction of brief and small possibilities but sometimes the destruction of long-lasting and large possibilities. Flourishing is not simply a name for real gains; it is also and at the same time and irreducibly a name for real losses. Any adequate account of flourishing must be attentive—more than attentive, it must be sensitive to and nuanced about—this butchering and this kind of loss.

[14] See the critical account of the "comprehensive view of the good life" and the recognition of the regular and irreducible conflicts among different goods of different domains of life that Lori Gallegos develops in "Navigating Irreconcilable Conflicts: Philosophical Thinking for Better Lives," her chapter in this volume.

8. This last point makes evident that if one wants to give an account of a *life* of flourishing, then even seemingly innocuous dictionary definitions of "flourishing" all fail. Standard dictionaries note that the English word "flourish" comes from the Latin word *floere* and the old French word *florir*: Both mean to flower. Flourishing thus is understood as flowering, blossoming, blooming, and displaying and abounding in vigor—and this plant-based or vegetative notion is extended to mean thriving and prospering, being successful, and being in one's prime. Precisely because this notion of flourishing is drawn from plant life, it is essentially seasonal and cyclical: Life consists of dormancy followed by rebirth and growth and then bloom and flourishing display which in turn give way to decline and death or dormancy again. This plant-based understanding limits flourishing to a season, not a whole life. On this account, flourishing is flowering; what happens before flowering and what happens after is not flourishing. We might say this idea is "summer-normative," and thus wonder why bare stems and branches or muted gold and rust colored leaves must be any less instances of thriving, flourishing, well-being, or being in prime form than are flowers and bright green new leaves. This dictionary notion of flourishing appears to implicitly do normative work—it locates greatest value in the blooms and flowers of life—but it is without any critical justification and, thus, application. Is a ten-year old human merely a preparatory stage to a thirty-year old, and a sixty-year old merely a faded after-glow in decomposition as winter approaches? Or should we throw out this plant-based idea in favor of a view of flourishing that allows for *different* kinds of flowering and blooming and growth in every season of human life? Should we think of flourishing in terms of whole lives and not just a season in the sun? And if we take this turn—essentially a (non-Aristotelian) temporalizing of means and ends and a recognition of intra-personal pluralism—then surely part of what it means to flourish at any given time is to develop the conditions for flourishing at a later time. Any adequate account of flourishing must be rooted (sorry!) in a means-end continuum and not confined to a single season. It must be a motion picture and not a still photograph.

9. Flourishing is often characterized as a life of meaning or purpose. This seems to be a mistake or confusion, perhaps another instance of taking one important strand or dimension of flourishing for its

sufficient condition. It is important here not to confuse a *meaningful* life with a *valuable* life. (I realize that people often say that something is "meaningful" to them when what they mean is that it is "valued" by them or "valuable" to them.) A life of abuse, suffering, frustration, rejection, loneliness, and sadness, for example, is *not* a life *without meaning*, without significance, and without sense. It is not a desirable life, a life of self-realization and happiness, a life of flourishing, a life that has received what Rebecca Newberger Goldstein, following William James, calls "appropriate attention" and the being morally worthy of attention.[15] Indeed, this lack of desirability is its very meaning. Accordingly, meaning in life is not sufficient for well-being. The important issue here for human well-being is not *whether* a life has meaning; it is *what* meaning life has.

Of course, to distinguish a valuable life from a meaningful life simply points to the need to explain what makes a life valuable— what makes particular lives instances of genuine well-being. So, if a flourishing life is a valuable life, what is the practical meaning of a valuable life? Here it is critically insufficient to say that it is a life of purpose or hope—or even to say, with Camus, that it is a life without hope. A life dedicated to killing supposed infidels or reaping the benefits of racial slavery or leading new recruits into a cult founded on the belief that God is uniquely on one's own side are lives with purpose and with hope. But the sheer presence of such purposes and hopes, many people would think, have nothing at all—or, at least, not everything—to do with leading a flourishing life. In fact, some purposes and hopes may be downright incompatible with a flourishing life. When flourishing or thriving is identified with meaning or purpose or hope but the normative core of these terms is not given practical meaning, no clear and sufficient account of flourishing can emerge.

10. If human beings are irreducibly social beings, then any adequate account of flourishing must apply not simply to individual humans but to social relations, societal associations and institutions, and to cultural practices more broadly. Any account of human flourishing as merely individual flourishing is wildly incomplete. If the self is

---

[15] Rebecca Newberger Goldstein, this volume (especially the "Normativity and Mattering" section).

social, flourishing must be understood in social and political terms and not simply in individual ethical terms. In this light, to account for flourishing is not to formulate a merely personal ethic. Rather, it is to detail and recommend diverse forms of community life and the means to their realization. In this context, John Dewey's characterization of democracy in its generic sense is telling and with little modification could serve as a practical and critical corrective of any overly individualistic or overly voluntaristic account of flourishing. Dewey wrote:

From the standpoint of the individual, it [democracy] consists in having a responsible share according to capacity in forming and directing the activities of the groups to which one belongs and in participating according to need in the values which the groups sustain. From the standpoint of the groups, it demands liberation of the potentialities of members of a group in harmony with the interests and goods which are common.[16]

A realization of the social, political nature of flourishing in turn points directly to a crucial substantive question: To what extent can an individual flourish in a society that is not flourishing? I am reminded here of Mary Wollstonecraft's observation that "virtue can only flourish among equals" and Adam Smith's assertion that "No society can surely be flourishing and happy, of which the greater part of the members are poor and miserable." As indicated earlier, this also raises a methodological question: What are the limits of an account of flourishing made from within largely non-flourishing social conditions? This concern also raises a crucial political questions: Who is authorized or empowered to put forward or to act on behalf of any particular account of flourishing? By contrast, who is silenced or excluded? To what extent is the flourishing of some parasitic on the non-flourishing of others, perhaps many more others? Who is so privileged as to be able to live blithely unaware of the impacts of one's own efforts to flourish on the lives of others? How can I genuinely flourish while so many others suffer and are deprived—and suffer in part to provide the very

[16] Dewey, *The Public and Its Problems, The Later Works of John Dewey, 1925-1953*, vol. 2 (Carbondale, IL: Southern Illinois University Press, 1984 [1927]), pp. 327–28.

resources and conditions of what I might take to be my personal well-being? These political questions highlight the *irreducibly normative* nature of any notion of flourishing—and thus the fact that any positive *psychology* of flourishing is at least in large part a philosophical *ethic* and a political *philosophy*. (If the notion of flourishing were not normative, it would make sense to ask for reasons why flourishing is something *prima facie* good). Finally, if any adequate account of flourishing is irreducibly political because the self is irreducibly social, so too any adequate account of flourishing must be irreducibly *environmental or ecological* because the self is irreducibly natural. Here too John Dewey put this nicely:

> An organism does not live in an environment; it lives by means of an environment . . . The processes of living are enacted by the environment as truly as by the organism; for they are an integration . . . . Natural operations like breathing and digesting, acquired ones like speech and honesty, are functions of the surroundings as truly as of a person. They are things done by the environment by means of organic structures or acquired dispositions.[17]

From Multiplicity to Clarity and Empirical Method

I have identified ten dimensions of flourishing and some of the pitfalls that accompany insufficient attention to them. Collectively all this constitutes a challenge to address in order to formulate a concept of human flourishing that has both practical or operational meaning and critical, normative use. As detailed in the prior section, these pitfalls and challenges are as follows:

1. Viewing flourishing in a wholly third-person or "objective" way
2. Conceiving flourishing only in a first-person or "subjective" way
3. Failing to recognize the limits of individual or aggregate preference claims
4. Taking homeostasis or like conditions as a sufficient basis or full model for human well-being;5. Under-estimating human differences

[17] Dewey, *The Later Works of John Dewey, 1925–1953*, vol. 16, p. 100.

and failing to provide a sufficiently pluralistic rather than one-size-fits-all account

6. Failing to take this pluralism as intra-personal as well as inter-personal

7. Overly minimizing the role of loss and tragedy in even realizations of ideals, goals, and goods

8. Embracing only a plant-based notion of flourishing as a brief flowering season rather than a complete life;

9. Conflating a life of meaning or purpose with a life of value (and some but not any and all meanings and purposes) and

10. Considering flourishing in overly individualistic or private terms abstracted from its constitutive social relations and cultural conditions.

The upshot of all this is *not* that the concept of human flourishing or well-being is irreducibly unclear and imprecise—or that human flourishing thus cannot be a subject of rigorous empirical measurement or scientific study. The upshot of all this is not a dead-end but, rather, an agenda for the future. The idea of human flourishing, often unclear and imprecise, must be—and can be—made clear. "Flourishing" is a multi-valent word: It is a (non-linear) polyseme—a word with multiple different but related senses. This requires that its practical meaning in any given context must be made explicit. This requires a five-dimensional account of flourishing that makes clear how the notion is being understood and used along all five of the following axes:

First, *an epistemic methodology axis*: By what criteria is the claimed relative presence or absence of flourishing determined? Is it, for example, a matter of first-person or subjective or self-reporting—all persons determining solely or finally their own level of well-being? And, if it is a matter of self-reporting, then what is it about one's self that a given self takes to be relevant—a feeling of satisfaction, a sense of purpose, a calculation of the maximization of one's choices, belief in the esteem of others, or something else? Or, is it a matter of third-person, objective, other-reporting—some particular person or particular group in the end determining the level of well-being in the lives of other people? And, if it is a matter of third-person reporting, who's reporting is taken as the basis or judged qualified or authorized to make this determination—family, friends, co-workers, strangers, trained (how?) experts and think tanks, psychologists, or psychiatrists? Moreover, what is being measured by these folks—economic output, disease or longevity, educational levels, presence of key social services, proximity to parks, clean air and water, levels of crime and war? Something else?

Second, *a semiotic content axis*: What does the idea of flourishing mean? What does it denote? In any given use of the notion, what is its reference? Is flourishing defined as some sort of persistence or biological homeostasis? Or, rather, is it a kind of change or growth or continual and creative self-re-creation? Is it a feeling of pleasure, a state of happiness, activities of flow, or experiences that are their own end and undertaken for themselves?[18] Is it a life in which one's desires are satisfied or the realization of one's choices maximized? Or is it a life in which one desires that things happen as they do or a life found worthy of the events that happen to it? Is it a life that is believed to be eternal? Is a flourishing life one that is meaningful in some sense or found to be purposeful, to matter, or to make some specific difference or to be marked by a particular kind of achievement? Is it a life that other people judge meaningful?

Third, *a normative judgment axis*: On what ethical basis is flourishing judged to be a moral value and what is its relation to other important moral values including, for example, tolerance, altruism and personal sacrifice,[19] responsibility, respect, justice, and equality? Is a flourishing life valuable because of the principles from which it issues? Because of its consequences? Or the character or commitments or sheer will of one who pursues it? Is a flourishing life good because it is somehow divine? These questions have practical and not just theoretical bite. When should concern with flourishing be primary? When should it yield to other values? Is the advancement of the well-being of one or some in some situations immoral? And, when the answers to these questions are deeply contested and divisive, is there either a genuine ethic or a genuine ethos of flourishing? If so, on what basis is concern with flourishing warranted under conditions of deep contestation about the nature of flourishing itself?

Fourth, *a temporal duration axis*: To what period of time does a claim or judgment about flourishing apply? Is it relatively short-term—reading one book chapter, a romantic fling, a leisurely dinner with friends, a day, a week, or a month? Or is it a longer span of time—one's years in elementary school,

---

[18] See Jennifer Hansen's account of autotelic activities in her chapter, "A Reconsideration of the Role of Philosophy in the Reconstruction and Promotion of Leisure," this volume. Hansen identifies philosophy as such an activity. While it is easy for me, as a philosopher, to agree with this, I think it is important for philosophers to be pluralistic about philosophy—and so to recognize that philosophical activities are autotelic for some people and not for others.

[19] Gallegos discusses often irreconcilable conflicts between individual flourishing and both moral virtue and social justice in sections "Caring for Others through Empathetic Response" and "The Pursuit of Social Justice" of her chapter, this volume.

life as a college or graduate student, the duration of military service, the years of a chronic illness, a multi-decades long intimate relationship, or a whole career? Or recalling Aristotle's question about whether it is possible to call people happy during their lifetimes and how easy it is to mistake good fortune for happiness if one thinks in a short-term way, is a claim about flourishing a claim about a whole life—and not just a claim about one period in that life or one aspect of it?

Fifth, *a scope of target population axis*: Whose flourishing does talk of well-being include? Is the focus on the flourishing of an individual? An aggregate of individuals, whether similar or diverse or randomly selected? Persons with particular habits or ways of thinking? Privileged individuals, culturally disenfranchised people, or those most vulnerable? A family? A neighborhood? A region or nation or diaspora? People alive at a particular time or past or future generations? A species? Whole eco-systems—a focus that would necessitate a trans-human scope and approach to human well-being?

If any notion of flourishing is to have practical, testable meaning and critical normative application, it must be explicitly clear along all five of these axes. This can be done in any number of ways because definitions are not right or wrong but, rather, clear or unclear. This is a pragmatic point: We should stop asking (and talking past each other about) which concept of flourishing is *really* the correct one and instead ask how and why it is illuminating and useful to take up any particular one in some particular context for some particular purpose. And so, for example, the claim that regular physical movement and strength-training is essential for flourishing could be made clear by specifying that clinical expert studies (epistemic methodology axis) suggest levels of pain and anxiety (semiotic content axis) may decrease and bring about more individual day-to-day pleasures and enjoyments (normative judgment axis) after the first month and as long as the exercise is continued (temporal duration axis) for US residents over age 70, above specific levels of wealth and education, and without cancer, chronic heart disease or memory-loss symptoms (scope of target population axis). Or, for a second example, the claim that the humanities and arts contribute nothing to human well-being could be made clear by specifying that one's drinking buddy, Willie,[20] self-reports (epistemic methodology axis) that he experiences philosophy and novels and concerts and art museums as tedious, boring, and frequently undecipherable (semiotic content axis) in ways that make him feel

---

[20] I take this character from John Lachs's essay, this volume.

his own life is meaningless, unimportant, and out of his control[21] (normative judgment axis) for several days on the rare occasions (temporal duration
axis) that he (scope of target population axis) gives them a try.

Specifying the notion of flourishing in this pragmatic kind of way allows
claims about flourishing, so specified, to be matters of empirical inquiry. This
inquiry, in turn, has pragmatic value in so far as it identifies the conditions on
which flourishing, so specified, depends. And it is the subsequent control of
these conditions that best may allow for greater future well-being.

Habits, Genius, and the Humanities

This pragmatic proposal to clarify the concept of flourishing in epistemic, semiotic, normative, temporal, scope dimensions is intended as a description
of a forward-looking and constructive research agenda. As such, this five-
dimension account of flourishing (see section From Multiplicity to Clarity
and Empirical Method) goes a long way in addressing successfully ten important ways (see section Multiple and Partial Dimensions of Flourishing)
in which the concept of flourishing often lacks sufficient practical clarity and
critical application.

In taking up this research agenda, it is tempting to formulate prerequisite
conditions for flourishing—to list physiological, environmental, psychological, social, aesthetic, and political conditions upon which a flourishing life
depends and without which a flourishing life is not possible. This approach
runs two very large risks: First, it often mis-identifies some necessary condition for flourishing as a sufficient condition for flourishing; and, second,
it often mis-identifies a necessary condition for the flourishing of some persons at some times and places as the necessary condition for the flourishing
of all persons at all times and places. To avoid these risks, it is crucial to take
up a temporal, situational, and pluralistic approach rather than one that is
universal, abstract, and general. Even doing this, however, it is impossible to
over-stress the diversity and pluralism of human life—the large differences
in lives, the large differences in the times and places of these lives, and the
large differences in the habits, meanings, and values forged and operative in

---

[21] Jessica Wahman focuses on the role of self-empowerment, narratives of self-empowerment, and
agency as aspects of human flourishing, this volume.

these different conditions. Speaking wisely about flourishing lives requires listening at length to diverse lives, to the narrative stories of diverse lives.

One way—there are other ways—to begin to do this is to recognize that human beings are creatures of habit—and thus to recognize that a life of flourishing (as distinct from an instant or sporadic moments of flourishing) is a life marked by particular habits. The work of William James can be especially helpful here. Viewing life as a bundle of habits and calling habit "the enormous flywheel of society" and "its most precious conservative agency, an unthinking perfect fluency," James advised that the "great thing, then, in all education, is to make our nervous system our ally instead of our enemy." He continued: "It is to fund and capitalize our acquisitions, and live at ease upon the interest of the fund. For this we must make automatic and habitual, as early as possible, as many useful actions as we can . . ."[22] What is habit and how is it possible to make things automatic? By observing that instincts facilitate the establishment of habits, James purposively blurred "the boundaries between instincts—pre-established electrophysiological current paths—and habits—reinforced and new paths "due to the plasticity of the organic materials of which [living] bodies are composed.[23]

On the basis of this physiological account of habit, James turned to their practical consequences for individuals and for society. "The first result," he wrote, "is that *habit simplifies the movements required to achieve a given result, makes them more accurate and diminishes fatigue.*" He added, "The next result is that *habit diminishes the conscious attention with which our acts are performed.*"[24]

James then detailed ethical and educational implications of this point. Here his concluding point was, "Keep the faculty of effort alive in you by a little gratuitous exercise every day,"[25] a point that repeats James's claim in "The Sentiment of Rationality" that "our dearest desires and most cherished powers" need motive to act, something that must be done and something to live *against*, opportunity for and opposition to our powers.[26] In effect, James thus replaced the Puritan work ethic with a more this-worldly physiological work ethic that teaches "the hell to be endured hereafter, of which theology tells, is no worse than the hell we make for ourselves in this world

---

[22] James, *The Principles of Psychology*, pp. 109, 125, 117.
[23] James, *The Principles of Psychology*, pp. 110, 112.
[24] James, *The Principles of Psychology*, pp. 117, 119.
[25] James, *The Principles of Psychology*, p. 130. See also pp. 124–31.
[26] James, *The Principles of Psychology*, p. 328, and James, "The Sentiment of Rationality," p. 70.

by habitually fashioning our characters in the wrong way" and that "every smallest stroke of virtue or of vice leaves its never so little scar."[27]

James also recognized, of course, the danger or negative dimension of habit and its efficiency given the reality of change. In a moving passage—or at least a passage that should resonate with anyone over the age of 20—James observed:

> Most of us grow more and more enslaved to the stock conceptions with which we have once become familiar, and less and less capable of assimilating impressions in any but the old ways. Old-fogyism, in short, is the inevitable terminus to which life sweeps us on. Objects which violate our habits of "apperception" are simply not taken account of at all; or, if on some occasion we are forced by dint of argument to admit their existence, twenty-four hours later the admission is as if it were not, and every trace of the unassimilable truth has vanished from our thought. Genius, in truth, means little more that the faculty of perceiving in an unhabitual way.[28]

Now, I suspect that genius involves not simply *perceiving* in an unhabitual way but also, on the basis of these perceptions, melioristic *acting* in new ways as well. But, this small point aside, I think here we have in short form an account of flourishing not as comfort but as genius: as an openness and flexible[29] responsiveness to unhabitual ways. In a life of flourishing, this openness and responsiveness must themselves become habitual—the cultivation of a habit of being open to the unhabitual in imagination, perception, conception, purpose, and action—in one's own life and in the lives of others. Life requires effective habits; flourishing (judged from both first and third-person perspectives, understood as growth, valued as both means and end, viewed over lifetimes, and manifest by both individuals and their communities), requires the habit of not allowing habits to go bad by binding us to routine, old-fogey responses long after the conditions that generated those habits have changed. If one accepts the reality of time and change, then a flourishing life also must be constituted by (and responsive to) time and change.

The practical, how-to development of this genius—of the habit of perceiving and acting in unhabitual ways—is the work of the humanities and

---

[27] James, *The Principles of Psychology*, p. 120.

[28] James, *The Principles of Psychology*, p. 754.

[29] See Wahman's account of "flexible habits"—i.e., habits of flexibility—in the "Flexible Habits and Flourishing," the penultimate section of her chapter, this volume.

arts.[30] They are the disciplines and activities that self-consciously and self-critically define, develop, and nurture habits of genius. They are any and all endeavors that purposefully aim to humanize. Indeed, the humanities and arts provide an immense wealth of resources for lives of growth.[31] Collectively they are a vast venture fund for genius. They are exercises of critical imagination, simultaneously challenging us and enabling us to renew ourselves through new, different, unhabitual possibilities—to speak and think and feel differently; to re-ask old questions, re-think old answers, and invent new questions; and to articulate new aims, advance new lines of criticism and appreciation, and produce expanded meanings and enlarged selves. To live for sufficient time, even if not forever, with Confucius and Buddha, Plato and Aristotle, the Bible and the Koran, Cervantes and Shakespeare, Rousseau and Wollstonecraft, Shelley and Mastretta, Douglass and Cooper, Addams and Ambedkar, Wright and O'Keefe, Achebe and Carson, Coltrane and Simone, Kushner and Schreck, or the authors of this volume is to develop as habit the skill of perceiving and acting unhabitually. In a time of rapid cultural change, unprecedented climate change, and the hijacking of reason by technological and market forces,[32] now more than ever a flourishing life requires this skill (in both its critical and affirmative dimensions).[33]

A concluding point: The humanities and arts do not foster flourishing lives all by themselves. To flourish over a lifetime, one cannot simply learn a language, read a book, see a painting, or attend a concert. Unhabitual new possibilities must be imagined, but this imagination alone does not realize those possibilities. If the possibilities imagined by the humanities and arts are not

---

[30] By "humanities and arts," I am not referring to departments or disciplines separated from natural and social science in present-day universities and colleges. I am referring to any type of inquiry and activity that self-consciously and self-critically makes the development of habits of genius its aim. I am taking the humanities and arts in a functional sense.

[31] Michele Moody-Adams provides a detailed, pluralistic account of human flourishing and art, particularly its capacity to transform: our sense of possibilities and to provide consolation in the face of the limits of those possibilities; and our sense of ourselves and our societies. "Philosophy and the Art of Human Flourishing," this volume.

[32] This concern with "technological rationality" and market forces is discussed by Jennifer Hansen in her "A Reconsideration of the Role of Philosophy [and the University] in the Reconstruction and Promotion of Leisure," this volume.

[33] I hope this does not need to be stressed, but just in case: the fact that we must avoid becoming what James called "old fogys" does not mean that habits per se interfere with flourishing or that all habits should be scrapped—as if that were even possible. See Louis Tay, James O. Pawelski, and Melissa G. Keith, "The Role of the Arts and Humanities in Human Flourishing: A Conceptual Model," *Journal of Positive Psychology*, 2017, DOI: 10.1080/17439760.2017.127920.7 The "human flourishing outcomes" that the authors identify as "psychological competencies" and "positive normative outcomes" seem particularly to dovetail with a Jamesian account of genius as a habit of unhabitual perception and action.

tied to and joined by structural reconstruction and social action—a politics of flourishing—they will not produce flourishing lives but, instead, only lofty and learned theories of flourishing. Thinking well about flourishing must not become a substitute for living well.

Works Cited

Dewey, John. The Public and Its Problems, The Later Works of John Dewey: 1882–1892, vol. 2, edited by Jo Ann Boydston. Southern Illinois University Press, 1984 [1927].

Dewey, John. Theory of Valuation, The Later Works of John Dewey, 1925–1953 (1939), vol. 13, edited by Jo Ann Boydston. Southern Illinois University Press, 1988.

Dewey, John. Essays, Typescripts, and Knowing and the Known, The Later Works of John Dewey, 1925–1953, vol. 16, edited by Jo Ann Boydston. Southern Illinois University Press.

James, William. "The Sentiment of Rationality," 1879, The Will to Believe and Other Essays in Popular Philosophy. Harvard University Press, 1979.

James, William. The Principles of Psychology, 1890, vol. 1 (Cambridge, MA: Harvard University Press 1981 [1890]), pp. 109, 125, 117.

McMahon, Darrin M. "From the Paleolithic to the Present: Three Revolutions in the Global Revolution of Happiness." E-Handbook of Subjective Well-Being, edited by ed. E. Diener, S. Oishi, and L. Tay. Noba Scholar, 2017.

Pawelski, James O. "Happiness and Its Opposites." Oxford Handbook of Happiness, edited by S. A. David, I. Boniwell, and A. C. Ayers. Oxford University Press, 2013.

Pawelski, James O. "Bringing Together the Humanities and the Science of Well-Being to Advance Human Flourishing." Well-Being and Higher Education, edited by D. Harward. Association of American Colleges and Universities, 2016.

Pawelski, James O. "Defining the 'Positive' in Positive Psychology: Part I. A Descriptive Analysis." The Journal of Positive Psychology, vol. 11, no. 4, 2016, pp. 339–56.

Pawelski, James O. "Defining the 'Positive' in Positive Psychology: Part II. A Normative Analysis." The Journal of Positive Psychology, vol. 11, no. 4, 2016, pp. 357–65.

Peterson, Christopher. "The Values in Action (VIA) Classification of Strengths." A Life Worth Living: Contributions to Positive Psychology, edited by M. Csikszentmihalyi and I. S. Csikszentmihaliy, pp. 29–48. Oxford University Press, 2006.

Seligman, Martin, and Mihaly Csikszentmihalyi. "Positive Psychology: An Introduction," American Psychologist, vol. 55, no. 1, pp. 5–14.

Tay, Louis, James O. Pawelski, and Melissa G. Keith, "The Role of the Arts and Humanities in Human Flourishing: A Conceptual Model." Journal of Positive Psychology, 2017, DOI: 10.1080/17439760.2017.127920.7.

Tucker, Don, and Phan Luu, Cognition and Neural Development. Oxford University Press, 2010.

8

Navigating Irreconcilable Conflicts

Philosophical Thinking for Better Lives

Lori Gallegos

Individual Responsibility for Wellbeing

If the popular self-care movement is any indicator, many people view the individual as largely responsible for preserving their own wellbeing.[1] The view underlying this trend is that people should commit themselves to self-improvement (by engaging in a variety of relaxation strategies, making changes to diet, or receiving life coaching, for example), because through such investments, they can protect or heal themselves from the harm to wellbeing that results from many of life's difficulties. While this view may often be helpful, those who hold the view may be tempted to overemphasize individuals' power to determine their own wellbeing.

There are at least two mistaken tendencies of thought that accompany such an overemphasis. The first is the tendency to believe too often that wellbeing is simply the result of one's own quality of character. Someone who holds this view might believe that if a person is disciplined, has their priorities straight, is self-respecting, and is committed to being a productive contributor, they will be able to successfully make the choices that result in their own wellbeing. The second mistaken tendency is having inflated expectations about what is humanly possible with regard to achieving greater wellbeing. Someone who holds this view might believe that one should be able to preserve their wellbeing in the face of all manner of hardships and life demands. Both of these mistaken tendencies result in people putting unrealistic expectations on themselves and others. They also may lead us to misidentify that which is actually detracting from wellbeing in a given circumstance.

---

[1] For a concise history of the mainstream self-care movement, see Harris, "A History of Self-Care."

Lori Gallegos, *Navigating Irreconcilable Conflicts* In: *Philosophy and Human Flourishing*. Edited by: John J. Stuhr, Oxford University Press. © Oxford University Press 2023. DOI: 10.1093/oso/9780197622162.003.0009

Although most of us seem to easily recognize our own lack of wellbeing, saying what exactly wellbeing *is*, is another matter. Wellbeing is a highly contested, contextually variable, socially constructed, and shifting concept (Ereaut and Whiting "What Do We Mean by 'Wellbeing'?"). Nevertheless, some shared features can be identified across a diversity of contexts in which the concept appears: It is taken to be positive and desirable; it is holistic, rather than fragmented (that is, it tends to connect, rather than compartmentalize aspects of the self, such as mind, body, and spirit); and it tends to include subjective elements (how the individual experiences themselves as faring) in addition to 'objective' indicators (such as income and life expectancy; White "Analyzing Wellbeing" 159–60). In this chapter, I take wellbeing to be a process that includes material, relational, and subjective dimensions (170–71). The material dimension includes factors like assets, life expectancy, and standards of living. The relational dimension includes social and personal relationships, access to public goods, capabilities, and attitudes toward life. Lastly, the subjective dimensions includes people's perceptions of their positions, as well as their cultural values, ideologies, and beliefs (161). Wellbeing is a process, rather than a state, because the three dimensions are co-constitutive and because people experience and evaluate the significance of each dimension in different ways in different spaces and at different times in their lives (165–66). While much more analysis of the nature of wellbeing is called for, I find that for the purposes of this chapter, this description is broad enough to include many of the ways in which wellbeing might be assessed, but also informative enough to allow us to identify specific detractors or contributors to wellbeing.

In order to resist the tendency to overemphasize individuals' capacity to determine their own wellbeing, I focus in this chapter on a set of challenges to wellbeing that do not result from individual failures. I show that pursuing factors that are significant for one dimension of wellbeing can come into conflict with factors that are significant for some other dimension of wellbeing. I take it that such conflicts are, in fact, a regular part of human life.[2] As finite beings, we often must choose to prioritize some aspects of our lives at the expense of others.

My aim in this chapter, however, is not merely to argue that these conflicts exist, but to show that these conflicts are exacerbated by oppressive social

---

[2] In the seventh point of the first section of his chapter in this volume, John Stuhr discusses this issue in terms of what he identifies as the irreducibly tragic dimension of life.

conditions--conditions that are primarily structural and which tend to impact individuals on the basis of their membership to particular social groups. They thus transcend individual agency. I dedicate the next section, Irresolvable Conflicts in Oppressive Social Conditions, to surveying contemporary scholarship that collectively supports this thesis. Then, having shown the ways in which this work contributes to our understanding of wellbeing, I turn in the third section, Navigating Irreconcilable Conflicts and the Contributions of Philosophy, to the question of how the discipline and practice of philosophy in general might be useful in light of the recognition that wellbeing for many people depends not merely on their personal psychological management, but rather on the transformation of oppressive conditions.

Irresolvable Conflicts in Oppressive Social Conditions

Inappropriately Adaptive Preferences

The first example of a conflict among the domains of wellbeing is the phenomenon of inappropriately adaptive preferences (IAPs). All of us have desires that are shaped by our social conditions. We adapt to the realities of our lives, limiting the extent to which we desire the impossible or lament the inevitable. We set up realistic expectations, temper our hopes, and prepare for disappointment in order to soften its inevitable blow. If we are living in social conditions that are particularly unjust, or where opportunities for flourishing are limited, this, too, will often shape our behaviors and desires. Such an influence is especially evident in the case of oppressed and severely deprived people who become complicit in perpetuating their own depravation. Global feminist ethicist Serene Khader employs the term "inappropriately adaptive preferences" (IAPs) to describe this sort of situation, in which people live in less than optimal situations, engage in behaviors that perpetuate their deprivation, and whose subjective states (beliefs, choices, and desires) indicate, to some extent, that they endorse their situation (*Adaptive Preferences and Women's Empowerment*," 2011). In other words, not only does the individual with an IAP engage in welfare-undermining behavior, but the individual autonomously engages in the behavior, often because they have values, desires, or commitments that lead them to choose the behavior. The ability to engage in autonomous action in accordance with one's values, desires, and commitments is no doubt a factor in wellbeing. In the case of IAPs, however, it conflicts with other key factors.

One example Khader provides of this phenomenon is a woman who holds the belief that a good woman sacrifices her own nourishment so that her husband may eat, and so she ensures that her husband is well-fed before eating whatever is left after he finishes, even if it means she is left hungry. The woman chooses to deny herself food, believing that by making this sacrifice, she is living in accordance with her own values. Another example might be a father who works at a miserable and exploitative job for decades because, in addition to being under financial pressure, he believes his purpose is to provide for his family and he does not believe he is entitled to a less grueling life or a life of greater prosperity. While the father may be over-worked and undercompensated, he believes that he is fulfilling his proper role as provider. Indeed, he might find that his very suffering is an expression of his integrity or his love for his family. In both of these cases, the individuals endorse their own depravation in the midst of far-from-ideal social conditions. Their choices are unquestionably constrained, but they nonetheless exhibit some agency in perpetuating their own deprivation.

IAPs are one example of how conditions of social inequality produce tensions between the domains of wellbeing. Indeed, one defining feature of IAPs is that acting in accordance with one's preferences is at odds with other key factors in wellbeing, such as physical health. IAPs are *inappropriately* adapted preferences precisely for this reason. Developing a preference for exercising in a society where people are under pressure to be physically fit would not necessarily be an IAP if the preference improves the wellbeing of the person who has it. On the other hand, a woman's physically and emotionally damaging fixation on improving her physical imperfections in a society that measures a woman's worth in accordance with her physical attractiveness would be an IAP.[3]

---

[3] The lines between these two cases can be blurry, precisely because in both the cases, society might be measuring the individual's worth by the appearance of their body in ways that are oppressive. I am arguing that the individual's *endorsement of the oppressive norm* is a necessary condition for something to count as an IAP. Often, though, it is not always easy to determine the source or nature of our motivations (that is, does my desire for toned muscles come from some authentic commitment to enjoying my physical strength or does it come from an internalized norm about what counts as attractive)? Furthermore, individuals might have an ambivalent relationship with a norm. One might experience a first- but not second-level endorsement of this norm (for instance, I may be self-conscious about the appearance of my body, but I might wish I didn't care about that). I thank Keisha Ray for prompting these considerations.

A second defining feature of IAPs is that people who have them seem to endorse the situations that undermine their own wellbeing. Consider the case of a woman who believes that a woman's proper place is in the home, and who feels shame and guilt about spending her time out of the house, so she remains isolated and confined. This woman may be said to have an IAP. However, if this woman instead held the belief that she *should* be able to participate in public life, and she desired to do so, but she stays home because she fears being harmed by others, she cannot be said to have an IAP. In the latter case, her preferences have not adapted to her situation. Hence, it is the endorsement of the preference that produces the tension between what one desires and their wellbeing.

Finally, a third defining feature of IAPs is that they emerge as a result of oppressive social conditions. Suppose someone engages in a certain self-destructive pattern of sabotaging all of their romantic relationships once they reach a certain level of emotional intimacy. Perhaps the person's pattern is rooted in a difficult relationship with their mother in early childhood. In this case, we can say that certain social conditions generated the self-undermining behavior. However, the behavior is not an IAP insofar as it is individual, psychologically isolated, and is not produced as a result of broader, unjust social context, because of one's belonging to a particular social group. The preference is not an adaptation to one's society. Instead, it emerges as a result of patterns of relating to a parent that the individual learned as a child. In a sense, the person is now adapting their preferences to their own emotional wounds, but not to broader social conditions.

One might object that many IAPs are not *deep* preferences because they may be corrected through deliberative interventions (with development practitioners, for example). These interventions involve helping people to reflect upon their own conception of flourishing and to make choices that align more closely with that view. In these cases, a person might be making choices that undermine their wellbeing because they have unquestioningly adopted harmful social norms. Given the opportunity to reflect more carefully on what they really value, however, they might realize that what they thought were their preferences are not actually their preferences at all. Khader seems optimistic that resolving some of the conflicts among the domains of life is possible through guided and deliberative philosophical reflection. Given the proper support, people can learn to recognize and resist norms that are inconsistent with their true conceptions of flourishing.

In reply to this objection, I contend that IAPs that could *potentially* be resolved through a deliberative intervention are still IAPs. That is, because of the subjective and relational dimensions of wellbeing, the conflicts between the agent's preferences and other factors in their wellbeing are still very real, even if they have the potential to be worked through. Their potential for resolution does not make them any less "deep" in the moments that they are actually experienced by the agent. Furthermore, it goes without saying that many people will not fully resolve their IAPs.

Caring for Others through Empathetic Response

Another often-irreconcilable conflict among the domains of wellbeing is the conflict between responding empathetically to others and preserving personal wellbeing. In moral life, we sometimes face decisions in which each of our available courses of action has some serious disadvantage, and where even pursuing the best possible option may cause lamentable harm to oneself. Personal sacrifice is often a justifiable part of moral action, but in some cases, the harm endured by the agent making the sacrifice would be great, and it becomes doubtful whether there is any right way to proceed. Although the challenge of finding a proper balance is a requirement of moral life generally, the difficulty or impossibility of doing so is exacerbated by unjust social conditions. Specifically, having and exercising certain virtues within an unjust society comes at a cost to other wellbeing factors. To demonstrate this point, I focus in this section on empathy, and I highlight two ways in which those who empathize may experience a decrease in aspects of their wellbeing as a result of their empathy.

The first case concerns the effect of empathy on women, who do the great majority of paid and unpaid care work. Professionally, women make up 92 percent of registered nurses, 98 percent of kindergarten teachers, and 79 percent of social workers, and they also make up three quarters of those caring for older relatives and two thirds of those caring for grandchildren (Hochschild "*So How's the Family? And Other Essays*" 35). Sociologist Arlie Hochschild also finds that, unsurprisingly, women tend to do most of what we might call "empathy-work," the work of creating and preserving community through emotional connection and support. Think, for instance, of the charge women take in preserving relationships with neighbors, coworkers, clients, and more distant family members; in mediating troubled relationships, often within families; in being an emotional pillar for husbands and children and aging parents; in checking in with others on the occasion of birthdays and anniversaries, or when people are ill; and in sending food or watching others' children when a community member is facing serious hardship.

This empathy work is vital: it is clearly essential to the relational aspects of wellbeing, and the ability to experience oneself as ethically responsive to others is likely an important factor in the subjective dimension of wellbeing. Unfortunately, psychologists have found a link between the comparatively higher rate of depression and anxiety in women and women's higher propensity to empathize. Psychologists Ronald Kessler and Jane McLeod explain that within social networks, the stress of some members ripple throughout ("Sex Differences in Vulnerability to Undesirable Life Events."). Women tend to be emotionally involved in the lives of those they care for, and deep concern for the wellbeing of a loved one results in personal distress. Hochschild suggests that the reason women experience more of this vicarious stress has to do with the social role women tend to occupy. Women participate in wider support networks than men, and women are more likely than men to be sought out for help and support for problems. Hochschild writes:

Women in [the Kessler and McLeod] study . . . were not just feeling down about their own bad news, or even their husband's or their children's bad news, but about the bad news of others in their larger circle of family and friends. There, they are the designated empathizers—the ones others relied on to stay tuned in. They held in mind the sad news of these others. They charted larger family-and-friend empathy maps. (34)

I contend that because of the way in which gender is socially constructed, women are left to perform a disproportionate amount of care work. Emotional care work, which often requires the practice of empathy, is also largely left to women and expected of women. It is likely that because this labor is not more evenly distributed among society, and because women engaged in this work often do not, themselves, receive adequate social and emotional support, their own psychological health is adversely affected. Simply stated, women are often put into the position of choosing between providing vital emotional care for their families, friends, and communities, on the one hand, and their own emotional wellbeing, on the other.

Lisa Tessman describes a different way in which empathy can detract from aspects of the wellbeing of empathizers in unjust social conditions. Rather than discussing the role of empathy in fostering connection and support for others generally, Tessman is concerned with the virtue of sensitivity and attention to suffering that is tied to injustice (for example, emotional suffering in response to others' experiences of poverty, child abuse, violence against women, political torture, slavery, and genocide; Tessman 84).[4] Unlike the empathy-work carried out disproportionately by women, the sensitivity to suffering caused by injustice applies both "to those who are themselves oppressed—for they can still care about others who are oppressed in the same or different ways—and to those who at least in some ways escape oppression themselves" (95).[5]

The tendency to empathize with those who are subject to oppression, exploitation, and domination is likely an important aspect of relational wellbeing, and it leads us to resist these types of preventable and human-caused forms of suffering (Hoffman "Empathy, Justice, and Social Change"). However, Tessman identifies this sensitivity as a "burdened" virtue because it detracts from aspects of the wellbeing of those who bear it (95). Specifically, Tessman explains, "sensitivity and attention to others' suffering entails taking on others' pain, being pained by their pain." Indeed, "one's actual felt pain is part of the response to the other that constitutes the morally recommended responsive action" (93). In other words, sensitivity is a virtue insofar as it conduces to a "noble" end (that is, it is morally wrong to not be pained by others' suffering, and being pained by others' suffering often leads us to try to alleviate that suffering). However, it detracts from flourishing because it "undermines the 'external' conditions for flourishing, including freedom from great pain" (153).

Tessman notes that the morally problematic alternative to this anguished sensitivity is coldly ignoring the great suffering of countless people (*Burdened Virtues* 2005). We are thus put in a morally impossible position: "In a world with masses of suffering people one necessarily turns one's back on many. Meanwhile, being fully sensitive and responsive to just a small portion of the

---

[4] Tessman suggests that she is not referring to mere sympathy—feeling *for* others—but also empathy, or feeling *with*, others. She writes, "The trait I am examining *does* involve taking on the pain of others" (90).

[5] Notably, though, evidence suggests that people with a higher sense of power empathize less with the suffering of others. See, for instance, van Kleef, et al.

suffering population requires taking on enormous pain" (85). In short, be-cause of the tremendous suffering caused by injustice all around us, we find ourselves in a position in which we either ignore it—thereby failing to exhibit sufficient virtue—or are sensitive and attentive to it, resulting in often over-whelmingly painful vicarious distress.

It is the background conditions—the broader context of the unjust world we live in—that create a situation in which it becomes "impossible to es-cape both the horror of indifference and the psychic pain (and perhaps ex-haustion) of sensitivity and attention" (85). There is no doubt that many of our most important virtues involve some degree of pain or self-sacrifice. Nevertheless, Tessman's work demonstrates that it is, specifically, widespread injustice that interferes with wellbeing in the case of empathy for sufferers of injustice. Such contexts, she concludes, require "certain virtues that are painful precisely because they are responses to the effects of oppression" (95). In this way, the conflict between having and exercising appropriate and im-portant socially directed emotional responses and the agent's freedom from emotional pain is exacerbated by the unjust context.

A likely objection to the claim that empathy undermines the wellbeing of the empathizer is that empathy comes in several varieties, and not all of them are called for or come at so high a cost to the empathizer. Emotional resonance—or feeling what another person feels—is central to what we typi-cally think of as empathy. Paul Bloom argues that this kind of empathy—often referred to more specifically as "affective empathy"—is often inappropriate, as it does not tend to generate optimal moral responses to others' suffering ("Against Empathy" 2014). He reasons that it leads us to become so affected by the feelings of others that it impedes our ability to act ethically. Bloom offers as an example an older relative who requires medical treatment, and who is anxious and uncertain about his health. This relative prefers doctors who do not share his emotional states. Rather, he benefits most from a doctor who is calm and confident. Hence, Bloom argues, a more detached kind of compassion—what is sometimes referred to as "cognitive empathy"—is preferable. With cognitive empathy, one intellectually recognizes another person's suffering and needs, and one wishes for the wellbeing of the other person, but one does not experience the same emotions that the other person is experiencing. This degree of emotional detachment allows for the cogni-tive empathizer to avoid experiencing painful sensitivity to the suffering of others. It also allows them, Bloom argues, to more effectively respond to the sufferer.

Although cognitive empathy can play an important role in supporting our capacity to meet another person's needs, I find that affective empathy undergirds some critical aspects of moral agency that cognitive empathy does not. For one, as Elisa Aaltola notes, people's emotional lives are not always rational, so attempting to grasp the experience of another person in non-affective terms may generate misunderstandings. Aaltola writes, "Efforts towards sheer detachment, aloofness and rational calculus will fail, in their emotional hollowness, to grasp the content of the emotions in others and will be inclined instead to search for logical reasons under the behavior of other subjects" (*Varieties of Empathy: Moral Psychology and Animal Ethics* 62). Affective empathy, in contrast, enables understanding of others' affective states via affective resonance, which provides critical supplementing information. Aaltola further surmises that affective empathy is a way of knowing others that is "firmly sculpted into our mentation and biology," making it "one of the most reliable sources of accessing others" (52). Indeed, at a very basic level of interpersonal exchange, the successful sharing of meanings is largely made possible through empathic modes like mimicry, classical conditioning, and direct association, which weave together affect and cognition in complex ways (Hoffman, *Empathy and Moral Development*). The capacity not only to experience emotions but also to identify and correctly interpret the emotions of others is necessary for evaluating meaning in others' speech and actions. The necessary role of affective resonance in interpersonal communication undermines the assumption that it is even possible to have a good grasp on others' experiences in an emotionally detached way, since a breakdown of these automatic affective functions would significantly impair normal communication.

More to the point, the sometimes subtle and nuanced information about the emotional states of others that we grasp through affective empathy often allows us to respond more appropriately to their needs. Bloom writes that his relative appreciates doctors "who are calm when he is anxious, confident when he is uncertain." It is not clear, though, that a non-empathetic doctor would recognize how to provide such appropriate emotional comfort. Ideally, a caregiver would recognize her resonant affects as supplying important information about her patient, and respond in a way that best meets the patient's needs. She would, for example, discern her patient's anxiety through emotionally sensitive perceptiveness and know that she could shift the affective climate by responding through warm care, or perhaps emotional neutrality and calm. It is not emotional detachment that provides this information, but emotional sensitivity.

A final point is that affective empathy does involve openness to being personally affected by the suffering of others, thereby making the empathizer vulnerable to experiencing emotional harm. Nevertheless, this same emotional availability to others deepens our relationships with others and is sometimes precisely the way in which we meet the needs of those who are most dependent upon us. Although we may not desire a feeling of emotional intimacy with some people, we no doubt need it from others, such as close friends and family members. It may be the case, as Aaltola argues, that cognitive and affective empathy frequently work best when they work in tandem with one another (54). The significant point here is that shutting down one's propensity to experience affective empathy would come at too high a cost.

The Pursuit of Social Justice

The third and final conflict to consider is that between the pursuit of social justice—a state that is comprised of fair access to relational, subjective, and material aspects of wellbeing—and the costs to physical and mental health that fighting for social justice might entail. There are many reasons why pursuing social justice may be important to someone. Certainly, this commitment often has a moral dimension, but is not reducible to it. People also commit to social justice causes because it has some meaning to them, personally. For some people, this commitment is based on the fact that they or someone about whom they care belongs to the group that is targeted by an injustice. The harm of some injustices extends to the deepest layers of the self, what is most meaningful to a person, and even to the way in which a person is able to find meaningfulness to begin with.

In the most obvious sense, some injustices involve the danger of being physically harmed or killed. Injustice is often a matter of life or death, such as when it involves direct violence or slower or mediated forms of violence (such as poverty, exposure to environmental hazards, and lack of access to health care). Numerous psychological studies indicate that in every studied minority group, prejudice and discrimination predicts negative health outcomes, including depression, substance abuse, increased physical symptoms of disease, and poor health behaviors (Pascoe and Richman).

Systemic injustices also involve harms that transcend the physical body. For one, a person who is oppressed might experience significant barriers to being able to engage in activities or pursue life paths that are deeply meaningful to them. A prejudiced environment undermines opportunity and the social conditions required for certain kinds of personal fulfilment (think, for instance, of the metaphor of the glass ceiling).

In addition, injustices can affect the very ways in which people make sense out of the world around them.[6] They shape the way in which people understand and experience themselves and others. With regard to the injustice of racism, thinkers such as W.E.B. DuBois, Ralph Ellison, Frantz Fanon, George Yancy, and Helen Ngo have articulated how a racialized existence in a white supremacist world is a not merely a moral or political problem, but also impacts people on the deepest, existential, levels. Drawing from Louis Gordon's work on the subject, Charles Mills proposes that the absurdity and tragedy of life for racialized subjects arises less from the realization that God is dead or of the "finitude of human existence in an indifferent universe," as well-known existentialists have proposed, than it does from "the day to day problems of negotiating a world shaped by a white domination aspiring to omnipotence and ensuring black existence falls below the human" (21).

Resisting injustice, then, is more than a matter of fulfilling a moral duty. It is a matter of fighting for one's life, for the lives of one's loved ones, and for a community to which one recognizes oneself as connected. A commitment to social justice is, therefore, a commitment to wellbeing in the deepest senses.

Yet this very commitment can also undermine factors that are a part of the activist's wellbeing. Targets of injustice may find themselves compelled into a position of resistance, where this resistance becomes a new center of meaning. For many, it is a meaning that is not chosen (one would rather not live in a world where they must center their lives around resisting police brutality, for instance), but they nonetheless whole-heartedly commit to it. This new center of meaning is riddled with additional hardships. If this is the case, then the one of the costs of committing one's life to political resistance often entails a loss of personal wellbeing.

This conflict is tragically evident in cases like that of MarShawn McCarrel, a well-known Black Lives Matters activist who, in 2016, took his own life on

---

[6] See José Medina's discussion of "insensitivity to lived experience," section 2 of his chapter in this volume. See also John Sadler's account of "value-blindness" in his chapter in this volume.

the steps of the Ohio Statehouse at the age of 23. Following his death, dozens of well-known activists began to reflect more openly about the emotional costs of activism—battles with depression, anxiety, insecurity, and despair (Lowery and Stankiewicz). One now finds hundreds of blog posts online dedicated to the topic of activist wellbeing. A deep commitment to social justice is gaining widespread recognition as having a personal toll on already vulnerable populations.

Navigating Irreconcilable Conflicts and the Contributions of Philosophy

I have thus far sought to demonstrate that central factors of wellbeing can conflict with one another and, furthermore, that these conflicts are exacerbated by oppressive social conditions. Those who suffer from injustice suffer doubly: Beyond the primary and immediate harm of the particular injustice suffered, conditions of social inequality also amplify the irresolvable conflicts that are a part of our lives. Given these conflicts, it is no wonder that the human experience is so often one of yearning, incompleteness, guilt, friction, exhaustion, and a sense of failure. We strive, in various ways, to master an impossible balancing act—to do our best, all things considered. At the same time, the way we navigate these irreconcilable conflicts gives content to our identity and defines our character.

The questions of what wellbeing is and how we should live in order to maximize it are classically philosophical questions. We might wonder, then, what philosophy today has to offer in light of the challenges for wellbeing. It should be stated, first of all, that philosophy cannot resolve the conflicts identified in this chapter. The reason, as the work of Bernard Williams and Harry Frankfurt illustrates, is that it cannot help us to identify an underlying, independent, source of reasons according to which we could evaluate other reasons for acting. It cannot always give us a clear and consistent way of knowing, for instance, how we ought to choose between a closer connection with people we care about or greater freedom from the pain of empathizing with their suffering without begging the question about which source of reasons is more fundamental. Nevertheless, I maintain that philosophy does provide us some resources for navigating life's irreconcilable conflicts. I briefly discuss three of those resources here, though there are no doubt additional items that could be added to this list.

First, in terms of its methodology, philosophy often calls on us to make conceptual distinctions. In the case of elucidating the conception of well-being, we might benefit from distinguishing between domains of wellbeing. It is not at all difficult to imagine lives that we would call deeply meaningful or admirably virtuous, but where the person living that life has had to make a genuinely lamentable sacrifice: A caregiver who meets the needs of dependent family members, but who continually disregards her own health; a migrant laborer who works nearly every waking hour in the fields so that their children can attend school and have the hope of greater opportunity; an artist or activist who abandons their duties to loved ones or to their own safety or in order to pursue their larger commitment or craft. It is far from obvious that we should judge these lives as irrational, unworthy, or as lacking altogether in wellbeing. Nevertheless, it seems essential to acknowledge that they are full of genuine sacrifice, loss, and suffering. Philosophical thinking allows us to make these important distinctions between the factors that make up wellbeing.

Philosophical thinking can also be used to clarify the distinction between the life conflicts that are a result of our finite human condition and those that are a result of human-caused injustice. With regard to those conflicts that result from our human condition, the second way in which philosophy is useful is through its corpus of works that directly address the difficulties of human existence. I opened this chapter by describing the mistaken tendency to over-emphasize what individuals can and should do to ensure their own wellbeing. When we face inevitable setbacks, we may be likely to think there is something wrong or deficient about us, and to dwell in self-blame. Through reading philosophical works, however, we are brought into connection with people throughout history who have grappled with similar concerns about the challenges of the human condition. Rather than blame ourselves, we learn the humbling lesson that we are finite and that our limitations are only partially within our control. We learn the humbling lesson that living is itself the imperfect artwork of trying to navigate irreconcilable conflicts, and the right way to fashion this artwork is not determined and cannot be fully prescribed. We thus engage in philosophical activity when we continue, each day, to reflectively compose our way of being, given our limitations and limited resources.

While reflection on our human condition may be a valuable practice in responding to our existential limitations, other strategies may be called for when the source of conflict between the domains of wellbeing is oppressive social conditions. In this case, philosophical thinking can play a practical role in helping us to diagnose the source of these conflicts. So, the third way in which philosophy can help us to navigate conflicts of wellbeing is by raising the sorts of questions that would aid us not only in understanding, but also addressing, the injustices that contribute to these conflicts. For example, with regard to the disparities in empathy between women and men, we can ask: What would it look like to better support women caregivers? With regard to activist burnout, we can ask: How are we going to do better as communities to support our most committed activists? With regard to addressing adaptive preferences, we can raise the question: What do culturally sensitive and competent and empowering interventions into adaptive preferences look like? In this way, the practice of critical reflection, guided by a commitment to empowering those who are oppressed, can contribute to improving the conditions that undermine wellbeing.

In this chapter, I have warned against overestimating individuals' power and responsibility to determine their own wellbeing. It is important, I have proposed, to recognize the ways in which we are also constrained by the social and structural conditions within which we find ourselves. Perhaps one conclusion to be drawn is that as long as we live in an unjust world, our best strategies for helping individuals to improve their own wellbeing can only get us so far. If we do not consider social, historical, and political conditions that shape individual lives, then we overlook a central problem.

Works Cited

Aaltola, Elisa. *Varieties of Empathy: Moral Psychology and Animal Ethics.* Rowman and Littlefield, 2018.

Bloom, Paul. "Against Empathy." *Boston Review*, Sept. 10, 2014. www.bostonreview.net/forum/paul-bloom-against-empathy#comment-list. Accessed September 20, 2018.

DuBois, W. E. B. *The Souls of Black Folk.* Yale University Press, 2015 [1903].

Ellison, Ralph. *The Invisible Man.* Random House, 1995 [1952].

Ereaut, Gill, and Rebecca Whiting. "What Do We Mean by 'Wellbeing'? And Why Might It Matter?" *Research Report DCSF-RW073.* Linguistic Landscapes, 2008. https://core.ac.uk/download/pdf/4158044.pdf. Accessed September 10, 2019.

Fanon, Frantz. *Black Skin, White Masks.* Grove Press, 2008. 1952.

Frankfurt, Harry G. *The Reasons of Love.* Princeton University Press, 2004.

Existentia Africana: Understanding Africana Existential Thought. Routledge, 2000.

Gordon, Lewis R. *An Introduction to Africana Philosophy.* Cambridge University Press, 2008.

Harris, Aisha. "A History of Self-Care." *Slate.com*, April 5, 2017. www.slate.com/articles/arts/culturebox/2017/04/the_history_of_self_care.html. Accessed September 7, 2019.

Hochschild, Arlie Russel. *So How's the Family? And Other Essays*. University of California Press, 2013.

Hoffman, Martin L. *Empathy and Moral Development: Implications for Caring and Justice.* Cambridge University Press, 2000.

Hoffman, Martin L. "Empathy, Justice and Social Change." In *Empathy and Morality*, edited by Heidi L. Maibom. Oxford University Press, 2014, pp. 71–96.

Kessler, Ronald, and McLeod, Jane. "Sex Differences in Vulnerability to Undesirable Life Events." *American Sociological Review*, vol. 49, 1984, pp. 620–31.

Khader, Serene. *Adaptive Preferences and Women's Empowerment*. Oxford University Press, 2011.

Lowery, Wesley, and Stankiewicz, Kevin. "'My Demons Won Today': Ohio Activist's Suicide Spotlights Depression among Black Lives Matter Leaders." *The Washington Post*, 2016. www.washingtonpost.com/news/post-nation/wp/2016/02/15/my-demons-won-today-ohio-activists-suicide-spotlights-depression-among-black-lives-matter-leaders/?noredirect=on&utm_term=.3fe217c8d8c9. Accessed April 13, 2018.

Medina, José. *The Epistemology of Resistance: Gender and Racial Oppression, Epistemic Injustice, and Resistant Imaginations*. Oxford University Press, 2014.

Medina, José. "Relational Insensitivity and the Interdependence of Flourishing and Withering." *Philosophy and Human Flourishing*. Edited by John J. Suhr, Oxford University Press, 2022.

Mills, Charles W. "Critical Philosophy of Race." *Oxford Handbook of Philosophical Methodology*, edited by Herman Cappelen, Tamar Szabó Gendler, and John Hawthorne. *Oxford Handbooks Online*, 2016. www.oxfordhandbooks.com/abstract/10.1093/oxfordhb/9780199668779.001.0001/oxfordhb-9780199668779-e-15?rskey=XuD7P2&result=1

Ngo, Helen. *The Habits of Racism: A Phenomenology of Racism and Racialized Embodiment*. Lexington Books, 2017.

Prinz, Jesse. "Is Empathy Necessary for Morality?" In *Empathy: Philosophical and Psychological Perspectives*, edited by Amy Coplan and Peter Goldie. Oxford University Press, 2011.

Pascoe, E. A., and Richman, L. S. "Perceived Discrimination and Health: A Meta-Analytic Review." *Psychological Bulletin* vol. 135, 2009, pp. 531–54.

Sadler, John Z. "Values Literacy and Citizenship." *Philosophy and Human Flourishing*. Edited by John J. Suhr, Oxford University Press, 2022.

Tessman, Lisa. *Burdened Virtues*. Oxford University Press, 2005.

Van Kleef, Gerben A., Oveis, Christopher, van der Löwe, Ilmo, LuoKogan, Aleksandr, Goez, Jennifer, and Keltner, Dacher. "Power, Distress, and Compassion: Turning a Blind Eye to the Suffering of Others." *Psychological Science*, vol. 19, no. 12, 2008, pp. 1315–22.

White, Sarah C. "Analyzing Wellbeing: A Framework for Development Practice." *Development in Practice* vol. 10, no. 2, 2010, pp. 158–72.

Williams, Bernard. *Ethics and the Limits of Philosophy*. Harvard University Press, 1985.

Yancy, George. *Black Bodies, White Gazes: The Continuing Significance of Race*. Rowman and Littlefield, 2008.

9

Relational Insensitivity and the Interdependence of Flourishing and Withering

José Medina

Attentiveness to Lived Experiences and Standpoints ("The Will to Believe")

In the Pragmatism lectures (esp. lectures II and IV), William James sketches a provocative pragmatic account that brings truth to the level of experience and action: our truth assessments are to be understood as ways of harmonizing our experiences and actions, of putting them in synch with the world we share. In James's view truth is a value that regulates our normative engagements with others.[1] Truth is therefore the source of solidarity, for it contributes to the sharing of experience and the coordination of action. When James defines truth as "whatever proves itself to be good in the way of belief" ("The Will Not to Believe: Pragmatism, Oppression, and Standpoint Theory" 42), he is referring not only to what we believe individually but also to what we believe together. But before beliefs can be candidates for truth or falsity, they have to make sense; intelligibility is a precondition for truth-candidacy. According to James's pragmatism, intelligibility is also to be grounded in experience, in possible experience: what is intelligible has to be identified not simply with what has been, is, or will be experienced, but more broadly with what is imaginable as connected with the realm of possible experience and action. On this view, the domain of what we find intelligible is the domain of what is relatable to the possible experiences and actions of

---

[1] Parts of this section and the next are drawn from my essay "The Will Not to Believe: Pragmatism, Oppression, and Standpoint Theory." *Feminist Interpretations of William James*, edited by Shannon Sullivan and Erin Tarver. Penn State University Press, 2015; pp. 235–60.

José Medina, *Relational Insensitivity and the Interdependence of Flourishing and Withering* In: *Philosophy and Human Flourishing*. Edited by: John J. Stuhr, Oxford University Press. © Oxford University Press 2023. DOI: 10.1093/oso/9780197622162.003.0010

particular subjects under some imagined circumstances; and of course, thus conceived, the domain of intelligibility can never be fully delimited: it remains forever open. This is a criterion of meaningfulness with a strong commitment to openness and inclusivity.

James typically talks about something *having meaning* in an existential sense, that is, as having significance or impact in someone's life under some circumstances; and given the wide variety of lives that people can have and the wide variety of contexts in which those lives can unfold, what is intelligible is always expanding. But what is deemed experience-able and meaningful at any given time—what is deemed live-able—has to be grounded in the embodied, lived experience of particular people in particular contexts. Giving priority to lived experience as a criterion of meaning is precisely one of the hallmarks of standpoint theory, as Patricia Hill Collins, for one, has argued (*Black Feminist Thought: Knowledge, Consciousness, and the Politics of Empowerment* 257–60). Collins finds the roots of this appeal to personal experience as a criterion of intelligibility in black feminists such as Sojourner Truth and her celebrated discourse "And ain't I a woman?" As Collins argues and Truth's discourse illustrates, this empiricist criterion of intelligibility has a tremendous critical and subversive potential, for it can be used by marginalized and oppressed subjectivities to interrogate received meanings and to make room for new meanings. As Collins goes on to argue, the criterion of lived experience makes us think of inquiring subjects as "connected knowers" (259), giving center stage to those who experience things in their own flesh, but also inviting everyone to feel involved and to think of themselves as *connected* with subjects whose experiences are the meaning- and truth-bearers of our discourses and investigations. Jamesian pragmatism and the kind of standpoint theory described by Collins converge in calling attention to communities built around relations of epistemic solidarity and epistemic care. And yet, how is it that only the latter but not the former has been developed into a critical epistemology that addresses the experiences of the oppressed?

The brief sketch of Jamesian pragmatic approach to truth and meaning that I have provided already reveals a deep convergence with the critical feminist epistemology of standpoint theorists such as Lorraine Code, Sandra Harding, and Patricia Hill Collins. Rather than thinking of knowers as detached and disengaged observers with nothing at stake who inspect things from a third-person perspective, both James and standpoint theorists depict knowers as experiencing and experimenting subjects who find meanings and truths in the first person (i.e., in themselves) or in the second person (i.e. in their fellow inquirers). In this section I explore how far the convergence between Jamesian pragmatism and standpoint theory can be taken, and where their paths start to diverge. To preview, I suggest that, although not lacking resources to do so entirely, James does not distinguish sufficiently between having an experiential and agential *perspective* and developing a *critical standpoint* that can recognize the limits and presuppositions of one's perspective.[2] This is where Jamesian epistemology needs supplementation and expansion to become a critical epistemology. But before we sketch this supplementation in the next section, let me start with the critical resources that we can find in James and the (expandable) convergence between his pragmatism and standpoint theory.

I want to highlight four points of convergence between Jamesian pragmatism and standpoint theory. In the first place, both James and standpoint theorists demand *attentiveness to embodied and situated experience*: we have to start and end with the experiences of actual people in actual contexts. On their view, epistemology is not about abstract (disembodied and decontextualized) subjects and their purely hypothetical cognitive activities; it is about actual people and their actual lives. On this situated and pragmatic perspective, epistemological analyses have a practical point: they are action-based and action-oriented; they are aimed at the melioration of people's lives, at the enrichment of people's experiences and practices.

In the second place, both James and standpoint theorists underscore the *normative* dimension of our cognitive life, arguing for a robust notion of *epistemic responsibility*. In their views, responsibility is to be understood both as *accountability* and as *responsivity*: subjects have to be held accountable for their beliefs and the impact that they have in their own lives and the lives of others; but subjects also have to be responsive to the perspectives of others, being consequent in their actions with the positionality of their perspectives and the relationality that binds them to the perspectives of others.

In the third place, both James and standpoint theorists see a deep connection between our cognitive life and our *affective and volitional* life. As James famously argued in "The Will to Believe," our "passional nature" is the engine of our cognitive life; people with different "passional natures" or "temperaments" conduct their cognitive activities differently, and the affective dimension of our epistemic activities has to be taken into account for the

---

[2] For an elucidation of the distinction between a mere perspective and a standpoint, see Harding (1991), p. 276 and Sullivan (2001), p. 212.

coordination of our perspectives. But as James remarks, the "willing nature" that is involved in our cognitive activities should not be understood simply as the capacity for "deliberate volitions," rather, "I mean all such factors of be- lief as fear and hope, prejudice and passion, imitation and partisanship, the circumspressure of our castle and set" ("The Will to Believe 96). Standpoint theorists have also emphasized the role of affect in our epistemic interactions and negotiations. In this sense, they have called attention to the importance of empathy in cognitive activities, the importance of speaking and listening "with the heart," as Collins puts it (*Black Feminist Thought: Knowledge, Consciousness, and the Politics of Empowerment* 262–64).

Finally, in the fourth place, both in James and in standpoint theory, we find a core commitment to *inclusivity and pluralism*. This is also a point of conver- gence between Dewey and standpoint theory that Sullivan highlights: "the ideal of radical inclusion as a guide for practice" (*Feminist Interpretations of John Dewey* 227). Both for pragmatists and for standpoint theorists, the nor- mativity of a critical epistemology has to be grounded in the ideal of radical inclusion: "Each particular situation must be examined for what it requires to maximize inclusion"; "radical inclusion should be the ideal toward which feminists, pragmatists, and others work, even if they fall short of it" (226). And short of it we always fall. On the one hand, we can find in James a com- mitment to an always unfinished project of inclusivity. As James puts it: "Ever not quite' has to be said of the best attempts made anywhere in the universe at attaining all-inclusiveness" (*A Pluralistic Universe* 145). But, on the other hand, James's pragmatism lacks a sufficiently critical awareness of exclusion and oppression. This deficiency affects the critical potential of James's plu- ralism and his commitment to inclusivity. In what way is Jamesian pluralism not radical enough? And how can it be supplemented to accommodate the ideal of radical inclusivity?

Elsewhere I have distinguished three very different attitudes with respect to epistemic differences and the plurality of heterogeneous perspectives that we can find in pluralistic accounts of truth and knowledge.[3] In the first place, in some classic pragmatists such as C. S. Peirce, we can find an approach to epistemic practices that places emphasis on the plurality of experiential perspectives, but nonetheless preserves a commitment to unification, so that all available standpoints must ultimately be subsumable under a *single per- spective*. This is what I call a *converging pluralism*. For converging pluralisms,

---

[3] See chapter 6 of Medina (2013).

the diversity and heterogeneity of conflicting perspectives are merely contingent and in-principle transitory features of our epistemic practices that we should aspire to eliminate or at least minimize. By contrast, in more thoroughgoing pluralistic views such as that of William James, diversity and heterogeneity are unavoidable features of our epistemic lives that can be hidden or repressed only with violence and exclusions, but can never be fully erased. But in Jamesian pluralism, though more radical, the possibilities for epistemic friction and resistance are qualified and constrained for the sake, not of consensus and unification, but of *coordination and cooperation*. This is what I call a *melioristic pluralism*.

In James's pragmatism, the openness to contestations and reinterpretations of our beliefs never goes away and constitutes the very normative core of our epistemic lives. However, although on this pluralistic view epistemic differences and conflicts are not erased, they are put at the service of mutual improvements. On this melioristic pluralism, epistemic contestations and negotiations among perspectives are aimed at maintaining their truths *alive*—that is, dynamic, adaptable, and integrated in the lives of those who hold those experiential perspectives. Although here there is no aspiration to combine and unify all perspectives into a single one, there is the normative expectation that the interactions among diverging perspectives will result in an increase of objectivity and in the improvement of the articulations and justifications of beliefs and epistemic appraisals. On this view, epistemic friction among perspectives is always an opportunity for learning from each other and correcting each other. Although I think that this melioristic pluralism goes in the right direction, I also think that it needs to be combined with a different and more radical kind of pluralism, a *guerrilla pluralism*, in order to allow for radical critique, for the inclusion of subversive voices and perspectives.[4] In my view, this more subversive pluralism is precisely what is needed to address *radical exclusions*. *Guerrilla pluralism* is what we need when equitable and fair melioration for all is not yet possible, that is, when in a fractured society the conditions are not given for beneficial epistemic friction that results in mutual corrections and a collective process of learning in which all social groups can participate.

For a *guerrilla pluralism*, epistemic frictions are no more tools for learning than they are tools for *unlearning*, for undoing power/knowledges. On this

---

[4] See also John J. Stuhr's discussion of this same issue in his "Flourishing: Conceptual Clarity and Practical Genius," this volume.

view, epistemic frictions are not merely instrumental or transitional—that is, tools for, or steps toward, harmony or conflict resolution. Epistemic frictions are sought for their own sake, for the forms of *resistance* that they constitute. *Guerrilla pluralism* is not a pluralism that tries to resolve conflicts and overcome struggles, but instead tries to provoke them and to re-energize them. It is a pluralism that aims not at the melioration of the cognitive and ethical lives of all, but rather, at the (epistemic and socio-political) *resistance* against exclusionary and privileged perspectives. This is a pluralism that focuses on the gaps, discontinuities, tensions and clashes among perspectives and discursive practices. This is a pluralism that addresses the relation between knowledge and power and focuses not only on knowledge, but also and more fundamentally on *ignorance*—a pluralism that pays as much attention to belief, memory, and the imagination, as it does to disbelief, oblivion, and counter-imaginations. This is what standpoint theorists (Code and Collins, for example) and other critical epistemologists (Mills, Sullivan, Tuana, etc.) have offered by developing *epistemologies of ignorance* that study interrelated regimes of knowledge-ignorance/power.[5] My argumentation in the next section will offer guidelines for developing an epistemology of ignorance out of James's pragmatism by supplementing its attentiveness to embodied experience, its focus on epistemic responsibility, and its concern for "passional natures" or epistemic sensitivities. How can a *guerrilla* pluralism that gives center stage to radical differences, to the subversive and destabilizing perspectives of oppressed subjectivities, transform the epistemological insights about the experiential, normative, and affective dimensions of our life offered by James's pragmatism?

Insensitivity to Lived Experiences
("The Will Not to Believe")

Despite James's interest in diversity and his acute sensitivity to diversity of temperaments and ways of life, we do not find in his writings an exhortation to cultivate a critical attentiveness to the experiences of those who have been marginalized and stigmatized, those whose experiences have been rendered unintelligible. What kind of pragmatism would James have developed

---

[5] This is of course inspired by Foucault's critical epistemology. For a Foucault-inspired epistemology of ignorance, see Code (2007), Sullivan (2007), and Medina (2013).

if he had given center stage to the experiences and concerns of marginalized and stigmatized subjects and groups? Take, for example, the case of transgendered subjectivities. Their experiences and actions, the transgendered lives they lead, deeply interrogate accepted gendered meanings and truths that are taken for granted in received paradigms of masculinity and femininity. But these interrogations do not go very far at all when the very intelligibility of transgendered subjectivities is called into question: if a transgendered life is not a life worth living, if a transgendered identity is not an identity that makes sense for anyone to inhabit, the presence of transgendered subjects as *freaks*, as living performative contradictions, reasserts the compulsory nature of a rigid gender binarism. As many queer theorists have emphasized, there is often a systematic distortion in listening to transgendered meanings, a failure to relate to and to engage with transgendered experiences, a failure to understand them in their own terms. This is a failure in *epistemic responsibility*: a failure to become responsive to others and their experiences, but also a failure to become accountable for one's own meanings and truths.

As Naomi Scheman has argued, in order to displace heterosexist gender binaries, it is not sufficient to simply give center stage to queer voices as if they alone had the responsibility of resisting heterosexism and liberating all of us from gender and sexual oppression. We need to center the queer, but we need to do so, as Scheman states, by *queering the center*, that is, by making mainstream heterosexual subject positions strange, unfamiliar, queer ("Queering the Center by Centering the Queer: Reflections on Transsexuals and Secular Jews"). It is a mistake to think that the forms of exclusion, subordination, and marginalization that we can find in mainstream culture can only be resisted from the outside, and not also from within. The activity of resisting and contesting established presumptions of normalcy is a critical task that befalls upon everyone, and especially upon privileged subjectivities. This involves making the familiar and obvious newly strange and queer, bringing to the fore the processes of exclusion and stigmatization that go into what has been deemed normal and paradigmatic. As Scheman argues, the gender-conformists and gender-privileged need to go through a process of self-estrangement that calls into question their comfort and easy conformity with the gender binary. The exclusionary and stigmatizing aspects of the male-female gender binary is felt more acutely by transsexual and gender-non-conformists whose lives and experiences have been rendered unintelligible, but "it ought to fall to those of us who occupy positions of relative safety and privilege to complicate our own locations, to explore the costs of

our comfort, and to help imagine a world in which it would be safe to be non-
, ambiguously, or multiply gendered" (Scheman, 133).

It is precisely this critical moment of *self-estrangement* that the Jamesian
epistemology lacks, although some seeds are there for its development. In
fact, James takes us to the very threshold of such critical process of self-
scrutiny in "On a Certain Blindness in Human Beings" (1899/1983). There
James offers critical insights into affective limitations of human sensibility: "the blindness with which we are all afflicted in regard to feelings of
creatures and people different from ourselves" (1). James deserves credit for
trying to identify this blind-spot in our ability to understand the affective life
of others. But he did not go far enough in his exploration of human insensitivity, for he restricted our affective "blindness" to what is *simply alien* to us,
that is, to what lies entirely outside our affective life, to experiences we do not
have and cannot appreciate. But what if this affective "blindness" or insensitivity were to extend even to our most intimate and familiar experiences?
What if there were elements in the experiences of those we share our life with,
and even in our own experiences, which we have become blind to? What,
moreover, if this affective blindness were constitutive of our experiential enjoyment, so that the very possibility of such enjoyment required our ignoring
how our experiences are entangled with the experiential frustrations of
others (and even frustrations of our own selves, in some cases)? This is where
a *guerrilla* pluralism is needed to expand the notion of affective blindness or
insensitivity and to link it to the workings of privilege and power/knowledge-
ignorance, which need unravelling and undoing.

In his discussion of "blindness" James focuses exclusively in our inability
to relate to the significance of what is *simply alien* to us. His essay does not
consider how one's "blindness" to the affective lives of others handicaps not
only our ability to understand *them* but also our ability to understand *ourselves*; but indeed such "blindness" reverts back to the affective life of the experiential subject herself and functions also a form of *self-blindness*. James's
limited focus on what is *simply alien* to us can be appreciated in the examples
he discusses. Consider James's example of an intimate inter-species relation
in the opening page of the essay: "Take our dogs and ourselves, connected
as we are by a tie more intimate than most ties in the world; and yet, outside
of that tie of friendly fondness, how insensible, each of us, to all that makes
life significant for the other!—we to the rapture of bones under hedges, or
smells of trees and lamp-posts, they to the delights of literature and art" ("On
a Certain Blindness in Human Beings"). James applies the same logic to his

exploration of insensitivity within human relations as well: the "blindness" occurs "outside of that tie" we share with other human beings and with respect to those experiences of others that are alien to us. As illustrated by James with multiple examples—the rural man versus the city man, the uneducated man versus the man of letters, etc.—his view construes our "blindness" with respect to the feelings and emotions of others as concerning only those experiences that we do not share and whose significance we cannot appreciate. But this only scratches the surface of "the blindness with which we are all afflicted." There are two aspects of this blindness that James does not recognize, key aspects that have been highlighted by standpoint theory and recent epistemologies of ignorance. In the first place, our "blindness" or insensitivity is not something purely negative and devoid of content, a gap or emptiness that affects only what is outside our experiential lives. Rather, such insensitivity is also positive and full of content: it operates by projecting our own truths and meanings on others, by distorting the significance of their experiences. We are dealing with a much more insidious and recalcitrant kind of insensitivity when this does not consist simply in seeing nothing but emptiness and lack of meaning, but it involves seeing distortions that hide people's lives, erasing their voices and suppressing their concerns, interests, and aspirations. And in the second place, unlike recent analyses in epistemologies of ignorance (especially Charles Mills's analysis of *white ignorance*), James's view does not account for the reflexive and relational aspects of "our blindness": how such "blindness" reverts to oneself and shapes one's sensibility, so that it is not just an insensitivity with respect to others, but also with respect to key aspects of oneself and one's own perspective and position. Let me say a bit more about these two key points that separate James's account of "blindness" and the richer and deeper account that can be found in recent epistemologies of ignorance.

According to James, the affective limitations in our relations with others concern experiential possibilities that we have not explored and cannot appreciate. But there is a much more intimate side to "the blindness with which we are all afflicted": this blindness also functions *inside* the affective ties we develop with others, inside human relations, and with respect to *shared* experiences. This "blindness" concerns not only experiences one does not have and cannot appreciate, but also experiences one does have but appreciates differently, that is, in a way that conflicts with the experiential appreciations of others. James is certainly right in urging us to critically inspect our "blindness" with respect to experiences that are alien to us, but we must also interrogate our "blindness" with respect to aspects of the familiar experiences of our neighbors, of our friends, of our partners, and even of ourselves! This is what has been termed the *alienated familiar*.

In recent epistemologies of ignorance in feminist theory and race theory we can find two different notions of what is experientially alien: the *simply alien* and the *alienated familiar*. As Charles Mills explains and illustrates this distinction, the *simply alien* comprises "experiences that are outside the hegemonic framework in the sense of involving an external geography" ("Alternative Epistemologies," 28). It is an exhibition of "the simply alien," for example, when "a muckraking Frederick Engels brings details of British slum conditions to the shocked attention of a middle-class audience" (28). Another illustration can be found in Nancy Tuana's account ("Coming to Understand: Orgasm and the Epistemology of Ignorance"; "The Speculum of Ignorance: The Women's Health Movement and Epistemologies of Ignorance") of how women's genitals and sexualities were rendered "simply alien" to a male-dominated medical science and body culture until very recently. But even more interesting for the critical purpose of recognizing the limitations of our perspective is the *alienated familiar*, which comprises "experiences that are outside because they redraw the map of what was thought to be already explored territory" (Mills "Alternative Epistemologies" 28). As Mills remarks, the alienated familiar is well illustrated by the feminist "claim that most 'seductions' have a coercive element that makes them more like rapes" (28). Confronting experiences that make you radically rethink your own is not easy. It can be quite shocking to hear that something you thought you knew well what it was (courting or seducing, for example) can be experienced by the other subjectivities involved quite differently (as sexual violence, for example). Indeed, confronting the alienated familiar is more disruptive than being exposed to the simply alien; and more resistances are mobilized to block that confrontation or to stage it so that the alienated familiar appears as pathological or unintelligible experience that can simply be dismissed. In particular, I want to emphasize that there is a *relational insensitivity* that protects the ignorance about the alienated familiar. This insensitivity includes the tendency to (mis)interpret the experiences of others all too quickly, that is, the tendency to arrogantly assume that one knows what things mean for the other and what the true significance of their experiences is.

As the insensitivity rooted in the alienated familiar shows perspicuously, our *relational insensitivity*—i.e. our inability to relate properly to the experiences, meanings and truths of others—is intimately related to how we relate to our own experiences, meanings and truths. Undoing our relational insensitivity and the affective disconnect between our perspective and those of others involves more than simply reconsidering facts about these others; it involves a deep interrogation of how our life experiences relate (or fail to relate) to theirs, a critical inspection of our own perspective—as it relates (or fails to relate) to that of others—and its habits and defense mechanisms. And this brings us to the reflexive and relational point about relational insensitivity: what James terms our human "blindness" concerns not only the shortcomings of our other-regarding attitudes and habits, but also those of our *self-regarding* attitudes and habits. James's analysis of "blindness" takes us there only part of the way with the epistemic policy of "live and let live" suggested by his pronouncements about epistemic humility[6] and about tolerance and respect for diverging perspectives even when they seem unintelligible to us.[7] James's claims about our obligation to make room for the perspective of each subject of experience no matter how different from ours sound, on the surface, quite similar to the claims of standpoint theory: "each observer gains a partial superiority of insight from the peculiar position in which he stands" (p. 11.) Standpoint theory has also underscored the partiality of perspectives and the potential epistemic advantage of different perspectives in different experiential domains. But, unlike the critical insights of standpoint theory, James's insights about the partiality of experiential perspectives are not tied to critical insights about the positionality and relationality of those perspectives: there is no requirement that guarantees critical awareness of one's perspective vis-à-vis those of others, there is no demand that subjects undergo a process of *self-estrangement* in which, to borrow Scheman's words, they can *queer the very center* of their sensibility. As Scheman puts it, we should all be required "to complicate our own locations" and "to explore the costs of our comfort" ("Queering the Center by Centering the Queer: Reflections on Transsexuals and Secular Jews" 133). This critical process of self-estrangement, this way of queering the core of who we are, is what we need to come to terms with in order to overcome our

---

[6] James underscores the importance of epistemic humility in the concluding paragraph of the essay: "neither the whole of truth nor the whole of good is revealed to any single observer" (1899, p. 11).

[7] James concludes that his analysis "forbids us to be forward in pronouncing on the meaninglessness of forms of existence other than our own; and it commands us to tolerate, respect, and indulge those whom we see harmlessly interested and happy in their own ways, however unintelligible these may be to us" (1899, p. 11).

"blindness" and what James's epistemology needs in order to be truly radical and transformative.

James's claims in the conclusion of his 1899 (1983) essay seem to amount to an epistemic policy of "live and let live" that does not pay sufficient critical attention to the entanglement of perspectives, to their mutual positionality and relationality. Relational insensitivity is not overcome by letting different perspectives flourish around or alongside your own if there is no commitment to the cultivation of critical engagements with those perspectives and to a sustained process of mutual transformation. We need more than a thoroughgoing pluralism, we need a *guerrilla* pluralism. With an epistemic policy of "live and let live" perspectives are left critically untouched and unfair relations among them (relations of subordination and marginalization, for example) are not meliorated. As standpoint theory has taught us, what is important is not *just* to come to terms with the limitations of one's experiential perspective, but rather, to develop a *critical standpoint*. Acquiring a critical standpoint (as opposed to simply having a perspective) requires developing a critical awareness of one's positionality and relationality. It is not enough just to say "these are my experiences and others have their own"; we need to be able to relate those experiences to those of others in critical ways. This is what a *guerrilla* pluralism demands: a process of mutual contestation among competing meanings and truths, which opens up possibilities for the deep transformation and rearticulation of perspectives and sensibilities. The critical insights of Jamesian epistemology can be deepened with a more radical and transformative pluralism in which different experiential perspectives are not simply "tolerated" or accommodated alongside each other, but they are, rather, summoned to interrogate and transform each other. When it comes to different experiential perspectives, what a truly critical epistemology should enable us to achieve is not simply to "tolerate, respect, and indulge" ("On a Certain Blindness in Human Beings" 11), but to seek and maintain critical engagements with those experiential differences and to pursue self-transformative processes: a deep self-interrogation through which subjects can develop a transformed sense of positionality and relationality in the world.

In "The Will to Believe" James emphasizes the characteristic opacity of our epistemic lives: "we find ourselves believing, we hardly know how or why" (96). We don't know the inner workings of our "passional nature"; we ignore the affective elements that control our epistemic lives: our fears and hopes, our prejudices and passions, etc. (see 96). This recognition of self-opacity could be the starting point for a critical process of self-estrangement that reveals and critically assesses the deepest presuppositions of our epistemic life. However, James only points in the direction of a limited reconstructive process, one that focuses only on the positive elements of our epistemic lives: on how trust and faith operate in our doxastic life, in our *will to believe*. Indeed, trust and faith are preconditions for important aspects of our epistemic activities. But what is left out of James's account is the key role that distrust and skepticism also play in our epistemic practices; they too are constitutive of key aspects of our epistemic lives. The affective side of our epistemic lives does not stop in the will to believe; there is also *the will not to believe*. Alongside a will to believe, we also find a resistance to acknowledge certain experiences, a refusal to engage with certain perspectives, in short, a will not to believe certain things. And these different elements in our epistemic lives, the positive and the negative, have to be studied not simply in juxtaposition, but as they interrelate and permeate people's epistemic attitudes. Trust and faith are key elements of our epistemic life in common, but so are the epistemic resistances that constrain our capacity for being truly attentive to diverse lived experiences and for responding to them. In order to be deeply transformed by the experiences of others, we need to unmask and uproot those resistance and fight against the relational insensitivity that prevents us to be attentive to relations of interdependence among our experiences and lives, and more specifically the interdependence of the flourishing of some and the withering of others.

Epistemic Activism: Fighting against Relational Insensitivity

Precisely because of the existence of affective resistances to be transformed by the perspectives of others who are very different from us—and especially those others who have a precarious social visibility and audibility, those whose standpoints have been obscured in social life (see Rogers "Knowing How to Feel: Racism, Resilience, and Affective Resistance")—we need confrontations that put pressure on subjects and publics to overcome their relational insensitivity. As I have argued, we need a socially transformative, *guerrilla* pluralism that requires that we mobilize our efforts to create epistemic friction among perspectives and use that friction to undo the relational insensitivity of power/knowledge-ignorance perspectives.[8] As recent epistemologies of ignorance and my own analysis suggest, individuals and groups will not become aware of their blind-spots by themselves or by mere exposure to different perspectives, since they have all kinds of protective mechanisms that will make them come out of those encounters not only unchanged, but affectively untouched, unmoved, unconcerned. We need to cultivate critical interventions and practices of interrogation that wake people up from their epistemic slumbers and trigger a process of deep epistemic engagement that can lead to new forms of relational sensitivity and attentiveness to the interdependence of our lives and perspectives. This is what I call *epistemic activism*.

What I call *epistemic activism* refers to critical interventions and transgressive forms of epistemic interaction that call attention to, and potentially disrupt, relational insensitivity and dysfunctional epistemic dynamics in which marginalized perspectives are not properly heard (if heard at all) and engaged with. As I have analyzed elsewhere in relation to activist practices that call attention to and critically engage with the social invisibility and inaudibility of imprisoned populations,[9] epistemic activism can augment the epistemic agency of unfairly disadvantaged subjects, amplifying their voices and facilitating the development and exercise of their epistemic capacities. It can also wake up potential audiences from their epistemic slumbers, inviting them to attend to contexts of epistemic marginalization and to the voices that come from those contexts, stimulating new and improved epistemic attitudes and habits across contexts, potentially leading to more just dynamics. The kinds of epistemic interventions and transformative epistemic practices that fall under the heading of *epistemic activism* have been recently discussed in feminist theory and disability studies, where the expressions "activist epistemology" and "epistemic activism" have been developed (Hamraie "Cripping Feminist Technoscience"). Calls for epistemic subversions and transformations have also been issued by intersectional approaches to racial, gender, and sexual oppression. This literature contains a broad and rich repertoire of strategies for epistemic activism, such as *epistemic disobedience* (Mignolo "Epistemic Disobedience, Independent Thought and Decolonial Freedom");

---

[8] On this point, see also the analysis of "inappropriately adaptive preferences" that Lori Gallegos provides in "Navigating Irreconcilable Conflicts: Philosophical Thinking for Better Lives," this volume.

[9] See my analysis of some of the programs of the Inside/Out Alliance in Medina and Whitt (forthcoming).

disorientating/tricking (Ahmed *Queer Phenomenology: Orientations, Objects, Others*; Lugones *Pilgrimages/Peregrinajes: Theorizing Coalition against Multiple Oppressions*); and *resistant logics/ languages/ imaginations* (Lugones *Pilgrimages/Peregrinajes: Theorizing Coalition against Multiple Oppressions* Medina *The Epistemology of Resistance: Gender and Racial Oppression, Epistemic Injustice, and Resistant Imaginations.*). It is not accidental that these activist perspectives in social epistemology have been developed by theorists who study the unfair treatment of intersecting identities in particular contexts and practices of oppression. It is only through the critical and practical engagement with the live experiences and embodied perspectives of marginalizes subjectivities that epistemic friction with privileged perspectives can be created. Privileged perspectives protect themselves from deep scrutiny and interrogation from underprivileged and oppressed perspectives; and special resistances are mobilized to fully acknowledge and remain attentive to our interdependences and especially to how the opportunities to flourish of some are closely linked to the lack of opportunities of others.

In order to uproot and displace the relational insensitivity that I have analyzed and criticized in this essay, it is crucial that, as argued above, we go beyond the epistemic policy of "live and let live," which leaves perspectives critically untouched and unfair relations among groups (relations of subordination and marginalization, for example) unexamined. The kind of *guerrilla* pluralism I have proposed calls for a process of mutual contestation among competing meanings and truths, which opens up possibilities for the deep transformation and rearticulation of perspectives and sensibilities. On this view, different experiential perspectives are not simply "tolerated" or accommodated alongside each other, but they are, rather, summoned to interrogate and transform each other. The flourishing of all requires inclusive communities in which relations of interdependence are not only acknowledged, but also felt and taken into account as we plan our life, undergo experiences, and evaluate our life experiences in common. In order to work toward such inclusive communities in the spirit of guerrilla pluralism, we need to cultivate epistemic activist practices that aim at making our sensibility vulnerable and contestable to the sensibilities of others. I want to emphasize here the role of public art for providing opportunities for the mutual interrogation of perspectives and mutual contestability. In particular, I want to illustrate how public art can be used to instigate processes of self-estrangement in which publics can become self-critical about the blind-spots of their perspectives in relation to other perspectives.[10] For this purpose, I will focus on public art that invite us to become self-critical about the relational insensitivities that occlude the dependence of the flourishing of some on the withering of others. In this respect, there may be no better contemporary examples than the public installations of the Colombian visual artist Doris Salcedo.

Salcedo's visual art aims at prompting subjects and communities to deeply interrogate how their identities and histories relate to other identities and histories, and to dwell on experiences of estrangement and mutual entanglement. Salcedo's most notorious installations are interventions in public spaces that make these familiar places appear unfamiliar or uncanny, planting carefully crafted material provocations in these spaces that call for the sharing of memories and the mutual interrogation of collective memories. Salcedo's powerful works address the importance of remembrance and mourning in relation to issues of violence, displacement and colonial oppression. She composes her pieces with everyday objects—such as chairs, desks, shoes, dresses, etc.—which are reminiscent of the lost lives to which they were connected. Some of Salcedo's pieces are public performances of mourning which echo experiences of violence without representing them (and underscoring the impossibility of their representation), and reenact ways of resisting the oblivion of traumatic events.[11] Salcedo's public installations are also performative and non-representational; they invite critical interaction and interrogation in subtle ways. Salcedo's provocative visual installations alter public spaces dramatically but in such a way that the alteration blends into the space and can remain unnoticed; on the surface, they can appear inconspicuous; but upon being noticed, they become disorienting, mesmerizing, hypnotic; we are drawn to them and they provoke in us experiences of the uncanny, de-familiarizing familiar spaces we pass by and interrogating our perspective and positionality in those spaces. These qualities are perfectly displayed by the untitled installation that Salcedo produced for the 8th International Istanbul Biennial. For this installation Salcedo chose a vacant lot in downtown Istanbul in which she crammed 1,550 wooden chairs stacked between two buildings, calling attention to the complex history of forced migration and displacement in the city. This piece has a complex emotional texture and it intimates experiences of being suffocated, of being

---

[10] In her chapter in this volume, Michele Moody-Adams argues that art makes crucial, vital contributions to satisfying and well-lived lives.

[11] For a lucid analysis of Salcedo's piece *Noviembre 6–7* (2002) in Bogota, Colombia, and how this piece performs mourning and resistance to oblivion, see Acosta López (2014).

stuck, of being entangled, of being pushed down by the weight of the lives of others, and of being forgotten. It brings to the fore in a vivid and dramatic way the close relationship between place and displacement, between the history of a place and histories of being displaced; and it invites us to interrogate our own positionality with respect to that place and the multiple forms of displacement that have shaped it, offering opportunities to connect our ordinary experiences of inhabiting a place with the experiences of multiple displaced others and to become critically transformed and affected by those experiences. This is how Salcedo summarizes her inspiration for this piece as a critical reflection on the interrelation between past displacement and present placement:

> I was visiting the city and walking in an area full of ruins. There were so many ruins in a central area that I started wondering why [. . .] There were legacies of a violent past where Jews and Greeks were forced out of their buildings, these buildings. It's the process of this placement—of forceful displacement that is taking place. (Salcedo, Interview with MCA Chicago)

Another example of public art that calls for a deep interrogation of one's positionality vis-à-vis that of others can be found in Salcedo's *Shibboleth* (2007–8), a provocative installation that calls attention to the fact that the very ground on which we stand is shaped by complex histories of colonial dominations and exclusions that remain invisible unless we look down and inspect the cracks of the ground on which we walk, decentering our perspective and taking into account the perspectives of others who may have fallen between the cracks. This installation is an enormous (548-foot-long) crack that Salcedo and her team created in the floor of the Turbine Hall at the Tate Modern in London, in order to call attention to the colonial and postcolonial fissures in society that still persist today. The crack is not only long and imposing, but also deep and richly textured inside, enticing people's imaginations about possible underworlds beneath them and inviting them to kneel down and inspect what might be hidden underneath. The term "shibboleth" that Salcedo used as a title for this installation comes from a story in the Bible in which invaders used the pronunciation of this word to identify and execute Ephraimites, whose dialect used a differently sounding first consonant. As the title suggests, the installation aims at provoking reflections about how cultural differences have been used to separate, exclude and stigmatize groups, and how stigmatization and cultural violence can become constitutive of one's world and part of the very ground on which we stand.[12] The installation also has a complex emotional texture, making us feel the disorientation of standing over a ground that opens up into the abyss, the vertigo of looking down between the cracks, the fear of not knowing what is beneath us, supporting our weight, enabling us to stand and walk. This is how Salcedo explains what the piece tries to express and create:

> It represents borders, the experience of immigrants, the experience of segregation, the experience of racial hatred. It is the experience of a Third World person coming into the heart of Europe. For example, the space which illegal immigrants occupy is a negative space. And so this piece is a negative space. (Salcedo, Interview with MCA Chicago)

What is remarkable about Salcedo's installations is that, rather than telling us a story, they open up unusual spaces for people to tell stories from eccentric, non-dominant perspectives, and to do so in such a way that they transform those spaces and invite new relations and entanglements of perspectives. In other words, they issue critical provocations and interrogations of our epistemic sensibility, of what we are attentive and inattentive to, of what we understand and know and of what we misunderstand and ignore. In this sense, Salcedo's visual artwork is exemplary of how public art can be viewed as a form of *epistemic activism*, that is, as a critical intervention in a public space designed to produced epistemic friction between different sensibilities. Of course, Salcedo's installations cannot guarantee that the publics that interact with them will critically engage with what is alien to them (the *simply alien* as well as the *alienated familiar*), that is, that they will engage in processes of self-estrangement and self-interrogation in which they critically examine the limits and blind-spots of their own perspectives in relation to the perspectives of others. But Salcedo's installations stage spaces of decentered interaction that facilitate critical reflection across perspectives and communicative processes of estrangement and mutual transformation, of becoming transformed and affected by each other's experiences and memories. Public art of this kind as well as educational initiatives in the humanities aimed

---

[12] Interestingly, although the crack was filled in after the exhibit ended in April 2008, a visible line in the floor remains, *as a scar*, reminding us of the forgotten and invisibilized underworlds we walk on. As the Tate Director, Sir Nicholas Serota, stated during the exhibit: "There is a crack, there is a line, and eventually there will be a scar. It will remain as a memory of the work and also as a memorial to the issues Doris touches on." (Interview with MCA Chicago)

at stimulating critical dialogues across perspectives and processes of self-estrangement and mutual interrogation are key components of the epistemic activism that we need to cultivate in order to resist relational insensitivity and to work toward new forms of relational sensitivity that enable us to become attuned to the interdependence of experiential standpoints and of their flourishing and withering.

The unexamined life may or may not be worth living, but it is epistemically and ethically objectionable and not conducive to responsible living. As this essay has tried to show, this can be appreciated by paying attention to the epistemic and ethical failures involved in relational insensitivity, in being numbed to the flourishing and withering of those who are very different from us but with whom we coexist, in cultivating forms of neglect and disregard for the ways in which human enjoyment and human suffering become entangled. Publically engaged art and the critical humanities provide venues for practicing epistemic activism that aims at unmasking, disrupting, and uprooting these forms of relational insensitivity, waking people up from their epistemic slumbers and facilitating mutual accountability and responsible relationality.

Works Cited

Acosta López, María del Rosario. "Memory and Fragility: Art's Resistance to Oblivion (Three Colombian Cases)." *CR: The New Centennial Review,* vol. 14, no. 1, 2014, pp. 71–97.

Ahmed, Sara. *Queer Phenomenology: Orientations, Objects, Others.* Duke University Press, 2006.

Gallegos, Lori. "Navigating Irreconcilable Conflicts: Philosophical Thinking for Better Lives." *Philosophy and Human Flourishing,* edited by John J. Stuhr. Oxford University Press, 2022.

Hamraie, Aimi. "Cripping Feminist Technoscience." *Hypatia,* vol. 30, no. 1, 2015, pp. 307–13.

Harding, Sandra. *Whose Science? Whose Knowledge? Thinking from Women's Lives.* Cornell University Press, 1991.

Hill Collins, Patricia. "Piercing Together a Genealogical Puzzle: Intersectionality and American Pragmatism." *European Journal of Pragmatism and American Philosophy,* vol. 3, no. 2, 2011, pp. 88–112.

Hill Collins, Patricia. *Black Feminist Thought: Knowledge, Consciousness, and the Politics of Empowerment.*, Unwin Hyman, 1990/2000.

James, William. "The Will to Believe." *The Pragmatism Reader,* edited by R. Talisse and S. Aikin. Princeton University Press, 1896/2011, pp. 92–108.

James, William. "On a Certain Blindness in Human Beings." 1899. Talks to Teachers on Psychology and to Students on Some of Life's Ideals. Harvard University Press, 1983. http://www.uky.edu/~eushe2/Pajares/jcertain.html.

James, William. The Meaning of Truth. Harvard University Press, 1975a.

James, William. Pragmatism: A New Name for Some Old Ways of Thinking. Harvard University Press, 1975b.

James, William. A Pluralistic Universe. Harvard University Press, 1977.

James, William. Essays in Philosophy. Harvard University Press, 1978.

Lugones, María. Pilgrimages/Peregrinajes: Theorizing Coalition against Multiple Oppressions. Rowman & Littlefield, 2003.

Medina, José. The Epistemology of Resistance: Gender and Racial Oppression, Epistemic Injustice, and Resistant Imaginations. Oxford University Press, 2013.

Medina, José, and Whitt, Matt. "Epistemic Activism and the Politics of Credibility: Testimonial Injustice Inside/Outside a North Carolina Jail." Making the Case, edited by Nancy McHugh and Heidi Grasswick. SUNY Press, 2021, pp. 293–324.

Mignolo, Walter. "Epistemic Disobedience, Independent Thought and Decolonial Freedom." Theory, Culture & Society, vol. 26, no. 7–8, 2009, pp. 159–81.

Mills, Charles. "Alternative Epistemologies." Blackness Visible: Essays on Philosophy and Race. Cornell University Press, 1998, pp. 21–39.

Rogers, Taylor. "Knowing How to Feel: Racism, Resilience, and Affective Resistance." Hypatia: A Journal of Feminist Philosophy, vol. 36, no. 4, 2021, pp. 725–47.

Scheman, Naomi. "Queering the Center by Centering the Queer: Reflections on Transsexuals and Secular Jews." Feminist Rethink the Self, edited by D.T. Meyers. Westview, 1997, pp. 124–62.

Sullivan, Shannon. "The Need for Truth: Toward a Pragmatist-Feminist Standpoint Theory." Feminist Interpretations of John Dewey, edited by C.H. Seigfrid. Penn State University Press, 2001, pp. 210–35.

Sullivan, Shannon, and Tuana, N., editors. Race and Epistemologies of Ignorance. SUNY Press, 2007.

Tuana, Nancy. "Coming to Understand: Orgasm and the Epistemology of Ignorance." Hypatia: A Journal of Feminist Philosophy, vol. 19, no. 1, 2004, pp. 194–232.

Tuana, Nancy. "The Speculum of Ignorance: The Women's Health Movement and Epistemologies of Ignorance." Hypatia: A Journal of Feminist Philosophy, vol. 21, no. 3, 2006, pp. 1–19.

10

Values Literacy and Citizenship

John Z. Sadler

In terms of the goals of the HHF Project for philosophy, one of the key questions offered was "Does philosophy contribute to well-being in any unique ways in which other endeavors do not?" My chapter intends to address this question through a modest and specific example. The context of my example is a focused but interrelated set of social problems that, I claim, interfere with flourishing in the public sphere. I do not focus on philosophical issues of defining eudaemonia and assume a conventional meaning of this term and related ones like "flourishing."

In the first part of the paper I will describe the contemporary problem of public civil discourse. I will provide an overview of others' works which frame a breakdown in civil discourse in the realms of political discourse, social media use, and the educational problem of teaching citizenship and civic engagement at the secondary and college levels. I provide some background on citizenship and citizenship education.

With this background, I turn to the second portion of the paper, in which I introduce the concept of "values literacy." My concept of values literacy, while inspired by E. D. Hirsch's term "cultural literacy," is a uniquely philosophical concept which addresses not a canon of crucial works on values, but rather the cultivation of a set of epistemic skills and attitudes in recognizing, analyzing, and interpreting values (*Cultural Literacy: What Every American Should Know*). I describe briefly how deficits in values literacy contribute to the problems in contemporary civil discourse discussed in the first section of the paper.

Having set up the problem and introduced the concept of values literacy as a constructive response, I then flesh out a philosophical method

John Z. Sadler, *Values Literacy and Citizenship* In: *Philosophy and Human Flourishing*. Edited by: John J. Stuhr, Oxford University Press. © Oxford University Press 2023. DOI: 10.1093/oso/9780197622162.003.0011

of values analysis and recognition that is based upon my prior work and which constitutes a portion of the skills implied by "values literacy."[1] I define "values" in an operational manner based upon the work of Hilary Putnam.[2] Values, under this account, are attitudes or dispositions, which are action-guiding and subject to praise or blame. With this understanding, texts or human discourses can be "searched" for value terms (words with required evaluative meanings), value semantics (sentences in which evaluations are semantically or pragmatically implied), and value entailments (practices which involve one or more evaluations). These philosophical concepts can then be applied in a concrete way to cultural artifacts–texts, talk–to identify the values explicitly or implicitly present. This method of values analysis is intuitive and teachable with concrete illustrations, which are provided. The problem of "values blindness" refers to our tendency not to recognize values we and others hold. Values blindness is addressed in my treatment here through presenting a hierarchical order of value types commonly encountered and structured by Western liberal democratic societies. The hierarchical value-types serve as heuristic tools in hypothesizing about implicit values in discourses.

In the fourth and concluding portion of the paper, I then make the case for how educating the polity in values-analysis can deepen and expand civil discourse, even in short communications such as tweets and media sound bites. The primary importance of values-analytic skills is empathy building among stakeholders and recognizing shared values is a first step to addressing non-shared values. Moreover, I show how values-analysis can aid the citizen in detecting insincere or guileful discourses. I argue these techniques can cultivate the secondary or college student into a conscientious consumer of communications, independent of ideological commitments, contents, and prejudices. Instead of taking values for granted, or simply accepting a claim to values (e.g., 'family values,' 'progressivism'), the sincere seeker of human flourishing can use values analysis to explode simplistic accounts into complex sets of value trade-offs and compromises, exposing the insincere while revealing potentials for common ground.

---

[1] Sadler 1997 "Recognizing Values: A Descriptive-Causal Method for Medical/Scientific Discourses"; 2013 "Values in Psychiatric Diagnosis and Classification"; 2015 "Values-Based Psychiatric Ethics."

[2] Putnam 1981 "Fact and Value"; 1990a "Beyond the Fact/Value Dichotomy"; 1990b "The Place of Facts in a World of Values."

Introduction and Background

In recent times many of us have been concerned about a perceived decline in the quality of public discourse, and what has come to be known as the "public sphere" has increasingly become polarized and divisive. Our Federal governmental leaders seem incapable of consistently executing effective public policy, and substantive factions of the polity seem to reject expertise, virtue, statesmanship, and perhaps rationality itself. Research has shown that mass media, including, and perhaps especially, social media, have substantively contributed to this divisiveness and incivility (Sunstein *#Republic: Divided Democracy in the Age of Social Media*). I do not believe a complex argument is needed to claim that a civil, competent public sphere is a component of democratic governments, as this has been the view of American political theorists since Thomas Jefferson. Moreover, a connection between civil discourse and human flourishing, for the purposes of this essay, will be assumed. Finally, I assume that a multipronged approach to restoring civil discourse is required for (at least) supporting human flourishing in the United States, and this paper aims to employ some methods of philosophy to sketch a very modest contribution to this larger need.

My basic thesis moves in several steps. The problem I want to address is an ongoing challenge in secondary education: how to prepare young people to be good citizens–how to foster "citizenship." The education of good citizens, after all, is aimed to contribute to improving the quality of public discourse. Variously called citizenship education, civil education, civic education, civics, and social studies, citizenship education (cit-ed) has occupied a small but brisk place in the education literature over the past 30 years. Two fundamental issues penetrate the cit-ed literature: (1) what is meant by citizenship, and (2) what should be taught to cultivate citizenship. This first part of the paper examines citizenship education and attempts to clarify some of the issues. In the second part of the paper, I introduce the idea of "values literacy" adapted from Hirsch's much older concept of "cultural literacy," the latter being what students need to know in order to be good citizens (Hirsch "*Cultural Literacy: What Every American Should Know*"). Hirsch's concept has had its own share of controversy. I flesh out what I mean by values literacy and describe it as a set of epistemic skills and attitudes which are teachable to secondary-school and college students (despite their high-falutin' philosophical roots) and enable students to more deeply engage discourses by revealing the kinds of values that "lurk" within them. Through this deeper engagement with the values behind people's talk, students can (hopefully) begin to better understand the standpoint of the other who does not agree with them, and perhaps, find common ground. I will also mention, though not argue, that values-literacy is intrinsically rewarding, as the values-laden portions of the discursive world are revealed and effectively explored, thereby enriching and diversifying one's cultural experience. For the third part of the paper, I introduce my methods of values-analysis as the core of values-literacy, the former based on my prior work in studying the values associated with psychiatric diagnostic schemes (Sadler 1997, 2013, 2015).[3] I provide examples from ordinary discourses. In the fourth and concluding part of the paper, I draw upon some of the research that has addressed divisive processes like polarization and indicate how skills in values-analysis can contribute to de-polarizing discourses and thus improve civil discourse.

Public Discourse, Citizenship, and Citizenship Education

One needn't look far, or hard, for discussions about the decline of civil discourse in the United States; see for instance Schall, Seib, Conner, Davidson, and Sunstein.[4] The reasons are many, including such social processes as polarization, affirmation bias, and "cybercascades," among others (Sunstein). Polarization is the tendency to elevate viewpoints consistent with one's own and marginalize or ignore those that are inconsistent. Affirmation bias in psychology is the phenomenon of ingroup members affirming their own viewpoints—viewpoints different from outgroup perspectives that, in turn, are ignored, dismissed, or marginalized. Cybercascades are media phenomena where concepts, ideas, or tropes undergo massive replication and promulgation through (typically, but not exclusively) social media communications like Facebook, Twitter, Instagram, and the like. Cybercascades are significant because the process may undermine the distinction between true and false information, as either kind of information can be propagated through instant and massive group-forwarding mechanisms. These

---

[3] Sadler 1997 "Recognizing Values: A Descriptive-Causal Method for Medical/Scientific Discourses"; 2013 "Values in Psychiatric Diagnosis and Classification"; 2015 "Values-Based Psychiatric Ethics."

[4] See Schall 2018 "The Death of Civil Discourse Is the Death of Us"; Seib 2017 "Civil Discourse in Decline: Where Does It End?"; Conner 2018 "The Decline of Civil Discourse and the Rise of Extremist Debate: Words Matter" 213–31; Davidson 2015 "The Decline and Fall of American Political Debate"; and Sunstein 2017 #Republic: Divided Democracy in the Age of Social Media.

processes are the mechanisms of pop culture phenomena like "fake news" and "echo-chambering" and share some features with older, now-quaint social-communications processes like gossip and moral panics (Cohen "Deviance and Moral Panics").

But framing the problem as one of poor "civil discourse" is overly simple. At its core the question about public discourse should consider citizenship as some kind of aspirational virtue. But what is citizenship?

Kymlicka and Norman, among others, describe the concept of citizenship as having three aspects or elements: (1) citizenship as legal status, (2) citizenship as being a political agent, and (3) citizenship as membership in a political community with a substantive identity (*Citizenship in Culturally Diverse Societies*). Aspect (1) is not of particular interest in my context, in that the particulars of one's place in the rule of law in a society, or which rights one has, is not specifically germane to my discussion here. Aspect (3) is of key interest, for reason of the problems of cit-ed to follow, which includes the problem of selecting curriculum in contemporary communities with diverse cultural, ethnic, religious, and political identities. But Aspect (2) is also important for my discussion here, in that my interests in public, civil discourse lands most closely to this aspect of citizenship, where people actively, or passively, engage in political communities.

Political philosophy has several matters of debate regarding the concept of citizenship, and some familiarity with these will aid in understanding the challenges of what and how to teach in cit-ed will be discussed shortly. In a review article, Leydet identifies three models of citizenship, spanning ancient philosophy to the present ("Citizenship"). Introducing these is of some orienting value as the tensions between these accounts are operative today, and the political changes of the post-digital world raise some new questions for them. The first account springs from Aristotle and others: the "republican" account, where citizenship has to do with civic self-rule, where citizens are actors in the public sphere and have direct input into political offices and issues. The republican citizen is an active decision maker—a political agent. The second, the "liberal" account, emerges, according to Walzer, from the Roman Empire, where conquered peoples were citizen-subjects under to the protections of common law, but not necessarily participating in lawmaking and governing ("Citizenship" 211–20). In this sense the liberal account falls more fully under the earlier aspect (1) citizenship as legal status. The third sense, what Leydet calls the "feminist" account, which is more contemporary, challenges the strict distinction between private and public spheres, recognizing that citizenship and political impact is potent in personal circumstances, whether in childrearing, or religious or cultural expressions, and racial, language, and gender relations ("Citizenship"). This conception of citizen as contextualized in multiple communities and multiple identities ("intersectionalism") then, in the cit-ed context, asks what content is suitable for education in citizenship—whether one, for instance, should teach about responses to teen pregnancy, Muslim immigration, or the Bill of Rights.

This challenge of diversity in the contemporary world has been characterized as a tension between "universalist" versus "differentialist" concepts of citizenship. In Marshall's account, the universalist concept of citizenship held that the same set of political, civil, and social rights should apply to all of the polity (*Citizenship and Social Class and Other Essays*). Citizenship, above all, should be equitable. In today's world this is a naive concept for many, as it ignores the range of different capabilities, opportunities, communal values, notions of the good, and ethnoreligious traditions that have different implications for political, civil, and social rights across various groups and identities. For example, the universalist concept of citizenship sets up the problem of majoritarian intrusion into minorities' lives because equal voting rights mean that minority interests are unlikely to prevail (Dahl *A Preface to Democratic Theory*). Being female, gay, Muslim, black, etc.—that is, being different from white heteronormative males—came to be recognized as politically relevant to citizenship, provoking a diversification of not just citizenship theory but political theory in general, generating a profusion of various, but more "differentialist," accounts of citizenship (e.g., Connolly *Politics and Ambiguity*; Kymlicka *Multicultural Citizenship*; Nussbaum *Frontiers of Justice*; Okin "Women, Equality, and Citizenship"; Rawls *A Theory of Justice, Revised Edition*; Young "Polity and Group Difference: A Critique of the Ideal of Universal Citizenship). Whether harbingers, provocateurs, or commentators, these voices in political philosophy were synchronic with debates within the cit-ed literature.

In his review of the politics of citizenship education, Ross notes that there is "widespread agreement that the appropriate aim of social studies is 'citizenship education,' or the preparation of young people so that they possess the knowledge, skills and values necessary for active participation in society" ("Negotiating the Politics of Citizenship Education" 249). In his view, the problem of cultural pluralism and recognition of diversity is through making *deliberation* the core skill of cit-ed, where students "engage in careful consideration and discussion of alternatives for the purpose of creating a better life" (251).

Banks in his treatment of cit-ed, engages, head-on, the problem of diversity and group identity in citizenship education ("Diversity, Group Identity, and Citizenship Education in a Global Age.") Adding "liberal assimilationism" to the universal and liberal concepts of citizenship (and by extension, cit-ed), Banks describes assimilationism as the contemporary process where "individuals from different groups have to give up their home and community cultures and languages to attain inclusion and to participate effectively in national civic culture" 1). He provides as examples the early American colonial missionary schools which aimed to "Christianize" Native American youth, as well as pressures for Mexican Americans to speak English in schools. He notes that assimilationism is found in history textbooks where the white majority histories predominate, and minority histories and cultures are absent.

In my home state of Texas today, the handling of iconic Texas historical moments is fraught with these latter conflicts. Controversy continues regarding the telling of the Alamo story in Texas schools from the white Texan perspective, the Mexican perspective, or the Tejano (Mexican citizens loyal to Texas independence) perspective (Casares "A Textbook on Mexican Americans that Gets Their History Wrong? Oh Texas"). The liberal assimilationist process asserts that once students are taught the modern, democratic pluralism their group affiliations will dissolve and the group members will be "assimilated" into the dominant culture. Banks reviews the social science literature that shows how this view has increasingly become untenable in our current world. Factors include the widespread migration and immigration throughout the world, making polyethnic groups common, and in some cases, the majority in Western nations. Kymlicka notes that "In very few countries can the citizens be said to share the same language, or belong to the same ethnonational group . . ." (*Multicultural Citizenship* 1). Banks notes that today, "identity is multiple, changing, overlapping, and contextual, rather than fixed and static" (5) making the question of cit-ed even more complex ("Diversity, Group Identity, and Citizenship Education in a Global Age" 5). He favors a philosophy of global citizenship, where allegiances and political actions are directed at the world community of human beings and their flourishing, such as in Martha Nussbaum's concept of cosmopolitanism (*Toward a Globally Sensitive Patriotism*).

This challenge of national and global citizenship, in the face of such diversity, then fuels the questions about what to teach in cit-ed. In a recent review

of American citizenship education, Alex Lin (see also Morgan et al.) identified three kinds of programs delivering cit-ed ("Citizenship Education in
American Schools and Its Role in Developing Civic Engagement: A Review of
the Research"). The first, *character education* programs, which are primarily
situated in primary schools and focus on developing ethical values or character virtues in students, are aimed at fostering the "personally responsible
citizen." A common example of character education in the primary school
setting is scouting programs that focus on cultivating virtuous conduct and
social action (and other aims such as campcraft and respect for nature). The
second form of American citizenship education identified by Lin's review is
political simulation. Aimed at older, secondary school and college students,
this program has students engage in simulated discussions about social issues. These objectives are addressed through role play and simulations of
political discussions or situations, such as mock campaigns and elections.
The third method for secondary education students involves *service learning*,
where worthy projects in the community are developed and delivered. The
values associated with being a participating citizen are intended to assimilate
in such experiences.

In a comparable review from the United Kingdom for the period 1995–
2005, Osler and Starkey use the term "education for democratic citizenship"
(EDC; "Education for Democratic Citizenship: A Review of Research, Policy
and Practice 1995–2005"). Osler and Starkey's research review emphasize
topical contents of EDC programs, de-emphasizing modes of delivery of such
content. In this sense, their review is complementary to Lin's. Both reviews
emphasize the growing importance of global citizenship and the need for
active engagement by students. Content themes identified by the team include (a) diversity and unity, addressing the aforementioned issue of recognizing minorities while building national unity; (b) global and cosmopolitan
citizenship; (c) children as citizens; (d) democratic schooling; (e) students'
understanding of citizenship and democratic processes; (f) the complementary roles of schools and communities; (g) European citizenship; and (h) the
practicalities of implementing EDC at the school level. The latter category
is of particular interest for this paper, in that the role of cross-curricular
learning is considered. The research in this domain indicates that substantive
room exists in existing school subjects to incorporate EDC learning. These
subjects included, for example, history, religion, science, environmental education, holocaust education, languages, and business studies, among others.
A second relevant aspect here within topic (h) is actual classroom practices.

They note several relevant themes of interest here: a paucity of research and standards about how to actually deliver EDC material; noting that teachers are uncomfortable about how to teach EDC learning (see, in particular, Oulton et al., "Controversial Issues: Teachers' Attitudes and Practices in the Context of Citizenship Education"), and that methods of delivery are diverse. Often, EDC learning converges upon a "special theme day" that balkanizes cit-ed (Osler and Starkey "Education for Democratic Citizenship: A Review of Research, Policy and Practice 1995–2005" 36.

Graham, in a white paper for civilpolitics.org, an academic organization focusing on moral psychology research in civic affairs, summarizes studies intended to show what kinds of interventions have scientific evidence "to improve intergroup relations" ("Interventions to Improve Intergroup Relations: What Works, What Shows Promise, and What This Means for Civil Politics." 2014). While aimed at the adult public, the principles would appear to be relevant to secondary and higher-ed approaches to cit-ed. The material is organized around the research base for various kinds of practices intended to improve community relationships. These include the following:

Improve personal relationships: This principle focuses on meaningful contact between ingroups and outgroups, with interventions that concern perspective-taking and empathizing with the other.

Emphasize superordinate goals: The focus of this principle is on interventions and goals that transcend group boundaries, such as global warming or crime reduction. By working together on such superordinate goals, in/out groups learn to understand and respect each other.

The following principles had a weaker evidence base but were presented as promising directions:

Reducing moral certainty: This principle focuses on "demoralizing" civic situations and having in/outgroups see situations in less morality-laden ways. "Demoralizing" in this sense does not mean losing hope for civics, but rather reducing the moral weight and acuity of civic perspectives. This is done in various ways, by marginalizing extremist views and by emphasizing financial or other sources of self-interest. (Interestingly, this approach does not focus on complicating moral positions or adding moral ambiguity to situations.)

Emphasizing shared humanity: This principle exposes participants to ordinary activities and challenges encountered by all people, presumably building empathy for outgroup members.

Expressing ingroup love without outgroup hate: In game settings, cultivating statements of team (ingroup) love reduces conflict with outgroups.

Reducing zero-sum perceptions: This principle focuses on interventions that reduce the perception of politics as a for-me-or-against-me activity and emphasizes, instead, that in working together one could accomplish more.

I draw several conclusions from this material for the purposes of this chapter. First, the cit-ed field is largely balkanized into its own, limited arena in educational programs. While exceptions do occur, cit-ed generally finds its way into dedicated courses, even dedicated days or periods, and is too-often removed from day-to-day classroom topics and activities. Second, the literature is dominated by knowledge-oriented approaches. If one takes the traditional task of education as cultivating knowledge, skills, and attitudes, the prevailing cit-ed approaches emphasize knowledge of (for instance) governmental structures and functions, political processes, and topics of civic interest. Only recently, notably in the Graham review, have intergroup processes—skills and attitudes—been considered seriously ("Interventions to Improve Intergroup Relations: What Works, What Shows Promise, and What This Means for Civil Politics." Finally, a third conclusion is that the actual consideration of discourses—of how people talk and write together—is nearly absent. To the latter I now turn for my own exposition.

Becoming Values Literate

In the 1980s, E. D. Hirsch, a University of Virginia English professor, articulated the concept of "cultural literacy," which, while controversial, has been very influential in American education through providing a way of conceptualizing what students should learn in order to participate in the larger society and culture (*Cultural Literacy: What Every American Should Know*). The basic idea is that students require a certain amount of cultural background knowledge in order to understand novel information, including standardized texts in schools. For example, a student has to know something about the US Civil War in order to understand new biographical material about Robert E. Lee. Hirsch's empirical research indicated that students' ability to understand new textbook information was proportionate to the amount of background knowledge on the subject. While not a particularly surprising finding, this insight was crucial at a time when US schools had focused on more process-oriented approaches to teaching, independent of any standard cultural "canon," which Hirsch believed contributed to the declining scores and academic achievements in schools (*Cultural Literacy: What Every American Should Know*). The educational focus on process over canonic content was in part a response to the dilemmas I have outlined above regarding cit-ed–namely, that a multicultural world poses serious problems for what is canon versus what is not. Hirsch's belief that the more traditional Western canon (which was largely white, male, English-speaking, Anglo-European, privileged), and was crucial to American cultural literacy, was simultaneously influential as well as controversial—as it is today. In addition, the concept of "literacies" extending beyond the usual reading, writing, and arithmetic, caught on in many educational fields, with all kinds of specialized "literacies" appearing, such as health literacy, economic literacy, etc.

In planning this chapter I had to figure out a simple term to refer to what philosophical skills I would like all secondary and college students to have, in order to be good citizen-participants. I picked "values literacy" as the imperfect best option. Values literacy as a concept is imperfect because it is not fully analogous with Hirsch's concept of cultural literacy. I am not insisting that students learn the meanings of lists of value terms and expressions, or learn a canon of works in one or more traditions. Hirsch's concept of cultural literacy was mostly about what facts, or educational contents, students should know, or learn. It was not about what students need to know *how*—or *how to do*. With this transition away from educational content (knowledge) and instead towards *know-how*.[5] I am proposing values literacy as what students *need to be able to do* in regards to recognize and use values in ordinary discourse. Values literacy as I am proposing here is about skills and attitudes, and much less about knowledge or educational contents and facts. As a skill, values literacy applies to any and all human conversation, whether written or spoken. In introducing this concept, I am also introducing a set

---

[5] In the context of this contrast between matter of fact knowledge and know-how or skills, see Jennifer L. Hansen's account of the reduction of know-how to "technological rationality," in "A Reconsideration of the Role of Philosophy in the Reconstruction and Promotion of Leisure," this volume.

of easy-to-understand philosophical methods that can help students engage with others—especially other citizens.

I wish to avoid making any more than a modest claim for the utility of these methods of values literacy or values-analysis to be described shortly. Moreover, my account here is at most introductory. However, as a set of skills and attitudes, values literacy has "value" in addressing several of the deep problems in citizenship education. Values literacy education eschews any need for a specific set of contents or facts to be learned. It is equally applicable to religious debates as to science, literary, and policy debates. Values analytic skills can be applied to all ethnicities, cultures, identities, and political dispositions. Moreover, understanding the values held by others sets the stage for empathic understanding of the other, which much of the research previously mentioned aims as a goal of cit-ed. Moreover, as a skill, it can be refined by practice, and applied to multiple contexts. The universal applicability of this skill set thereby enables cit-ed to avoid being balkanized into "teaching days" and courses, but allows consideration of values relevant to citizen participation in virtually any course, and so cit-ed can be, with the teacher's will and institutional support, applied to many kinds of coursework.

So what kind of skills are we talking about? And what do I mean by values? Let me respond to these questions by describing my "discovery."

Years ago I became interested in discerning the value judgments that were implicit in psychiatric diagnostic categories, as imbricated in the American Psychiatric Association's *Diagnostic and Statistical Manual of Mental Disorders* (the DSMs), currently in fifth edition—*DSM-5®*. While at the time a few scholars argued that value assumptions and commitments of various kinds were endemic in psychiatric diagnosis, there was no method in clinical or philosophical literatures I could find that described how one could survey, in a systematic way, the value judgments, commitments, and assumptions in the DSMs, or for that matter, other kinds of discourses. Philosophers as well as many psychiatrists were aware, for example, that diagnostic criteria for "Antisocial Personality Disorder" seemed to be laden with descriptions of wrongful conduct and even criminal conduct, and subject to negative social judgments, but what about the other 300 or so disorders in the DSMs? I wanted to explore these questions, among others, but how to proceed?

A key step was encountering Harvard logician Hilary Putnam's then-contemporary work on values. Putnam was interested in how values worked in discourses, and his account framed the semantic concept of "value" in a way that could enable a reader/listener to identify values, even "scan" for them, by using a few simple rules. Putnam defined a value as a descriptor or condition which would (a) be a guide to human action and (b) be subject to praise or blame within a human community. I later reformulated Putnam's understanding to describe values as *attitudes or dispositions which are action-guiding and subject to praise or blame.*[6] A second clue came from my friend and colleague, K. W. M. "Bill" Fulford, who also shared an interest in how values operate in psychiatric discourse (*Moral Theory and Medical Practice*). Fulford had been trained in analytic and ordinary-language philosophy, and mentored by the moral philosopher Richard M. Hare. Fulford was interested in the use of "value terms" in psychiatry. Here value terms are words which identify concepts that are irreducibly evaluative—such that the word loses its meaning if one tries to extract the evaluation. So, for instance, "blue," the color, is not a value term, but "blue," the mood state, is, because being "blue" influences my actions, and is subject to praise or blame. My example explains the importance of pragmatic context of use of value terms and phrases–that what the word means depends upon its use in discourse. Just to keep readers clear where I am going with this, my definition of values can be translated into "high-schoolese" in this way:

Values are attitudes or tendencies to do things which people more-or-less like, or don't.

But the key for philosophy and teaching is "Show, don't tell." The standard grown-up example I give for how to find values in discourses is this one, which is the first paragraph in the Introduction to DSM-IV (APA xv, under-lining mine):

Our highest <u>priority</u> has been to provide a <u>helpful</u> guide to clinical practice. We hoped to make DSM-IV <u>practical</u> and <u>useful</u> for clinicians by striving for <u>brevity</u> of criteria sets, <u>clarity</u> of language, and <u>explicit</u> statements of the constructs embodied in the diagnostic criteria. An additional goal was to <u>facilitate</u> research and <u>improve</u> communication among clinicians and researchers. We were also <u>mindful</u> of the use of DSM-IV for <u>improving</u> the collection of clinical information and as an educational tool for teaching psychopathology.

[6] Sadler 1997 "Recognizing Values: A Descriptive-Causal Method for Medical/Scientific Discourses"; 2013 "Values in Psychiatric Diagnosis and Classification"; 2015 "Values-Based Psychiatric Ethics."

I ask the audience to identify the value terms, which in this case are done for you here through underlining them. This activity poses a fun puzzle or even a game. People pick up on this very quickly.

Here is a Twitter feed example:

> Donald J. Trump @ realDonaldTrump (27 April 2018 tweet, underlining and italics added)
>
> Kanye West has performed a <u>great service</u> to the Black Community - <u>Big things</u> are happening and *eyes are being opened* for the first time in Decades - <u>Legacy Stuff!</u> Thank you also to Chance and Dr. Darrell Scott, they *really get it* (lowest Black and Hispanic unemployment in history).

Though this tweet from President Trump exhibits his characteristic hyperbole, one can recognize that "great service," "Big things," and "Legacy Stuff" are value terms, as for Trump, one wants to pursue all of these, and he is eager to shower praise or blame accordingly.

But the italicized phrases pose a puzzle–are these value terms? "Getting it" and "having your eyes opened" seem to be action-guiding, and praise/blameworthy, but they are phrases, not words or "value terms." So then how do we identify value phrases and sentences?

In *Values and Psychiatric Diagnosis* and Classification (32) the example I gave of the problem is this one:

John will do anything to get a grant.

Here there is no value term, yet in ordinary usage it's clear that John is a ruthless, greedy miscreant who is subject to blame. I called this sentence a "value semantic," because its ordinary meaning meets the definition of a value. Ditto for "Getting it" and "having your eyes opened" because in these cases it is clear from context Trump's use is praiseworthy and action-guiding. Detecting a value semantic is more challenging. First, one has to understand the point of the sentence or phrase in common usage. Then, one must evaluate it for whether it is an instruction (action-guiding) and praise/blameworthy. So this poses a deeper puzzle for students.

In my philosophy of psychiatry work, I developed and used a more granular account of values-analysis in considering not just value/not-value decisions, but also how the value functions in a discourse (e.g. as a commitment, an entailment, or a consequence) as well as characterized values by kinds (e.g., ethical, pragmatic, epistemic, ontological, aesthetic; see Sadler "Recognizing Values: A Descriptive-Causal Method for Medical/Scientific Discourses" and "Values in Psychiatric Diagnosis and Classification" for more). But at this juncture in this paper, I want to turn my attention to the direction that most cit-ed discussions go. That direction I claim is social ethics (e.g., ethics directed at how we are going to get along with each other), involving ethical values in an evaluative "field" with other kinds of values. In this brand of so-cial ethics ethical values are not the only ones to be considered—and could include "folk" values like religious values, political allegiances, and personal preferences. For consideration then on these relationships of values-in-play with other individuals, communities, or discourses, I turn to some of my work on what I call "values-based ethics" (Sadler "Values-Based Psychiatric Ethics").

Values-based ethics (VBE) is not a philosophical ethical theory, at least not in the usual sense of ethical system-building in philosophical ethics. Rather, it is a response to some shortcomings in using philosophical ethics for clinical ethics activities, e.g., questions about right action in health care settings. This embeddedness of VBE in health care decision making makes for an attrac-tive implementation in cit-ed settings because both contexts require working with people who are not philosophers and the terms of discourse are com-monsensical and nontechnical. Several other features of VBE suit both the clinical ethics and cit-ed context. These include particularity. Both contexts demand a particular response to a particular situation. Philosophical ethics generally argue from the universal (e.g., the categorical imperative) to the particular (should I withdraw life-sustaining treatment [clinical] or should we more tightly regulate end-of-life treatment decisions [cit-ed]). Second, VBE, and cit-ed decisions about policy, require decisional closure in a way that philosophical ethics does not. In the former, decisions must be made and actions taken. Third, VBE and cit-ed are gritty and messy, meaning discussions in these contexts are concrete and involve multiple parties with diverse values, capabilities, prejudices, and virtues, and are embedded in concrete contexts with differential histories, cultures, and traditions, as op-posed to the aspirations to universalism characteristic of most philosophical ethics. Fourth, VBE and cit-ed both face a problem of "value blindness"–that the depth of value awareness characteristic of philosophy and philosophers are often absent in the on-the-ground, public discussions of VBE and cit-ed. Fifth, this value-invisibility contributes to a problem of value-translation. What the "principle of autonomy" means varies by individual and cultural background. An example I use here is the puzzle of what "autonomy" means for family-centered, communalist cultures in Asia. Sixth, the weighting of values varies from culture to culture and individual to individual. For example, values regarding personal taste or preference find little consideration in philosophical ethics, but in practical settings may be much more important. For example, you may blandly prefer to have a single room when you are in the hospital, but a painfully shy person from a culture of modesty may consider a private room something to fight for.

Another distinction in VBE of relevance to cit-ed has to do with this issue of evaluative weighting of ethical values. In identifying and discussing the values amongst a group or community, a presupposed or theoretical weight to particular values is unlikely. The principle of autonomy may be considered alongside matters of personal taste as in the above example. Indeed, in participating in the "moral conversation" the whole point is to identify the relevant values amongst the group and then negotiate what the priorities are, and identifying the potentials for resonance, resolving conflict, or finding common ground.

With this background, I turn to the problem of value-blindness. To be clear, value-blindness is the tendency of people to presuppose or not be aware of their own or other's values and interests.[7] As teachers of students and my practice as a clinical ethics consultant, we can likely agree that one of the challenges in ethics education, (and correlatively, cit-ed education) is helping students recognize values in discourses that heretofore they didn't recognize. In VBE, I use as an ethics consultant a "trumps hierarchy" as a *heuristic tool* to help people come to recognize values that the individual may not be fully aware of–including values of one's own. The fundamental assumption of the trumps hierarchy is that a socially-shaped and implicit moral order structures most values, both in clinical ethics and in cit-ed situations in which social policies and their impact on individuals are considered. The trumps hierarchy or "order" is not a rigid definition of which kinds of values trump others, but rather sketches a layered, hierarchical approach to the *conventions* of liberal democracies with civil liberty commitments. (The latter are crucial to the trumps-hierarchy, it doesn't apply to societies without substantive commitments to civil liberties and democratic principles.) The trumps hierarchy sketches how our values are typically, but not exclusively, organized in civil discourse. As a heuristic tool it helps students and

---

[7] See Jessica Wahman's account of the ways in which broad cultural narratives impact our understanding of our environment, other persons, ourselves, and our own agency in her "Pragmatic Stories of Selves and Their Flourishing," this volume

people recognize hidden or assumed values and weigh these from their own, personal standpoints. Once recognized, the weighting of particular values is then open for discussion.

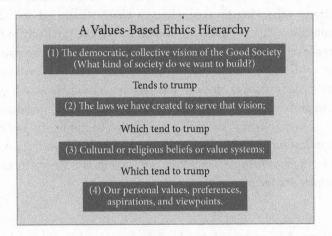

The figure above describes these trumps-hierarchical social conventions. Personal preferences and tastes (item 4) is the lowest in the presumed weighting. The higher-level categories of values in 1–3 generally "trump" these tastes and simple preferences. As noted earlier however, in practice it's possible, even common, for this presumed trumps order to be inapplicable in regard to a particular set of values. For example, one of our female, Muslim, psychiatry residents decided, after much deliberation, to discontinue wearing a hijab in the hospital, (level 3, religious belief), because relief from the hassle of harassment from some patients and intolerant others was worth her deviation from the religious orthodoxy of wearing a hijab. While the social convention is that religious beliefs are more important, or "weighty" than freedom from hassles (a personal value or preference), she elected to reverse this weighting of values.

The point of the trumps hierarchy is, in a sense, building a hypothesis about what values may be operative in a particular situation where a moral conversation is occurring. For example, consider the earlier example of students discussing the question of including, or substituting, the Mexican perspective on the story of the Alamo. It's possible that personal preferences are operative, but unlikely. However, cultural and ethnic beliefs about Mexican identity and sovereignty would likely be relevant, as would the Texas/US cultural beliefs about manifest destiny and the like. The students may think laws relevant to the United States, Texas, and Mexico may be relevant, but which ones, and how relevant, could be debated. However, in this case, much of the inquiry would revolve within Level 1, about "What kind of society should we have?" where important value considerations about the meaning of sovereignty, why it is good or not, and the relations of the frontier values with the relations with endogenous peoples may also be discussed (for instance). These considerations as public/social policy decisions are likely to "trump" the lower-level considerations for many. Yet, values around recognition of identities—identity politics—may surface and could be identified as the importance of (for instance) Mexican and Tejano perspectives as well as Native American perspectives, not to overlook white majoritarian considerations.

Space does not permit providing an extensive, beginning-to-end example of the application of these values-literacy principles, but in the concluding section I can provide some illustrative applications and synergisms with cited principles and techniques.

Values Literacy and Analysis in Citizenship Education

In his review of the literature about how to improve "intergroup relations," Graham identifies trends in the literature which are demonstrated, or are promising, for applications like cit-ed. The first of these is "improving personal relationships" ("Diversity, Group Identity, and Citizenship Education in a Global Age"3). He notes that intergroup relations are "improved by interventions focused on perspective-taking and empathizing with members of the outgroup." Let us reconsider the earlier April 27, 2018 tweet from President Trump (underlining and italics added):

> Donald J. Trump @ realDonaldTrump
> Kanye West has performed a <u>great service</u> to the Black Community - <u>Big things</u> are happening and *eyes are being opened* for the first time in Decades - <u>Legacy Stuff!</u> Thank you also to Chance and Dr. Darrell Scott, they *really get it* (lowest Black and Hispanic unemployment in history).

In this same-day news summary from CBS News online, Chance the Rapper apologizes for his tweets involving approval of Trump's message:

> "Anyone who knows me knows how passionate I am about my city and my loved ones. Kanye West is not just a mentor or big homie to me," Chance

said in the statement. "He's my family. No matter how much I may disagree with him, it's hard for me to watch people talk about someone I love-even if they were justified in doing so." The "No Problem" singer then clarified that he did not "speak up because I agree with what Kanye had to say" or that he supports Mr. Trump. He also said he was upset that his comments are "being used to discredit my brothers and sisters in the movement" and that he "can't stand by and let that happen either."

"I'd never support anyone who has made a career out of hatred, racism and discrimination," Chance wrote in an apparent reference to Mr. Trump. "I'd never support someone who'd talk about Chicago as if it's hell on earth and then take steps to make life harder here for the most disenfranchised among us."

Chance the rapper also addressed his comment about black people not needing to be Democrats, saying while the statement is true, it was also "a deflection from the real conversation and stemmed from a personal issue with the fact that Chicago has had generations of democratic officials with no investment or regard for black schools, neighborhood or black lives."

"But again, I said that s**t at the wrongest time," he added.

Chance also said that while West is his "brother-in-Christ" and a person who "does really want to do what is right, it's not my job to defend and protect him. It's my job to pick up the phone and talk to him about it."

This very brief exchange provides a nice example of how social media discourse could be placed under a cit-ed/values-analysis lens to understand exchange and its relevance to Trump's policies and the African-American community.

The questions for values-literate students in this context might be,

A. What are the things (values) that are important to Trump that we can tell from this tweet?
B. Why do you think he sent this tweet?
C. What are the values that Chance is discussing in the response?
D. How do you know?
E. Do they understand each other?
F. What values are shared? Which ones fit together?
G. Whose style of communication would you like to adopt? Why?

An examination of Trump's values from the context of this tweet would be that "getting it" is an appreciation that prominent African-Americans are understanding the positive impact of his policies, and the lowest unemployment rate in history is a good thing. But because Trump's dialogue with the media is often minimal, not much elaboration of this tweet communication is possible. In contrast to Trump, Chance both tweets on the same "riff" and is willing to elaborate on his values in the news excerpt. In identifying the value-semantics in the excerpt, we can recognize his loyalties to his community and his friendship to Kanye West, despite disagreement. Chance points out the negative values of racism and discrimination he believes are held by Trump. Further, he recognizes (perhaps along with Trump, but not from evidence in this discourse) that Democratic politicians in Chicago have failed to aid progress in the Chicago black community, citing some "common ground" with Trump about shared values in the role of government. He finishes with a statement of empathy and exemplifies the value of responsibility in friendship to "talk to him [West] about it."

The process of this analysis will likely lead to a mirrored discussion in the classroom among fellow students. Here the teacher can ask the students to clarify the values they hold that contribute to their opinions, including asking students to identify the values of students they disagree with. Thus the discussion finds its way to empathy-building; even in the face of disagreement, as with Kanye and Chance.[8]

The second empirically validated strategy for improving intergroup relations identified by Graham is to "emphasize superordinate goals." ("Diversity, Group Identity, and Citizenship Education in a Global Age" 6) The latter are those that "transcend group boundaries, often requiring cooperation between the groups" (6). So under my values-analysis rubric, this principle might be amended to "emphasize superordinate values," which might lead to the following classroom questions:

A. What values do you think President Trump and Chance the Rapper share?

B. [How would you find out?] (in case puzzled looks prevail)

---

[8] Lori Gallegos discusses the role of empathy in personal well-being and in virtuous lives in the section, "Caring for Others through Empathetic Response" of her chapter in this volume, "Navigating Irreconcilable Conflicts: Philosophical Thinking for Better Lives."

   C. What are the political methods to achieve these goals? Do Trump and
       Chance agree there? Why/why not?

   D. Would you like to weigh in on Twitter yourself? What would you write?

The latter question, on weighing- in yourself, is an implied call to direct civic engagement, though with a (hopefully) heightened awareness.
Weinstein conducted a qualitative study of the social media styles of previously civic-engaged students aged 15 to 25 ("The Personal Is Political on
Social Media: Online Civic Express Patterns and Pathways among Civically
Engaged Youth." She found three characteristic styles that she called 'blended,'
'bounded,' and 'differentiated.' A blended style meant the civic activities and
viewpoints students engaged in outside of social media were essentially similar to the viewpoints expressed in their social media activities. That is, the
students active in their political party posted about these activities on social
media. A bounded style meant social media activities were kept distinct from
their political/civic activities they engaged in actual (rather than virtual) life.
And a differentiated style meant distinct social media for distinct purposes—
such as a student who keeps Facebook postings personal and apolitical and
uses her Twitter account for civic/political communications.

The query about actually weighing in for discussion question D above
then offers a classroom opportunity for discussing one's developing identity
as a civic participant, and what makes for a good civic participant.

To this latter point, Antoci et al., in a white paper for the (German)
IZA Institute for Labor Economics, summarized a substantive literature
supporting that people who witnessed a civil discussion of a matter of public
interest were more likely to trust the information and the participants in
later communications ("Civility and Trust in Social Media"). Trusting others'
sincere communications seems to be the kind of goal citizenship education
should be cultivating.

Of course, this very sketchy discussion of the role of values analysis in citizenship education is at best indicative, not definitive. Much more elaboration
and structure is needed. However, helping students become values literate
has the virtue of being neutral and adaptable to almost any kind of civic issue,
topic, or debate. It welcomes multiple identities and the diverse values they
bring. It is friendly to the media discourse that young people today take for
granted. It cultivates empathy and aids in identifying common values and
common ground. I suggest it should be explored further as a component of
citizenship education.

Works Cited

Albala-Bertand, Luis. "What Education for What Citizenship?" *International Bureau of Education Educational Innovation and Information*, no. 82, 1995, pp. 3–11.

Althof, Wolfgang, and Berkowitz, Marvin W. "Moral Education and Character Education: Their Relationship and Roles in Citizenship Education." *Journal of Moral Education*, vol. 35, no.4, 2006, pp. 495–518.

American Psychiatric Association. *Diagnostic and Statistical Manual of Mental Disorders (DSM-IV-TR)*. American Psychiatric Association Publishing, 2000.

American Psychiatric Association. *Diagnostic and Statistical Manual of Mental Disorders (DSM-5®)*. American Psychiatric Association Publishing, 2013.

Antoci, Angelo, et al. "Civility and Trust in Social Media." *IZA Institute of Labor Economics, ICA DP*, white paper no. 11290, 2018.

Banks, James A. "Diversity, Group Identity, and Citizenship Education in a Global Age." *Educational Researcher*, vol. 37, no.3, 2014, pp. 129–39.

Casares, Cindy. "A Textbook on Mexican Americans that Gets Their History Wrong? Oh Texas." *The Guardian*, May 31, 2016, https://www.theguardian.com/commentisfree/2016/may/31/texas-textbook-mexican-american-heritage-public-schools-us-history. Accessed August 18, 2018.

CBS News. "'My Fault Yo': Chance the Rapper Apologizes for Defending Kanye West on Trump," April 27, 2018. www.cbsnews.com/news/my-fault-yo-chance-the-rapper-apologizes-for-defending-kanye-west-on-trump/. Accessed April 29, 2018.

Cohen, Stanley. "Deviance and Moral Panics." *Folk Devils and Moral Panics: The Creation of the Mods and Rockers*. St. Martin's Press, 1980, pp. 9–26.

Conner, Timothy W. "The Decline of Civil Discourse and the Rise of Extremist Debate: Words Matter." *Tennessee Journal of Law and Policy*, vol. 12, no. 2, 2018, pp. 213–31.

Connolly, William E. *Politics and Ambiguity*. University of Wisconsin Press, 1987.

Dahl, Robert A. *A Preface to Democratic Theory*. University of Chicago Press, 1956.

Davidson, John D. "The Decline and Fall of American Political Debate." *The Federalist*, Sept. 21, 2015, http://thefederalist.com/2015/09/24/the-decline-and-fall-of-american-political-debate/. Accessed August 29, 2018.

Davies, Ian, et al. "Education for Citizenship: A Case Study of 'Democracy Day' at a Comprehensive School." *Educational Review*, vol. 50, no. 1, 1998, pp. 15–27.

Duggan, Maeve. *Online Harassment*. Pew Research Center, October 22, 2014. pewinternet.org/2014/10/22/online-harassment/. Accessed 29 August 2018.

Fulford, Kenneth W. M. *Moral Theory and Medical Practice*. Cambridge University Press, 1989.

Graham, Jesse. "Interventions to Improve Intergroup Relations: What Works, What Shows Promise, and What This Means for Civil Politics." 2014, http://www.civilpolitics.org/?s=Graham Accessed September 12, 2018.

Hirsch, Eric D., Jr. *Cultural Literacy: What Every American Should Know*. Houghton Mifflin, 1987.

Junco, Reynol, and Chickering, Arthur W. "Civil Discourse in the Age of Social Media." *About Campus*, vol. 15, no. 4, 2010, pp. 12–18. DOI: 10.1002/abc.20030. Accessed August 18, 2018.

Kymlicka, Will. *Multicultural Citizenship*. Oxford University Press, 1995.

Kymlicka, Will, and Norman, Wayne J. "Return of the Citizen: A Survey of Recent Work on Citizenship Theory." *Ethics*, vol. 104, no. 2, 1994, pp. 352–81.

Kymlicka, Will, and Norman, Wayne J. "Citizenship in Culturally Diverse Societies: Issues, Contexts, Concepts." *Citizenship in Diverse Societies*. Oxford University Press, 2000, pp. 1–43.

Leydet, Dominique. "Citizenship." *The Stanford Encyclopedia of Philosophy*. Edited by Edward N. Zalta, Fall 2017, plato.stanford.edu/archives/fall2017/entries/citizenship/. Accessed August 18, 2018.

Lin, Alex R. "Citizenship Education in American Schools and Its Role in Developing Civic Engagement: A Review of the Research." *Educational Review*, vol. 67, no. 1, 2015, pp. 35–63. dx.doi.org/10.1080/00131911.2013.813440. Accessed August 18, 2018.

Lukensmeyer, Carolyn J. "Key Challenges Facing the Field of Deliberative Democracy." *Journal of Public Deliberation*, vol. 10, no. 1, art. 24, 2014, pp. 1–5. http://www.publicd eliberation.net/jpd/vol10/iss1/art24.

Marshall, T. H. *Citizenship and Social Class and Other Essays*. Cambridge University Press, 1950.

Morgan, Blaire, et al. *Empathy and Authenticity Online: The Roles of Moral Identity and Moral Disengagement in Encouraging or Discouraging Empathy and Authenticity Online*. University of Birmingham, Jubilee Centre for Character and Virtues, 2017.

Mrowicki, Mike. "Decline in Civil Discourse Threatens the Heart of Democracy." National Institute for Civil Discourse, May 6, 2015, https://nicd.arizona.edu/news/decline-civil-discourse-threatens-heart-our-democracy. Accessed August 18, 2018.

Nussbaum, Martha C. *Frontiers of Justice: Disability, Nationality, Species Membership*. Harvard University Press, 2006.

Nussbaum, Martha C. "Toward a Globally Sensitive Patriotism." *Daedalus*, vol. 137, no. 3, 2008, pp. 78–93.

Okin, Susan M. "Women, Equality, and Citizenship." *Queen's Quarterly*, vol. 99, no. 1, 1992, pp. 56–71.

Osler, Audrey, and Starkey, Hugh. "Education for Democratic Citizenship: A Review of Research, Policy and Practice 1995–2005." *Research Papers in Education*, vol. 24, no. 4, 2006, pp. 433–66.

Oulton, Christopher, Day, Vanessa, Dillon, Justin, and Grace, Marcus. "Controversial Issues: Teachers' Attitudes and Practices in the Context of Citizenship Education." *Oxford Review of Education*, vol. 30, no. 4, 2004, pp. 489–507.

Putnam, Hilary. "Fact and Value." *Reason, Truth, and History*. Cambridge University Press, 1981, pp. 127–49.

Putnam, Hilary. "Beyond the Fact/Value Dichotomy." *Realism with a Human Face*. Harvard University Press, 1990a, pp. 135–41.

Putnam, Hilary. "The Place of Facts in a World of Values." *Realism with a Human Face*. Harvard University Press, 1990b, pp. 142–62.

Rawls, John. *A Theory of Justice, Revised Edition*. Harvard University Press, 1999.

Rheingold, Howard. "Using Participatory Media and Public Voice to Encourage Civic Engagement." *Civic Life Online: Learning How Digital Media Can Engage Youth*. Edited by W. Lance Bennett. MIT Press, 2008, pp. 97–118.

Ross, E. Wayne. "Negotiating the Politics Of Citizenship Education." *Political Science and Politics*, vol. 37, no. 2, 2004, pp. 249–51.

Sadler, John Z. "Recognizing Values: A Descriptive-Causal Method for Medical/Scientific Discourses." *Journal of Medicine and Philosophy*, vol. 22, no. 6, 1997, pp. 541–65.

Sadler, John Z. "Values in Psychiatric Diagnosis and Classification." *Oxford Handbook of Philosophy and Psychiatry*. Edited by Kenneth W.M. Fulford, et al. Oxford University Press, 2013, pp. 753–78.

Sadler, John Z. "Values-Based Psychiatric Ethics." *Oxford Handbook of Psychiatric Ethics*. Edited by John Z. Sadler, et al. Oxford University Press, 2015, pp. 474–92.

Schall, James V. "The Death of Civil Discourse Is the Death of Us." *The Hill*, Jan. 4, 2018, thehill.com/opinion/civil-rights/367370-the-death-of-civil-discourse-is-the-death-of-us. Accessed August 18, 2018.

Seib, Gerald F. "Civil Discourse in Decline: Where Does It End?" *Wall Street Journal*, May 30, 2017, wsj.com/articles/civil-discourse-in-decline-where-does-it-end-1496071276. Accessed August 18, 2018.

Serratelli, Arthur. "No God, No Truth, No Civil Discourse." *Catholic News Agency*, Sept. 7, 2017, catholicnewsagency.com/column/no-god-no-truth-no-civil-discourse-3821. Accessed August 18, 2018.

Sunstein, Cass R. *Republic: Divided Democracy in the Age of Social Media*. Princeton University Press, 2017.

Torney-Purta, Judith, et al. "Mapping the Distinctive and Common Features of Civic Education in Twenty-four Countries." *Civic Education across Countries: Twenty-Four National Case Studies from the IEA Civic Education Project*. Edited by Judith Torney-Purta, et al. International Association for the Evaluation of Educational Achievement (IEA), 1999, pp. 12–36.

Young, Iris M., "Polity and Group Difference: A Critique of the Ideal of Universal Citizenship." *Ethics*, vol. 99, no. 2, 1989, pp. 250–74.

Walzer, Michael. "Citizenship." *Political Innovation and Conceptual* Change. Edited by Terence Ball et al. Cambridge University Press, vol. 11, 1989, pp. 211–20.

Weinstein, Emily C. "The Personal Is Political on Social Media: Online Civic Express Patterns and Pathways among Civically Engaged Youth." *International Journal of Communication*, vol. 8, 2014, pp. 210–33.

Zogby, James. "The Importance of Civil Discourse: Polarizing hostile discourse will only breed more division while, at the same time, making real debate over issues less likely." 23 Sept. 2017. huffingtonpost.com/entry/the-importance-of-civil-discourse_us_59c5782be4b08d6615504261. Accessed 18 August 2018.

11
Teaching Philosophy

The Love of Wisdom and the Cultivation of Human Flourishing

James O. Pawelski

What is the goal of teaching philosophy? One way to answer this question is to examine what philosophy teachers say when trying to attract students. Perhaps the easiest way to access these communications is by browsing through philosophy department pages on college and university websites. These pages tend to extol three basic benefits of studying philosophy. First is the acquisition of academic skills. Prospective students are told that a study of philosophy will develop their general problem solving skills, their communication and writing skills, their powers of persuasion, and their ability to understand other disciplines. Second, prospective students are told that the study of philosophy has specific vocational benefits. It can help them score higher on standardized exams, gain entry to a variety of professional schools, succeed in their jobs, and even earn more money over the course of their careers. Less attention is paid to a third category of benefits. Students are sometimes told that by following the fascinating questions raised by philosophy they will acquire a deeper understanding of the world, gain greater self-knowledge, develop personally, find connections to people in different times and places, and be more informed citizens.

The goals most emphasized by contemporary teachers of philosophy when trying to attract students are not unworthy, but they are instrumental aims, extrinsic to the study of philosophy. Philosophy was not created for the purpose of developing academic skills; rather, academic skills (at least some of them) are instrumentally important for the study of philosophy. Nor was philosophy established primarily as a means of career advancement. Although such advancement can result from the study of philosophy, it is an extrinsic benefit of this study. More central to the traditional aims of philosophy is the category of benefits least emphasized on the departmental

James O. Pawelski, *Teaching Philosophy* In: *Philosophy and Human Flourishing*. Edited by: John J. Stuhr, Oxford University Press. © Oxford University Press 2023. DOI: 10.1093/oso/9780197622162.003.0012

websites. The desire to acquire a deeper understanding of the world, to develop as an individual and a citizen, to become a better person, to live a richer and fuller life—in short, the desire to cultivate individual and collective human flourishing—is one of the perennial themes at the core of philosophical inquiry.

In this chapter, I look more closely at historical connections between the teaching of philosophy and the understanding and fostering of human flourishing, note a number of current obstacles to this connection, and explore basic questions aimed at supporting its renewal and further development. What is human flourishing? How can philosophy advance its conceptualization and cultivation? What is the proper role of the philosophy teacher in this process? How can philosophy teachers know when their efforts are successful? These are not merely theoretical questions, of course, particularly since so many students are not flourishing these days. I have been wrestling with these questions over the course of more than thirty years of teaching philosophy in various contexts, and I will share some of my experiences in the hope that they may help to inspire readers who are—or are planning to be—philosophy teachers to think in new ways about the connections between their own classes and the flourishing of their students (as well as their own flourishing). I hope that more conversations along these lines will result in the renewal of human flourishing as a central goal in the teaching of philosophy. I hope that such reflections also invite teachers of other disciplines in the humanities and across the university to consider the relation between their teaching and human flourishing, and that these perspectives encourage administrators and policy makers to consider ways of structuring teaching requirements and learning environments in ways that are more conducive to human flourishing. Ultimately, I hope that a greater focus on these topics will help educators in general support the well-being[1] of their students more effectively.

Historical Connections

Human flourishing has traditionally been one of the key goals of education. Many approaches to education are rooted in ancient and medieval

---

[1] Although various distinctions are sometimes made between human flourishing and well-being, I use these terms interchangeably in this chapter.

programs for educating individuals to live life well and become good citizens. In ancient Greece, *paideia* was a program of education intended to produce citizens of excellence who would flourish and also help the *polis* to thrive. To support their intellectual, moral, and physical development, students were given instruction in a wide range of subjects including language, philosophy, mathematics, science, and the arts, as well as training in gymnastics and wrestling. The ancient Romans built on this program of study, including many of the same subjects to create what they came to call the liberal arts (*artes liberales*), referring to the range of general skills needed by free persons to live well and participate actively in civic life. Eventually, these areas of study came to be codified as the trivium (grammar, logic, and rhetoric) and the quadrivium (arithmetic, geometry, music, and astronomy). In medieval universities, students mastered these seven liberal arts before proceeding to more specialized professional training in medicine, law, or theology.

Similar to the Greek *paideia* and the Roman liberal arts, the humanities were initially developed as a program of study intended to lead to human flourishing. Rooted in these ancient traditions, the humanities were first defined as a distinct domain and approach to education during the Renaissance. In a sense, the humanities are the gift of a pandemic. An outbreak of the bubonic plague known as the Black Death was the deadliest pandemic in history, killing an estimated 200 million people across Europe, Asia, and North Africa in the 14th century. One of the most powerful witnesses to the devastation caused by the Black Death was the Italian scholar and poet Francesco Petrarca, known to the English-speaking world as Petrarch. He found solace and strength in the wisdom of the Greek and Roman classics, and he advocated for their careful study as a way of coping during the devastation wrought by the pandemic. His followers, who took up his approach and developed it further, came to be known as "humanists," after Cicero's phrase *studia humanitatis* (literally, "studies of humanity"). Humanists reacted against the scholastic approaches to learning dominating medieval universities, arguing that the way contemporary scholars focused on the seven liberal arts overemphasized logic and linguistic analysis, prioritizing techniques of abstract thinking and resolution of textual contradictions and not the improvement of students' lives. Instead, they emphasized the study of history, philosophy, and poetry, along with grammar and rhetoric, subjects they saw as valuable for leading students toward wisdom, for the clarification of the nature of happiness and its relation to virtue, and for the provision of sound guidance for their lives (Kristeller *Renaissance Thought II: Papers on Humanism and the Arts* 178; Proctor *Defining the Humanities: How Rediscovering a Tradition Can Improve Our Schools* 10, 38–39). In brief, humanists turned away from scholasticism and toward a renewed interest in the classics as a way of cultivating human flourishing.

Each of these general programs of education—*paideia*, the liberal arts, and the humanities—have had individual and collective flourishing as a central goal. And each of these traditions considered philosophy to be a foundational area of study. Not surprisingly, questions of human flourishing have historically been key concerns within philosophical inquiry itself. In Greek philosophy, for example, Socrates believed that "the unexamined life is not worth living" and argued that all public and private goods come through the cultivation of virtue (Plato *The Dialogues of Plato* 420). Prior to Socrates, the prevailing view in the ancient world was that human flourishing was a matter of luck and good fortune, not something that could be controlled or changed (McMahon *Happiness: A History* 7–11, 19–24). By contrast, Socrates and those who followed him argued that a philosophical approach to life could lead to increased flourishing. Plato wrote dialogues exploring the nature of virtue, justice, courage, piety, truth, pleasure, creativity, beauty, and love. In his most famous dialogue, "The Republic," he suggested ways politics could support human flourishing through the creation of a just state (*The Dialogues of Plato* 591–879). Plato's student Aristotle wrote extensively in the *Nicomachean Ethics* about ethics and politics as well, arguing that human flourishing (*eudaimonia*) is the goal of all human activity. He held that human flourishing is best cultivated through the life-long practice of virtue, which he defined as the relative mean between vices of excess and deficiency. He used this perspective to analyze a variety of virtues, including courage, temperance, and modesty, not merely as a theoretical exercise, but with a practical goal in mind:

> As then our present study, unlike the other branches of philosophy, has a practical aim (for we are not investigating the nature of virtue for the sake of knowing what it is, but in order that we may become good, without which result our investigation would be of no use), we have consequently to carry our enquiry into the region of conduct, and to ask how we are to act rightly; since our actions, as we have said, determine the quality of our dispositions. (Aristotle *Nicomachean Ethics* II. ii. 1)

Post-Aristotelian schools of thought also emphasized the practical aims of philosophy. As Pierre Hadot has argued, these schools understood philosophy to be a "way of life," and the practices they cultivated were intended not just to inform, but also to form, their members (*Philosophy as a Way of Life* 264–276). The Stoics, for example, cultivated *apatheia*, freedom of control by the passions, and the Epicureans sought *ataraxia*, freedom from worry, anxiety, and trouble. Epicurus went beyond Aristotle to claim that all knowledge has human tranquility as its goal:

> ... we must not suppose that any other object is to be gained from the knowledge of the phenomena of the sky, whether they are dealt with in connexion with other doctrines or independently, than peace of mind and a sure confidence, just as in all other branches of study. (Epicuras "Letter to Pythocles" 57)

Leaders of these schools drew metaphors from medicine and sport to emphasize the practical nature of philosophy as they understood it. The Stoic Epictetus claimed that "the lecture-room of the philosopher is a hospital; you ought not to walk out of it in pleasure, but in pain. For you are not well when you come ... (Arrian *Discourses of Epictetus* III. xxiii. 30). He also pointed out that there are many costs to consider when becoming a philosopher and that it takes the same kind of dedication and perseverance to become a philosopher that it takes to be an Olympic athlete (Epictetus *Encheiridion* 29.2–7).

In the Roman world, Cicero also valued philosophy for its practical effects. Using an agricultural metaphor, he wrote:

> ... philosophy is the culture of the mind: this it is which plucks up vices by the roots; prepares the mind for the receiving of seeds; commits them to it, or, as I may say, sows them, in the hope that, when come to maturity, they may produce a plentiful harvest. (*Tusculan Disputations* 69)

The implication of Cicero's argument is that just as the cultivation of a field results in the flourishing of the plants, so the cultivation of the mind results in the flourishing of a person. He noted that there are things that must be removed (weeds/vices) and things that must be introduced (seeds/virtues) to enable that flourishing. He noted further, just before the quoted passage, that because philosophy is eminently practical, philosophers who do not live their philosophy are like grammarians who speak incorrectly or music teachers who sing out of tune.

A practical emphasis on human flourishing is also at the root of the wide range of religious and philosophical traditions developed from about the 8th to the 3rd century BCE, a period referred to by Karl Jaspers as the "Axial Age" (Jaspers *The Origin and Goal of History* 8–29). Hinduism, Buddhism, Confucianism, Daoism, and Judaism, along with the later Christianity and Islam, all emphasized questions of human flourishing. Like ancient Greek and Roman philosophy, these traditions held that popular pathways for seeking happiness like pleasure, wealth, power, and fame often lead in the wrong direction and can actually cause increased suffering. They advocated a different approach to happiness, teaching that a disciplined cultivation of virtue can lead to a connection to something higher, larger, and more enduring than any individual life or momentary pleasure (McMahon, "From the Paleolithic to the Present," 4–5; Ivanhoe "Happiness in Early Chinese Thought" 263–65).

Although the educational, philosophical, and religious traditions I have mentioned all aimed to increase human flourishing, they were by no means perfect. Intellectual historian Darrin McMahon points out that they all shared the limitation of being intended for the few and not the many. The Greek *paideia* and the Roman liberal arts were available only to young men privileged enough to be citizens in those societies and wealthy enough to be provided with this education. Traditions that were open to a wider cross-section of the population in the ancient world often required a total life commitment to become a monk, sadhu, or sage, a commitment few individuals were able to make. Many people were perceived to be too tied to their accustomed lives of seeking happiness through pleasure or status, or seen as not disciplined enough to cultivate the recommended virtues. In addition to these obstacles, the harsh realities of trying to survive in austere conditions put beyond the reach of much of the population the kind of human flourishing advocated by many of these traditions (McMahon "From the Paleolithic to the Present" 4–6).

Current Obstacles

Although equal access to education for all remains an unachieved ideal in our contemporary world, there has been a dramatic expansion in the scope of individuals deemed eligible for it. Education today is considered by many to be a basic human right, and it is available to more people around the world than ever before. Still, even for those who have access to education, there are numerous obstacles to the cultivation of flourishing. Similar to what is emphasized on philosophy department web pages, education today is often seen as a means of teaching certain academic skills and of preparing students for the work force, with questions of well-being often considered less important or taken to be outside the purview of formal education. Although early institutions of higher learning in the United States, for example, understood one of their chief missions to be the moral formation of their students, the rise of modern research universities led to a shift of priorities in higher education toward the creation of new knowledge. Although these new priorities have led to significant breakthroughs in research, they have come at a cost. They have reoriented faculty away from questions of living life well and toward narrow points of scholarship. Since most instruction in philosophy today occurs within higher education, this shift has had a deep impact on who teaches philosophy and on how they teach it. Philosophy faculty are shaped by the values, norms, and systems of recruitment, retention, and reward of the institutions by which they are employed. In most colleges and universities, they have become professional academics, encouraged to select a particular area of specialization within philosophy and to spend most of their time and energy focused on writing books and articles whose primary audience is other scholars with a similar specialization. Secondarily, these academics have responsibilities for teaching their specialization to students and for supporting their institution and the discipline of philosophy through various service roles. Rarely, however, are they required to link their scholarship, teaching, or service to human flourishing.

The practical aims that initially inspired early philosophers and that continued to remain at the core of philosophical inquiry for millennia are thus often supplanted by the theoretical and methodological demands of the kind of disciplinary scholarship required for success as a professional philosopher in academia today. Moreover, McMahon argues that the topical focus of much of philosophical inquiry over the past 150 years has drifted away from questions of the good life. He cites Nietzsche's critique of the quest for happiness in favor of the will to power as a key early shift in this direction ("The History of the Humanities and Human Flourishing" 50). Whatever the catalyst, there is a case to be made that questions of human happiness were largely eclipsed by questions about power or language or consciousness, by narrow debates on fine points of scholarship, by reconstructions of the thought of historical figures, and by similar scholarly projects. Although each of these areas of inquiry arguably has some at least distant connection to human flourishing, they are often pursued with such a narrow focus or with such an imbalanced critical emphasis on what obstructs human flourishing that they contribute little to an overall conceptualization of the actual nature of human flourishing or to the means of its practical cultivation.

The conditions under which philosophy is typically taught in colleges and universities today provide a number of obstacles to the advancement of students' well-being. Philosophy courses all too often emphasize knowledge over wisdom, critical problems over creative solutions, and course credits over eudaimonic outcomes. Grades, the institutional gold standard of success in the study of philosophy, may or may not be good indicators of how well students understand the concepts studied, but they are not good markers of well-being. Indeed, the notion of philosophy as the love of wisdom that could help cultivate well-being often seems foreign to the academic environment. I remember one of my professors in graduate school sneering about the undergraduates knocking on his door looking for wisdom, as though what he studied and taught could provide useful guidance for their lives. In the academy, the philosophical curriculum has largely become a way of knowing, with ways of living relegated to student services staff. In addition to these obstacles, students in higher education are feeling increasing vocational pressures, so when they register for philosophy classes, it is frequently to satisfy a requirement for their degree, to acquire various academic skills they can put to use elsewhere, or to make themselves more attractive to employers.[2]

I do not mean to paint too bleak a picture here. In spite of all these obstacles, of course, there are many philosophy teachers who care deeply about human flourishing and wish to help their students cultivate it. And there are many students who find in their philosophy courses insights that help them understand flourishing more deeply and make progress in cultivating it, both on a personal and a community level. My concern is that there seems to be a misalignment between the conditions under which philosophy is currently typically taught, including the academic and vocational needs students often bring to their study, and one of the central and most enduring

---

[2] For more detail on some of the barriers to focusing on flourishing in American colleges and universities, see Jennifer L. Hansen's "A Reconsideration of the Role of Philosophy in the Reconstruction and Promotion of Leisure" in this volume.

questions at the root of philosophical inquiry and practice. Given this reality, what can be done to bring philosophy teaching more in line with its historical roots and the present needs of students? What can be done to support a *eudaimonic turn* in philosophy, an acknowledgment of the centrality of human flourishing as a theme of study and as a practical goal of philosophy? Given the historical roots of philosophy in well-being, perhaps it would be more accurate to call this a eudaimonic *return*—not to an idealized past, but to many of the questions and concerns that gave rise to philosophy in the first place and that have been at its core for so much of its history. Of course, this return must take into account current knowledge, perspectives, and cultural realities if it is to be successful in opening up new possibilities for flourishing in our contemporary world.[3]

Student Opportunities and Needs

Before discussing these ideas in more detail, it is worth considering the great and growing eudaimonic needs of students today. In the case of traditional students, college is typically a time of rapidly expanding horizons. Many students live outside their parental home for the first time during these years. They encounter other students with very different experiences and perspectives, and their coursework opens them up to new ways of seeing the world and their place in it. Recent neuroscientific research indicates that this is also a time of great brain plasticity. The adolescent brain, from puberty through the early twenties, is primed for learning. Although neuroplasticity is now understood to last throughout our lifetimes, it is especially strong in adolescence (Jensen and Nutt *The Teenage Brain* 65–85). William James's claim that in most of us our character is set like plaster by the time we are thirty (*The Principles of Psychology* 126) is too extreme, but it is true that change becomes more difficult in adulthood. Because so many of the changes in our brain that occur in adolescence are likely to endure for the rest of our lives, it is especially important that students develop healthy intellectual, social, and moral habits during their college years. Thus, a college education that helps students achieve what James identified as the great goal of

---

[3] See Pawelski, "What Is the Eudaimonic Turn?" 17 and "The Positive Humanities: Culture and Human Flourishing" 26 for further discussions of the eudaimonic turn and return in the humanities disciplines.

education, making "our nervous system our ally instead of our enemy" (*The Principles of Psychology* 126), is likely to increase their flourishing both in adolescence and over the entire course of their lives.

For this reason, the current and rapidly decreasing levels of flourishing in college students is particularly tragic. Data on student well-being is gathered in regular surveys conducted by the American College Health Association (ACHA), which represents over 800 institutions of higher education. Twice each year, ACHA administers a National College Health Assessment (NCHA) to track a number of health-related metrics in college students in the United States.[4] In the fall of 2015, 36.1% of undergraduate respondents to this assessment indicated that they had been so depressed at some point in the last twelve months that it was difficult to function, 58.6% of respondents reported feeling overwhelming anxiety in the last twelve months, and 10.3% reported seriously considering suicide in that time frame (American College Health Association, "American College Health Association-National College Health Assessment II: Reference Group Undergraduates Executive Summary Fall 2015" 14). Shocking and disturbing as these numbers are, they deteriorated significantly over the next four years. By the spring of 2019, 46.2% of respondents reported having felt so depressed it was difficult to function (a 28% increase), 66.4% reported having felt overwhelming anxiety (a 13% increase), and 14.4% reported having seriously considered suicide (a 40% increase; American College Health Association, "American College Health Association-National College Health Assessment II: Reference Group Executive Summary Spring 2019" 14). The COVID-19 pandemic has taken a further toll on student well-being. Of students responding to a revised NCHA survey in the fall of 2020, 23% reported having been diagnosed with depression at some point in their lives, up 20% from respondents a year earlier. And more than 30% reported having been diagnosed with anxiety at some point in their lives, up more than 30% from a year earlier (American College Health Association, "American College Health Association-National College Health Assessment III: Undergraduate Student Reference Group Executive Summary Fall 2020" 14).

Although some of these increases may be due to greater awareness and less stigma about mental health and a resulting increased willingness to admit to having symptoms of depression, anxiety, and suicidality, it is unlikely that

---

[4] Visit www.acha.org/ncha for biannual reports aggregating undergraduate and graduate student data.

this is the sole cause of these rapidly rising numbers. Whatever the exact nature of the underlying causes, efforts to combat the problem are being largely shouldered by student mental health centers on college and university campuses. According to a report published in 2019, ten years of data from the annual Healthy Minds Study (administered to more than 150,000 students on nearly 200 campuses) indicated that the number of students seeking mental health treatment within the past year nearly doubled, going from 19% to 34% from 2007 to 2017, with many of those students seeking services from their campus counseling centers (Lipson, Lattie, and Eisenberg "Increased Rates of Mental Health Service Utilization by U.S. College Students: 10-year Population-Level Trends (2007–2017)" 60–63). As a result, colleges and universities are expanding their capacity to serve the mental health needs of their students by adding counselors, making their services more accessible, and promoting the learning of life skills for developing resilience.

The need is so great, however, that student counseling centers should not be expected to bear this burden alone. Mental health and well-being are not just matters for therapists and other student services personnel to deal with. They are also matters that connect to the research and teaching missions of colleges and universities. This point is increasingly being demonstrated by work in the relatively new field of positive psychology. A brief discussion of this work can shed light on ways teaching philosophy may be able to help as well. In 1999, Martin Seligman began teaching courses on positive psychology to undergraduates at the University of Pennsylvania. Seligman, a philosophy major who went on to earn a Ph.D. in psychology, had launched the new field of positive psychology the year before as president of the American Psychological Association. In his presidential address, he argued that psychology was half-baked, that it had made great strides in the treatment of mental illness but that it had neglected another part of psychology's mission: to make the lives of all people better ("The President's Address (Annual Report)." Noting that work on psychopathology was important, he advocated that it be supplemented by the scientific study of how to build the best things in life (e.g., hope, wisdom, creativity, and courage) and by the empirical investigation of "what actions lead to well-being, to positive individuals, to flourishing communities, and to a just society" (560). He contended that an understanding of optimal human functioning can both help increase well-being and decrease pathology, since one of the most effective ways of buffering against mental illness is cultivating human strengths. One of the first scientific projects in the field of positive psychology was the creation of a classification and assessment of character strengths to complement the American Psychiatric Association's *Diagnostic and Statistical Manual of Mental Disorders*.[5]

In his classes, Seligman combined the study of the science of well-being with exercises and activities intended to actually cultivate well-being in his students. These classes were very well received at Penn, and professors at other universities began to develop and teach similar courses. In the spring of 2006, Tal Ben-Shahar made news headlines when more students at Harvard University enrolled in his course on positive psychology than in any other course at Harvard that semester. More than 800 students, about one in eight Harvard undergraduates, attended the course. More recently, Laurie Santos developed a positive psychology course called "Psychology and the Good Life" at Yale University. When she taught it for the first time in the spring of 2018, some 1200 students—nearly a quarter of Yale undergraduates—signed up, making it the largest class in the history of the university. In addition to traditional academic requirements, like reading, quizzes, and a midterm, she also included "rewirements," where students were asked to complete experiential assignments like performing acts of kindness or forming new social connections. Santos believes students were attracted to the class because they had prioritized academic success over well-being in their lives and were suffering the adverse consequences to their mental health (Shimer "Yale's Most Popular Class Ever: Happiness"). Positive psychology courses are not always this large and do not always make the headlines, but many are taught each year at universities around the world, and they typically emphasize both an understanding of the scientific research on well-being and the application of that research in students' lives.[6] A growing number of instructors are using psychological measures to assess the degree to which these courses are actually helping to increase the flourishing of their students.[7]

---

[5] See Peterson and Seligman *Character Strengths and Virtues: A Handbook and Classification*, and American Psychiatric Association *Diagnostic and Statistical Manual of Mental Disorders*, 4th ed.

[6] The Positive Psychology Center at the University of Pennsylvania has collected syllabi from a number of these courses, and they can be found at https://ppc.sas.upenn.edu/resources/course-syllabi-teachers.

[7] For examples, see Goodmon et al. "Positive Psychology Course and Its Relationship to Well-Being, Depression, and Stress"; Lefevor et al. "An Undergraduate Positive Psychology Course as Prevention and Outreach"; Lambert "A Positive Psychology Intervention Program in a Culturally-Diverse University: Boosting Happiness and Reducing Fear"; and Smith et al. "The Effects of a Character Strength Focused Positive Psychology Course on Undergraduate Happiness and Well-being."

A Eudaimonic Turn in the Teaching of Philosophy

With all this in mind, what role can the teaching of philosophy play in the conceptualization and cultivation of human flourishing? A eudaimonic turn in the teaching of philosophy requires a renewed focus on the nature of human flourishing itself. There are many historical sources teachers can turn to in which philosophers of the past have taken up this question in various ways. These historical sources extend far beyond the few examples from the ancient world I noted at the beginning of this chapter.[8] Such historical sources are essential, of course, but because human flourishing is so closely connected to culture, it is also important to consider this question within the context of more current cultural realities. Amartya Sen and Martha Nussbaum, for example, have developed the influential capabilities approach to human development.[9] L. W. Sumner's book *Welfare, Happiness, and Ethics* has helped shape current philosophical thinking around well-being, as has Richard Kraut's more recent book *What Is Good and Why: The Ethics of Well-Being*. More and more work is being done in this area by analytic philosophers, and we can certainly see the beginnings of a eudaimonic turn at work in this domain. Two of the leaders of this turn, Daniel Haybron, author of *The Pursuit of Unhappiness: The Elusive Psychology of Well-Being*, and Valerie Tiberius, author of *The Reflective Life: Living Wisely With Our Limits* and of *Well-Being as Value Fulfillment: How We Can Help Each Other to Live Well*, are contributors of chapters in this volume.[10] This volume itself is intended to further the eudaimonic turn by encouraging a diverse group of philosophers to consider directly how their work connects to human flourishing. It is also intended as an invitation to readers to engage in similar considerations about their own work in whatever domain of philosophy they are engaged.

One foundational point to keep in mind is that, as I noted when discussing Cicero earlier, culture and human flourishing are agricultural metaphors. This figurative language both opens up new possibilities and presents potential dangers for thinking about these issues (Pawelski,

---

[8] See McMahon *Happiness: A History*; and Ivanhoe "Happiness in Early Chinese Thought."

[9] Sen and Nussbaum have made extremely important contributions to the understanding of human flourishing. I believe their contribution would be enhanced by adding positivity as a substantive capability (see Jayawickreme and Pawelski "Positivity and the Capabilities Approach").

[10] See Daniel M. Haybron's chapter on "Well-Being: Taking Our Selves Seriously" and Valerie Tiberius's chapter on "Well-Being, Value Fulfillment, and Valuing Capacities: Toward a More Subjective Hybrid" in this volume.

"The Positive Humanities: Culture and Human Flourishing" 35–36). In "Flourishing: Toward Clearer Ideas and Habits of Genius," an insightful chapter in this volume, John J. Stuhr points out that any notion of flourishing is *"irreducibly normative,"* but he also cautions against norms that are too restrictive. If we take too literally the etymological meaning of flourishing (which comes from the Latin *floere*, to flower), we may come to think of thriving as merely a seasonal instead of a life-long endeavor. Stuhr also points out that flourishing involves pluralism—both in the sense that different people flourish in different ways and that the same person flourishes in different ways over the course of their lifetime. He notes, too, that flourishing is not just a matter of particular persons but also involves social and natural environments.

It is important for philosophy teachers to help students learn about and reflect on various conceptualizations of human flourishing. But this in itself is insufficient. Human flourishing also has practical dimensions and requires more than just theoretical knowledge. As Stuhr likes to put it, in academia, theory and practice often become "theory about theory and theory about practice."[11] With human flourishing, it is essential to go beyond theory about practice to practice itself. Just as Aristotle wrote about virtue that the purpose of studying it is not merely to know what it is but to become good, so the purpose of studying human flourishing is not simply to know what it is but to increase one's well-being. Similarly, Cicero's agricultural metaphor is a practical one. Harvests depend not just on the study of agriculture but also on the actual planting of seeds and pulling of weeds.[12]

The Mexican muralist José Clemente Orozco created a powerful visual critique of what can happen if academics remain disconnected from the practical world. Between 1932 and 1934, he painted *The Epic of American Civilization* murals in the Baker Library at Dartmouth College. One of the panels, called "Gods of the Modern World," depicts a group of academicians attending the birth of a child. The mother is lying on a bed of books, and the newborn is wearing a mortarboard. What is striking about this panel is that all of the figures in it are skeletons. Dead academics are replicating

---

[11] More specifically and more formally, Stuhr has frequently explained that pragmatism cannot be merely the unity of theory and practice *in theory*. See, for example: "Looking Toward Last Things: Pragmatism Beyond Its First Century"; "A Terrible Love of Hope"; "From Consciousness of Doom to Criticism"; and "No Consolation: Life without Spirituality, Philosophy without Transcendence."

[12] Michele Moody-Adams in her chapter in this volume on "Philosophy and the Art of Human Flourishing" also emphasizes the practical outcomes of the study of philosophy.

themselves, passing along useless knowledge to new generations of students. Furthermore, these learned professors have their backs to a conflagration that can be seen in the background. The world is on fire, but the academics are oblivious to it, focused not on the burning issues of the day, but on the dissemination of lifeless ideas. A eudaimonic turn in the teaching of philosophy cannot simply be a detached, theoretical examination of abstract ideas; it must remain connected to the world and to the real experience of teachers and students in that world.

These are matters I have wrestled with during my more than three decades of teaching philosophy in various contexts, and I would like to share some of my experiences attempting to connect my teaching in robust and practical ways to the flourishing of my students. I share these experiences not because I think I have landed on the correct way of accomplishing this or because I think my attempts have been a complete success, but because I hope they will encourage readers to consider steps they might take in the direction of the eudaimonic turn in their own teaching.

I experienced a turning point early in my academic career when one of my students wrote on an exam that she was happy to be studying the philosophy I was presenting in class because it was helping her clarify her ideas, but that she was also frustrated because she did not know how to apply it. I found her comment puzzling. The class in which she was enrolled was a senior seminar in pragmatism. And as one of its founders, William James, pointed out, pragmatism "is derived from the same Greek word πράγμα, meaning action, from which our words 'practice' and 'practical' come" (*Pragmatism* 28). How could my student not know how to apply a philosophy that was all about practice?

The more I thought about my student's response, however, the more I realized she was right. Pragmatism is a method of understanding philosophical ideas in terms of their practical effects. But like any method, it is possible to have a theoretical understanding of it but have difficulty with its application. This is precisely why so many science courses have lab sections. It is one thing to have a theoretical understanding of the scientific method or of a particular formula in one of the scientific disciplines. It is quite another thing to step into the lab and set up an experiment to test these processes for oneself. Students quickly learn that theoretical understanding is not the same thing as practical knowledge. Both are necessary if one is to truly grasp the science.

The more I thought about my student's comment, the more it seemed to me that philosophy courses ought to have lab sections. I remember my college philosophy professor recounting that one of the students in his ethics class had been expelled for academic dishonesty. My professor reported asking the student whether he saw any connection between his problematic behavior and the ethics class he was taking. The student seemed puzzled by the question and responded in the negative. Perhaps if his ethics class had had a lab section, he might have more readily made connections between the academic study of ethics and its application in his own life.

In the case of pragmatism, there is both irony and tragedy in approaching it in the theoretical and intellectualistic way I had been teaching it. Although typical in academia, this type of pedagogy is ironic in that it undercuts the message of pragmatism itself. James defined intellectualism as "the belief that our mind comes upon a world complete in itself, and has the duty of ascertaining its contents; but has no power of redetermining its character, for that is already given" (*Some Problems of Philosophy* 111). Elsewhere, James cited two opposing intellectualistic views of the world. Optimism holds that the salvation of the world is inevitable, and pessimism holds that it is impossible. Between these two views, he argued, is meliorism, which holds that the salvation of the world is possible and that it depends on the efforts of human beings. "It is clear," he wrote, "that pragmatism must incline towards meliorism" (*Pragmatism* 137). Here is how he described what a melioristic world looks like:

> The melioristic universe is conceived after a *social* analogy, as a pluralism of independent powers. It will succeed just in proportion as more of these work for its success. If none work, it will fail. If each does his best, it will not fail. Its destiny thus hangs on an *if*, or on a lot of *ifs*—which amounts to saying (in the technical language of logic) that, the world being as yet unfinished, its total character can be expressed only by *hypothetical* and not by *categorical* propositions. (*Some Problems of Philosophy* 115)

John Dewey, another of the founders of pragmatism, agreed with James that both optimism and pessimism are problematic. In spite of their differences in orientation, he argued, they are similar in "benumbing sympathetic insight and intelligent effort in reform." Building on James's views, Dewey contended that meliorism is the opposite of paralyzing in that it "encourages intelligence to study the positive means of good and the obstructions to their realization, and to put forth endeavor for the improvement of conditions" (*Reconstruction in Philosophy* 182).

The tragedy of teaching pragmatism in a merely theoretical way is that it does not provide students with actual opportunities to "put forth endeavor for the improvement of conditions." They are not taught how to apply pragmatism and they and the world lose out on the improvement of conditions they might otherwise have been able to effect.

In light of these perspectives, I decided I needed to teach pragmatism differently. I needed to create a philosophy class with a lab section, and I began developing a course I called "Applied Pragmatism." Instead of merely teaching students theoretically about the individual and collective habits of thinking, feeling, and behaving emphasized by pragmatism, I wanted them to be able to identify those habits for themselves, to learn to reinforce the ones they found conducive to human flourishing, and to change the ones they found obstructive of well-being.

A course in Applied Pragmatism could invite students to focus productively on a wide variety of habits.[13] There are many ways in which students could work toward the salvation of the world, as James put it—or at least toward its improvement. In this context, I wanted to invite students to focus on the habits that constituted their own character. In the lectures James gave to teachers applying psychology to education, he stated, "Your task is to build up a character in your pupils; and character, as I have so often said, consists in an organized set of habits of reaction" (*Talks to Teachers on Psychology* 108). The notion that character is composed of habit goes back at least as far as Aristotle, who argued that "character (ηθος) is the product of habit (εθος), and has indeed derived its name, with a slight variation of form, from that word" (*Nicomachean Ethics* II. i. 1). Given the developmental stage of my college students, however, I thought it less appropriate to try to "build up a character" in them than to help them learn to shape their own character through their own selection and adoption of habits.

The practical aims of Applied Pragmatism went beyond making sure students had a theoretical understanding of the texts I asked them to read. I wanted to provide a space within which students could work together to apply pragmatic principles to help them improve the conditions of their own flourishing through the self-shaping of their character. In many ways, such a class resembles less a typical disciplinary course in philosophy and more

---

[13] See Jessica Wahman's chapter on "Pragmatic Stories of Selves and Their Flourishing" and John J. Stuhr's chapter on "Toward Clearer Ideas and Habits of Genius" in this volume for insightful discussions on connections between habits and human flourishing.

the integrated learning of *paideia*, the liberal arts, and the humanities that I discussed earlier in this chapter. Thinking of philosophy as part of a larger program of education broadens possibilities. Accordingly, I invited a psychology professor, Dr. Jane Marie Clipman, to team-teach the class with me. Together, we created a curriculum based in pragmatism, positive psychology (which was just emerging as a new field at the time), and personal development. Our goal was to help students develop awareness of a whole range of habits governing their thinking, their communication with themselves and others, their emotions, their interpretation of events in the world, what they ate, how they exercised, how they carried themselves, and so forth. We engaged in a number of exercises together to help them become aware of these habits and reflect on how supportive they were for their well-being, and then to take action to reinforce the habits they wanted to keep and to change the habits they wanted to modify.[14]

We taught the course for the first time at Albright College during the January interim term in 2000. When I moved to Vanderbilt University two years later, I modified the course and taught it as "Foundations of Character Development." It was through the course that I became involved with the field of positive psychology, and in 2005 I was invited by Martin Seligman to join him at the University of Pennsylvania to co-develop, direct, and teach in the inaugural Master of Applied Positive Psychology program. At Penn, I have taught elements of this course in the master's program and to undergraduates in a course I developed on "The Pursuit of Happiness" and in one I co-taught (with Religious Studies professor Justin McDaniel) on "Happiness and Despair."

In each of these contexts, students have responded to this approach with great appreciation. Virtually all of the students have found it to be significantly helpful and many have reported it to be transformative. Course evaluations have contained the following statements: "This class challenged me more—by far—than any other class I have taken . . . Every single reading and class period I learned something of ULTIMATE significance to my life." "We learned about things that would help us grow personally, which is something that no other class has ever done." "My favorite class ever in my entire academic career." Students have appreciated the shared positive vulnerability of learning about themselves and each other in a place of respect, where there

---

[14] For a description of some of these exercises, see Pawelski, "Character as Ethical Democracy: Definitions and Measures," pp. 11–17; and Pawelski, "Teaching Pragmatism Pragmatically: A Promising Approach to the Cultivation of Character," pp. 133–40.

is both deep acceptance of who they are and strong support for who they want to become. They have learned to see their classmates as people, different from them in their personalities and life experiences but similar in their shared humanity, and they have sometimes come to feel even closer to their classmates than to their friends outside of class. The growth students experience seems to be long-lasting. It is not uncommon for students to reach out to me years after the class to let me know that they are continuing to apply what they learned and that it is continuing to make a positive difference in their lives.

To supplement the information students shared with me directly and through course evaluations, I reached out to research psychologists for help identifying, administering, and analyzing the results of validated psychological measures to see what kinds of effects the courses were having. This involved getting permission from the college or university's Institutional Review Board (IRB). For the Foundations of Character Development course I taught at Vanderbilt University, these measures indicated an increase in optimism and hope, an improvement in attributional style, and a decrease in hopelessness. These results are linked to a range of practical outcomes, including increased physical, psychological, and relational well-being and decreased depression and suicidality.[15] For courses intended to help increase student flourishing, using a range of methods including personal communications, course evaluations, and psychological measures can be important for understanding the actual effects on students and for improving future iterations of the course.

What is the proper role of philosophy teachers in supporting the well-being of their students? This is a question I have asked myself repeatedly over the course of my teaching career. Philosophy teachers are not therapists. We should be clear on this point ourselves and also communicate it clearly to our students. Even for philosophy teachers who have psychological training and certification, the role they are playing in the classroom is that of an instructor and not of a therapist. With that said, some therapies have deep roots in philosophy. Cognitive behavioral therapy (CBT), for example, was greatly inspired by Stoicism. And the work of philosophy professors in Introduction to Logic classes helping students examine the validity and soundness of

[15] For a full list and description of the measures I used, along with more information on the results, see Pawelski, "Character as Ethical Democracy: Definitions and Measures," pp. 18–20, 23–43.

arguments can resemble the work of CBT therapists helping clients challenge the assumptions behind faulty thinking. I remember the first time I looked in a CBT manual, I was struck by how similar it was to the texts I used in my logic classes. Helping students be aware of the faulty thinking in arguments they encounter online or in their own heads can be an important part of what philosophy teachers do, and it makes sense that this work could have a profoundly positive effect on students' well-being, even though philosophy teachers must be clear that their proper role in the classroom is not the treatment of mental illness.

Another role philosophy teachers must avoid is that of evangelist. It is to be hoped that philosophy teachers take an interest in their own flourishing and that they have found approaches that have worked for them. Philosophers who want to teach others about flourishing but have no interest in working on it in their own lives are likely to come across as somewhat hypocritical. They resemble Cicero's grammarians who speak incorrectly or his teachers of music who sing out of tune. This does not mean, of course, that teachers must "have it all figured out" before they offer any courses on the subject. In fact, I think believing one has human flourishing all figured out is likely to be a problem in itself, and may result in an evangelical zeal to make students over in one's own image. Just like a major mistake teachers often make is assuming that all their students learn in the same way they do, it would be a major mistake with regard to human flourishing to think that the very same approach to well-being that works for the teacher will necessarily work in the same way for the student. It is important to keep Stuhr's point in mind here that human flourishing is normative but should not be approached in an overly restrictive way. There are some basic characteristics of human flourishing, but each student will realize these characteristics idiosyncratically, finding their own ways of flourishing. Using a different metaphor, the job of philosophy teachers is to help students find their own paths up the mountain, not to force them onto the paths they themselves have taken.

I also want to add that it is important for philosophy teachers interested in making the eudaimonic turn in their teaching to do so in a way that is fitting for them, for their students, and for the context in which they are teaching. I have shared aspects of my own experience not because I think everyone needs to begin teaching courses in Applied Pragmatism, but because I hope it will help readers think about how they can leverage their own interests, experience, and philosophical expertise to support the flourishing of their students more effectively.

Furthermore, I want to be clear that I do not see the goal of these kinds of practical courses in philosophy to be merely demonstration projects. Unlike many scientific lab courses, where the aim is simply to give students a practical understanding of well-established scientific results, human flourishing requires real experimentation. Lab sections in philosophy classes should not be merely for the purpose of demonstrating the supposed truth of philosophical ideas, but rather for the purpose of testing and refining—and when necessary, revising or replacing—those ideas. Thus, these courses should be seen, not merely as ways of applying philosophical ideas, but as ways of developing them further. Thus, the practical application of philosophy is, itself, philosophy.

Conclusion

Given the eudaimonic opportunities and needs of students today, it is crucial for more philosophy teachers to focus on ways they can develop their teaching to support human flourishing. These developments need to be authentic and carefully thought through, but they will also need to push the boundaries of higher learning environments where professional, academic, and economic interests often eclipse the eudaimonic interests at the root of education and the core of philosophy. I have focused on undergraduate teaching here, but the need for a eudaimonic turn in the teaching of philosophy is also great in other contexts, including K–12, graduate, and non-traditional courses. And the need for a eudaimonic turn extends beyond just the teaching of philosophy. It is a defining element of the new field of the Positive Humanities and it is important for all academic disciplines.[16] I hope conversations on these topics will help more faculty, administrators, and policy makers see student well-being as part of the research and teaching mission of colleges and universities, allowing them to share more deeply in the important work currently being undertaken by student services staff. Although much has changed since the days of the Ancient Greeks and Romans, the cultures of the Axial Age, and the curriculum of Renaissance universities, the broader purposes of education continue to be to help students thrive and participate fully and

---

[16] See Pawelski "The Positive Humanities" and McMahon "The History of the Humanities and Human Flourishing" for more on the eudaimonic turn and the historical and conceptual underpinnings of the field of the Positive Humanities.

effectively in civic life. By working together to change our own pedagogical habits and reform the entrenched patterns of our educational institutions, we can do better by our students, ensuring that more of them have access to educational experiences of ultimate significance to their lives, better equipping them, in the words of John Dewey, "to study the positive means of good and the obstructions to their realization, and to put forth endeavor for the improvement of conditions" (*Reconstruction in Philosophy* 182).

Acknowledgments

This chapter was made possible, in part, through the support of a grant from the Templeton Religion Trust. The opinions expressed in this publication are those of the author and do not necessarily reflect the views of the Templeton Religion Trust.

I would like to thank my parents for modeling good teaching, John Lachs for believing in "Applied Pragmatism" from the beginning, John Stuhr for reading and providing very helpful comments on drafts of this chapter, Sarah Sidoti for her behind the scenes support, and my students over the years for their trust.

Works Cited

American College Health Association. "American College Health Association-National College Health Assessment II: Reference Group Undergraduates Executive Summary Fall 2015." American College Health Association, https://www.acha.org/documents/ncha/NCHA-II_FALL_2015_UNDERGRADUATE_REFERENCE_GROUP_EXECUTIVE_SUMMARY.pdf, 2016.

American College Health Association. "American College Health Association-National College Health Assessment II: Reference Group Executive Summary Spring 2019." American College Health Association, https://www.acha.org/documents/ncha/NCHA-II_SPRING_2019_UNDERGRADUATE_REFERENCE%20_GROUP_EXECUTIVE_SUMMARY.pdf, 2019.

American College Health Association. "American College Health Association-National College Health Assessment III: Undergraduate Student Reference Group Executive Summary Fall 2020." American College Health Association, https://www.acha.org/documents/ncha/NCHA-III_Fall_2020_Undergraduate_Reference_Group_Executive_Summary.pdf, 2021.

American Psychiatric Association. *Diagnostic and Statistical Manual of Mental Disorders*, 4th ed., Text Revision, American Psychiatric Association, 2000.

Aristotle. *Nicomachean Ethics*. Translated by H. Rackham, Harvard University Press, 1934.

Arrian. *Discourses of Epictetus*. Translated by W. A. Oldfather. *Epictetus*, 2 vols., edited by J. Henderson, Harvard University Press, 1925.

Celenza, Christopher S. *Petrarch: Everywhere a Wanderer*. Reaktion Books, 2017.

Cicero, Marcus Tullius. *Tusculan Disputations*. Translated by C. D. Yonge, Harper & Brothers, 1877.

Dewey, John. *Reconstruction in Philosophy. John Dewey: The Middle Works, 1899–1924, Vol. 12*, edited by Jo Ann Boydston, Southern Illinois University Press, 1920/1982, pp. 77–201.

Epictetus. *Encheiridion*. Translated by W. A. Oldfather. *Epictetus*, 2 vols., edited by J. Henderson, Harvard University Press, 1925, pp. 479–537.

Epicurus. "Letter to Pythocles." *Epicurus: The Extant Remains*. Translated by Cyril Bailey, Clarendon Press, 1925, pp. 57–81.

Goodmon, Leilani B., Ashlea M. Middleditch, Bethany Childs, and Stacey E. Pietrasiuk, "Positive Psychology Course and Its Relationship to Well-Being, Depression, and Stress." *Teaching of Psychology*, vol. 43, issue 3, 2016, pp. 232–7, doi:10.1177/0098628316649482.

Hadot, Pierre. *Philosophy as a Way of Life*. Blackwell, 1995.

Hansen, Jennifer L. "A Reconsideration of the Role of Philosophy in the Reconstruction and Promotion of Leisure," this volume, 2022.

Haybron, Daniel M. *The Pursuit of Unhappiness: The Elusive Psychology of Well-being*. Oxford University Press, 2008.

Ivanhoe, Philip J. "Happiness in Early Chinese Thought." *The Oxford Handbook of Happiness*, edited by Susan A. David, Ilona Boniwell, and Amanda Conley Ayers, Oxford University Press, 2013, pp. 263–78.

James, William. *Pragmatism*. Harvard University Press, 1975.

James, William. *Some Problems of Philosophy*. Harvard University Press, 1979.

James, William. *The Principles of Psychology*. Harvard University Press, 1981.

James, William. *Talks to Teachers on Psychology*. Harvard University Press, 1983.

Jaspers, Karl. *The Origin and Goal of History*. Translated by Michael Bullock, Routledge, 2021.

Jayawickreme, Eranda, and James O. Pawelski. "Positivity and the Capabilities Approach." *Philosophical Psychology*, vol. 26, no. 3, 2013, pp. 383–400. doi:10.1080/09515089.2012.660687.

Jensen, Frances E., and Amy E. Nutt. *The Teenage Brain*. HarperCollins, 2015.

Kraut, Richard. *What Is Good and Why: The Ethics of Well-Being*. Harvard University Press, 2007.

Kristeller, Paul O. *Renaissance Thought II: Papers on Humanism and the Arts*. Harper & Row, 1965.

Lambert, Louise, Holli-Anne Passmore, and Mohsen Joshanloo. "A Positive Psychology Intervention Program in a Culturally-Diverse University: Boosting Happiness and Reducing Fear." *Journal of Happiness Studies*, vol. 20, 2019, pp. 1141–62.

Lefevor, G. Tyler, Dallas R. Jensen, Payton J. Jones, Rebecca A. Janis, and Chih Han Hsieh. "An Undergraduate Positive Psychology Course as Prevention and Outreach." PsyArXiv, 5 Dec. 2018. Web.

Lipson, Sarah Ketchen, Emily G. Lattie, and Daniel Eisenberg. "Increased Rates of Mental Health Service Utilization by U.S. College Students: 10-year Population-Level Trends (2007–2017)." *Psychiatric Services*, vol. 70, issue 1, 2019, pp. 60–3. doi:10.1176/appi.ps.201800332.

McMahon, Darrin. M. *Happiness: A History*. Atlantic Monthly Press, 2006.

McMahon, Darrin. M. "From the Paleolithic to the Present: Three Revolutions in the Global History of Happiness." *Handbook of Well-being*, edited by Ed Diener, Shigehiro Oishi, and Louis Tay, DEF Publishers, 2018, pp. 1–10. doi:nobascholar.com.

McMahon, Darrin. M. "The History of the Humanities and Human Flourishing." *The Oxford Handbook of the Positive Humanities*, edited by Louis Tay and James O. Pawelski, Oxford University Press, 2022, pp. 45–56.

Moody-Adams, Michele. "Philosophy and the Art of Human Flourishing," this volume, 2022.

Nussbaum, Martha C. "Capabilities as Fundamental Entitlements: Sen and Social Justice." *Feminist Economics*, vol. 9, 2003, pp. 33–59.

Orozco, José Clemente. *The Gods of the Modern World*. Dartmouth College, Hanover, New Hampshire, 1932–4.

Pawelski, James O. Character as Ethical Democracy: Definitions and Measures. *Journal of College and Character*, vol. 5, issue 9, 2004, pp. 1–43, doi:10.2202/1940-1639.1398

Pawelski, James O. "Teaching Pragmatism Pragmatically: A Promising Approach to the Cultivation of Character." *Contemporary Pragmatism*, vol. 3, 2006, pp. 127–43.

Pawelski, James O. "What Is the Eudaimonic Turn?" *The Eudaimonic Turn: Well-being in Literary Studies*, edited by James O. Pawelski and D. J. Moores, Fairleigh Dickinson University Press, 2013, pp. 1–26.

Pawelski, James O. "The Positive Humanities: Culture and Human Flourishing." *The Oxford Handbook of the Positive Humanities*, edited by Louis Tay and James O. Pawelski, Oxford University Press, 2022, pp. 17–42.

Peterson, Chris and Martin E. P. Seligman. *Character Strengths and Virtues: A Handbook and Classification*. Oxford University Press and the American Psychological Association, 2004.

Plato. *The Dialogues of Plato*, translated by B. Jowett, Vol. 1, Random House, 1920, pp. 401–23, 591–879.

Proctor, Richard E. *Defining the Humanities: How Rediscovering a Tradition Can Improve Our Schools*, 2nd ed., Indiana University Press, 1998.

Seligman, Martin E. P. "The President's Address (Annual Report)." *American Psychologist*, vol. 54, 1999, pp. 559–62.

Sen, Amartya K. "Capability and Well-being." *The Quality of Life*, edited by Martha C. Nussbaum and Amartya K. Sen, Clarendon Press, 1993, pp. 30–53.

Shimer, David. "Yale's Most Popular Class Ever: Happiness." *The New York Times*, January 26, 2018. https://www.nytimes.com/2018/01/26/nyregion/at-yale-class-on-happiness-draws-huge-crowd-laurie-santos.html.

Smith, Bruce W., C. Graham Ford, Kelly Erickson, and Anne Guzman. "The Effects of a Character Strength Focused Positive Psychology Course on Undergraduate Happiness and Well-being." *Journal of Happiness Studies*, vol. 22, 2021, pp. 343–62. doi:http://dx.doi.org.proxy.library.upenn.edu/10.1007/s10902-020-00233-9.

Stuhr, John J. "From Consciousness of Doom to Criticism." *Pragmatism, Postmodernism, and the Future of Philosophy*, Routledge, 2003, pp. 132–3.

Stuhr, John J. "No Consolation: Life without Spirituality, Philosophy without Transcendence." *Pragmatism, Postmodernism, and the Future of Philosophy*, Routledge, 2003, pp. 199–201.

Stuhr, John J. "Looking Toward Last Things: Pragmatism Beyond Its First Century." *100 Years of Pragmatism: William James's Revolutionary Philosophy*, edited by John J. Stuhr, Indiana University Press, 2010, pp. 194–207.

Stuhr, John J. "A Terrible Love of Hope." *Pragmatic Fashions: Pluralism, Democracy, Relativism, and the Absurd*, Indiana University Press, 2016. p. 201.

Stuhr, John J. "Flourishing: Toward Clearer Ideas and Habits of Genius," this volume, 2022.

Sumner, Leonard W. *Welfare, Happiness, and Ethics*, Clarendon Press, 1996.

Tiberius, Valerie. *The Reflective Life: Living Wisely with Our Limits*. Oxford University Press, 2008.

Tiberius, Valerie. *Well-Being as Value Fulfillment: How We Can Help Each Other to Live Well*. Oxford University Press, 2018.

Wahman, Jessica. "Pragmatic Stories of Selves and Their Flourishing," this volume, 2022.

12

A Reconsideration of the Role of Philosophy in the Reconstruction and Promotion of Leisure

Jennifer L. Hansen

Political debates in the United States concerning the proper function and organization of the university, typically heating up during election cycles for at least the last 40 years, tacitly belie a more fundamental clash of views over the specific democratic ideals it serves. The locus of the clash centers primarily on different interpretations of how various liberal democratic civic institutions serve and/or prepare citizens. To put this differently, the political debate springs from factions differently weighting values[1]—whether that be technical progress and economic expansion theoretically aimed at lifting the quality of life for all (the *homo economicus* view) *or* the cultivation of certain dispositions requisite for responsible citizenship (the *homo liber* view). The humanities often serve as the battleground for this clash of values; the camp promoting technical progress and economic expansion fail to see their *utility* and consequently propose either the downsizing or elimination of humanities departments.[2] Arguments so framed by utility threaten to win the day

---

[1] John Sadler proposes a widespread adoption of "values-analysis" education in the service of "citizenship education" that improve all or our capacity to identify the different and often clashing personal values guiding individuals—including how such individuals may conceptualize education, democracy, and the university. See Sadler "Values, Literacy, and Citizenship," this volume.

[2] For example, see Rifkin "What's Wrong with the Proposal to Eliminate Small Majors." One of the important observations that Rifkin makes concerning this Wisconsin state-wide initiative to eliminate majors at University of Wisconsin campuses based on how "productive" they are—which is problematically measured by numbers of majors—is that it flies in the face of the "Wisconsin Idea" that its public university system is committed to public service and "improving the human condition." Rifkin points out that among the majors likely to be eliminate under this metric are humanities departments (history, philosophy and languages), the very departments in which students are challenged to "study, analyze and understand important political, social, cultural and economic challenges in their state or region, in the country, and across the planet more generally." See also Harris "The Liberal Arts May Not Survive the 21st Century.", who reports that Governor Scott Walker seeks to "tweak" the Wisconsin Idea from a "search for truth" to "a charge to 'meet the state's workforce needs.'"

Jennifer L. Hansen, *A Reconsideration of the Role of Philosophy in the Reconstruction and Promotion of Leisure*
In: *Philosophy and Human Flourishing*. Edited by: John J. Stuhr, Oxford University Press. © Oxford University Press 2023.
DOI: 10.1093/oso/9780197622162.003.0013

given the unsatisfactory and infrequent defenders of a vision of the university as deeply concerned with citizenry. One important exception here is Roosevelt Montás, who directs the Core Curriculum at Columbia University:

> [t]o 'educate' is to nurture an individual into a particular community. We must recognize plainly that all education is education for citizenship. What we teach, how we teach it, and whom we teach it to necessarily describes a vision of society and the types of individual we want to prepare for that society. ("Democracy's Disappearance")

To put this differently, in the context of a liberal democracy, the university is an institution committed to cultivating important intellectual and practical habits—or virtues—that should its citizenry possess may promise the state supports greater flourishing for all, including eliminating structural conditions that create profound social inequality[3] beyond job creation.

Given that presently the *homo economicus* view is winning out in legislatures and university budgeting processes, the humanities, including philosophy, which shall be the focus of this essay, are facing a legitimacy crisis, and therefore sorely need to recruit better arguments that both articulate and provide evidence of their value to the American university. While the current legitimacy crisis gained new steam from the Trump administration,[4] the assaults on the humanities—and the liberal arts more broadly—are as old as the American university itself.[5] However, current critics of the humanities—whether fiscally conservative state legislators, shills plumping for conservative political causes, fervent champions of STEM-focused

---

[3] In her chapter in this volume, "Navigating Irreconcilable Conflicts: Philosophical Thinking for Better Lives," Lori Gallegos clarifies how the background conditions of social inequality in the United States forces those oppressed by patterns of domination into a unfair bargain where fighting for social justice comes at the cost of personal flourishing.

[4] In the budget report for the 2020 Fiscal Year, the Trump administration proposed to begin shutting down both the NEA and NEH, asserting that both find private sources of funding. In other words, the Trump administration did not recognize public investments in the arts or the humanities as valuable for its citizenry. See *A Budget for a Better America. Promises Kept. Taxpayers First.*

[5] Many historians have chronicled the rise of the American university in the late 1800s, which principally offered a Classical education (*artes liberales*) modelled on the English university for elite men who seeking respectability, and then, in the post-Civil War era, influenced by the German model of scientific research, practically banished the humanities so that the American university might serve Agriculture or Industry, and then returned in the early twentieth century to a debate that seems to never quite be settled over the proper role of the humanities in higher education. For the historical analysis of this debate, see, for example, Veysey *The Emergence of the American University,* and Hofstadter and Hardy *The Development and Scope of Higher Education in the United States.* For more contemporary analyses, see Giamatti, *A Free and Ordered Space: The Real World of the University* and Menand, *The Marketplace of Ideas: Reform and Resistance in the American University*).

education deeply concerned about the competitiveness of the United States in the global technology economy, or more commonly, anxious parents and students wanting to make sure courses and majors actually translate into secure jobs—each disclose in their "why the humanities?" objection the *homo economicus* view. Included within this particular view are the following: the university is a business, or a commodity, or should serve private industry, or exists solely to provide vocational and/or professional training.

Offering a potentially powerful rebuttal to the pervasive *homo economicus* view, James O. Pawelski encourages fellow philosophers to begin collaborations with positive psychology researchers and therein find a "unifying rationale" for the humanities in the articulation of another paradigm of values—"eudaimonic values"—that, he persuasively argues, drives many—if not more—of our decisions than do than the market values subtending the *homo economicus* position (Pawelski "Bringing Together" 209). Eudaimonic values promote and preserve what help us flourish, as well as mitigate or prevent what diminishes our flourishing (211). Here, flourishing is not gauged by epidemiological or economic metrics such as real family income, standard of living, length of workweek, life-expectancy, prevalence of disease—it is not synonymous with merely or exclusively hedonic goods. Rather, for the field of positive psychology, flourishing can be measured in the quality of subjective emotional and mental states, character traits, and civic institutions. "Well-being is a notion that resonates deeply with those outside academia," argues Pawelski, and by ". . . [u]sing the language and rationale of well-being could help scholars in the humanities guide and frame the work they do in a way that could connect powerfully with administrators, funding organizations, government agencies, and the general public" ("Bringing Together" 209).

Martin Seligman helpfully explains that positive psychology rests on three pillars: (1) positive subjective emotions, (2) positive virtues or characteristics, and (3) positive intuitions and communities ("Foreword," xvi–xvii).[6] Pawelski's proposal that the humanities, and philosophy in particular, from the lens of this collaboration would be characterized as promoting eudaimonic values (as opposed to market values)—or referring to the pillars, focused mainly on (2) and (3).[7] *Prima facie*, I am decidedly in favor of doing

---

[6] See also Martin E. P. Seligman and Mihalyi Csikszentmihalyi, "Positive Psychology: An Introduction," *American Psychologist* 55, no. 1: (2000).

[7] While I do not have the space to defend this thesis, my own view, which is highly influenced by the work of John Dewey, is that the positive emotions (1) emerge insofar as our civic institutions are so arranged to cultivate eudaimonic traits (this would be an argument parallel to Dewey's consistent

this work; much of my previous work is best understood as both phenom-enological descriptions of positive virtues or characteristics that promote human flourishing and feminist, pragmatic evaluations of norms and values that either interfere with or cultivate said virtues.[8,] However, the fruitfulness of this collaboration depends on how we define, describe, and then defend positive virtues, positive institutions, and positive communities.

Before delving further into how positive psychology may supply persua-sive arguments for the value of philosophy, I must register a worry that even if we could broadly (read: thinly) agree on what eudaimonic values consist in, as well as the important role they ought to play in our lives—especially insofar as they may progressively advance liberal American democratic ideals—one could, nonetheless, imagine how quickly those values could be subsumed into market values. Unless the promotion of a "eudaimonic turn" in the university includes an intelligent, Deweyan, pragmatic stance towards[9] what Zachar and Scott Bartlett characterize as technological ra-tionality, the momentum and force of the *homo economicus* view threatens to co-opt it (37–39). Zachar and Bartlett's notion of technological rationality captures the conflation of rational thinking with currently valued technolog-ical methods available for dealing with *certain* kinds of problems. To further explain, consider the following two examples: (1) under the sway of "tech-nological rationality" many of us in the university have been increasingly subjected to instruments for quantitatively measuring student outcomes or (2) the medical profession has adopted the gold-standard of evidence-based medicine (i.e., only those treatments and therapies empirically verified in clinical trials). The crucial insight of Zachar and Bartlett's concept is that in both of these cases the role of expertise and judgment are downgraded to less rigorous or, perhaps, plainly irrational in favor of information or data that is procured through *currently* more valued methods, i.e., statistical methods. Given the thesis that many of our institutions, including the university, are

view that civic institutions, such as education, are crucial to cultivating democratic habits which are the necessary condition for a flourishing democracy).

[8] See Hansen, "A Virtues-Based Approach"; Hoffman and Hansen, "*Is Prozac a Feminist Drug?*"; and Hoffman and Hansen, "Prozac or Prosaic?" for more.

[9] For Dewey, intelligence is the critical, social capacity to reorganize our natural and social environments—experimentally—to yield the particular goods we seek from them. Dewey's notion of intelligence is drawn largely from the natural sciences—inquiry, hypothesis testing, revision of hypotheses in light of results, and so on. Dewey asserts, "[Intelligence] is disposition of activity, a quality of that conduct which foresees consequences of existing events, and which uses what is fore-seen as a plan and method of administering affairs" (Dewey *Experience and Nature,* 126.

becoming increasingly myopic in their understanding of good learning outcomes under the rule of technological rationality, I could imagine, if by promoting eudaimonic values one is criticizing this very myopia, that the study of philosophy is a necessary, but not sufficient condition for human flourishing. Insofar as the study of philosophy cultivates positive virtues that promote human flourishing and, *in theory*, the university provides fertile conditions for students to richly study philosophy, then the study of philosophy could increase the likelihood of a flourishing life, and perhaps as a consequence a flourishing democracy. Nonetheless, I am worried that in practice, in order to influence university administrators during times of examining budget priorities or in providing a rationale for grant proposals, eudaimonic values will be treated as functionally equivalent to *utility* or *optimality* which are values central to the currently dominant and seeming intractable paradigm of technological rationality.

My plan is first to contribute to the expression of the peculiar tone of eudaimonic values, drawing on the work of one of the pioneers of positive psychology, Mihalyi Cskikszentmihalyi. In particular, I will focus on his concept of "autotelic" or "flow experience" as a way of characterizing philosophical activity (Navigating Irreconcilable Conflicts: Philosophical Thinking for Better Lives 67). In so doing, I will argue that philosophical activity may promote human flourishing both insofar as it cultivates positive traits and positive emotions. Drawing on John Sadler and Borgmann's acute analyses of how the values of technological rationality tend to overwhelm all other values and their defense of engagement as a possible suspension of Borgmann's rule of technology" (*Technology and the Character of Contemporary Life: A Philosophical Inquiry* 199), I will extend Jeanne Nakamura and Cskikszentmihalyi's recent work on autotelic activities as transactions between organisms and environments that open up the possibility for greater control and creativity over those environments (Sadler *Values and Psychiatric Diagnosis*; Nakamura and Csikszentmihalyi "The Concept of Flow"; Nakamura and Csikszentmihalyi "The Construction of Meaning"). Second, I will attempt a reconstruction[10] of the idea of leisure as

---

[10] "Reconstruction" is a technical term used by Dewey. It designates a critical process of making explicit the historical roots and methods that generated concepts and values embedded in our tradition and then discovering how we can intelligently alter our means/methods, drawing from empirical, experimental methods, to better achieve them in the future. Not all concepts, for Dewey, necessarily need to be reconstructed. However, insofar as a concept/value, such as leisure, persists in our cultural imagination, I posit it is worthwhile to undertake rescuing the aspirations within this concept and employing better tools for achieving them so that all human beings have an opportunity to partake in its benefits. See Stuhr, *Genealogical Pragmatism: Philosophy, Experience, and Community*

an important democratic ideal that the university ought to help citizens cultivate. Human engagement in autotelic activities contrasts dramatically with the conventional norms of contemporary living in the technological age. Drawing on the work of A. Bartlett Giamatti, I characterize the qualitative, experiential difference between autotelic and exotelic (instrumental) activity as *leisure*, which denotes a space for play, creativity, autonomy, and joy (*A Free and Ordered Space: The Real World of the University*; and *Take Time for Paradise: Americans and Their Games*).

A Reconsideration of the Study of Philosophy as Autotelic Activity

From the standpoint of psychology, Aristotle's concept of *eudaimonia* (often translated as flourishing), is construed, or at the very least measured, as a subjective state of mind, which is the first pillar on which Seligman erects the fundamental axioms of positive psychology. Csikszentmihalyi identifies "flow" as an emotional state of mind belonging to the class of traits or experiences that fall under the umbrella concept *eudaimonia*.[11] In In "The Concept of Flow," Nakamura and Csikszentmihalyi assert "*a good life is one that is characterized by complete absorption in what one does*" (89). An individual in a flow state experiences a sense of enjoyment, argues Csikszentmihalyi, that is qualitatively superior to pleasure (or for our purposes here, more conducive to human flourishing); in *Flow: The Psychology of Optimal Experience*, he observes,

> [e]njoyable events occur when a person has not only met some prior expectation or satisfied a need or desire [pleasure] but also gone beyond what he or she has been programmed to do and achieved something unexpected, perhaps something even unimagined before. Enjoyment is characterized by this forward movement: by a sense . . . of accomplishment (46).

for an excellent account of Deweyan-influenced pragmatism as a reconstruction of philosophy and experience.

[11] Many other researchers in the field of positive psychology study other traits or subjective states of mind that could each comprise—but not exhaust—eudaimonia. Included among the studied traits/subjective states of mind is: optimism, hope, resilience, grit, perseverance, mindfulness, or self-esteem. The field also makes a distinction between emotional and cognitive states of mind.

Csikszentmihalyi attributes the fact that flow is experienced as enjoyment, rather than pleasure, to the unique features that describe the activities that produce flow states, activities he describes as autotelic.

The neologism, autotelic, drawing on the Greek words for self (*auto*) and end/goal/purpose (*telos*), denotes activities undertaken for their own sake, for the enjoyment they bring when one is engaged in them, rather than activities undertaken instrumentally. Among the important features of autotelic activities are

(a) Challenges (need not necessarily involve competition with others) that stretch one's skills (neither too easy, nor too difficult)
(b) Clear goals
(c) Clear rules clarifying the successful achievement of goals
(d) Opportunities for feedback on one's progress toward meeting goals

A quick glance at these features makes clear that one engaged in an autotelic activity is not a consumer. To put this differently, the act of consuming, whether media, material goods, or technological devices, does not produce flow states and its attendant enjoyment; consumption may produce pleasure, but pleasure, from the standpoint of flow theory, does not lead to lasting human flourishing. Pleasure merely returns the individual to homeostatic states that can restore some order to consciousness after a grueling, chaotic, or depleting day of work (*Flow*, 46); pleasurable states do not lead, importantly, to further growth or complexity of the self, both of which, Csikszentmihalyi argues, afford one greater control and freedom over consciousness and, in turn, over forces in our environment that may try to coerce us in directions at odds with well-being (*Flow*, 61, 69, 120). For example, dragging oneself to the couch, turning on the latest episode of *The Walking Dead* with a full glass of Pinot Gris in hand, might start to melt away the physical and mental exhaustion and stress of one's day—in such a scenario, one might steal a moment of respite from maddening conversations with colleagues echoing in one's mind, unanswered emails, looming deadlines, anxieties over one's children, or fretting over imminent and necessary repairs to one's roof, *ad nauseum*. However, this temporary order amidst chaos is wasted time rather than truly free time; one is not *meaningfully* liberated from the tedium. Borgmann pointedly makes the same point this way: "[t]elevision . . . [is] a palliative that cloaks the vacuity and relaxes the tensions of the technological condition"

(*Technology and the Character of Contemporary Life: A Philosophical Inquiry* 143).

Csikszentmihalyi considers a variety of candidates for autotelic activities (and has researched and measured the effects of many of these), including rock climbing, chess, dancing, tennis, and reading. In his national best-seller, *Flow: The Psychology of Optimal Experience*, Csikszentmihalyi also devotes a chapter to autotelic intellectual pursuits (as opposed to activities that stress more physical action), with explicit mention of philosophy. His particular take on philosophy, however, is that only when one is engaged in philosophy in (what he takes to be) its root meaning—the love of wisdom—rather than caught up in the internecine battles waged between professional philosophers within the pages of journals or the halls of departments—does flow becomes a distinct possibility. Of course, this makes some sense insofar as once a philosopher depends upon her activity to pay the bills, then what may have first attracted her to this rather peculiar way of thinking, starts to become mere labor (*negotium*), rather than liberation (*otium*) of the mind. As Giamatti, former president of Yale, puts it starkly: "work in this life is at its heart a negotiation with death, a bargain made in a thousand different ways until the strength to make that daily deal wanes ..." (8). Hence, I do think one should, with caution, consider philosophical activity as an autotelic activity. Csikszentmihalyi does allow that many activities are mixed (both autotelic and exotelic)—we may take them up because we are forced (philosophy distribution requirement at a Jesuit College) or we may continue to read and write philosophy as a profession (it becomes work). However, the fact that an activity, such as doing philosophy, may be mixed, does not rule out that it may still be potent with Aristotelian enjoyment.

In this vein, I posit that the study of philosophy, thinking philosophically, writing arguments, and partaking in philosophical discussions and debates all count as autotelic activities. One could argue that philosophical activity meets the four conditions enumerated above [(a)–(d)], drawn from Csikszentmihalyi's research, that characterize autotelic activities. Reading itself is a challenge that requires skill; to read one must first learn how to decode symbols and the rules of language. Philosophy builds on literacy and stretches it to new limits insofar as it demands that one not only decode the word-as-symbol, but also begin to decode word-symbols that denote abstract concepts and arguments, definitions, and trains of thought represented without out words, but rather logical symbols. Reading philosophy is challenging, but one can find a place to begin that isn't too challenging (e.g., the early dialogues of Plato) in order to further develop his skills for reading philosophical texts. One could also move through philosophical texts historically in order to begin to identify the major questions, concepts, lines of argument, and debate. The point here is that the study of philosophy offers challenges to any reader—whether novice or expert—and thus is unlikely to ever become too easy or unchallenging.

Moving to the other three criteria unique to autotelic activities, one must admit that the goals of philosophical activity are by no means objectively clear within the field. In fact, what constitutes philosophy, and the metaphilosophical debates that regularly emerge whenever this question is raised, often leads to vicious, if not pointless, infighting. However, for our purposes here, we need not settle larger metaphilosophical debates in order to determine whether or not this is an activity with objectively clear and specifiable goals, rules, and mechanisms for feedback. The idea of identifying the goals and rules of philosophical activity may seem less fraught if we consider philosophy as an amateur sport. Csikszentmihalyi clarifies, after all, that for the amateur (deriving from the Latin *amare*, to love), the goals (b), the rules (c) one applies in order to evaluate how well one has met those goals, and the feedback (d) one attends to calibrate how well she stands in relation to her goals are internal (55, 140). One's personal goals with philosophy emerge over time (just as they would with rock climbing, running, gardening, or gourmet cooking); the longer one hones and deepens his skills in reading, understanding the history of, writing, crafting arguments, reflecting on experience, and discussing philosophy with others, the more likely he will begin to formulate specific goals, rules, and venues for feedback. For example, Ginger may set out to identify which argument(s) concerning the nature of a mental disorder best fit with their own experience, Mark might hope to discover a school of thought that radically transforms what he formerly took for granted concerning the field of ethics (i.e., following objective moral rules), and Jessica might make it her life's goal to specialize in and further develop the field of modal logic. Whatever one sets out to achieve in engaging in philosophical activities, it seems quite plausible that many persuasive arguments, as well as phenomenological descriptions of one's experience with philosophy, could be advanced to demonstrate a fit with description of autotelic activities.

If we grant that philosophical activities are autotelic activities, and therefore have potential to develop into flow activities, then it follows that philosophy, as one of the humanities, may contribute toward human flourishing.

Philosophy, that is, brings about an enjoyable emotional state that reasonably counts as one candidate out of many other states conveyed in Aristotle's concept of *eudaimonia*.

Before moving to a discussion of how philosophy as an autotelic activity presents us with an opportunity to reconstruct leisure as desirable goal for democratic states, it is crucial to first point out that for Csikszentmihalyi, flow states—enjoyable emotional states—are organically connected with strenuous, challenging, autotelic activity. One cannot replicate flow states, on his argument, by more direct means (i.e., neurotechnologies, psychopharmacological compounds, or virtual reality simulations; Borgmann 202). To help clarify this point, I will turn to the work of Borgmann and Sadler, specifically their notion of engagement, to extend Csikszentmihalyi's recent, ecological thinking on flow states (in fact Nakamura and he reconsider flow as "vital engagement"; "The Instrument Metaphor"; *Values and Psychiatric Diagnosis*).

Nakamura and Csikszentmihalyi have clarified the dynamic, transactional relationship between the human organism and her environment pre-existing development of any coordinated habits, skills or, especially, autotelic activities; human organisms are not "abstracted from context" but rather adapt and respond to the specific environments, both natural and cultural, within which they develop ("The Concept of Flow," 90). Evan Thompson brings a naturalistic, phenomenological frame for characterizing the fundamental relationship of organism to environment; drawing on the work of Humberto Maturana and Francisco Varela, Thompson describes the (human) organism as a self-making, self-organizing process, employing Maturana and Varela's neologism, *autopoiesis* (again drawing on Greek roots denoting self [*auto*] and production or making [*poeisis*]). Human beings are not machines, designed for specific, fixed purposes or ends, both of which can become obsolete over time. Human beings are organisms; they are dynamic, open systems, in constant transaction with their environments. This transactional relation creates the condition for the possibility of their autonomy from their environments, and thereby some degree of control over their environments, as well as the material basis of their basic reproduction and maintenance as a living system. Given that human beings are very sophisticated, complex organisms, autotelic activities, alongside basic survival and acculturated habits, belong to their autopoietic structure. In fact, Nakamura and Csikszentmihalyi describe the fact of autotelic activities as a feature of human consciousness "emergent motivation" insofar as the unique potentials of a given a thoroughgoing transaction between an individual's genetic endowment, social position, historical moment with the unique possibilities awaiting in her environment ("The Concept of Flow," 91). Heavily influenced by American pragmatism, they explain:

> there is no objectively defined body of information and set of challenges within the stream of the person's experience, but rather the information that is selectively attended to and the opportunities for action that are perceived . . . it is not meaningful to speak about a person's skills and attentional capacities in objective terms; what enters into lived experience are those capacities for action and those resources and biases (e.g., trait interest) that are engaged by this presently encountered environment. ("The Concept of Flow," 91)

Essentially, the flow states that may accompany autotelic activities, are created by individuals out of set of possibilities arrayed in the environment to which they are attracted given the selections of attention therein, which are directed by their temperament.

Borgmann, drawing inspiration from Martin Heidegger's phenomenological critique of technology, depicts autopoietic, autotelic activities as "engagement with focal things," that is things or artifacts that convey a pre-technological[12] attitude, orientation to the world. Things (human artifacts), Borgmann and Sadler point out, have embedded in them larger cultural values; things are never just things, they are part of a larger, organized network of meanings (Heidegger's word is "worlds"), including dominant values that govern the ways humans interact with others, their environments, and what they actually see (e.g., marshy land that could be drained for housing construction or precious wetland ecosystems that protect water quality). Borgmann invokes "focal things" to recall certain valued relationships to and ways of being in the world that have been eclipsed or marginalized by the rule of technology. Consider the different values communicated in the following: a BPA-free, portable, eco-friendly coffee mug, a 10% post-consumer recycled paper disposable paper cup, a hand thrown, ceramic mug made by a local artisan, or bone-china coffee cup sitting on a matching saucer. Each of those things conjure different ways of moving through the world, specifically,

---

[12] Borgmann's compelling argument shows that we cannot easily or permanently "switch off" a technological attitude. He thus proposes to develop focal practices to suspend, for a time, the domination of technological thinking, perceiving, and valuing.

ways of approaching the drinking of coffee—efficiency, disposability, eco-friendly, convenience, coziness, craftsmanship, family tradition, daily ritual, formal encounter, etc. The rule of technology, or technological rationality, that pervades are current age, continually promises that technological devices and solutions (including the BPA-free, portable, eco-friendly mug and the 10% post-consumer recycled paper cup) will free up our time. What our time is free up for, however, is the disappointment of the technological age—we get our coffee on the go so we can hustle back to work (Borgmann 128). The artisanal cup, or the formal china—both pre-technological age artifacts (whether they actually pre-existed or are made in opposition to mass production)—are the better indicators of free time. Technological revolutions all throughout human history, Darrin McMahon points out, do not necessarily usher in deeper human happiness (1–10). Taking one of his examples, the Agricultural Revolution, while it created a surplus of food and allowed humans to settle in regions rather than follow their food, it also ushered in inequality, slavery, war, less nutritious diets, monotonous and physically demanding labor, proneness to crop failure, etc. (McMahon 3).

From the dominant perspective of technological rationality, we too easily forget the purposes or ends for which humans, as auto*poietic* creatures, have invented technological devices (e.g., prevent diseases, preserve food, more widely disseminate information, amusement), and instead "the *means* [the technological devices] often dictate the *ends* . . . we sometimes choose to work on problems because the tools are available" (Zachar and Bartlett "Technological Rationality in Psychiatry" 37). In other words, we stop inquiring into fundamental questions concerning what constitutes well-being, the good life, or human flourishing, and instead follow along the pathways paved by dominant American cultural norms that promote either instrumental (market and technological) values of consumption, efficiency, optimality, convenience and productivity or fall victim to the dubious "belief that for every problem there is technological expertise which can take over the burden of solution" (Sadler *Values and Psychiatric Diagnosis*, 344–345; Borgmann *Technology and the Character of Contemporary Life* 137).

Sadler and Borgmann promote focal practices as buffers from the otherwise total domination of technological values—and the danger that technological thinking and solutions are the only justifiable ones. Sadler elaborates on how engagement—a way of describing how one relates to the world and others in focal practices—may better serve psychiatrists and their patients; "engagement," moreover, is among alternative modes of orienting oneself

toward the world that Sadler, following Heidegger, calls "poietic," or creative. Psychiatrists—perhaps far more than psychologists—are ensnared
in the disease-model approach to mental health; Sadler observes that
mental health practitioners are captivated by the "instrument metaphor"
"[w]hen people are used and regarded primarily as instruments in larger
social projects . . . " ("The Instrument Metaphor, Hyponarrativity, and the
Generic Clinician" 30). Sadler further clarifies that from the instrument
metaphor point of view, clinicians assess whether or not psychopathology
is present in a given individual if he or she does not succeed in "fulfilling
the technological values of productivity, efficacy, and efficiency" (31.) Armed
with value-laden symptom checklists that measure presence or absence of
psychopathology—evaluative instruments often created after researchers
observed changes in behavior in subjects who had taken antidepressant
medications and thus the symptom check-list is directly tied to the effects
of psychopharmaceuticals (i.e., circular reasoning), the clinician elicits
what Sadler calls the "hyponarrative" from the patient. In coining the term
"hyponarrativity," Sadler wishes to highlight the underdevelopment of any
given patient's story—the flattening of a patient's dimensionality into a yes or
no checklist. This technologically value-laden approach to healing is in stark
opposition to engagement, namely, "the intimate interplay of environmental
event, individual response, and historical unfolding that characterize important clinical information such as the personal meaning of events, development of the personality, and sensitivity to environmental or interpersonal
context" (Sadler *Values and Psychiatric Diagnosis* 177). Engaging in the therapeutic relationship in this way is labor and time-intensive; it also more difficult to measure efficacy unless one utilizes one of validated therapies, such
as Cognitive Behavioral Therapy. However, engaging with the patient in this
way might also align better with the enterprise of healing, caring, and promoting well-being that initially draws people to medicine (elsewhere I have
made parallels between this kind of therapeutic encounter and liberal arts
teaching). Sadler notes that operating from the virtue of engagement (as well
as empathy, genuineness, relatedness, etc.) has the added benefit that one's
work starts to feel less like toil (*negotium*) and more like human flourishing
(*otium*):

> [the] doctor-patient encounter is not characterized as problematic or goal
> oriented, it is not characterized as a means to a particular end; rather, it is
> described as a worthy end in itself, one in which healing is not an objective

or goal but is *intrinsic to* the encounter process. The goal of the existentialist encounter [one animated by non-technological values] is not to produce a particular outcome, not to initiate therapeutic changes, nor to address symptoms, but rather to have a genuine, real, or 'authentic' relationship with another person. Healing is an accompaniment rather than a goal. (*Values and Psychiatric Diagnosis* 340)

Borgmann selects the word "focal" to capture both senses of the root Latin word, focus, namely, central and gather (as the hearth gathers the family by its warmth). He elaborates "a focus gathers the relations of its context and radiates into its surroundings and informs them. To focus on something or to bring it into focus is to make it central . . ." (Borgmann *Technology and the Character of Contemporary Life: A Philosophical Inquiry* 197). This phenomenological perspective on the interactions of humans with their environments is a variation on a more naturalistic (Darwinian), pragmatist perspective that describes the conditions for the possibility for human creativity, free play, and inventiveness—all of which assert their autonomy. Focal practices, for Borgmann, provide the occasion—the time and place— for fully engaging with our environment, registering the metaphorical temperature, testing our mettle, and appraising our powers to achieve unimaginable feats. Borgmann regularly offers the example of running as a focal practice that puts us into a different, non-instrumental relationship with our environment:

Running is simply to move through time and space, step-by-step. But there is splendor in that simplicity. In a car we move of course much faster, farther, and more comfortably. But we are not moving on our own power and in our own right. We cash in prior labor for the present motion. Being beneficiaries of science and engineering and having worked to be able to pay for a car, gasoline, and roads, we now release what has been earned and stored for transportation. But when these past efforts are consumed and consummated in my driving, I can at best take credit for what I have done . . . driving, requires no effort, and little or no skill or discipline . . . But in the runner, effort and joy are one . . . if I have trained conscientiously, my past efforts will bear fruit in a race . . . My strength will be risked and enacted in the race which is itself a supreme effort and an occasion to expand my skill. (*Technology and the Character of Contemporary Life: A Philosophical Inquiry* 203)

Too, the study of philosophy—a "chalk and talk" discipline—can be considered a focal activity (as much as an autotelic one). The insight here—whether we use the pragmatic, Darwinian paradigm of autopoietic autotelic activity or the phenomenological one of focal practices that imbue meaning and value into a set of things and relationships within one's environment—is human flourishing may need to appeal to a different set of values, what I will now describe as the "leisure values" of the *homo liber* perspective. In the best case, philosophical activity embodies those leisure values, and thus promotes human flourishing.

A Reconstruction of Leisure: Freedom in Order

Before further exploring how the cultivation of skills or virtues associated with autotelic activities (Seligman's 2nd pillar of positive psychology) may better deliver on the promises of technology, namely free time or leisure, I must first address the quite understandable concern that many have with the concept of leisure, at least as it was concretely exercised in Western culture (e.g., depending on slavery, indentured servitude, colonialism, and the subjection of women). I wish to reconstruct the notion of leisure and put it in service of democratic ideals. "Leisure" as well as "Civilization" are damaged words, but hopefully, not beyond repair. Insofar as the notions of leisure and leisure classes still conjure images of Colonial imperialism and American chattel slavery, for example, arguments for enshrining the ideal of leisure in our civic institutions, including our universities, will be a dangerous proposition. However, Giamatti and Csikszentmihalyi present a perspective on leisure—partly insofar as it is a counterweight to market values—that encourages me to make the attempt.

Giamatti traces "leisure" to its root in Ancient Greek—*schole*—which is the same root for school—but a notion of school as a liberal education—the education of *homo liber* (15). Education was a prerequisite for enjoying leisure time, insofar as in pursuing the liberal arts

> the muscle that is the mind was disciplined and toughened and thereby made more free, to pursue new knowledge, and just as that freedom in the mind became a freedom for the mind, which freedom is the precondition to and guardian of political or social freedom . . . so was the pursuit of these studies undertaken in, and meant to perpetuate, a

condition of leisure. (Giamatti *Take Time for Paradise: Americans and Their Games* 16)

If we count philosophy as an autotelic activity, then Giamatti's point is deepened. Leisure, he argues, is an ideal to be achieved, a state of existence where one experiences herself to be free from coercion, manipulation, drudgery, and boredom. In leisure, Giamatti further argues, we are fully alive to the potency of the moment, we seize upon it to exercise our creativity and thereby realize our imaginations. To be skilled enough to seize the moment, to be fully alive and freely engaged in the world, we must first cultivate the skills and traits that are preconditions to experiencing leisure. And Csiskzentmihalyi gives us insight into how autotelic activities, such as philosophy, transform our inner experience—our consciousness of ourselves and the world. Autotelic activities, he explains, enlarge our sense of control. "Entropy is the normal state of consciousness," claims Csikszentmihalyi, which is "a condition that is neither useful nor enjoyable" (*Flow: The Psychology of Optimal Experience* 119). Engaging in autotelic activities, or Borgmann's focal practices, demands the concentration of attention to such a degree that one has no psychic energy left over to jump from one worry, anxiety, distraction to another; the activity demands total commitment. If this total commitment is not passively consuming, but actively making, constructing, engaging, and producing—if our entire organism is singularly devoted to the activity, then we find ourselves in a flow state. The flow state itself—a total absorption in an activity such that time expands and tedium dissipates—is the achievement, for however long it lasts, of human flourishing. In flow states, humans efficaciously push back just enough on the encroachment of work, toil, and other forms of coercion bound up with the values promoted by the technological rationality paradigm to make space for self-transformation (Giamatti *Take Time for Paradise: Americans and Their Games* 26). We become free because we transcend the otherwise obstructive disorder of our minds—the dispersal and fragmentation of our attention that we experience, Cskiszentmihalyi claims, as painful (whether in the form of depression, anxiety, or boredom). Without psychic order, without physical coordination, we are helpless and therefore at the mercy of external forces; without psychic order we are unfree.

Before closing, I want to briefly note that treating philosophy as necessary to human flourishing—as a precondition for leisure and thereby the enjoyment that accompanies the free direction of our energies to create—requires civic institutions to promote access and the valuable skills and traits one gains from engaging in autotelic activities, such as philosophy. The role of the university, as an important civic institution to our democracy, could try to promote the humanities in order to promote a reconstructed culture of leisure. But, as I shared in my worry earlier, and in many ways throughout this chapter, I fear that the autotelic activity, the eudaimonic value, or even leisure itself can all too easily be co-opted into the rule of technology and thereby undermine the project of human flourishing, at least as I have articulated my sense of it here.

Works Cited

Borgmann, Albert. *Technology and the Character of Contemporary Life: A Philosophical Inquiry.* The University of Chicago Press, 1984.

A Budget for a Better America. Promises Kept. Taxpayers First. Fiscal Year 2020. U.S. Government Publishing Office, 2019.

Csikszentmihalyi, Mihalyi. *Flow: The Psychology of Optimal Experience.* Harper Perennial, 1990.

De Grazia, Sebastian. *Of Time, Work and Leisure.* Vintage Books, 1994.

Dewey, John. *Human Nature and Conduct.* Southern Illinois University Press, 1988.

Dewey, John. *Experience and Nature.* Southern Illinois University Press, 2008.

Gallegos, Lori. "Navigating Irreconcilable Conflicts: Philosophical Thinking for Better Lives." This volume, 2022.

Giamatti, A. Bartlett. *A Free and Ordered Space: The Real World of the University.* W.W. Norton & Company, 1988.

Giamatti, A. Bartlett. *Take Time for Paradise: Americans and Their Games.* Bloomsbury, 1989.

Hansen, Jennifer. "A Virtue-Based Approach to Neuro-Enhancement in the Context of Psychiatric Practice." *Oxford Handbook of Psychiatric Ethics*, vol. 2, section 10, edited by John Z. Sadler, K.W.M. Fulford, and Cornelius Werendly van Staden. Oxford University Press, 2015, pp. 1228–49. DOI: 10.1093/oxfordhb/9780198732372.013.42

Harris, Adam. "The Liberal Arts May Not Survive the 21st Century." *The Atlantic*, December 13,2018, https://www.theatlantic.com/education/archive/2018/12/the-liberal-arts-may-not-survive-the-21st-century/577876/

Hoffman, Ginger, and Jennifer Hansen. "Is Prozac a Feminist Drug?" *International Journal of Feminist Approaches to Bioethics*, vol. 4, no. 1, 2011, pp. 89–120.

Hoffman, Ginger, and Jennifer Hansen. "Prozac or Prosaic Diaries? The Gendering of Psychiatric Disability in Depression Memoirs." *Philosophy, Psychiatry, and Psychology*, vol. 24, no. 4, 2017, pp. 285–98.

Hofstadter, Richard, and C. DeWitt Hardy. *The Development and Scope of Higher Education in the United States.* Columbia University Press, 1952.

Maturana, Humberto R., and Francisco J. Varela. *Autopoiesis and Cognition: The Realization of the Living.* D. Reidel Publishing Company, 1979.

McMahon, Darrin M. "From Paleolithic to the Present: Three Revolutions in the Global History of Happiness." *Handbook of Well-Being*, edited by E. Diener, S. Oishi, and L. Tay. DEF Publishers, 2018, pp. 1–10. DOI:nobascholar.com

Menand, Louis. *The Marketplace of Ideas: Reform and Resistance in the American University*. W. W. Norton & Company, 2010.

Montás, Roosevelt. "Democracy's Disappearance." *The Chronicle of Higher Education, Review*, vol. 64, no. 6, October 1, 2017, p. 11. https://www.chronicle.com/article/Democracy-s-Disappearance/241303

Nakamura, Jeanne, and Mihaly Csikszentmihalyi. "The Concept of Flow." *Handbook of Positive Psychology*, edited by C.R. Snyder and Shane J. Lopez. Oxford University Press, 2002, pp. 89–105.

Nakamura, Jeanne, and Mihaly Csikszentmihalyi. "The Construction of Meaning through Vital Engagement." *Flourishing: Positive Psychology and the Life Well-Lived*, edited by Corey L. Keyes and Jonathan Haidt. American Philosophical Association, 2003, pp. 83–104.

Pawelski, James O. "Bringing Together the Humanities and the Science of Well-Being to Advance Human Flourishing." *Well-Being and Higher Education: A Strategy for Change and the Realization of Education's Greater Purposes*, edited by Donald Harward. Bringing Theory to Practice, 2016, chapter 23.

Rifkin, Benjamin. "What's Wrong with the Proposal to Eliminate 'Small Majors?'" *Inside Higher Ed*, November 28, 2018, pp. 207–16. https://www.insidehighered.com/views/2018/11/28/university-wisconsin-systems-proposal-cut-programs-confer-few-degrees-wrongheaded.

Sadler, John Z. *Values and Psychiatric Diagnosis*. Oxford University Press, 2005.

Sadler, John Z. "The Instrument Metaphor, Hyponarrativity, and the Generic Clinician." *Philosophical Perspectives on Technology and Psychiatry*, edited by James Philips, pp. 23–33. Oxford University Press, 2009.

Sadler, John Z. "Values, Literacy, and Citizenship." This volume, 2022.

Seligman, Martin E. P., and Mihalyi Csikszentmihalyi. "Positive Psychology: An Introduction." *American Psychologist*, vol. 55, no. 1, 2000, pp. 5–14.

Seligman, Martin E. P. "Foreword: The Past and Future of Positive Psychology." In *Flourishing: Positive Psychology and the Life Well-Lived*, edited by Corey L. Keyes and Jonathan Haidt. American Philosophical Association, 2003, pp. xi–xx.

Stuhr, John J. *Genealogical Pragmatism: Philosophy, Experience, and Community*. State University of New York Press, 1997.

Tay, Louis, James Pawelski, and Melissa G. Keith. "The Role of the Arts and Humanities in Human Flourishing: A Conceptual Model." *Journal of Positive Psychology*, vol. 13, no. 3, 2017, pp. 215–25. DOI: 10.1080/17439760.2017.1279207

Thompson, Evan. *Mind in Life: Biology, Phenomenology, and the Sciences of Mind*. Harvard University Press, 2007.

Zachar, Peter, and Scott Bartlett. "Technological Rationality in Psychiatry: Immanent Critique, Critical Theory, and a Pragmatist Alternative." *Philosophical Perspectives on Technology and Psychiatry*, edited by James Philips, pp. 35–54. Oxford University Press, 2009.

Veysey, Laurence R. *The Emergence of the American University*. University of Chicago Press, 1965.

13

Philosophy and the Art
of Human Flourishing

Michele Moody-Adams

Understanding what promotes human flourishing is a matter of enduring philosophical concern. A central philosophical debate has focused on the question of whether engagement with art—as a spectator, a creator, or perhaps both—might be a vital component of a satisfying and well-lived human life. In recent contributions to this debate, philosophers such as Iris Murdoch, Arthur Danto and Richard Shusterman have answered this question in the affirmative. But they have also reminded us that in the first sustained philosophical discussions of the question, Plato declared a kind of war on art (Murdoch *The Fire and the Sun*; Danto 171–89; Shusterman *Pragmatist Aesthetics*). From his disdain, in the *Ion,* for art that he believed to issue from imitation without knowledge; to the plan, in the *Republic,* to exclude dramatic poets from the ideal polis; to the defense of censorship in the *Laws,* Plato seemed committed to what Danto calls the "philosophical disenfranchisement of art." Commenting on the development of philosophical thought after Plato, Danto suggests that philosophy has mostly offered "codicils to the Platonic testament" concerning art and thus that, in its traditional mode, philosophy "may just be the disenfranchisement of art" (176).

Yet although Plato would have excluded tragedy from the ideal polis, Aristotle's *Poetics* acknowledged the social and political value of tragedy's cathartic effects (Secs. II and III). Moreover, in the *Aesthetics,* Hegel maintained that *Antigone* is "one of the most sublime and in every respect most excellent works of art of all time," and his analysis of *Antigone* presented the suffering of the tragic hero as a profoundly significant means of resolving conflicts between important values (464).[1] Of course, Bentham's utilitarianism involved the claim that all poetry is "misrepresentation," but his disciple John

---

[1] See also Hegel, *Phenomenology of Spirit*, pp. 111–18.

Michele Moody-Adams, *Philosophy and the Art of Human Flourishing* In: *Philosophy and Human Flourishing*. Edited by: John J. Stuhr, Oxford University Press. © Oxford University Press 2023. DOI: 10.1093/oso/9780197622162.003.0014

Stuart Mill insisted, in contrast, that utilitarianism ought to celebrate the capacity of poetry to stimulate imagination and to strengthen sympathy and social feeling (Mill "Bentham" 114; Mill *Autobiography* vol. 1). Still further, although most twentieth-century empiricists and positivists in philosophy have taken science to be the arbiter of rationality in argument and inquiry, the analytic philosopher Nelson Goodman argued in *Ways of Worldmaking* "that the arts must be taken no less seriously than the sciences as modes of discovery, creation, and enlargement of knowledge in the broad sense of advancement of the understanding."[2] Philosophy does not, therefore, have to be at war with art. Ancient and modern philosophers, alike, have sometimes defended the value of art to human well-being, and a growing body of research in contemporary social sciences and in medicine confirms that there is good reason to do so (Tay, Pawelski, and Keith 215–25). This essay seeks to build on the insights of philosophical accounts that recognize the value of art, and on relevant empirical research, to argue that philosophy best supports and advances human flourishing when it acknowledges, and then seeks to deepen understanding of, the contributions that art can make to a satisfying and well-lived life.

My view rests on some important background commitments about the nature and sources of art. Following John Dewey, I presume that we can fully understand the contributions that art might make to human well-being only when we think and theorize about art in ways that, as Dewey urges, help "restore continuity between the refined and intensified forms of experience that are works of art and the everyday events, doings and sufferings that are universally recognized to constitute experience" (Dewey *Art as Experience* 2). The project of properly restoring continuity between "art" and "everyday experience" involves recognizing that the art that contributes to human flourishing must be understood fairly broadly. Thus, on my account, artistic activity involves the exercise and application of imagination, creativity, and skill in many domains of human interest and concern. Art, on this stance, is not confined to those activities and projects often labelled "fine arts;" or to products of that mysterious capacity we call artistic "genius;" or to objects, products and activities typically displayed in museums or presented in formal performance spaces.

---

[2] See, for instance, Ayer, *Language Truth and Logic* and Quine "On the Nature of Moral Values" pp. 471–80.

But my call to restore continuity between art and everyday experience also involves four main *positive* commitments. First, I claim that some objects, products and activities that initially appear primarily "useful" may sometimes count as art, and indeed, as the kind of art that can make a profound contribution to human flourishing. As Dewey contends, "the intelligent mechanic" who does his work well can be artistically engaged. For the same reason, the 'building arts'—principally architecture—can sometimes be the highest expression of artistic achievement.[3] That is, we can reasonably construe the Parthenon, or Christopher Wren's St. Paul's Cathedral, for example, as both great art and great architecture. But, second, drawing on the work of the art critic John Berger, I contend that we must find a way of talking and theorizing about fine art, itself, that does not presume that is properly the preserve of those with material privilege and specialized training. It may be true that one cannot *fully* understand the nature and value of certain works of art without "initiation" into specialized ways of talking about art interpretation and appreciation. This may mean that engagement with "fine art" can fully contribute to human flourishing only if we can provide widespread access to educational institutions that teach the conventions governing its deepest appreciation. But fine art can still contribute to the flourishing of the neophyte, who may approach it with ways of seeing that enlighten even the "expert" observer. Third, there is no good reason to insist that only those creative products that count as fine art or "high culture" can qualify as art. I follow Shusterman in holding that "the blanket rejection of popular art as aesthetically illegitimate and socio-culturally corruptive" cannot be defended, and that we can make sense of the continuity between art and everyday experience only if we are open an "aesthetic pluralism" that resists easy distinctions between "high art" and "low art," and rejects the notion that while the fine arts contribute to human flourishing the art of "popular culture" must always tend to diminish it (*Pragmatist Aesthetics* 34–35). Fourth, as theorists such as Walter Benjamin and Cynthia Freeland have suggested, we must accept that some of the art that matters to human flourishing—particularly certain kinds of photography and film—may be most important for its capacity to broaden the *reach* of art and enlarge our capacity to appreciate it.

Yet even as I propose aesthetic pluralism, I continue to hold that a satisfying and well-lived human life will include opportunities to appreciate (and

---

[3] See Nelson Goodman, "How Buildings Mean," pp. 642–53; and Joseph Maresca, *WPA Buildings: Architecture and the Art of the New Deal.*

sometimes to participate in) the "fine arts"—including "serious" music, and "great" literature, drawing, painting, sculpture, theater, and dance. In fact, the fine arts are so important to human well-being that every well-ordered political community should recognize the value of supporting them even in times of economic distress. This was the wisdom that guided America's Depression era policymakers who supported the fine arts through initiatives such as the Federal Arts Project, the Federal Writer's Project, and the Federal Theater Project as part of the Works Project Administration. Moreover, even as America conducted "an unconditional war on poverty," the notion that art—including "fine art"—is critical to human flourishing rightly led to the creation, in 1965, of the National Endowments for the Arts and for the Humanities. These initiatives rightly presumed that having opportunities to be engaged with the arts (in the broadest sense) is an important element of individual flourishing and a critical support of the benefits of democratic citizenship and the political institutions which protect it.

With this broadly Deweyan stance regarding the nature, sources, and potential of art, my argument begins in the first section, Art as a Vehicle of Individual Transformation, by discussing the connection between art and individual flourishing. In this context, art matters most as *a vehicle of transformation* in three domains: in the development of affective and cognitive faculties and capacities, in shaping the individual's sense of the nature and limits of human possibility, and in strengthening and refining the capacity for self-reflection. The second section, Art as a Vehicle of Social and Political Reconciliation, explores the link between art and flourishing from the perspective on persons as social and political beings. Here, art functions primarily as *a vehicle of reconciliation*, in two important senses of "reconciliation." First, art has the potential to promote reconciliation in the sense of social harmony, "agreement" and balance. But, second, when that harmony has been undermined or extinguished by injustice, serious conflict and social division, art can play a significant part in projects meant to move a society past current antagonisms and help restore—or create—social harmony. This promotes reconciliation in the sense of moral repair of social and political divisions. Finally, in the third section, The Consolations of Art, I explore the contributions that art can make when it addresses our persistent vulnerability to suffering, loss and adversity. From this perspective, art matters most as *a vehicle of consolation*. But the consolations of art are not simply a function of art's capacity to provide comfort and solace. Consolation, on my account, is fundamentally the lessening of sorrow and disappointment, and the art that lessens sorrow and disappointment sometimes works by unsettling us, rather than comforting us. Each section—that is, the discussions of transformation, reconciliation and consolation—will offer what I hope to be compelling examples and provocative suggestions concerning the precise ways in which art contributes to well-being.

Art as a Vehicle of Individual Transformation

It may seem prosaic to insist on the transformative power of art. Yet many of the most essential dimensions of art's transformative power, and their roles in promoting well-being, remain poorly understood and undervalued. This is, in part, because many discussions of these topics begin by adopting a conception of art that tends to mask the sources of art's transformative power. But Dewey's description of art as "refined and intensified forms of experience" can provide a helpful corrective (Dewey *Art as Experience* 2). The central idea of Dewey's description is best captured by an observation attributed to the contemporary "light and space" artist Robert Irwin, on which art is a "continuous examination of our perceptual awareness and a continuous expansion of our awareness of the world around us."[4] In this section, I consider, first, how engagement with art—as the examination and expansion of our awareness of the world—can constructively influence the functioning and development of basic human faculties and capacities. I then discus the power of art to enlarge one's understanding of human potential and possibility—with a special focus on its capacity to depict what John Stuart Mill described as "experiments in living." Finally, I reflect on the means by which engagement with art can sometimes deepen and enrich individual self-understanding, largely in virtue of its capacity to show that we sometimes understand ourselves best by becoming *immersed* in the experience of others.

A good place to begin reflection on the ways in which engagement with art can develop perceptual and cognitive capacities is with John Berger's contention that although there is an important sense in which, developmentally, seeing comes "before words" and "can never be quite covered by them," seeing is never really a question of "mechanically reacting to stimuli" (*Ways*

---

[4] Irwin is best known for works that shape environments through light and space. He is also an insightful theorist of art and its value. The characterization referred to here is from Cynthia Freeland, *But Is It Art?* p. 207.

of Seeing 8). That is, seeing is never as spontaneous and natural as is sometimes supposed, but is always partly dependent on what we believe to be important, on what we actually look at and for, and on what we think we know about those things we look for. Berger plausibly argues that some of what we think we know, and some of what we believe to be important, will be shaped by the visual arts that have gained cultural dominance in one's culture (129–154). But this suggests that sometimes art will have the potential to challenge what we believe, and what we claim to know, and thereby help us look for different things and come to see those things in a different way. Such challenges may be most effective when art comes from unconventional sources or portrays unconventional subject matter with unusual materials or methods. But sometimes even conventional art from conventional sources may unsettle accepted patterns and conventions of seeing. When this happens, art may even improve our ability to attend to certain features of the world to which our familiar cultural habits and conventions have made us insensitive.

In a striking example of this phenomenon (whereby even "conventional" art can challenge existing ways of seeing), it has been shown that training in the formal elements of the observation of visual art can substantially improve visual diagnostic skills of medical students—most of whom become dependent upon lab tests and elaborate technology to make diagnoses that their predecessors could make from physical exams alone (Naghshineh, Hafler, and Kaz).[5] Building on this evidence, some medical schools require their students to take art courses that involve "training the eye." These courses have been shown to enhance the capacity to make sense out of ambiguity, to pick up visual "cues" of health or disease that might otherwise be missed, and to better understand the human form, human movement, and the variety of human expression—all in ways that enhance the delivery of health care.[6] Indeed, there is evidence that training in art observation can enhance what art historian Amy Herman calls our general "visual intelligence": a capacity that enhances individual performance in a variety of occupations, including occupations in fields such as law enforcement and the military, in which the difference between life and death may rest on the practitioners' ability to overcome their implicit, unreflective biases (2016). Herman's well-regarded

[5] See also Dhruv Khullar, "What Doctors Can Learn From Looking at Art."
[6] Harvard Medical School at one time required a course, "Training the Eye: Improving the art of physical diagnosis for 1st and 2nd year medical students."

"Art of Perception" course uses the study of painting, sculpture, and visual art more generally, to teach participants how to better "assess, analyze and articulate" what—and how—they see, and then how to effectively "adapt ... behavior" to respond to what they see.

But just as sustained engagement with, and attentive study of, visual art can enhance our capacity to fully appreciate the depth and complexity of experience, it has been well-documented that serious engagement with literature strengthens the ability to use, understand, and appreciate the value of language. For instance, there is compelling evidence that students who read widely—across historical periods and cultures, and within different literary genres—will develop larger and more sophisticated vocabularies when they approach the texts with the right kind of attention (Pennington and Waxler *Why Reading Books Still Matters*; Nagy, Herman, and Anderson 233–53; Sternberg 89–106). Reading widely and attentively has also been shown to make one a better writer, as masters of the craft have long urged.[7] Perhaps most intriguing, using fMRI technology, some neuroscience studies of brain function have suggested that when we engage in "close reading" of a complex novel such as Jane Austen's *Mansfield Park* we are developing a cognitive "flexibility" with benefits likely to be realized across a range of human activities (Goldman).

But perhaps most important, reading widely gives one a special and immediate access to a remarkably broad array of what Mill called "experiments in living." To be sure, in *On Liberty,* Mill was most concerned to assert the value of *actual* experiments in living, both as a way of promoting human progress and as an expression of the importance of respecting individuality. But Mill would surely agree that literature provides some of the most valuable, and the least risky, sources of knowledge about of human possibility. Moreover, given his belief in the value of "higher pleasures" in human life, he would surely have agreed that literary experiments in living are important not just for the varieties of human possibility they present, but also for the ways in which they engage our distinctively human capacities of imagination and understanding. Of course, one of Mill's best known defenses of literature is his discussion, in the *Autobiography*, of the ways in which Romantic poetry helped him recover from a period of severe depression. Others may find that the most affecting literary experiments are those that we encounter in novels, short stories, plays, and epic poetry. Yet whatever the source of one's most

---

[7] See, e.g., Stephen King's *on Writing: A Memoir of the Craft.*

valued literary experiments in living, such experiments play a critical role in promoting human flourishing especially when our engagement is serious and sustained, as when we return to a familiar novel more than once over the course of a lifetime.

In my view, we must also acknowledge the power of films to present valuable experiments in living, and to do so in ways that vividly and powerfully encourage examination and expansion of our awareness of the world. To be sure, as Erwin Panovsky once observed, some critics may object that film cannot really be art because it seems to invert the typical pattern whereby "an artistic urge" gives rise to "the discovery and gradual perfection of a new technique" (93). But Panovsky compellingly argues that the "technical invention" that allowed us to record movement on film truly "gave rise to the discovery and gradual perfection of a new art" and that "in modern life the movies are what most other forms of art have ceased to be, not an adornment but a necessity" (122). More than any other single force, Panovsky writes:

> it is the movies that mold . . . the opinions, the taste, the language, the dress, the behavior, and even the physical appearance of a public comprising more than sixty per cent of the population of the earth. If all the serious lyrical poets, composers, painters and sculptors were forced by law to stop their activities, a rather small fraction of the general public would become aware of the fact and a still smaller fraction would seriously regret it. If the same thing were to happen with the movies the social consequences would be catastrophic. (94)

This passage reminds us that it is partly because of their accessibility to large populations that movies—unlike the fine arts—have come to play such a critical role in human flourishing, and we therefore have reason to take seriously their status as art—even as we recognize that, in the movies as elsewhere, not all art is good art.

But when we contemplate the power of art to transform our understanding of human possibility, we cannot ignore the role that art can play in transforming our sense of ourselves and, in particular, in transforming our ability to consider how much of our individual experience is an expression of what it is to be human. As the novelist and essayist James Baldwin once observed, "You think your pain and your heartbreak are unprecedented in the history of the world but then you read. It was Dostoevsky and Dickens who taught me that the things that tormented me most were the very things that connected me with all the people who were alive, or who had ever been alive."[8] Of course, in contemporary culture, a potent blend of post-modern skepticism and old-fashioned cultural relativism continues to dominate the way in which many cultural observers react to the idea of a "shared human experience." But Baldwin is surely right to contend that one of the things that art does—again and again—is remind us of just how much we have in common with others, despite the very real and profound differences, which it is sometimes the purpose of art to express. This is why Dewey was right to claim, in *Art and Experience*, that art (at its best) can be helpfully understood as a "universal language."

One of the most effective ways to learn the "language" of art may be through active participation in the creation of art. Moreover, there is compelling empirical evidence that participation in aesthetic activities helps encourage constructive transformations in the capacities and talents of participants, and helps to strengthen their sense of how developing these capacities and talents might improve their individual well-being.[9] If we care about human flourishing, we ought thus to lament the decline—and sometimes even the extinction—of arts education programs in many contemporary school systems.

But if we can be transformed by art, and if some transformations effected by art can contribute to human flourishing, any effort to understand the contribution that art makes to human flourishing must reject appeals to any "metric" that takes human desires and preferences as essentially fixed. The transformations that art makes possible are not simply increases in visual intelligence and enhancements of cognitive flexibility, but transformations in our sense of ourselves, of our connections to other beings, and of our place in the world we share with them. We cannot get an accurate picture of the *value* of such transformations if we simply take subjects' desires and preferences as fixed, and ask whether art somehow increases those subjects' capacity to satisfy those desires and preferences. This is because art has the capacity to help us develop new desires and preferences, and thus to see our most fundamental interests in new ways. Far too much empirical literature in this domain continues to ignore this possibility and thus remains insufficiently attentive to insights that might help us understand the most important sources of human well-being. Many conventional psychometric assumptions

---

[8] Baldwin made this observation more than once. The best (most complete) version is in a 1963 interview with a writer for *Life Magazine* (89).

[9] There are many relevant studies. See, for instance, "Critical Evidence: How the Arts Benefit Student Achievement" at https://files.eric.ed.gov/fulltext/ED529766.pdf.

about "objective" measurement of outcomes may be inadequate to generate understanding of how some of the consequences of engagement with art unfold, over time, in the course of a well-lived life.

Art as a Vehicle of Social and Political Reconciliation

Drawing on Baldwin's claims about the transformative power of literature, I have argued that art, more generally, can transform our self-conceptions and reshape our understandings of our relationships to others and their experiences. Baldwin's stance is especially valuable for his recognition that even as art sometimes confirms the diversity of human experience, it also has the capacity to confirm our commonality and depict the reality of *shared* human experience. In this section, I argue that is in virtue of this capacity—this capacity to confirm our common humanity—that art may become a vehicle of social and political projects that promote human flourishing.[10]

A critical task of any such project is to preserve, and sometimes to create, harmony and "balance" among individuals and groups—that is, to produce outcomes that can be understood as some kind of "reconciliation." Of course, as Danto urged, following Plato's example many philosophers have been mistrustful of art's capacity to produce politically stable reconciliation, or—as a Rawlsian might say—to produce such reconciliation "for the right reasons." But in contemporary social and political contexts of extreme cultural and doctrinal pluralism, if we want to defend liberal democratic ideals such as equality and liberty we must encourage the kind of art that best reflects and embodies such ideals, seeking non-coercive reconciliation that respects individual autonomy and acknowledges participant equality. Moreover, in the morally non-ideal contexts of many contemporary societies, that is, societies in which social solidarity and harmony have been endangered by injustice and social division, the art of social protest can sometimes provide the most effective, non-coercive challenges to injustice and social division and creating the prospect of a more just reconciliation.[11]

---

[10] John Sadler discusses the skills, including those provided by the arts, that can expand civic discourse and deepen citizenship, "Values Literacy and Citizenship," this volume.

[11] In this context, see also José Medina's contrast in his chapter in this volume, "Relational Insensitivity and the Interdependence of Flourishing and Withering," between the "coordination and cooperation" of what he terms "melioristic pluralism" and the "epistemic friction" and unlearning that are at the heart of "guerrilla pluralism."

As a start to understanding how art might promote non-coercive social harmony we can consider the social and political roles of civic art and architecture—perhaps, especially, the art and architecture of civic remembrance. Civic art and architecture play a critical role in human flourishing for two main reasons. First, as Jeremy Waldron argues in *The Harm in Hate Speech*, the way a society looks, sounds, and feels is a principal means of "conveying assurances to its members" that they can count on being treated justly. It is a way of communicating that all of a society's members can expect to be treated with what Stephen Darwall (1977) calls "recognition respect": that is, as equally entitled to be taken seriously in public deliberations and decisions (Waldron 82, 85). Philosophy ought to care about "political aesthetics," Waldron rightly urges, because the way in which a society "choreographs" official ceremonies, shapes displays of public power, and creates and preserves public projects of remembrance, profoundly influences its capacity to provide "general and diffuse" assurance of just treatment as a fundamental public good (75). But, second, as the anthropologist Benedict Anderson argues in *Imagined Communities*, when public projects of remembrance embody solidarity-generating values, such as an uncoerced commitment to shared sacrifice, they can help create a sense of "deep horizontal comradeship." Indeed, though I cannot make the case here, public projects of remembrance which embody solidary-generating values can promote political *stability* where rational consensus on principles, alone, cannot.[12] Philosophy ought to help us to recognize what such projects of remembrance look like and to understand the social and political processes that produce them.

The civic art of remembrance sometimes promotes the right kind of reconciliation by expanding perceptual space—in particular, by expanding our capacity to perceive commonality between persons or groups initially deemed as fundamentally different, and as having potentially irreconcilable interests. It is thus that, at the end of the 19th century, sculptor Augustus St. Gardens produced Boston's *Memorial to Robert Shaw and the Massachusetts 54th Regiment* that challenged the racial ideology of its time: depicting the willingness of black soldiers to sacrifice their lives to end slavery, and displaying the possibility of "deep horizontal comradeship" between white and black soldiers. Regrettably, though the memorial was meant to commemorate the commemorate the July 1863 battle of Fort Wagner, South Carolina, it was not completed and dedicated until 1897, one year after the US Supreme Court's

---

[12] This draws on my in-progress manuscript for *Renewing Democracy*.

1896 decision in *Plessy v. Ferguson*, which C. Vann Woodward once called America's "national decision against equality" (229). But as commentators have noted, the memorial was remarkable and *singular* in many respects, perhaps especially for Saint-Gaudens' decision to place the figure of Colonel Shaw in the midst of the figures of the regiment's soldiers, rather than having him ride in front of the soldiers or depicting him as riding alone as a more conventional Civil War memorial might have done. The philosopher William James delivered one of several orations at the 1897 dedication, describing the memorial as a "noble work of bronze" that, in depicting courageous black soldiers fighting *beside* courageous white officers, captured the "true meaning" of the War for the Union ("Oration by Wm. James" 64). On my account, Saint Gaudens's defiance of the conventions of 19th century commemoration was an important source of the memorial's expressive power, making it unexpectedly open to expressing values that challenged some elements of the official racial ideology of its time to promote the possibility of racial reconciliation.

It must be noted, however, that the memorial suffered an extended period of neglect, in large part because *Plessy v. Ferguson* was not overturned for another 58 years, with the 1954 decision in *Brown v. Board of Education*, and because America was still dismantling many of the legal structures of segregation for much of the 20th century. It should not be surprising that continued inconsistency between the ugly reality of American life and what William James had described as the "true meaning" of the memorial might initially diminish the memorial's expressive power. Still further, despite its singularity, the memorial was not entirely free of the dominant racial ideology of 19th century America: while the names of all the white officers who died at Fort Wagner were listed on the monument, the black soldiers who died were referred to simply as "the black rank and file." The citizens' committee that spurred restoration of the memorial in 1980 eventually decided to have all recoverable names of the regiment's black soldiers inscribed on the base of the memorial, despite objections that doing so would obscure the truth about 19th century race relations. In my view, whatever the cost in historical accuracy, inscribing the names on the memorial helped to complete the memorial's most important expressive goal, which was to expand perceptual space by displaying the possibility of commonality and comradeship that might cross the divide created by American racial apartheid. This expansion of perceptual space eventually helped to strengthen scholarly efforts to reassert the truth of African American military sacrifice and civic contributions.

It also influenced broader cultural life in America through the release of one of the finest Civil War films ever made: the 1989 film *Glory*, which (finally) told the full story of the Massachusetts 54th.

If the St. Gaudens memorial helped expand *perceptual* space, nearly two decades before Brown *v. Board of Education*, Marian Anderson's 1939 concert at the Lincoln Memorial helped expand *conceptual* space for national debate about whether *Plessy v. Ferguson*—and the Jim Crow laws that it allowed—had wrongly declared racial segregation to be compatible with constitutional principles. The very idea of holding Anderson's concert at the Lincoln Memorial emerged in response to the decision of the Daughters of the American Revolution to deny Anderson the right to sing in Washington D.C.'s Constitution Hall. Ironically, the Lincoln Memorial had been dedicated in 1922 in a ceremony that, by all accounts, amounted to tacit acceptance of Jim Crow segregation as a "proper" condition of national reconciliation after the Civil War. But an audience of 75,000 listened on the grounds of the Lincoln Memorial while millions more listened to the radio broadcast of the concert. In so doing, they helped transform the Memorial into an affirmation of the importance of racial justice, at the same time reclaiming Lincoln's legacy in support of a more just project of national reconciliation. In 1963, the Lincoln Memorial became the physical focal point of the 1963 March on Washington that (among other things) helped forward the passage of the Civil Rights Act of 1964 and the Voting Rights Act of 1965 as powerful steps toward a hoped-for project of racial reconciliation.

But near the end of the 20th century, Maya Lin's *Vietnam Veterans Memorial* provoked a very different kind of reflection about the possibilities of national reconciliation. The memorial became part of a largescale challenge to America to try to reintegrate soldiers who had fought in a contested war back into networks of social relationships that connect citizens to each other and that might make deep comradeship possible once again. That challenge was made more difficult by the fact that when any commemorative public art is created with the intent of fostering a morally reparative, or politically restorative, reorientation towards a nation's past, it will bear an extraordinary burden of social expectations. Such projects have an especially urgent and direct connection to the search for political stability, but they are often produced in a context of deep disagreement about an acceptable path to stability. The Vietnam Veterans' Memorial was conceived by a small group of Vietnam veterans who established a charitable foundation to create a public memorial that would recognize the service of American veterans of the Vietnam War and help "begin a national process of reconciliation." So, the project needed, first, to address the feelings of disenfranchisement that plagued so many returning veterans. But, second, it needed to be the focal point for broader collective memory of one of the most divisive eras in American history, symbolically uniting those who had served in a bitterly contested war with those who had not and reconciling those who had opposed the war with those who viewed that opposition as a principal cause of the failure to achieve "victory."

Lin's core design—"two walls of polished black granite" listing the names of the 58,000 US citizens who were lost or went missing in the war—is now thought by many to be a compelling response to the challenges of fostering reconciliation and symbolically addressing veteran disenfranchisement.[13] Like the Saint-Gaudens memorial, many of the VVM's most notable achievements are a function of its singularity, in particular, its departures from the "codes of remembrance" that shaped earlier war memorials (Sturken 46–54). It departs from these codes in a material sense, through Lin's use of polished black granite rather than the white stone of other memorials on the National Mall. Further, rather than creating a towering presence on the landscape, Lin deliberately set the Memorial below grade as a quiet invitation to contemplation and reflection. Still further, the VVM is still the only American war memorial to list the names of all the Americans who died or went missing over the course of an entire war. These departures reflect Lin's preference for many of the vernacular values that find expression in the practices of those who visit the memorial, and it is a mark of the subtlety of Lin's vision that drawing on vernacular values in this way, the memorial is still able to challenge us to see the world in a new way. Yet even morally robust art can never be a substitute for the hard work of human moral reflection, and those who expected the Vietnam Veterans' Memorial to be more than a catalyst for reflection have simply failed to appreciate the limits of art.

But civic art and architecture are not the only important means of promoting social reconciliation, especially in response to the kinds of social ruptures sometimes produced by severe oppression, discrimination, and injustice.[14] In *Art as Experience,* Dewey argued that art is a form of

---

[13] The making of the monument is discussed in Kirk Savage, *Monument Wars,* esp. Ch. 6 "The Conscience of a Nation"; and Maya Lin, "Making the Memorial."

[14] Lori Gallegos provides an account of ways in which struggles for justice can conflict with individual well-being and meaningfulness in the section "The Pursuit of Social Justice" of her chapter in this volume.

communication that has the power to break down many of the most important barriers that divide us.[15] Dewey understood that one of the special challenges of any effort to create perceptual space for justice is how often it requires that we become able to see the world, and our place in it, in a new way. Dewey thus plausibly urged that literature is one of the most important means of bridging social and political divides in pursuit of progress toward morally just reconciliation, particularly in virtue of its capacity to depict the nature and consequences of injustice and oppression in need of redress. In works as varied as *Uncle Tom's Cabin,* Upton Sinclair's *The Jungle;* Steinbeck's *The Grapes of Wrath;* Ellison's *Invisible Man* and Margaret Atwood's *The Handmaid's Tale* literature is often able to help create space for stable and just reconciliation. Of course, sometimes the power of literature to create space for justice is most fully realized by narratives that depict the experience of oppression, discrimination and injustice "from the inside." But like Baldwin, I believe that the literature of moral reconciliation might sometimes be the product of those who are not themselves the victims of a particular injustice under scrutiny. Charges of "cultural appropriation" with which such literature is sometimes met risks silencing much needed sources morally insightful reconciliation.

At some moments in history, and sometimes for certain kinds of injustice, visual culture—including painting, drawing, sculpture, photography and film—may be the most effective means of using art to create perceptual space for justice. This is surely why Picasso's 1937 painting *Guernica,* depicting the horrors of the Nazi devastation of the town of Guernica during the Spanish Civil War, continues to be valued as one of the most powerful expressions of the horrors of war. Further, at least since the American Civil War, photography has been an especially reliable means of communicating the human suffering and social damage that can be created by war, social division, and injustice. This is one of the most important lessons of the New Deal Photography Project, which relied on the talents of some of America's most gifted photographers to help create support for New Deal programs meant to address the condition of one-third of the nation that, in the words of Franklin Roosevelt, was "ill-housed, ill-clad and ill-nourished." Still further, some contemporary artists combine painting and photography in a single work, creating space for justice by confronting us with the "immediacy"

---

[15] See John J. Stuhr's discussion of the ways in which the humanities and arts can forge what he, following William James, calls "habits of genius"—habits of perceiving and acting in unhabitual, imaginative, flexible ways: "Flourishing: Toward Clearer Ideas and Habits of Genius," this volume.

of photographic images of injustice through a painterly lens. In a haunting example of this process, a triptych by contemporary painter Kerry James Marshall, entitled "Heirlooms and Accessories," uses elements of a well-known photograph of a 1930 lynching in Marion, Indiana to challenge his audience to confront the terror of, and the question of responsibility for, contemporary racial violence (Caldwell, "Responding to Terror").[16]

In the twentieth century, music played an especially prominent role in exposing the reality and the depth of social oppression, and in articulating the existence of politically significant discontent about failures to address that oppression. The extraordinary cultural impact of Marian Anderson's concert at the Lincoln Memorial made it a singular example of this phenomenon, but so did her decision to change the lyrics of a critical line in "My County tis of thee" from "Of thee I sing" to "Of thee we sing." Yet many would argue that the music of social protest has been especially important to the project of creating space for justice. In 1939—ironically, the same year in which Anderson sang at the Lincoln Memorial—Billie Holiday debuted one of the most influential protest songs of the twentieth century: the haunting "Strange Fruit," which tackled the horror of lynching in a deceptively lyrical mood. The song is a bold challenge to the notion that a work must uplift us, or even produce any ordinary kind of pleasure, to qualify as art. In fact, like the art of social protest, more generally, "Strange Fruit" is perhaps best understood as an example of the phenomenon that Bernard Bosanquet once characterized as "difficult beauty." A central attribute of difficult beauty is a kind of "tension of feeling"—an unease at confronting troubling subject matter—and, at its best, the art of social protest serves to produce just such unease (Three Lectures on Aesthetics, Lecture Three). To be sure, even at its best, the difficult beauty of the art of social protest may not seem capable of directly promoting reconciliation. But it plays a critical indirect role in making truly just reconciliation possible by providing memorable and powerful depictions of the social ruptures in need of moral repair.

Any decision to rely on the power of any art to expose injustice, to depict remediable human suffering, and to create empathy and strengthen fellow-feeling in response to suffering and injustice, may raise concern about the dangers of turning art into propaganda. But I am not troubled by this possibility since, like W.E. B. DuBois and George Orwell, I contend that "all art is propaganda" (DuBois "Criteria of Negro Art;" Orwell All Art Is Propaganda).

---

[16] See also Leigh Raiford, "Photography and the Practices of Critical Black Memory," 112–29.

I nonetheless believe that we can plausibly distinguish between morally le-gitimate art that promotes human flourishing, by seeking to create space for repairing social division, injustice and suffering, and morally illegitimate images that undermine human flourishing by promoting hatred and cruelty and rationalizing the horrors of war and destruction (Moody-Adams "Moral Progress and Human Agency" 153–168). That is, if our concern is to promote human flourishing we need not be reluctant to allow that there are *aesthetically relevant moral differences* between the sort of paintings, photography, and posters that were meant to further the aims of the New Deal, for instance, and those that were meant to rationalize the horrors of fascism and Nazism.

There is also a critical *political* difference between these two types of propaganda—if I may use that word—and that is the difference between sys-tems that seek to realize democratic ideals and systems built on hate-filled, xenophobic authoritarianism. Indeed, as Dewey writes in his 1939 essay, "Creative Democracy: The Task before Us": "the task of democracy is forever that of creation of a freer and more humane experience in which all share and to which all contribute." Dewey also argues in that essay that "democracy is belief in the ability of human experience to generate the aims and methods by which further experience will grow in ordered richness," and given his conviction concerning the importance of art to human flourishing, we have to presume that he takes art (of the right sort) to constitute an important element of those "aims and methods." We can only hope for continued pro-duction of art that is conducive to the "ordered richness" of democratic institutions and practices that genuinely contribute to human flourishing.

The Consolations of Art

Of courses, as Mill reminds us in Chapter Five of his *Autobiography*, some-times the most important contributions that art makes to human well-being emerge in the context of our vulnerability to suffering and adversity, when we turn to art for its powers of consolation. Yet the consolations of art are only partly a function of art's capacity to provide solace and comfort. Consolation, as I understand it, is fundamentally a matter of the lessening of grief, sorrow or disappointment and sometimes that is achieved by projects that have little to with providing comfort and solace. This because, sometimes, the consolations of art are a reflection of its capacity to remind us that disap-pointment, adversity, and loss are inescapable features of human life, and to help us learn both to bear up under these strains and to recognize that what we accomplish when we do so is a form of human flourishing. For many, a masterful example of such consolation is provided by Richard Strauss's *Vier letzte Lieder,* four songs which set to music a series of poems about life's difficult transitions—including death—written by Herman Hesse and Joseph von Eichendorf. As the critic David Mermelstein writes, the songs "provide a certain succor, suggesting that death is less an ending than a transition—though to what is left unspoken" ("Masterpiece"). The idea that a "certain succor" providing no ordinary pleasure of resolution can be a source of human flourishing is one of the central insights embodied in Mill's distinction, in Chapter Two of *Utilitarianism,* between higher and lower pleasures. Strauss's masterful song cycle yields some of the best evidence possible that "it is better to be a human being dissatisfied than a pig satisfied; better to be Socrates dissatisfied than a fool satisfied."

Yet the power of art to console is not confined to music, and whenever we think that poetry might be "dead" or dying, we would do well to remember the almost unparalleled power of poetry to provide solace in the face of loss. The contemporary poet Kevin Young contends that "often, in death, everything else fails. We are left only with the music and the meaning of poetry" (*The Art of Losing*). He adds that we often turn to poetry in times of grief because the best poems have the capacity to "render a complex fate simply; to render chaos as chaos; or to examine the unseen complexities of seemingly simple, even everyday experience." If we can plausibly generalize Young's analysis of the power of elegiac poetry—which I think we can—we can understand the consolations of art, more generally, and appreciate the critical role they play in making it possible for us to constructively confront suffering, loss, and adversity.

Mill is best known for his appreciation of art as the source of more "ordinary" comforts: his encounter with Wordsworth's poetry engaged and reawakened emotions with the potential to soothe. But his description of that encounter helps confirm the wisdom of the tendency to seek comforting music or poetry when we grieve the loss of someone we value. That wisdom grounds our confidence in the power of singing a simple hymn like "Amazing Grace," or reciting a verse from a poem like W.H. Auden's "Funeral Blues," at a funeral or a memorial service. In addition, this capacity of art to comfort in the context of psychological suffering confirms its more comprehensive power to heal. A rich array of empirical studies strongly supports the idea that providing patients some kind of engagement with art can aid in the treatment of various physical and mental illnesses, and sometimes prevent, or at least diminish susceptibility to, some kinds of illness.

Conclusion

This essay has explored the role of the creative arts in promoting human flourishing and asserted the importance of philosophical recognition of that role. Engagement with art can constructively transform our capacities and talents; produce social reconciliation and promote democratic stability; and console us when we confront suffering, adversity, and loss. But I have also assumed that we can articulate and defend the value of art in a satisfying and well-lived life without appeal to any particular definition of art. In fact, as I understand it, even Irwin's Deweyan claim that art is a continuous examination and expansion of perceptual awareness is really a description rather than definition, since it does not purport to provide necessary and sufficient conditions for calling something "art." But seeking a definition of art is not the most plausible approach to providing a comprehensive "picture" of art. If we want to allow for the most useful and expansive aesthetic pluralism, art may be most compellingly understood as a complex "cluster concept" which cannot be defined (Gaut, 'The Cluster Account of Art Defended").[17]

Finally, like Nelson Goodman, I presume that the most important question to ask is usually not "what is art?" but "when is art?" ("When is Art?" pp. 57–70). The best answers to the "when is art?" question will, of course, refer to the role of human creative imagination in producing some object, event, or activity. If we can identify some "product" that results, at least in part, from the exercise of human creative imagination and that helps to deepen and enrich our understanding of the world by encouraging us to examine or expand some aspect of our awareness, it will be reasonable in that context to treat that product as an instance of art. Taking Goodman's question as central is especially important to the Deweyan project of restoring continuity between everyday experience and the "refined and intensified" forms of experience that constitute art. The Deweyan project is, in turn, critical to any serious effort to create and identity the kinds of "objects," events, and activities that can promote constructive individual transformation, support morally defensible forms of social and political reconciliation, and offer consolation in the face of suffering, adversity, and loss. Picasso is reported to have said that "[E]very child is an artist. The problem is how to remain an artist once we grow up." But the more fundamental challenge is to remain

---

[17] In this context, see also John Lachs's focus on the importance of pluralism for an understanding of human flourishing, "The Allure of the 'All,'" this volume.

engaged with art in "everyday life" in ways that acknowledge its multi-faceted power to promote human flourishing.

Works Cited

Anderson, Benedict. *Imagined Communities*. Rev. ed. Verso, 2016.

Aristotle. *Poetics*. Translated by A. Kenney. Oxford University Press, 2013.

Ayer, Alfred Jules. *Language Truth and Logic* 1946. Pelican Books, 1971.

Baldwin, James. Interview with Jane Howard, "The Doom and Glory of Knowing Who You Are." *Life Magazine*, May 24, 1963, p. 89.

Berger, John. *Ways of Seeing*. Penguin Books, 1990, pp. 129–54.

Bosanquet, Bernard. *Three Lectures on Aesthetics*. MacMillan, 1915, Lecture Three.

Caldwell, Ellen C. "Responding to Terror: The Art of Kerry James Marshall." *JSTOR Daily*, July 16, 2015. https://daily.jstor.org/art-of-kerry-james-marshall/

Danto, Arthur. "The Philosophical Disenfranchisement of Art." *Grand Street*, Vol. 4, No. 3, Spring 1985, pp. 171–89.

Darwall, Stephen. "Two kinds of respect." *Ethics*, Vol. 88, No. 1, , 1977, pp. 36–49.

Dewey, John. *Art as Experience*. 1934. Perigree Books, 1990.

Dewey, John. "Creative Democracy: The Task before Us," *John Dewey: The Later Works, 1925–1953*, vol. 14. Southern Illinois University Press, 1998 [1939], pp. 224–30.

DuBois, W. E. B. "Criteria of Negro Art." *The Crisis*, Vol. 32, October 1926, 290–97. http://www.webdubois.org/dbCriteriaNArt.html accessed May 26, 2022.

Freeland, Cynthia. *But Is It Art?: An Introduction to Art Theory*. Oxford University Press, 2001.

Gaut, Berys. "The Cluster Account of Art Defended." *British Journal of Aesthetics*, vol. 45, no. 3, pp. 273–88, July 2005.

Goldman, Carrie. "This Is Your Brain on Jane Austen, and Stanford Researchers Are Taking Notes." *Stanford Report*, Sep. 7, 2012 https://news.stanford.edu/news/2012/september/austen-reading-fmri-090712.html accessed Jan. 5, 2019.

Goodman, Nelson. "How Buildings Mean." *Critical Inquiry*, vol. 11, no. 4, June 1985, pp. 642–53.

Goodman, Nelson. "When Is Art?." *Ways of Worldmaking*, Hackett, 1978, pp. 57–70.

Hegel, G. W. F. *Aesthetics*. Translated by T. M. Knox. Oxford University Press, 1975. Reprint, 1998.

Hegel, G. W. F. *Phenomenology of Spirit*. Translated by A. V. Miller. Clarendon, 1977.

Hegel, G. W. F. *Philosophy of Right*. Translated by T. M. Knox. Oxford University Press, 1967.

Herman, Amy. *Visual Intelligence*. Mariner Books, 2016.

James, William. "Oration by Wm. James." *Essays in Religion and Morality*, edited by Frederick Burkhardt and Fredson Bowers. Harvard University Press, 1982, p. 64.

Khullar, Druv. "What Doctors Can Learn from Looking at Art." *New York Times*, Dec. 2, 2016.

King, Stephen. *On Writing: A Memoir of the Craft*. Scribner, 10th annual edition, 2010.

Lin, Maya. "Making the Memorial." *New York Review of Books*, Nov. 2, 2000 https://www-nybooks-com.ezproxy.cul.columbia.edu/articles/2000/11/02/making-the-memorial/

Maresca, Joseph. *WPA Buildings: Architecture and the Art of the New Deal.* Shiffer Publishing, 2016.

Memelstein, David. "Masterpiece: Confronting Death with Music and Verse." *Wall Street Journal,* December 20, 2014, Section C:13.

Mill, John Stuart. "Bentham." *The Collected Works, Vol. 10, Essays on Ethics, Religion and Society.* Edited by J. M. Robson, University of Toronto Press, 2006, p. 114.

Mill, John Stuart. "Autobiography." *The Collected Works, Vol. 1, Autobiography and Literary Essays,* edited by J. M. Robson and Jack Stillinger, University of Toronto Press, 1981, pp. 5–290.

Moody-Adams, Michele. "Moral Progress and Human Agency." *Ethical Theory and Moral Practice,* vol. 20, no. 1, 2017, pp. 153–168.

Murdoch, Iris. *The Fire and the Sun.* Viking Press, 1991.

Naghshineh, Sheila, Hafler, J. P., Miller, A. T., . . ., and Kaz, J. T. "Formal Art Observation Training Improves Medical Students Visual Diagnostic Skills." *Journal of General Internal Medicine,* vol. 23, no. 7, July 2008, pp. 991–97.

Nagy, William, P. Herman, and R. C. Anderson. "Learning Words from Context." *Reading Research Quarterly,* vol. 20, no. 2, 1985, pp. 233–53.

Orwell, George. *All Art Is Propaganda.* Mariner Books, 2008.

Panofsky, Erwin. "Style and Medium in the Motion Pictures." *Three Essays on Style,* edited by Irving Lavin. MIT Press, 1997, p. 93.

Pennington, Martha, and Robert Waxler. *Why Reading Books Still Matters: The Power of Literature in Digital Times.* Routledge, 2017.

Raiford, Leigh. " Photography and the Practices of Critical Black Memory." *History and Theory* vol. 48, December 2009, pp. 112–29.

Roosevelt, Franklin Delano. "One Third of a Nation." Second Inaugural Address. January 20, 1937. http://historymatters.gmu.edu/d/5105/ accessed May 26, 2022.

Ruppert, Sandra. "Critical Evidence: How the Arts Benefit Student Achievement." National Assembly of State Art Agencies. 2006. https://files.eric.ed.gov/fulltext/ED529 766.pdf

Shusterman, Richard. *Pragmatist Aesthetics: Rethinking Beauty, Living Art.* 2nd ed., Rowman and Littlefield, 2000.

Savage, Kirk. *Monument Wars.* University of California Press, 2005.

Sternberg, Robert J. "Most Vocabulary is Learned from Context." *The Nature of Vocabulary Acquisition,* edited by Margaret McKeown and Mary Curtis. Lawrence Erlbaum Associates, New York, 1987, pp. 89–106.

Sturken, Marita. *Tangled Memories.* University of California Press, 1997, pp. 46–54.

Tay, Louis, James O. Pawelski, and Melissa Keith. "The Roles of the Arts and Humanities in Human Flourishing: A Conceptual Model." *Journal of Positive Psychology,* vol. 13, no. 3, 2018, pp. 215–25.

Quine, W. V. "On the Nature of Moral values." *Critical Inquiry* vol. 5, no. 3, Spring, 1979, pp. 471–80.

Waldron, Jeremy. *The Harm in Hate Speech.* Harvard Press, 2012.

Woodward, C. Vann. "The National Decision against Equality." *American Counterpoint: Slavery and Racism in the North/South Dialogue.* Little Brown, 1971, pp. 212–33.

Young, Kevin. *The Art of Losing: Poems of Grief and Healing.* Bloomsbury Press, 2010.

Index

For the benefit of digital users, indexed terms that span two pages (e.g., 52–53) may, on occasion, appear on only one of those pages.